A Potent Moment

A Potent Moment

Building Social Equity into Cannabis Legalization

Jeffrey Moyer

LEXINGTON BOOKS
Lanham • Boulder • New York • London

Published by Lexington Books
An imprint of The Rowman & Littlefield Publishing Group, Inc.
4501 Forbes Boulevard, Suite 200, Lanham, Maryland 20706
www.rowman.com

86-90 Paul Street, London EC2A 4NE

British Library Cataloguing in Publication Information Available

Library of Congress Cataloging-in-Publication Data

Names: Moyer, Jeffrey, 1990- author.
Title: A potent moment : building social equity into cannabis legalization / Jeffrey Moyer.
Description: Lanham : Lexington, 2023. | Includes bibliographical references and index. | Summary: "This book describes the history of cannabis criminalization in the United States and details the legalization movement that has evolved over the past decade. It forcefully argues that the historically racist enforcement of cannabis prohibitions means that racial justice and social equity goals should be part of future legalization efforts"-- Provided by publisher.
Identifiers: LCCN 2023043836 (print) | LCCN 2023043837 (ebook) | ISBN 9781666918076 (cloth) | ISBN 9781666918083 (ebook)
Subjects: LCSH: Marijuana--Law and legislation--United States--Criminal provisions--History. | Drug legalization--United States--History. | Drug control--United States--History. | Crime and race--United States--History. | Discrimination in criminal justice administration--United States.
Classification: LCC KF3891.M2 M69 2023 (print) | LCC KF3891.M2 (ebook) | DDC 345.73/0277--dc23/eng/20231002
LC record available at https://lccn.loc.gov/2023043836
LC ebook record available at https://lccn.loc.gov/2023043837

Contents

Acknowledgments

This work is absolutely a product of community, including those in academia who have influenced me in the past decade as I developed my interest in this topic, as well as those in the cannabis community who have welcomed me and helped to impart their knowledge and wisdom over the last several years. I hope that these experiences and perspectives come across in this book.

My professors and fellow students at UMass Boston formed a key professional support network, and their insights and inspiration are a key part of who I am today. Professors Mark Warren and Michael Johnson helped ensure my dissertation went smoothly and according to schedule, and they gave me the framework to continue my own research for years to come. Members of my doctoral cohort, including Caitlin Carey, Marcia Mundt, Andrew King, and Sean Mossey, were a great group to share the irreplaceable doctoral candidacy experience with. I also can't leave out George Chichirau, with whom I shared both the cohort experience and countless other personal and professional moments since then. I treasure the opportunity to follow the work of all of these committed scholars, whether they are inside or outside the academy.

I have also been lucky to work with a growing network of students and fellow faculty at Northeastern University. I'd like to thank the School of Public Policy and Urban Affairs for allowing me to expand my teaching portfolio, including the opportunity to teach economics. Various students helped me with my earlier research into cannabis policy and previous publications, including Tracy Chen and Jacob Masli. Likewise, my student research team for this book—Brooke Williams, Ellie Witman, Brendy Jerome, and Aida Zilkic—supported my efforts to research the cases within this text and did crucial work to validate my examples and provide their own perspectives, all of which have strengthened my analysis. I'd also like to thank everyone else who agreed to read earlier versions of this text and provide feedback.

I also must thank my outside editor for this book, Nicholas Osborne. He was willing to take on the thankless work of helping me turn my early drafts into a coherent and accessible narrative, and I could not have completed this project without his incisive attention to detail and consistent ability to help me meet arduous self-imposed deadlines. I am lucky I was able to work with such a scholar who has a common appreciation for the topic and could even suggest similar areas of inquiry which later became focal points of my narrative. Thanks also to Mackenzie Dietz, who served as my editor for my dissertation and other related work I have published in this topic area, as well as to Emy Christodoulou, who helped visualize my subject matter on the cover of this text. Thanks to everyone at Lexington Books for giving this manuscript an opportunity to be read more widely, particularly Becca Beurer and Sara Noakes for their supportive encouragement during the drafting process, as well as all the support staff at the press for their own contributions.

Lastly, I would like to emphasize that this work is entirely my own, including any mistakes or omissions. Likewise, nothing in this text should be attributed to any organization that I have, had, or could in the future have an employment relationship with.

I humbly hope that this text provides the reader with some insight about the stakes of racial equality for cannabis legalization and regulation more broadly. I welcome any feedback or thoughts that the reader might have.

Jeffrey Moyer
Boston, Massachusetts
July 2023

Introduction

> The federal government has screwed up marijuana policy in this country for a generation. We lied to people about the effects of marijuana. And then we used marijuana as a cudgel to incarcerate wide swaths of communities, particularly in African American communities. So I am not offended by the concept of restorative justice in marijuana policy because we can't honestly say the war on drugs impacted suburban white communities the same way it impacted urban black communities. We can't say marijuana enforcement was happening the same way on the corner that it was happening in the fraternity house. We have an opportunity to fix that problem. The war on drugs—much like many of our "forever" wars—has been a failure. If there has been a war on drugs, drugs have won that war.
>
> —US Representative Matt Gaetz[1]

Uttered by seemingly one of the least likely political figures today to speak positively about the concept of "restorative justice," the above quotation nevertheless manages to concisely lay out the legacy of the War on Drugs. This war has been fought not against a foreign enemy, but rather against Americans of every color and creed over the last few decades—Black and brown Americans disproportionately so—with little to show in terms of positive outcomes on the front lines for the decades of harm it has caused.

In the current political discourse, there is a particular risk in going "woke"—in other words, centering the historical and material legacy of prior discrimination in an effort to account for, and ultimately "restore," the damages that have been caused by these injustices.[2] The state of Florida—which counts Matt Gaetz, the speaker of the above words, as one of its congresspeople—even recently passed the so-called "Stop WOKE Act," which purports to limit the teaching of critical race theory in state-funded schools. Skeptics of critical theories today frequently claim that these "woke" lessons will cast guilt on students and distract them from the lessons they need in order to be successful in today's workforce.

I do not agree with this perspective.

Instead, I argue that scholars and activists—indeed, all citizens—must engage issues such as racial injustice and economic inequality in order to build a more just world. Recent developments in cannabis legalization, the specific topic of this book, demonstrate that it is one of the most promising areas of cultural and political discourse today with the potential to make authentic connections across ideological lines. After all, if even a politician such as Gaetz—generally perceived to be one of the most conservative members of the House of Representatives[3]—can see the War on Drugs as a damning lesson about racial inequity and in response call for restorative justice actions, then it's easy to imagine the extent of common ground that might be found among politicians, scholars, and activists of all persuasions on this topic. I hope that this book, even if only in some marginal way, helps advance this cause.

LEGAL CANNABIS TODAY

It is a Saturday in Massachusetts, where cannabis has been recreationally legal for more than six years. As in over twenty other states, residents of the Commonwealth are free to purchase cannabis at a licensed store without threat of prosecution or other legal interference. As a scholar of drug policy generally and of cannabis policy in particular, living here affords me the advantage of a front-row seat to the development of this new market. And so this weekend I have opened a browser, typed "cannabis near me" into my search bar, and come up with dozens of stores and dispensaries within ten miles of my home—each offering a dizzying array of flower, edibles, vape products, oils, and more.

My trip to the store is brief, but I am required to display my ID at multiple points during the process to verify that I am over twenty-one. In a somewhat clinical-feeling process, I survey a menu and am invited to inquire about the properties and experience associated with any products that interest me. The store employees are kind and helpful; they seem to speak from firsthand knowledge. When I take my selection to the counter, I have the option of paying with cash or a debit card. I go with the latter. The employee who rings me up processes the transaction as an ATM withdrawal—fee included.

This quick errand to a licensed shop (which also provides pickup or delivery service) represents the legal purchasing option for both local and visiting cannabis customers. However, the unregulated market continues—for the moment—to offer alternatives.

There are, for example, Boston's many head shops. Storefronts display colorful glassware that can be used to smoke cannabis flower. While all are careful to stress publicly that they do not sell cannabis itself, in some of these places, for customers in the know, the right words will still unlock access to products behind the counter. Offerings overlap with those available at licensed stores. Some are labeled as having come from other states, most commonly California. Others are distinct from those on the legal market, with flashier packaging that often adopts images from popular culture or trademarked logos. Here, I can pay with a credit card.

Alternatively, I could access a delivery network to which an acquaintance has referred me. The process in this case starts by confirming phone numbers with my contact. Next, I pick from several available products and a delivery agent is dispatched. I meet the driver in their car, place my cash in the drink holder, and receive my purchase in a paper bag. Pricing in this market is more flexible, with sellers offering volume discounts and first-time customer benefits.

I could also go the route of the "social supply." Within most extended social networks, odds are good that at least one person can be found who both uses and sells a narrow selection of cannabis products in small amounts. To unlock this connection requires a strong bond of trust and mutual interest.

My own experience pursuing any of these options carries fewer risks for me than those faced by Americans of color who may also want to access cannabis. Still, these and other illegal avenues for the purchase of cannabis are well established and accessed daily, in every state, by millions of Americans across class and color lines. Tax revenue cannot be collected beyond the regulated market, of course, and regulators are limited in their ability to impact all but those licensed establishments. But the market is still young.

PURPOSE OF THIS BOOK

Whenever I am asked about my research focus, I am faced with a choice. The simplest answer, "cannabis legalization," inevitably elicits some good-natured ribbing, and any follow-up questions tend toward a general curiosity about the prospects for legalization. Such was the standard exchange when I was a graduate student and my interests first settled in this area. As I began to recognize the profound racial justice issues in the cannabis sphere, my answer more often became: "social equity in cannabis legalization." This answer triggers an entirely different conversation. "What is social equity?" "What does that have to do with cannabis?" The questions are understandable—cannabis legalization is far more complicated than is commonly discussed or portrayed in the media. But answering them in a way that does justice to the issues is difficult, especially within the conversational space of an elevator pitch, and my attempts to do so sometimes risk leaving the asker more confused than before I started talking. As such, these questions deserve a thorough, nuanced response.

That is why I wrote this book.

There is a great deal of discussion on the topic of "social equity" as it relates to cannabis today, but this term is often vaguely defined and means different things to different people. For some, it represents an opportunity to introduce "diversity" into the market, while for others it is a profound racial justice response to damage wrought by cannabis criminalization. Such ideas will be explored here, but I won't presume to provide a concrete definition of social equity in cannabis. Instead, I'd like to think this book can provide the basis for further discussion of the various kinds of social equity approaches and their relative merits.

Much of the complexity of pursuing social equity in cannabis policy rests in figuring out how to respond to the interlocking institutions that converged to ensure that the lion's share of the damage of cannabis criminalization would fall upon Americans of color while white citizens could in many cases choose to consume cannabis with few or no legal repercussions. With legalization's arrival, some of those same white Americans were able to transition into owning cannabis businesses, while many of those who had faced criminal consequences—disproportionately, people of color—were shut out of these opportunities. To those whose lives have been shaped by the fight against racism and poverty, this disparity is utterly unsurprising. Given that historic and ongoing injustice, it seems understandable that many activists would like to see the reparation of past wrongs accompany any attempts to prevent harm in the future. In this view, it seems particularly unfair that people would continue to serve prison sentences, for example, for something they did a few years ago that is no longer considered a crime.

Yet there are those, even among legalization activists, to whom social equity advocacy in this sphere is perceived as the unnecessary, unreasonable demand of antagonists who ought to be happy with a decisive victory. For them, legalization is about the future. According to this logic, if racial disparities were a product of criminalization, then presumably legalization will put an end to the problem. If legalization is associated with any color for people who subscribe to this view, it is green—that is, the color of money. Advocacy motivated by this perspective largely focuses on enforcement costs and potential tax revenues, removing race from the argument altogether. With so much money on the table, who wants to talk about justice?

I know that I do. By explicitly identifying cannabis legalization as a matter of racial justice, I aim to complete the picture both for those interested in drug policy but less knowledgeable about its ramifications for people of color, as well as for social justice audiences curious about the specificities of cannabis regulation. I also hope to highlight a pressing social equity issue for undergraduate and graduate students in fields such as criminology, sociology, law, social work, and political science, among others. Many of these budding scholars struggle to unpack the structural status of inequality and disparity, and I believe this book is an applied contribution to this exercise.

CHAPTER OVERVIEW

American policymakers have often framed changes in drug policy as explicit responses to the perceived failures of earlier regulatory regimes, so I begin this book with three chapters that sketch out the key developments in this area over the past century. Specifically, the legislators and policymakers who established the regulated cannabis market in recent years have often done so at least in part to respond to the perceived racial injustices that informed decades of prior criminalization. I therefore contextualize drug regulation generally and cannabis criminalization specifically within the social and political history of American racism and the legal and economic regimes that racist motivations have supported. Considering how this history has informed recent regulatory actions demonstrates that the new legal market is ironically plagued by those same injustices and is on course to reproduce cycles of incomplete racial liberation, ultimately enriching and protecting white participants while excluding and harming Americans of color.

Given that more than a quarter century has passed since the first significant steps toward legalization were taken, it is perhaps unsurprising that extensive criticism of cannabis regulation has grown up alongside the market. So, after reviewing the history of criminalization, I devote a series of chapters to case studies of individual states and the social equity programs they have pursued—or failed to pursue—in response to the burgeoning injustices of legalization. Because numerous states have envisioned, designed, implemented, and evaluated them, these programs vary in scope and depth. In some ways, therefore, an examination of them must be taxonomic: an attempt to first classify and define in order to compare. In particular, I seek to identify which of these programs have provided—or have the potential to provide—some benefit to communities of color. In so doing, my point is not to pass moral judgment on those who supported previously unsuccessful models of social equity (something I sometimes encounter in my research). Rather, I offer this critical evaluation in the spirit of policy innovation and entrepreneurship, with the hope that my insights can help to build a pathway for activists and policymakers to improve existing policy.

To that end, the five cases I focus on represent the range of political and legal processes that have led to cannabis legalization over the last decade, the different strands of legalization, and the methods of adoption. The first,

Colorado, typifies many Americans' conceptualization of legal cannabis, with its ubiquitous dispensaries seemingly part of the retail fabric, akin to liquor stores in many other places. Ohio, the second state I discuss, has only legalized medical cannabis, but past and ongoing campaigns for recreational legalization there show how ideas about how or whether to incorporate social equity considerations into legalization have evolved. The next, Massachusetts, is the first state where a social equity emphasis was adopted as part of legalization itself. As we will see, this has led to learning moments for equity activists and a frustratingly incomplete adoption of equity measures through the legal cannabis market. Illinois and New York, the final states I will look at, claim to have learned from the example of Massachusetts. This is possible in part because both states adopted legalization through the legislative process. Indeed, one thing that the five case studies collectively show is how each state's legalization method has been immensely consequential for the development of social equity policies. These policies have developed in the shadow of institutional power and are often limited by the entrenched resistance of the organized political elite. In fact, some social equity programs have invited determined opposition even in cities such as Evanston, Illinois, and Cambridge, Massachusetts, that are otherwise regarded as fiercely progressive.

Throughout these case studies, I discuss two bases by which commentators often evaluate social equity programs: first as reparations for individuals and communities who have been negatively affected by cannabis criminalization, and second as a way of spurring future economic development opportunities for those same individuals and communities. While compelling in different ways to both racial justice activists and elected officials, I argue that either model will fall short of achieving social equity so long as it fails to incorporate the input of those people and communities most harmed by criminalization. Much as cannabis legalization has almost exclusively succeeded through popular action at the ballot box, social equity in cannabis will only be achieved with active participation in the decision-making process about how to spend money earned from tax revenues on legal cannabis sales by those who were once the most marginalized by its illegality.

Because cannabis legalization has mostly happened at the state level, attention to social equity has understandably been focused on state actions. Nevertheless, the federal government has played a role in social equity conversations of the past and must be part of such discussions in the future. A chapter on the federal government takes up this theme, considering its role in continuing criminalization policies and its potential future impact on legal cannabis. My final chapter considers the policy landscape related to contentious aspects of legalization—including youth use—while also summarizing some of the common themes that emerge from comparing the various time periods and jurisdictions examined in the book. My goal is to suggest some of the key questions that will need to be answered in coming years as both the legal status of cannabis and its political, cultural, and economic place in the United States continue to evolve.

METHODOLOGY

Before describing my approach, it is important to acknowledge my own positionality: I am a relatively privileged white male who grew up in a more rural area. In the past, I at times held at least a basic sympathy toward the idea that taking race into account in public policy was a relic of the past, an attitude exemplified by commentaries after Barack Obama's 2008 election victory that proclaimed the dawn of a post-racial America. As such, I take care throughout this book to avoid prioritizing my own voice over the voices of those who grew up and survived—and many times thrived—in communities with little political representation or access to wealth, which were also often overburdened by legal enforcement of criminal statutes. This is a primary reason that I work as a qualitative scholar and focus on equity questions in cannabis policy and beyond, as well as why I make sure to provide quotations from those who actually do this work. I have my mentor Mark Warren, a proud scholar-activist who studies education organizing, to thank for the example he has set in this regard through his relentless commitment to the belief that research should speak to the disempowered and question existing power structures.

My approach to interviews and other first-person accounts builds on Warren's original research into the attitudes and motivations of white anti-racist activists.[4] Many of the people I interacted with for this book who work or worked in the cannabis legalization space fit Warren's profile of individuals who have thought a great deal about race and racial justice in their day-to-day work and view their activism as fulfilling a vision of justice for all. They certainly know the data that demonstrates how drug enforcement has historically been focused in minority neighborhoods, and they also believe that cannabis legalization should serve in some way to build economic opportunities for people and communities of color.

In addition to the limited original interviews I conducted for this book in order to confirm my understanding of key details, I was able to access the voices of many more individuals through a variety of news sources, podcasts, recorded events, and government records, among other sources. The modern era is kind to the qualitative scholar in many ways, but none more gracious than the drove of podcast hosts looking for new and unique material to discuss, the easy capacity to access recordings of panels and public events recorded in recent years, and the software that is now available to easily transcribe this rich video and audio content. Many of the quotations I provide here come from recordings of this content, most of which I downloaded, auto-transcribed, and verified. I treated these podcasts as equivalent in all ways to the interviews I was able to personally conduct, though I assumed rather than independently confirmed that the participants had consented to their words being attributed to them given their public activism on this compelling topic.

I do not extensively use quantitative data to analyze the effectiveness of social equity programs that have since been implemented, primarily because many of them are too new to be fully assessed in this way. Even where data is available and where I bring it into my analysis, it is usually clear that its quality and depth in this space stems from the information produced by a flawed criminal justice system that imprisoned millions of Americans and that struggles even today to account for the records of these innumerable injustices. My hope is that should social equity policies continue to develop across America, the coming years will give future researchers the ability to more comprehensively answer the important additional questions that can best be pursued with quantitative data.

The lack of any comprehensive national database that tracks cannabis-related criminal enforcement shows the enduring importance of local- and state-specific histories and dynamics in American policymaking. This is further demonstrated by the case study approach that I've taken in the second half of this book. Still, for these chapters I tried to choose states that are in many ways representative of those others that legalized cannabis at roughly the same time (often in the same election cycle). By this comparison, one can see the strength of state innovations on the larger national culture as well as the corresponding strength of national narratives on developments in each state. Moving forward in time, social equity considerations were a nonexistent or small part of the discussion in Colorado until relatively recently, and this was true as well in other earlier states to legalize, such as Washington, Oregon, and Alaska. The next two states covered here, Ohio and Massachusetts, represent the more mature second wave of legalization referendums where questions of social equity became a more central part of the conversation—as they were in a wave of ballot initiative campaigns in 2016 and 2018, including in California and Michigan. The last two state cases, Illinois and New York, represent the newer wave of legalizations that have been adopted by state legislatures. Common themes from this thread of legalization can also be found around similar efforts in other states, including Connecticut, New Jersey, and Maryland.

WHY YOU SHOULD READ THIS BOOK

In writing this book, I have been fortunate to encounter the work of many passionate activists across the country. One of them, Robin Rue Simmons—a city councilor from Evanston, Illinois, who has been credited with passing one of the nation's first reparations programs (which will be explored further in chapter 7)—explained the nature of her own work. She noted that "that is how I like to lead: I identify the problem and get right to identifying a solution and put some action behind that. But we can't work so swiftly with [racial justice work]; there are generations and decades and layers of problems, damages, responsible institutions, and practices. The more I learn and the more I get accomplished, it seems like the more there is to do."[5]

Much like the fight for racial justice, this process of action and reflection has been a central theme of drug policy for more than a century. What often seem like simple binary choices instead reflect a complicated and nuanced set of decisions that only reveal themselves once a preceding action has been taken. As historians are inclined to remind us, only those who know history are in a position to learn from past experiences and be empowered to potentially chart a different path forward. Of course, this is not as straightforward a process as we would like to think. For one, identifying whose history is being recorded and told, and to whom, is certainly as important as it is that those who hear the history and learn from it are in a position of power to potentially change the future.

My desire is that those who read this book get an understanding of the material forces that have shaped the War on Drugs and how the racial wealth gap, particularly economic disparities involving access to housing and financial services, has impacted both the way cannabis was criminalized and the legacies of that criminalization. Likewise, I want these material facts to directly impact how we design proposed solutions. My argument is that we must evaluate those policy designs that have already been adopted in terms of the needs of communities that have been most affected by the criminalization of cannabis specifically and the War on Drugs more generally. We should be willing to learn as much from the recent past of early attempts at cannabis legalization as we can from the longer history of criminalization, adapting and proliferating what has been helpful and shifting course when we identify policy failures in our efforts to achieve social equity. Much like previous scholars in the cannabis policy space, I seek to illuminate the questions we should be asking rather than settle the debates, which will only be resolved through patient engagement in the public sphere and ballot box. I hope that this introduction—and the book at large—will convince readers of the importance of considering social equity issues when designing and implementing cannabis legalization policies.

You should especially read this book if you are a student and your professor told you to do so—okay, I am biased there, but my hope is that this book will help anyone who considers themselves to be a praxis-oriented learner to gain insight into issues of social and racial justice. While it is not a stretch to think that many legalization advocates will agree with the basic idea that pursuing social and racial justice is worthwhile, you should also read this book if you think the War on Drugs was a good idea and are wary of a world of legal cannabis. I hope that it will help you to understand why we need better solutions than criminalization to address the harms that drugs can cause, be they cannabis or some other substance. You should also read this book if you want to understand the broader implications of choosing regulation instead of criminalization as an effective model for state intervention in markets of all kinds—not just for those substances that most Americans currently think of as drugs. I examine a number of such markets, especially in my first three chapters.

If you think the War on Drugs has been unjust, you should read this book if you'd like to better understand why. You should read this book if you would like to understand how the political motivations of reactionary leaders—from Harry Anslinger to Richard Nixon and directly through to Donald Trump—create public policy that reinforces social and economic divisions in American society. You should read this book if you believe that simply ending criminalization is not enough to help the communities and individuals impacted by the War on Drugs and you'd like to understand the details of policies that have been proposed to address these harms. You should read this book if you want to better understand at least some of the economic and social barriers that Americans of color continue to face today. You should read this book if you'd like to get a better sense of at least some small steps that might be taken to redress the harms caused by those barriers.

NOTES

1. "Proud to Support the MORE Act," video, Gaetz.House.Gov, September 30, 2021, https://gaetz.house.gov/media/videos/matt-gaetz-proud-support-more-act.

2. Merriam-Webster, s.v. "woke," https://www.merriam-webster.com/dictionary/woke.

3. See Amy Davidson Sorkin, "The G.O.P.'s Matt Gaetz Problem," *New Yorker*, April 19, 2021, https://www.newyorker.com/magazine/2021/04/19/the-gops-matt-gaetz-problem.

4. Mark Warren, *Fire in the Heart: How White Activists Embrace Racial Justice* (New York: Oxford University Press, 2010), 9–14.

5. Erika Alexander and Whitney Dow, dirs., *The Big Payback: Fear and Reparations in the American Suburb* (Color Farm Media, 2023).

Chapter 1

The First Era of Drug Regulation

From the Great Binge to the Great Society

In the first half of the nineteenth century, two families emigrated from the country of Ireland, then under British domination, to the city of Boston.[1] These families—the Fitzgeralds and the Kennedys—would form the legacy and the name of the thirty-fifth president of the United States, inaugurated a century later in 1961. The first generation of their children born in Boston included Patrick Joseph "P. J." Kennedy, who was elected to the Massachusetts Legislature and operated as a political boss in the state's Democratic Party. Kennedy made his business career by opening saloons and later entering the whiskey importation trade. P. J.'s son, Joseph, continued his father's business but also expanded into other industries, including banking and the film arts. More notably, Joe Kennedy advanced farther into national politics than his father had by serving as the head of federal agencies and ambassador to Great Britain during the lead-up to World War II, though his stance toward Germany in 1940 caused an abrupt stop to his intended ascent to the presidency. Joe may not have become president himself, but many of his children fulfilled both his and their own high ambitions: three became US senators, and one of those served as an attorney general, and, in John F. Kennedy, a US president.

The storied imagery of the Kennedys' Camelot narrative has always had a darker side that haunted the family as well as the politics of the nation they served. For example, two members of the Fitzgerald family operated a drugstore in the 1920s where they took advantage of exceptions in Prohibition laws to provide alcohol to patients who had prescriptions from doctors, while also selling liquor out the back door at high prices.[2] Likewise, Joe Kennedy has been the subject of decades of speculation that he was involved with alcohol smuggling during Prohibition, in part because he provided the alcohol for his alumni party at Harvard, possibly from stores of whiskey that his family had stocked from importation. That said, David Nasaw, one of Joe Kennedy's more recent biographers, examined these claims and found little credible evidence that the family participated in bootlegging.[3] Nevertheless, it is indisputable that alcohol played a key role in creating the material wealth and social status that the Kennedys and the Fitzgeralds enjoyed in Boston, both before and after Prohibition. At the same time, intoxicating substances have stalked some of the more troubling aspects of the Kennedy legacy, such as Edward "Ted" Kennedy's infamous car crash in 1969, which took the life of a young aide and led to numerous questions of whether it was caused in part by alcohol.[4] There was also the trial of Michael Skakel—a Kennedy cousin who himself struggled with alcohol dependence—for the murder of Martha Moxley.[5]

More recently, another member of the Kennedy family has taken up a prominent role in the national debate on drug use. Patrick Kennedy, Ted's son, became the last scion of the Kennedy family to serve in elected office when he left his House seat representing Rhode Island in 2011. Patrick's prior struggles with cocaine, Oxycontin, and alcohol were the subject of public discussion and news spanning his political career. In 2006, for example, he made headlines after crashing his car in Washington, DC, and later seeking treatment for addiction.[6] After leaving Congress, he founded a group called Smart Approaches to Marijuana (SAM), using his own prior struggles with mental health and drug addiction to guide his advocacy work.[7] Speaking about his experience in 2014, he stated that "incarceration is a powerful motivator—that does it for a lot of people. That's the turning point: hearing that judge say treatment or jail."[8] Kennedy has argued for decriminalization of cannabis but against legalization and the kinds of regulated markets present in many states today, as he believes that this will create incentives for the legal market to exploit health and safety in order to increase profits.[9]

The Kennedy clan's deft early investments in the alcohol industry may have helped them build wealth and political access, but Patrick Kennedy's observation speaks to a more common experience: for generations of Americans who have even been *suspected* of possessing cannabis, the legal and political outcomes of this criminalized regulation have been different and generally much more negative. Regulation and taxation of controlled substances—and the resistance to these processes—have been part of the lifeblood of American political culture for basically as long as there has been an American culture, dating back to fights over the British government's edicts about tobacco and tea in their colonial territories. Yet all too often the story has been one where the system of regulation becomes one of oppression. As Michelle Alexander famously points out in her seminal book about racial inequity in the American criminal justice system, *The New Jim Crow*, these systems are dynamic and respond to the existing institutional and political debates of the moment in which they are created.[10]

In order to understand current debates about cannabis legalization, then, as well as the larger critique of drug criminalization that has come along with them, readers first need to understand how the United States has arrived at the current system of drug regulation in force today. That is what this chapter will discuss. Chapter 2 will then turn to the actual enforcement of this regulatory regime and the staggering consequences that it has had, especially for Americans of color.

A BRIEF HISTORY OF IRREGULAR REGULATION

It is likely that any intoxicating substance that you can easily imagine—cannabis, yes, but also coffee and tea, alcohol and tobacco, and what we would today consider "hard" drugs such as opium and cocaine—has a long history of use in the United States. In many cases, this history is one that stretches back in the Americas to a time before there even *was* a United States.[11] But it was not until the end of the nineteenth and turn of the twentieth century that states and then the federal government began to regulate intoxicating substances' production and distribution, setting them apart from most other consumable goods.

As this first era of drug regulation evolved, it maintained some general features: a focus on policing producers and distributors (even if the goal was ultimately to prevent consumption), a relatively small list of targeted substances, and enforcement mechanisms that relied heavily on state and local police forces and judicial systems rather than the federal government—even when the former was responding to guidance or legislation produced by the latter. The nationwide prohibition on alcohol that was enshrined in the Constitution from 1918 to 1933 was in a certain sense the most ambitious of these policies, although it was riddled with exceptions and ultimately failed. In its wake, a seemingly less bold but nevertheless far more draconian prohibition on "narcotics" would instead take over much of the attention of governments, leading to decades of legal restrictions on the production, sale, transfer, marketing, and possession of a whole array of substances. At the same time, other consumable products which are arguably as (and, in some cases, more) dangerous in terms of their potential for addiction and direct health consequences—most notably tobacco—have merited much less restrictive treatment.

With this in mind, it is useful to examine a few of the most prominent kinds of substances—tobacco, alcohol, and the ill-defined yet ubiquitous category of "narcotics"—from the history of debates over regulating intoxicating substances in order to get a better sense of why American policymakers and police forces alike have treated certain ones differently than others. Doing so will help to reveal the social and political consequences of those choices—consequences which undoubtedly are shaping current debates about whether and how to revisit our state and federal governments' most recent regulatory decisions.

Tobacco: Big Money, Big Power

Tobacco has a history of use that long predates the establishment of the United States and which continued, despite some recent declines in rates of consumption, unabated into the twenty-first century. It also has a lengthy history of first European and later American observers condemning its ills. Unlike substances such as alcohol, opium, or cannabis, however, tobacco not only historically failed to attract an institutionally sustained movement to prohibit its use but also largely escaped regulation of any kind until well into the twentieth century.[12] This is despite the fact that the health dangers of tobacco use have been apparent and recognized for centuries. None other than England's King James I wrote a treatise against the use of tobacco in 1604—several years *before* granting a charter to the colony that would become Virginia. For his part, James made his case by pointing to patterns of overuse and the scourge of addiction. He was particularly concerned by the tendency to add other adulterating substances to tobacco in order to make use more tempting.[13]

Long used in the Western Hemisphere for recreational and mystical reasons,[14] tobacco was introduced to Europeans during the colonial era and was in turn distributed throughout the world. From an early point in the history of the British colonies, slaves were coerced into growing and harvesting tobacco in plantation settings—first in Virginia, then later in places such as Maryland and North Carolina. These slaves produced incredible wealth for already-wealthy English landlords. The connection between cash-crop tobacco and the slave labor needed to sustain production at economically profitable rates ensured the continued existence of the colonies that grew it. It also established slavery as the backbone of the economic system that spread throughout much of the American South even after tobacco declined in relative importance.[15]

As Virginia and other states with large enslaved workforces used their wealth and relative size to wield political power in the early American republic, slave owners and others who benefited from slavery captured political institutions and made them subservient to their whims.[16] Early efforts by James I and his son to ban tobacco and restrict its production and importation to England itself gave way to those merchants who made a fortune smuggling it in anyway (and more generally resisting the regulation and taxation system).[17] Perceived threats to an American economic system that relied on valuable products such as tobacco would continue to shape political realities for centuries thereafter. Samuel Adams, one of the original organizers of colonial resistance to British authority that led to the American Revolution, made a brisk trade among his brethren by smuggling everything from tea to whiskey. He also famously led a group of Boston men in 1773 in what has become known as the "Boston Tea Party," sending tons of government-sanctioned Indian tea—intended to crowd out local merchants such as himself from the colonial market—to the bottom of the city's harbor.[18]

Once the war actually came, the British recognized tobacco's central role in the colonial economy. During the last stages of fighting in 1780 and 1781, British troops engaged in a form of economic warfare against the colonists, burning tobacco crop harvests and freeing many of the slaves used for tobacco production.[19] Unsurprisingly, the political consequence of this was to harden slave owners' resolve for independence. Several generations later, the threat of losing the labor provided by slavery similarly drove the slave-owning leaders of Virginia and other southern states to secede in 1861, leading to a bloody civil war and a wrecked economy. Yet even long after the end of both wars and the abolition of slavery, tobacco continues today to be an important part of the economy of states such as North Carolina and Kentucky.[20]

Indeed, over the course of the twentieth century, tobacco companies and products proliferated, and American culture widely celebrated them. Then-movie star Ronald Reagan appeared in a series of advertisements in the late 1940s for the cigarette brand Chesterfield, alongside other tobacco advertisements that today would seem utterly bizarre and anachronistic.[21] The core reality behind this trend came from a similar kind of regulatory capture that helped to spark the Civil War—the political representatives of states such as Virginia and North Carolina that had large populations of tobacco farmers worked with wealthy and politically connected tobacco companies to keep citizens ignorant or at least in doubt about the scientific consensus that tobacco smoking was harmful to individual health. Among other tactics, they formed seemingly independent front groups that called for more research before federal legislation or court cases could begin.[22] In the coming decades, tobacco's negative health effects would become more and more publicized, however. Even Ronald Reagan eventually quit smoking—famously using a rigorous course of jelly beans to combat his cravings.[23] This public awareness finally gave political support to regulate the use and sale of tobacco products in the later half of the twentieth century, albeit in a way that maintained their legality and wide availability.

Throughout this history, tobacco has never been subject to the same form of social control that alcohol and many other recreational drugs have faced at one time or another. It took decades of sustained political organizing for the federal government to take up the task of regulating tobacco. Even this shift occurred only after the tobacco industry first took sustained financial blows from a deluge of product safety lawsuits—frequently led by state officers.

One of the largest of these blows came in the early 1990s, as the flood of evidence around smoking's negative health effects led populist political leaders such as Alabama Attorney General Mike Moore—later joined by lawyers representing nearly every other state—to file lawsuits against tobacco companies on the basis that they had fraudulently suppressed information about the dangers of tobacco and had unduly burdened state government health care plans with millions of dollars in costs related to the medical consequences of tobacco use. These companies, along with the industry at large, lobbied the federal government to get involved to sort out the proliferating claims. Several developments resulted, including the national Tobacco Master Settlement Agreement, in which the major tobacco companies agreed to pay individual state governments for the costs of treating tobacco-related health conditions for people in subsidized health systems such as Medicaid and state retiree health care plans. In exchange for these payments, the federal and state governments indemnified the traditional tobacco industry against further product liability lawsuits.[24]

This political settlement governs the federal regulation of many tobacco products, including chewing tobacco, cigars, and cigarettes. It has also permitted states to fund an array of antismoking programs and has led to increased taxes and restrictions on advertising and packaging. This, along with other messaging by public health advocates, has led to a slow but steady decline in the weekly use of tobacco over the last half century. In the mid-1960s, more than four in ten American adults smoked weekly. This rate halved by 2020, settling around 15 percent.[25] Both influencing and reflecting this decline, tobacco use has often been recast as deviant—portrayal of tobacco products in popular culture rarely conjures an image of glamour, if they're even present at all.

A surge in the use of vaping products in the early twenty-first century has led to a more complicated regulatory landscape. While upstart companies like Juul and Evali were innovators in developing vaping technologies and products that were in general lightly controlled when they first came to market, questions about the health relationship between vaping and legacy nicotine products and the appropriate manner of regulation of the former have increased as ownership in the vaping industry has become more consolidated, with legacy tobacco companies such as Altria taking large ownership stakes in vaping companies. Juul, in particular, has been accused of advertising to children and marketing many youth-friendly flavors. This in turn has led to intense regulatory scrutiny of the industry, something which will be discussed in this book's conclusion. As the vaping market has evolved and investigators have learned more about the technology, its uses, and its effects, federal officials have increasingly applied many of the same legal devices they previously used with cigarettes in order to restrict marketing and content of vaping products—especially to young people.

Still, vaping companies were able to bring their nicotine-based product to market in relatively short order with few initial regulatory questions. None of them are currently contributing to the Tobacco Master Settlement Agreement. And vaping is still legal and its products are still widely available. All in all, the story of vaping in its early years is one that suggests the distinct regulatory and cultural space that tobacco still maintains compared to many other intoxicating substances.

Alcohol: A Failed Model of Prohibition?

Visitors to the National Pharmacy Museum in New Orleans arrive at a world unfamiliar to our modern-day sensibilities. There you can see the wide variety of substances, tools, and other cures available to a mid- to late nineteenth-century pharmacist, who was often charged with developing treatments for every imaginable disease. Many of these treatments involved a healthy dose of substances that the Food and Drug Administration today claims have "no currently accepted medical use" and/or "a high potential for abuse."[26] This includes opium, heroin, cocaine, morphine, and—most importantly for this book—cannabis. Treatments of the era may have included one or more of these substances in combination with other questionable or even poisonous ingredients. Most of these substances would eventually be classified as narcotics and afterward be regulated and prohibited under an increasingly criminalized system.[27] Others would not—including, perhaps most notably, alcohol.

Today many Americans—as well as the Drug Enforcement Administration (DEA)—understand "narcotics" to primarily mean derivatives of opium like morphine and other similar highly addictive substances used for pain management and sometimes recreation.[28] This word was once used more flexibly, however, covering any substance that dulled the senses, including cannabis, peyote, and even alcohol.[29] This tendency to lump together very different substances helps explain why the national regulatory expansion that began in the early twentieth century sought to cover so many substances in similar ways at different times, despite the fact that their social history and patterns of use were dramatically different. Unsurprisingly, the outcomes of these regulatory pursuits have included widely varying results depending on which substance and which moment in time you consider. Alcohol's shifting status—from a widely consumed substance with an important role in the American economy during the first parts of the 1800s, to the only substance ever regulated via a US Constitutional amendment in the early 1900s, back to the widely available and licit recreational product that it is today—perfectly illustrates how social conceptions of a substance can influence its legal and regulatory position far more than anything inherent in the substance itself or its physiological effects.

During the early twentieth century, for example, fears about alcohol's social role—especially around the groups who might consume it and what harms they might enact if drunk—facilitated a political coalition of culturally conservative suffragettes to join forces with a power structure in American politics that was dominated by Protestant politicians who felt threatened by the increasing number of Catholic immigrants (particularly in major urban areas in the Northeast). Together, they worked to codify a federal prohibition on alcohol production and consumption.[30] While the popular idea of Prohibition is focused on the federal passage of the Eighteenth Amendment and the Volstead Act, the fight against alcohol was actually initiated and grown from the local and state levels and represents one of the first mass movements to try to drive social reform through legislation in American history.[31]

Among the groups that formed the core of the movement in favor of Prohibition included the Woman's Christian Temperance Union (WCTU, founded in 1874) and the Anti-Saloon League (ASL, founded in 1893), each of which campaigned for a multitude of state-level dry laws before the campaign for a federal constitutional amendment took shape. Both the WCTU and the ASL began as Christian evangelical movements focused on pressure campaigns aimed at consumers and purveyors of alcohol, but when the social problems stemming from alcohol addiction continued to impact society, advocacy turned toward governmental action to curb the supply of alcohol.[32]

State-level organizing for alcohol prohibition and efforts to restrict Black voting rights in the South were explicitly connected for many whites. In many Southern states, membership in organizations like the WCTU and the ASL was limited to white elites, many of whom were also members of the Ku Klux Klan, a situation that sometimes led to tensions with national coalition partners.[33] Still, it is perhaps unsurprising that a movement devoted to proscribing people's individual choices would appeal to a certain strain of white supremacists—restricting Black people's alcohol consumption was a natural complement to a belief that it was necessary for white people to protect Black people from themselves by restricting their access to anything that could lead to "deviant" behavior.[34] Southern states had long prohibited selling alcohol and other drugs to Black people and Native Americans on the assertions that they could not be trusted to control themselves and that the main barrier to community success for these groups was access to intoxicating substances—and not the poverty and social exclusion forced on them by society.[35]

There was also a general fear among white people that alcohol consumption would lead to disorderly behavior among Black Americans in particular. This fear—similar to the racist tropes that developed around cocaine, as discussed below—drew on a long history dating to the slavery era of worries about the ability of white people to protect themselves from unruly Black people (especially for white men to protect white women).[36] One of the first feature-length movies ever produced, D. W. Griffith's *Birth of a Nation* (1915), reinforced this narrative by explicitly connecting saloon drinking among Black men with behavior outside the social order.[37] Alcohol was also seen as inflaming social tensions that would culminate in episodes of poor white people committing racially motivated violence in places throughout the United States, especially in the South. Immediately following one episode of racially motivated violence in Atlanta, lawmakers in Georgia passed a 1907 bill—ratified by state voters—that took the right to vote away from tens of thousands of Black citizens.[38]

That said, a separate strain of support for Prohibition did exist among Black Americans—Frederick Douglass, for one, was a noted prohibitionist.[39] Black prohibitionists, especially women, generally viewed their work to limit the liquor trade as synonymous with the broader fight for racial liberation and economic justice—a variation on generic pro-temperance arguments about the personally degrading effects of alcohol that was tailored the specific situation of Black Americans.[40] If nothing else, this points to the complicated politics of Prohibition, which divided political parties and the country as a whole for years prior to World War I. Indeed, it suggests how the relative popularity of Prohibition was often directly related to more general social and political conditions that went well beyond alcohol consumption.

This relation to the general cultural moment was belied by one of World War I's prominent domestic effects as well. Acts of German aggression against Americans—such as the sinking of the *Lusitania* and the Zimmerman Telegram—set off a wave of anti-German propaganda, which led to the marginalization of German American citizens even before the US had formally entered the war. Since many German Americans at that time opposed Prohibition, this anti-German wave played a significant role in driving other Americans to support the movement.[41] The war proved a boon to prohibitionists in other ways as well. Claiming the need to conserve grain, prohibitionists successfully won legal limits on alcohol production as a war measure—limits which conveniently aligned with the goals of the preexisting moral crusade against alcohol.[42]

Indeed, not four months after Congress declared war on Germany in April 1917, the Senate first acted on a constitutional amendment to provide the authority for the federal government to prohibit alcohol, which it formally adopted that December. The Eighteenth Amendment achieved ratification by the constitutionally required three-fourths of the states a little more than a year later, in early 1919. By the end of that year, Congress passed the Volstead Act, which prohibited the production and sale of intoxicating alcoholic beverages beyond a 0.5 percent concentration of alcohol by volume and regulated the production of spirits for uses other than consumption as beverages.[43] The period of federal enforcement lasted from 1919 to 1933, when the Eighteenth Amendment was repealed.

Even when Prohibition was technically in force, however, two factors in particular led it to mostly fail at its overt goal—at least in the early 1920s. First, the Volstead Act, which implemented the ban, allowed for the continued consumption of alcohol for certain reasons, including religious uses and medical treatment under the supervision of a doctor. These exceptions were fairly broad and allowed many Americans to continue to consume alcohol, even if in limited portions.[44] Second, despite the popularity demonstrated by the passage of the constitutional amendment, the federal government failed to provide the resources necessary to disrupt and control the market for alcoholic beverages.[45] Prohibition was far from the first and would certainly not be the last social program that Congress underfunded. In this case, poor and inconsistent enforcement often targeted less fortunate Americans, while the privileged elite were allowed to take advantage of the exceptions built into the Volstead Act. For those still blocked from access to alcohol, organized crime filled the gap since the law did little to reduce demand but vastly increased the incentives to participate in the new illicit market.[46] The result was often dangerous, with unregulated alcohol products severely injuring or even killing consumers while producers and retailers evaded accountability and reaped an enhanced cut of the profits.[47]

In response to both spotty enforcement and these kinds of negative outcomes, public confidence in Prohibition slowly eroded over the course of the decade. The Association Against the Prohibition Amendment, a national organization in favor of repeal, continued to grow and adapt.[48] With the economic collapse and the beginning of the Great Depression in 1929, the political logic of Prohibition continued to crumble and the coalition that supported it lost much of its previous power. By the time Franklin Roosevelt ran for president in 1932, anti-prohibitionists had gained the upper hand in the Democratic Party. While Roosevelt himself was a reluctant anti-Prohibitionist, his campaign took careful advantage of the political context to mobilize voters by making clear that Democrats would initiate and support a repeal of the Volstead Act.[49] After Roosevelt won, the dam broke and the lame-duck Congress initiated a repeal amendment which was sent to the states in early 1933 and rendered much of the Volstead Act unconstitutional and therefore void when it was ratified as the Twenty-First Amendment at the end of that year.[50]

Given that many of the first states to legalize cannabis starting in the 1990s did so through ballot initiatives rather than legislative action—a history which will be discussed in later chapters—it is worth noting that the drafters of the Prohibition repeal amendment opted for a ratification method not previously attempted in American history, nor since. While every other amendment to the US Constitution was adopted through ratifications by state legislatures, the resolution sending what became the Twenty-First Amendment to the states specified that special elected conventions consider ratification. This allowed repeal supporters to sidestep state legislatures, which often embodied the worst of institutionalism and corruption that might be expected to oppose or frustrate a repeal amendment. It also meant that repeal supporters could directly engage voters on the question of alcohol prohibition, as conventions were elected solely on the question of support or opposition of the repeal amendment. Repeal was uncontroversial in some states—Massachusetts ratified the amendment almost unanimously and the state convention sat for only a brief meeting—though it was much closer elsewhere. Still, the required number of states had ratified the amendment by December 1933, ending the era of Prohibition.[51]

Prohibition's unique cultural and political legacy, however, lives on. Most Americans are taught as a standard lesson in school that Prohibition was a failure and a prime example of social policy gone too far. This plays into Americans' skepticism of authority and is sometimes drawn into political discussions about issues such as drug policy, gun control, and social welfare. This "standard lesson" is not exactly incorrect, but viewing Prohibition as a simple failure—both as a government policy and a moral cause—risks misunderstanding what it actually did and failing to recognize important parts of its legacy.

The fact is, Prohibition did have some successes, at least in terms of what its supporters envisioned for it. Alcohol consumption was initially reduced by over half, only rebounding on the back of organized crime and underwhelming federal enforcement.[52] Problem drinking and the saloon culture that had been the bane of religious movements and suffragists was also significantly disrupted. And as Prohibition ended, states took the opportunity to build an alcohol regulatory system intended to prevent the worst impacts of overconsumption and backsliding into that earlier era.[53] Both the long campaign leading to it and the experience of Prohibition itself also provided Americans with a real opportunity to consider the social benefits and costs of alcohol against those of prohibitionist policies themselves.

Considering Prohibition on these terms helps to make sense of what otherwise might appear to be a paradox: the prohibitionist impulse continues to hold sway today—both in political posturing about executing a "War on Drugs" and actual laws and policies which strictly restrict access to a range of substances—despite the widespread belief that the legal regime, which is popularly considered to be the paradigmatic application of that impulse, is also popularly considered to have been itself a failure.

Narcotics: Where Prohibition Lived On

While the temperance movement was growing in popularity, a parallel campaign led by muckraking journalists, scientists, and progressive campaigners called for regulation of many other ingestible substances, both intoxicating and non-intoxicating alike. Many of these were grouped under the general heading of "narcotics," and attempts to address the perceived dangers of products including these substances began in the decades after the Civil War at the state and local levels.[54] Much like alcohol prohibition, this state-level political pressure eventually pushed the federal government to act, first by passing the Pure Food and Drug Act in 1906. This law did not prohibit any substances that people regularly consumed—even cocaine or heroin—but it did require that labels for products containing them be accurate. It also created a regulatory regime to limit interstate transfer of covered substances, while mandating that improperly shipped products could be seized and destroyed.[55]

This relatively light touch for substances that most people today consider "hard" drugs was followed by a stricter regime adopted in 1914. The Harrison Narcotics Tax Act sought to implement the 1912 International Opium Convention—a pioneering multilateral agreement to control and limit the trade in potentially addictive substances by asking signatory countries to focus on policing providers—by imposing high taxes on those selling and producing narcotics, though it notably did not directly target users. Narrow exceptions were made for medical provision, though a series of court decisions made these exceptions nearly meaningless.[56] Medical providers who had been providing maintenance doses for addiction treatment were forced to drop their patients. As a result, many consumers and suppliers for these substances moved to the illicit market.[57] Along with this increasingly precarious legal situation, a cloud of cultural and societal pressure redefined what had often been considered medicine in the late nineteenth century—whether prescribed by a doctor or by oneself—as dangerous, addictive, and a gateway to moral failing.[58] This framing was similar to the view of alcohol that was current in the temperance movement at the same time. Yet, as with alcohol prohibition, demand could not simply be legislated away.

When considered in the abstract as a movement to ensure the purity and safety of medical treatments, this regulatory push sounds well intentioned, especially considering that the campaign to restrict opium and related substances was connected to a broader effort to ban fraudulent "patent medicine" treatments that either did nothing or that we would today consider to be actively harmful. Yet, even at the time, it was difficult to miss the social and power dynamics that shaped this policy design.

Opium, for example, had long been prescribed for a variety of conditions, particularly among upper-class white women.[59] Despite this, there was a long-established racialized association between opium use and Chinese immigrants in the American West that one might imagine could have provoked a backlash against the substance at many prior points. But it wasn't until the second decade of the twentieth century—as support for government regulation of individual consumption in many realms became more common—that the perception of out-of-control opium use and addiction created the political drive to regulate usage.

When the impulse to control consumption of opium did emerge, it swiftly built on the existing racist narrative and combined it with the long-held belief that women needed special protection from predation. Rather than users exercising their own agency, white women were portrayed as the victims of drug trafficking directed by Chinese communities, with the drugs inviting an unfavored amount of racial mixing between those Chinese communities and white elites.[60] At around the same time, media narratives also swept Black Americans into the moral panic about intoxication in ways that extended the similar discussion surrounding race and alcohol. For the first time, claims that drugs like cocaine made Black people "savage" and violent became common, portraying both the substances and Black people as threats to the existing social order and justifying new enforcement mechanisms to keep these threats at bay. To this end, cocaine was also covered in much of the early federal narcotics legislation, including the Harrison Act, seeking to further limit its supply and control access to it.[61]

This result was another instance of politics making strange bedfellows, just as had been the case with the coalition of suffragettes, old-school politicians, anti-German "patriots," and white supremacists who helped push alcohol prohibition over the line. During this early twentieth-century political moment, American progressives concerned about consumer safety and social uplift allied with traditionalist politicians to target drugs associated with ethnic minorities—though these drugs were also used by many white people. Working together, they imposed what became a harsh regulatory framework cloaked in the lab coat of scientific purity and backed by the power of law and social repression.[62] Meanwhile, the more widely used intoxicants of choice for socially elite whites, such as tobacco, were subjected to little legal scrutiny or, as with alcohol, were easily acquired, along with the full spectrum of illegal drugs, even when they became illegal.[63]

Even as alcohol was marching toward prohibition and more powerful narcotics were slowly being brought under government control, cannabis at first attracted no special scrutiny. Much like alcohol and tobacco, cannabis has a social history of use going back millennia, and it was generally legal and unregulated. Cannabis is mentioned in historical sources from India, China, Egypt, Greece, and Mesopotamia, among other civilizations.[64] Viewed as a lower-potency medicine, it was used as a home remedy for pain management and a treatment for venereal disease, sexual dysfunction, and even as an aid in childbirth.[65] Cannabis use by Europeans was documented by the early nineteenth century, and through this and other channels, information about the substance spread to the United States and the Western Hemisphere more generally.[66]

Within this broader context, most of the patterns of cannabis use we recognize today were brought to the United States by Mexican workers beginning in the early twentieth century as they emigrated in pursuit of better economic conditions and to escape violence.[67] The political and legal legacy of that transfer is built into our legal system even today—beginning with the name that we call the substance itself. Several states, as well as the federal government, adopted laws regulating cannabis that used an alternate spelling of the term "marijuana" with an "h" in place of the "j."[68] This other name reminded the largely white population of many states of the "foreign" nature of cannabis, and reinforced a need to regulate or even prohibit its use.

Along with "marihuana" itself, Mexican migrations also brought the cultural context of the substance's association with social disorder and chaotic behavior. Historian Isaac Campos has demonstrated that Mexico has a long and contested history with cannabis, with both colonial and post-independence authorities seeking to limit access to the drug over several centuries. By 1919, the Mexican government sought to prohibit "marihuana" completely, with authorities viewing users as immoral and degenerate. Officials in the US West heard of these developments and states such as Colorado became among the first to pass laws prohibiting cannabis (a history explored more in the beginning of chapter 5).[69]

While the exact use patterns of cannabis in the United States before the second half of the twentieth century remain difficult to approximate given limited data, it seems likely that even at the time the common emphasis on it being associated first with Mexican migrants—and later with African Americans—was a misstatement of reality. More recent data, including results from the national Monitoring the Future study, demonstrate that racial patterns of youth use of cannabis are relatively consistent between demographic categories, with all racial groups except Asian Americans maintaining levels of use between 10 and 20 percent across decades of data.[70] Despite a long history of widespread use, however, cannabis became subjected to increasing legal and criminal scrutiny in a way that mirrored other intoxicating substances during the early to mid-twentieth century. But, as with the temperance movement owing its success as much to factors only indirectly related to alcohol itself, the fact that cannabis was swept up in the prohibitionist regime was as much an accident of historical circumstance as anything else.

Before the end of Prohibition but with its future shaky, Harry Anslinger, the head of the Federal Bureau of Narcotics, desperately needed a new purpose for his agency's existence.[71] Building on growing cultural awareness about cannabis, in part derived from the Mexican narratives about users being violent and degenerate, Anslinger used the media to create a panic.[72] Beginning in 1930, he collected stories of crimes supposedly committed under the influence of cannabis—at least in his interpretation. The stories usually featured a person of color perpetrating a crime against a white victim. By sharing these contrived stories at some gripping congressional hearings, Anslinger ensured that his fabricated vision of a cannabis-induced, racially charged crime wave would be publicized across the country.[73] While cross-border Mexican media infiltration had played an early role in associating "marihuana" with violence within the public consciousness, Anslinger's publicity campaign emphasized the foreign roots of cannabis and solidified the link between shockingly violent crime and cannabis, even when the actual evidence of cannabis directly causing said violence was nonexistent.[74]

Congress quickly passed the Marihuana Tax Act (MTA) in 1937, giving the federal government the power to enforce high taxes and fees on cannabis use and sales.[75] Similar to the Harrison Act, the central enforcement mechanism of the MTA was a requirement that those seeking to buy, sell, or possess cannabis would need to purchase stamps from the federal government in order to avoid arrest and prosecution. This mechanism is the origin of the oft-repeated assertion familiar to many cannabis activists that the motivation behind cannabis criminalization was less a concern for the supposed victims of Anslinger's stories than a desire by investors in the US timber industry (namely Andrew Mellon and William Randolph Hearst) to use a protectionist tax to secure their economic interests against the domestic hemp market.

In any case, the high cost to comply with the MTA effectively achieved its primary purpose of criminalizing cannabis use at the federal level. This was in part because many states had already individually criminalized cannabis by attaching strict criminal penalties for its possession and sale, which provided a strong disincentive to pay for a federal tax stamp that could itself serve as evidence for a state-level criminal prosecution.[76] For the most part, states that criminalized cannabis did so when they adopted the Uniform Narcotic Drug Act, a product of the Uniform Law Commission, an obscure but incredibly powerful nonprofit legal institution that even today still drafts model state bills for legislatures across the country. By 1932, it was circulating this particular bill among legislators in states and territories throughout the country.[77] Despite the fact that cannabis is not actually a narcotic, the Uniform

Narcotic Drug Act considered it to be one, a decision with consequences that we still see today.

Including cannabis within the law's purview doesn't seem to have initially been a high priority for many legislators or other political actors—other than those who viewed it as a plus, as they promoted the law as part of Anslinger's campaign during the early 1930s to pressure state legislatures to adopt it.[78] Tellingly, one of Anslinger's primary arguments for passing this law was to fulfill the terms of the federal government's commitments under the Hague Convention on narcotics limitations. While state passage was initially slow, a later push by Franklin Roosevelt in 1935 was successful in eventually leading all states to adopt this form of drug control. Including cannabis in a scheme that had political traction for other reasons was therefore perhaps simply a means to an end for Anslinger and his fellow travelers, who sought some sort of legal prohibition in the face of still marginal public concern about the use of cannabis. Later, unsatisfied with the pace and scope of state action, Anslinger would shift his attention to federal prohibition of cannabis specifically.

One outcome of going the federal route was that it gave federal agents a basis to investigate anyone deemed to be "subversive." Anslinger, whom even his peers in the 1930s considered to be a racist, quickly used this as a pretext to target African Americans. For example, federal agents went after Billie Holiday on cannabis-related charges after she released her famous song "Strange Fruit," which was intended to highlight the contemporary national scourge of mob-driven lynchings across the South.[79] Anslinger also targeted Black centers of power more generally, collecting stories about jazz musicians and their cannabis use and executing coordinated dragnets of the jazz industry.[80] While the full-control regimes that we see today would not come to exist for decades to come, the culture of race-fueled fear around cannabis was set.

The injustice of this turn of events is thrown into even sharper relief when considering that this government response to cannabis use—especially by people of color—closely coincided with the development of a markedly different approach to the growing use of many other substances which were culturally associated with big business and white users. For as federal officials focused on criminalizing an ever-increasing set of substances that were clearly defined in the public's mind as corrupting and harmful, governments at both the federal and state levels struggled to even get their bearings on a silent but increasingly more dangerous threat to public health originating from the boardrooms of corporate America rather than the criminal underground. Historian David Herzberg has documented this divergence—part of what he calls the "drug-medicine" divide—that developed over the twentieth century, as pharmaceutical companies and doctors sought to preserve their market power to sell drugs to consumers in legal markets while minimizing or even ignoring their potential for abuse or addiction.[81] During the 1940s and '50s, new pharmaceutical products such as Miltown, Librium, and Valium led to surges in addiction, though formal attention to these public health threats was minimal.[82] Even with increased public attention to pharmaceutical regulation in the decades since, legal pharmaceutical products remain one of the largest threats to public health, with the opioid crisis leading to trillions of dollars in economic losses as well as the deaths of hundreds of thousands of Americans as of 2020.[83]

THE CONTROLLED SUBSTANCES ACT: THIS MEANT WAR

Enforcement penalties at both the federal and state levels were enhanced in the two decades that followed the initial wave of narcotics criminalization. Emblematic of this trend was the Boggs Act, passed in 1951, which responded to the perceived softness of federal judges for narcotics offenders by creating mandatory minimum sentences and leading to decades in prison for growing numbers of federal drug offenders. Many states followed suit. However, by the 1960s, cannabis in particular came to represent social change and increased freedom, being used by Black and white Americans alike, often when they were together.[84] Given that the fall of legal segregation in the 1960s had set off a racially oriented backlash among many white conservatives, cannabis was a seemingly inevitable political target. Much like the prior wave of legislation that had first criminalized cannabis, the reassertion of criminalization required a new political moment of chaos and disorder to justify its backers' regressive tendencies.

By the late 1960s, the United States seemed to many people to be exactly that—a society that was spinning out of control and sorely in need of policies to restore order. The connection between violence and perceived societal disorder had little better example than the Democratic National Convention hosted in Chicago in August 1968. A year of disorienting public spectacles—including the Tet Offensive, Lydon B. Johnson's decision to forgo reelection, and the assassinations of both Martin Luther King Jr. and Robert Kennedy—led to intense public discontent with the status quo, as well as a restive group of activists who were intent on pressuring the Democratic Party establishment over the costs of the Vietnam War and who used the convention to focus media attention on the disconnect between the political sausage being made on the convention floor and the aspirations of many of the party's voters. Later investigations would demonstrate that the Chicago police were responsible for inciting nearly all of the violence that occurred that August, though the image of street fighting on American televisions did not give then-vice president and Democratic nominee for President Herbert Humphrey a clear mandate, contributing to his narrow defeat to Richard Nixon three months later.[85]

By the late 1960s, the ramshackle system of "narcotics" criminalization that had been constructed in the first half of the twentieth century was also spinning out of control. Cannabis use had become more widespread and had grown to include upper-class white people who attended college, exposing some of them to increased scrutiny by law enforcement and even criminal charges. In states across the country, both legislatures and courts were also beginning to question the classification of cannabis as a "narcotic" on the basis that its physiological effects were notably distinct from substances such as heroin, though these challenges often faced mixed results.

The major blow came at the end of the decade when the Supreme Court decided that the way Congress had used the tax code to regulate individual activity via laws such as the Marihuana Tax Act was unconstitutional. In *Marchetti v. United States* (1968) and *Leary v. United States* (1969), the Supreme Court overturned tax stamp provisions designed to prohibit gambling and cannabis use, respectively. Yet rather than opening up a new era of legal cannabis use, these rulings gave Nixon—newly inaugurated and holding a belief that he had a mandate to address the social disorder voters had feared so much—an opportunity to re-create the entire structure of federal narcotics regulation. Even as state officials used the breakdown of federal gambling restrictions to scale down criminalization and create government monopolies to capture gambling revenue in the form of lotteries,[86] Nixon closed off any possibility that states would develop a similar regulatory system for cannabis by including it in the Controlled Substances Act (CSA) of 1970.

Much as alcohol prohibition was motivated in part by a desire from more conservative and rural voters and elected officials to control and discipline the urban immigrants that dared speak and vote "out of line," the War on Drugs that the CSA ushered in was infused with the desire to assert political control through the regulation of substance use. Nixon himself was under no impression that cannabis was a real threat to public health or safety. Nixon's own expert investigatory body, the Shafer Commission, actually recommended that cannabis be federally decriminalized.[87] But so-called hippie liberals had become associated with using cannabis as a "protest" drug, and this presented an opportunity to disrupt the left that Nixon could exploit.[88]

Evaluating these years in hindsight, Nixon's former chief of staff made this connection explicit:

> The Nixon campaign in 1968, and the Nixon White House after that, had two enemies: the antiwar left and black people. You understand what I'm saying?

> We knew we couldn't make it illegal to be either against the war or black [people], but by getting the public to associate the hippies with marijuana and blacks with heroin, and then criminalizing both heavily, we could disrupt those communities. We could arrest their leaders, raid their homes, break up their meetings, and vilify them night after night on the evening news. Did we know we were lying about the drugs? Of course we did.[89]

Nixon's declaration of a War on Drugs was intended to fulfill the political aim of marginalizing his enemies. It is telling that the way he went about it was to take behaviors that were culturally linked to minorities and other disfavored populations—regardless of actual use patterns—and suggest a causal relationship between them and perceived social disorder. This may have demonstrated Nixon's inherent talent to appeal to the more primal pressures of politics, but it also helped to establish a basis for decades of inequitable enforcement of drug laws.

Most importantly, Nixon declared this war on the scourge of drugs in the early 1970s with the passage of the CSA. This law consolidated previous drug control regimes into one statute and built an enforcement system that harmonized state and federal efforts. While few but the most dedicated insiders know the specific details of the CSA, most Americans instinctively know the drug classification regime that it created. Nearly all of the substances for which possession and sale carry severe penal consequences are classified as Schedule I, or those drugs for which the federal government recognizes a high potential for abuse and no accepted medical use, even under the direct supervision of a doctor. Schedule I substances include heroin, peyote, psilocybin, and cannabis. As far as the CSA is concerned, there is nearly no legal way to access these substances since doctors are prohibited from prescribing them and production, transportation, marketing, retailing, transfer, and possession are all separately and concurrently illegal under federal law.[90] Tellingly, Schedule II drugs are similarly defined as having a "high" potential for abuse, "may lead to severe psychological or physical dependence," and are generally considered dangerous.[91] Yet unlike Schedule I drugs, the recognition that they have a medical use leads the government to allow physicians to prescribe these substances—including many synthetic opioids such as oxycodone, the active ingredient in Oxycontin, among other medications. This has remained true even as there have been more than 10,000 overdose deaths involving prescription opioids in the United States every year since 2006.[92]

It is on this structure that the last five decades of criminal drug enforcement have been built. While there was a short period of legal and political activism in the early 1970s that was successful in decriminalizing cannabis in at least eleven states, this period of liberalization was short and ended with the so-called parents movement and the Reagan administration's enhancement of the War on Drugs only a decade later (both of which will be discussed in chapter 2).[93] Cannabis was again criminalized in nearly every state and remained so until 1996, when the first adoptions of medical cannabis broke the legislative logjam. The resistance to this political regime included a futile 1972 California ballot initiative, defeated by nearly two-thirds of the vote (Nixon himself garnered about 11 percent less support in his landslide reelection win).[94] One of the few places in the United States with something less than full criminalization was Alaska, where the state supreme court found in 1975 that state regulation of individual cannabis use violated the privacy rights of citizens. Cannabis was later largely recriminalized there via ballot measure, though some legal protections around personal possession remained after that.[95]

REGULATION OF DRUGS AND SOCIAL IMMOBILITY

The CSA explicitly prohibits the inclusion on Schedule I of the two substances that have perhaps the richest history of both medical and recreational use in the United States—tobacco and alcohol. This means that the federal government is prohibited from using the provisions of the CSA to regulate or restrict access to these substances—there is a prohibition on prohibition, at least for alcohol and tobacco. Yet each kill hundreds of thousands of Americans per year as a result of directly causing chronic health conditions, with alcohol additionally contributing to violence, social disorder, accidents, and suicide. Despite this, providers in each market are given economic protections that are not seen in other industries. Their legacy in American culture, history, and material conditions have given alcohol and tobacco a special protected status in law and social regulation.[96]

The exclusion of alcohol from the CSA specifically reflects the bitter lessons learned during the enactment of alcohol prohibition, yet these lessons did not carry over to the substances the CSA does prohibit. One possible explanation is that although discussions of alcohol prohibition sometimes involved racist arguments, they were rarely the main point of debate in the way that they were with the movement to ban substances such as opium and cannabis. Likewise, the substances brought under strict regulation in the CSA were not nearly as widely used by Americans—especially not in popular social settings such as bars—by the time the CSA came into force, partly because of prior restrictions on their use. Intersecting with the divisions engendered by racism, this may have further limited the possible base for a political backlash. Whatever the reasons, the question of why alcohol prohibition did not cause a broader reconsideration of substance regulation is one that undoubtedly bears further examination by future researchers.

Regardless of the full explanation, the undoubtedly racist motivations of and messaging surrounding cannabis regulation under both the pre- and post-CSA regimes developed during a crucial century for Black Americans seeking economic and political acceptance in American society. The Civil War had removed the chains from formerly enslaved people, but with little economic security or legal protections—especially compared with the average white person. This disparity, some characteristics of which I will discuss in depth in chapter 2, has left Black Americans vulnerable to the kind of state intervention and surveillance that has characterized campaigns to regulate or criminalize substances and behaviors over the course of the last century.

Drug policy scholars Richard Bonnie and Charles Whitebread noted nearly a half century ago "that drug use or other minority behavior is more likely to be viewed with anxiety (and to be indicted as a 'menace') . . . when the dominant social order is thought to threatened—by economic woes, by internal disruption of lawlessness, or by external aggression." The result in these moments is that "policymaking is likely to be defensive, lashing out at behavior perceived to be associated with general societal fears."[97] Narcotics regulation has had a much more pervasive and resilient policy life than this might imply, in part because the successful cultural and political association of drug use with racial minorities has made it an evergreen choice for politicians seeking to win over the larger bloc of white voters. Such policies are much more than political ploys, however—narcotics regulation today still serves as one of the major engines of mass incarceration and social control of racial minorities in the United States. Even as alcohol prohibition swept the nation and then cracked under the pressure of the incoherency of its origins and alcohol's widespread popularity, the ability to associate narcotics use with a much smaller proportion of the American population—one that politicians like Nixon have long been effective at stigmatizing in one way or another—has made the political utility of controlling it far more enduring.

By contrast, consider the story of the Kennedy family that opened this chapter. They, along with many other white families in the nineteenth and twentieth centuries, achieved rapid social mobility despite their participation in a trade (saloon ownership) that was often widely socially and sometimes legally disfavored in many parts of the country. The ability to make a trade related to this substance meant that their family members moved from poor immigrants to the height of political power within the space of a century. Conversely, the political decisions to criminally prohibit specific other substances, including cannabis, drove a wave of social and economic exclusion of racial minorities that is still present today. The fact that this remains true nearly three decades after the first cracks in the criminalization regime of cannabis began to emerge suggests just the depths of criminalization's effects.

The remainder of this book is dedicated to understanding the mechanics of this challenge as well as efforts to address it.

NOTES

1. John F. Kennedy Presidential Library and Museum, "John F. Kennedy and Ireland," https://www.jfklibrary.org/learn/about-jfk/jfk-in-history/john-f-kennedy-and-ireland.

2. Doris Kearns Goodwin, *The Fitzgeralds and the Kennedys* (New York: Simon and Schuster, 1987), 442–43.

3. David Nasaw, *The Patriarch: The Remarkable Life and Turbulent Times of Joseph P. Kennedy* (New York: Penguin, 2013), 81.

4. The Boston Globe, "Ted Kennedy and the Chappaquiddick Incident | Boston Globe," YouTube video, August 26, 2009, https://www.youtube.com/watch?v=ZNHbDikvXlU&ab_channel=TheBostonGlobe.

5. *New York Times*, "How the Skakel-Moxley Murder Case Unfolded Over Four Decades," November 2, 2020, https://www.nytimes.com/article/skakel-moxley-murder-case.html.

6. Bill Frist, "How Former US Representative Patrick Kennedy's Own Experience with Addiction Led Him to Become One of Our Nation's Most Ardent Mental Healthcare Champions," *Forbes*, June 21, 2021, https://www.forbes.com/sites/billfrist/2021/06/21/how-former-us-representative-patrick-kennedys-own-experience-with-addiction-led-him-to-become-one-of-our-nations-most-ardent-mental-healthcare-champions/?sh=6380bf59232e.

7. Patrick McGreevy, "Kennedy Group Puts $2 Million into Fight Against Pot-Legalization Measures, *Los Angeles Times*, August 1, 2016, https://www.latimes.com/politics/la-pol-ca-patrick-kennedy-marijuana-legalization-opposition-20160801-snap-story.html.

8. *NBC News*, "Treatment or Jail: Patrick Kennedy Wages Anti-Pot Crusade," February 17, 2014, https://www.nbcnews.com/storyline/legal-pot/treatment-or-jail-patrick-kennedy-wages-fierce-anti-pot-crusade-n22256.

9. *NBC News*, "Treatment or Jail."

10. Michelle Alexander, *The New Jim Crow: Mass Incarceration in the Age of Colorblindness* (New York: New Press, 2010).

11. *PBS*, "A Social History of America's Most Popular Drugs," Frontline: Drug Wars, October 2000, https://www.pbs.org/wgbh/pages/frontline/shows/drugs/buyers/socialhistory.html. See also Michael Pollan, *How to Change Your Mind: What the New Science of Psychedelics Teaches Us About Consciousness, Dying, Addiction, Depression, and Transcendence* (New York: Penguin, 2018).

12. Iain Gately, *Tobacco: A Cultural History of How an Exotic Plant Seduced Civilization* (New York: Grove Press, 2001), 222.

13. Gately, *Tobacco*, 67–68.

14. Gately, *Tobacco*, 44.

15. Gately, *Tobacco*, 110–13.

16. James Horn, "Transformations of Virginia: Tobacco, Slavery, and Empire," forum introduction, *William and Mary Quarterly* 68, no. 3 (2011): 327–31.

17. Gately, *Tobacco*, 99–100.

18. Commonwealth Museum, Boston, Massachusetts, "The Stamp Tax Crisis of 1765," Traveling Exhibit: Road to Revolution, https://www.sec.state.ma.us/mus/pdfs/Stamp-Tax-Crisis.pdf.

19. Gately, *Tobacco*, 142. See also Peter Andreas, "Drugs and War: What Is the Relationship?" *Annual Review of Political Science* 22, no. 1 (2019): 63, https://doi.org/10.1146/annurev-polisci-051017-103748.

20. Gately, *Tobacco*, 354.

21. *Christian Science Monitor*, "Tobacco, Government, and the Reagan Team," January 2, 1981, https://www.csmonitor.com/1981/0102/010218.html.

22. Douglas G. Altman et al., "Tobacco Farmers and Diversification: Opportunities and Barriers," *Tobacco Control* 5, no. 3 (1996): 192, https://www.jstor.org/stable/20207199.

23. Ronald Reagan Presidential Library and Museum, "Jelly Belly® Jelly Beans and Ronald Reagan," https://www.reaganlibrary.gov/reagans/ronald-reagan/jelly-bellyr-jelly-beans-and-ronald-reagan.

24. National Association of Attorneys General, "The Master Settlement Agreement," https://www.naag.org/our-work/naag-center-for-tobacco-and-public-health/the-master-settlement-agreement/.

25. Gallup, "Tobacco and Smoking," In Depth: Topics A to Z, accessed February 24, 2023, https://news.gallup.com/poll/1717/tobacco-smoking.aspx.

26. US Food and Drug Administration, "FDA Regulation of Cannabis and Cannabis-Derived Products, Including Cannabidiol (CBD)," FDA.gov, content current as of January 22, 2021, https://www.fda.gov/news-events/public-health-focus/fda-regulation-cannabis-and-cannabis-derived-products-including-cannabidiol-cbd.

27. Richard J. Bonnie and Charles H. Whitebread, *The Marihuana Conviction: A History of Marihuana Prohibition in the United States* (Charlottesville: University of Virginia Press, 1974), 13–22.

28. US Drug Enforcement Administration, "Narcotics," Drug Fact Sheet, April 2020, https://www.dea.gov/sites/default/files/2020-06/Narcotics-2020.pdf.

29. Bonnie and Whitebread, *Marihuana Conviction*, 28.

30. David E. Kyvig, *Repealing National Prohibition*, 2nd ed. (Kent, OH: Kent State University Press, 2000), 7.

31. Ronald G. Walters, *American Reformers: 1815–1860*, rev. ed. (New York: Hill and Wang, 1997), 125–46.

32. Kyvig, *Repealing National Prohibition*, 7.

33. Doris Marie Provine, *Unequal Under Law: Race in the War on Drugs* (Chicago: University of Chicago Press, 2007), 47, 52.

34. Provine, *Unequal Under Law*, 53. See also Denise A. Herd, "Prohibition, Racism and Class Politics in the Post-Reconstruction South," *Journal of Drug Issues* 13, no. 1 (1983): 81, https://doi.org/10.1177/002204268301300105.

35. Mark Lawrence Schrad, *Smashing the Liquor Machine: A Global History of Prohibition* (New York: Oxford University Press, 2021), 198.

36. Jennifer Wriggins, "Rape, Racism, and the Law," *Harvard Women's Law Journal* 6 (1983): 106–8.

37. Provine, *Unequal Under Law*, 56.

38. Kaylynn Washnock, "Prohibition in Georgia," *New Georgia Encyclopedia*, last edited July 20, 2020, https://www.georgiaencyclopedia.org/articles/history-archaeology/prohibition-in-georgia/.

39. Provine, *Unequal Under Law*, 51; and Donald Yacovone, "The Transformation of the Black Temperance Movement, 1827–1854: An Interpretation," *Journal of the Early Republic* 8, no. 3 (1988): 285–86, https://doi.org/10.2307/3123691. See also Frederick Douglass, "Frederick Douglass on Prohibition," *San Marcos* (TX) *Free Press*, May 19, 1887, https://texashistory.unt.edu/ark:/67531/metapth295657/m1/1/?q=frederick%20douglass.

40. Mark Lawrence Schrad, "The Forgotten History of Black Prohibitionism," *Politico*, February 6, 2021, https://www.politico.com/news/magazine/2021/02/06/forgotten-black-history-prohibition-temperance-movement-461215.

41. Kyvig, *Repealing National Prohibition*, 10, 36–37.

42. Kyvig, *Repealing National Prohibition*, 11.

43. Kyvig, *Repealing National Prohibition*, 13; and US Senate Historical Office, "The Senate Overrides the President's Veto of the Volstead Act," https://www.senate.gov/artandhistory/history/minute/Volstead_Act.htm.

44. Bonnie and Whitebread, *Marihuana Conviction*, 24–26.

45. Kyvig, *Repealing National Prohibition*, 113; and Bonnie and Whitebread, *Marihuana Conviction*, 30.

46. Mark Thornton, "Alcohol Prohibition Was a Failure," Cato Institute Policy Analysis No. 157, July 17, 1991, https://www.cato.org/policy-analysis/alcohol-prohibition-was-failure#notes.

47. Deborah Blum, "The Chemist's War," *Slate*, February 19, 2010, https://slate.com/technology/2010/02/the-little-told-story-of-how-the-u-s-government-poisoned-alcohol-during-prohibition.html.

48. Kyvig, *Repealing National Prohibition*, 83–84.

49. Kyvig, *Repealing National Prohibition*, 166; and Jean Edward Smith, *FDR* (New York: Random House, 2007), 252–54.

50. Kyvig, *Repealing National Prohibition*, 169–71.

51. John Dinan and Jac C. Heckelman, "Support for Repealing Prohibition: An Analysis of State-Wide Referenda on Ratifying the 21st Amendment," *Social Science Quarterly* 95, no. 3 (2014): 636–51, https://doi.org/10.1111/ssqu.12077.

52. Jeffrey A. Miron and Jeffrey Zwiebel, "Alcohol Consumption During Prohibition," *American Economic Review* 81, no. 2 (1991): 242–47, https://www.jstor.org/stable/2006862; and *PBS*, "Unintended Consequences of Prohibition," *Prohibition: A Film by Ken Burns and Lynn Novick*, https://www.pbs.org/kenburns/prohibition/unintended-consequences.

53. Harry G. Levine and Craig Reinarman, "From Prohibition to Regulation: Lessons from Alcohol Policy for Drug Policy," *Milbank Quarterly* 69, no. 3 (1991): 461–94, https://doi.org/10.2307/3350105; and Mark Lawrence Schrad, "Let's Raise a Glass to What Prohibition Accomplished," *Politico*, December 4, 2022, https:

//www.politico.com/news/magazine/2022/12/04/liquor-capitalism-prohibition-repeal-day-00072067.

54. Bonnie and Whitebread, *Marihuana Conviction*, 14.

55. Jonathan Rees, *The Chemistry of Fear: Harvey Wiley's Fight for Pure Food* (Baltimore, MD: Johns Hopkins University Press, 2021), 112–16; and Bonnie and Whitebread, *Marihuana Conviction*, 15.

56. *Webb et al. v. United States*, 249 U.S. (1919), https://tile.loc.gov/storage-services/service/ll/usrep/usrep249/usrep249096/usrep249096.pdf.

57. Provine, *Unequal Under Law*, 76.

58. Bonnie and Whitebread, *Marihuana Conviction*, 7.

59. Provine, *Unequal Under Law*, 65.

60. Provine, *Unequal Under Law*, 68–73; and Bonnie and Whitebread, *Marihuana Conviction*, 9.

61. Provine, *Unequal Under Law*, 74–75; and Bonnie and Whitebread, *Marihuana Conviction*, 30.

62. Martin A. Lee, *Smoke Signals: A Social History of Marijuana—Medical, Recreational, and Scientific* (New York: Scribner, 2012), 43; and Provine, *Unequal Under Law*, 30–32.

63. Provine, *Unequal Under Law*, 65.

64. Bonnie and Whitebread, *Marihuana Conviction*, 1–3.

65. Lee, *Smoke Signals*, 14–34; and Bonnie and Whitebread, *Marihuana Conviction*, 53–55.

66. Bonnie and Whitebread, *Marihuana Conviction*, 2–3.

67. Bonnie and Whitebread, *Marihuana Conviction*, 38–41.

68. Cannabis Regulatory Agency, State of Michigan, "Why Is Marijuana Sometimes Spelled with an 'H' and Other Times Spelled with a 'J'?" https://www.michigan.gov/cra/faq/licensing-list/additional-new/why-is-marijuana-sometimes-spelled-with-an-h-and-other-times-spelled-with-a-j.

69. Isaac Campos, *Home Grown: Marijuana and the Origins of Mexico's War on Drugs* (Chapel Hill: University of North Carolina Press, 2012).

70. Katherine M. Keyes et al., "Race/Ethnicity and Marijuana Use in the United States: Diminishing Differences in the Prevalence of Use, 2006–2015," *Drug and Alcohol Dependence* 179, no. 1 (2017): 379–86, https://doi.org/10.1016/j.drugalcdep.2017.07.027.

71. Lee, *Smoke Signals*, 49.

72. Campos, *Home Grown*, 127–33.

73. Lee, *Smoke Signals*, 51–57.

74. For example, see H. F. Anslinger, "Marijuana—Assassin of Youth," with Courtney Ryley Cooper, *Reader's Digest*, February 1938, reprint available at https://www.druglibrary.org/schaffer/history/e1930/mjassassinrd.htm. One of the cases cited by Anslinger was that of Victor Licata, a Tampa man who in 1933 murdered multiple members of his family with an axe. Local authorities found no evidence that cannabis use played a role in Licata's crimes, or that he even used cannabis. Despite this, Anslinger and a chorus of media voices seized on the case to support their cause.

75. Lee, *Smoke Signals*, 54; and Provine, *Unequal Under Law*, 83–85.

76. Bonnie and Whitebread, *Marihuana Conviction*, 115.

77. Bonnie and Whitebread, *Marihuana Conviction*, 77.

78. *New York Times*, "Roosevelt Asks Narcotic War Aid," March 22, 1935, reprinted at Schaffer Library of Drug Policy, https://www.druglibrary.net/schaffer/History/e1930/rooseveltasks.htm; and Bonnie and Whitebread, *Marihuana Conviction*, 114–15.

79. Lee, *Smoke Signals*, 57.

80. Lee, *Smoke Signals*, 57; Jessica Winter, "Pot, Porn, and Strawberries," *Village Voice*, May 6, 2003, https://www.villagevoice.com/2003/05/06/pot-porn-and-strawberries/; and Rund Abdelfatah and Ramtin Arablouei, "Strange Fruit," podcast, 31:00, in *Throughline*, produced by Rund Abdelfatah et al., August 22, 2019, https://www.npr.org/transcripts/752909807.

81. David Herzberg, *White Market Drugs: Big Pharma and the Hidden History of Addiction in America* (Chicago: University of Chicago Press, 2020). For the drug-medicine divide, see especially 11–13.

82. Herzberg, *White Market Drugs*, 181–86.

83. US Senate Joint Economic Committee Democrats, *The Economic Toll of the Opioid Crisis Reached Nearly $1.5 Trillion in 2020*, issue brief, 2021, https://www.jec.senate.gov/public/_cache/files/67bced7f-4232-40ea-9263-f033d280c567/jec-cost-of-opioids-issue-brief.pdf.

84. Bonnie and Whitebread, *Marihuana Conviction*, 224.

85. Melvin Small, "The Election of 1968," *Diplomatic History* 28, no. 4 (2004): 523, https://doi.org/10.1111/j.1467-7709.2004.00428.x.

86. Matthew Vaz, *Running the Numbers: Race, Police, and the History of Urban Gambling* (Chicago: University of Chicago Press, 2020), 85.

87. National Commission on Marihuana and Drug Abuse, *Marihuana: A Signal of Misunderstanding* (New York: Signet, 1972), https://babel.hathitrust.org/cgi/pt?id=mdp.39015015647558&view=1up&seq=6.

88. *ABC News*, "Tapes Reveal Nixon's Prejudices Again," March 22, 2002, https://abcnews.go.com/GMA/story?id=126236&page=1.

89. Quoted in Dan Baum, "How to Win the War on Drugs," *Harper's Magazine*, April 2016.

90. Joanna R. Lampe, "The Controlled Substances Act (CSA): A Legal Overview for the 117th Congress," Report no. R45948, Congressional Research Service, updated February 5, 2021, 13–22, https://sgp.fas.org/crs/misc/R45948.pdf.

91. Lampe, "The Controlled Substances Act," 7–8.

92. National Institute on Drug Abuse, "Drug Overdose Death Rates," Figure 4, https://nida.nih.gov/research-topics/trends-statistics/overdose-death-rates.

93. Emily Dufton, *Grass Roots: The Rise and Fall and Rise of Marijuana in America* (New York: Basic Books, 2017), 123–25.

94. Lee, *Smoke Signals*, 128–33.

95. Megan Edge and Laurel Andrews, "Timeline: Notable Moments in 40 Years of Alaska's History with Marijuana," *Anchorage Daily News*, April 14, 2014, https://www.adn.com/cannabis-north/article/alaska-weed-history/2014/04/14/.

96. Lampe, "Controlled Substances Act," 37.

97. Bonnie and Whitebread, *Marihuana Conviction*, 31.

Chapter 2

Racial Inequity and the War on Drugs

Akele Parnell is an African American man from the South who trained as a lawyer and began his professional career recently in the city of Chicago. He is also one of the few people of color today who has made at least some progress establishing himself as a cannabis entrepreneur. As regulated cannabis markets have continued to mature and the gap between white and Black owners in the industry has persisted, the policy and material challenges of providing opportunities to people of color have become increasingly clear, with few easy fixes in sight.

Parnell spoke in 2022 about his motivations for pursuing a cannabis business, noting that "I'm a fan of the plant and its ability to foster human connection and creative expression. . . . I [also] wanted to help shape the industry to provide Black and brown communities with the opportunity to build generational wealth from a plant that has been used to oppress our communities for generations."[1] Parnell did not have any formal experience in commercial cannabis before becoming in-house counsel for Green Thumb Industries, a Chicago cannabis product manufacturer. From there, he moved on to serve as head of equity partnerships for the national cannabis delivery company Lantern, as well as serving at the Chicago Lawyers' Committee for Civil Rights to work toward racial equity in the cannabis industry.

Then, in 2019, Parnell began a yearslong effort to start his own cannabis business. He was one of the first Black individuals awarded a license from the State of Illinois, which "felt like, one, it was a stamp of legitimacy, because now it's like I'm an owner. I felt like it was, in a lot of ways, life-changing. . . . To be one of the first social equity, one of the first Black licensees in the state of Illinois, in the city of Chicago, was historic. . . . [My] dream at that point was to have our own cannabis brand. This is one of my dreams that actually came true."[2]

Today, Parnell's business is still not open, primarily because of a web of challenges that lie at the intersection of the political and financial efforts to diversify the cannabis industry and ensure those with previous experience in the industry are included. These challenges will be explored more fully in coming chapters, but two of the most important relate to the general lack of intergenerational wealth controlled by Black people and the historic—and in some cases ongoing—unequal access that Black Americans have had to financial institutions and other vehicles for advancing their businesses. This chapter will therefore review the repeated policy failures over the last century that have limited the generation of wealth in communities of color and in turn have made it extremely difficult to pursue new businesses such as those that cannabis legalization has nominally made possible.

This is important to do because the current moment of cannabis legalization threatens to repeat some of the same policy mistakes related to the conditions under which Black people can engage with the economy that originally led to the urban ghettos where many of them continue to live today. At multiple points over the century-and-a-half since Lincoln signed the Emancipation Proclamation, Black people have sought to assert their economic place in the United States only to meet the violent backlash or malign indifference of white people holding power. Cannabis criminalization wasn't the only mechanism that led to this inequity, but it was one of them—and its legalization therefore presents a unique opportunity to redress at least the economic wrongs that criminalization wrought.

Parnell views his work with cannabis in this light, noting:

> You can't criminalize cannabis for all these years, throw millions of Black and brown folks in jail, completely ruin their lives, meanwhile, the wealthy white person down the street is doing the exact same thing, they have no consequences, go on to live great lives, and then legalize cannabis and then they can make all the money, and we're just still sitting around with devastated communities and completely locked out of the industry. It's just fundamentally unfair as a matter of social policy. It's important for us to be able to have an opportunity to build wealth, one, as just part of repairing the harms of the war on drugs, in addition to all the other forms of systemic racism that we still haven't really made an attempt to dismantle and repair the harms of.[3]

Drug criminalization had always reflected the darker impulses of racism and social control, but Parnell's insight points to the fact that a reversal of criminalization in and of itself will not reverse the effects of racism or the continuing social control of Black people's lives that it engenders. To see why, it is important to understand how inequity—especially economic inequity—has been the result of far more than a single policy or moment in time.

OBSTACLES TO BLACK INTERGENERATIONAL WEALTH FORMATION

In the years immediately after the Civil War, for every dollar that Black families had in wealth, white families had nearly sixty. This ratio decreased to 20:1 by the end of Reconstruction, and gradually settled into a range of around 7:1 by the end of the twentieth century.[4] Among other things, this suggests that none of the major economic and political reforms that nominally aided the rights and welfare of the Black population during the course of the previous century made a lasting impact on Black family wealth. During the Civil Rights Movement era from 1950 to 1980, Black family incomes increased at a higher relative rate than those of white people, reducing the wealth gap. But after 1980 this reduction first stagnated, then eventually even retreated somewhat. Current trends show the wealth gap is actually getting worse, but even if marginal progress on closing the income and savings gaps continued, it would take until 2200 to reduce the racial wealth gap to only 2:1. When viewed as a whole, the Black population controlled approximately 0.5 percent of the national wealth of the United States in 1860, a figure which has increased to approximately 2.5 percent today despite African Americans comprising roughly one-eighth of the nation's population.[5]

This wealth gap represents a chicken-and-egg challenge for the social and economic condition of Black Americans today. White Americans have historically dispossessed communities of color in a variety of ways—during the slavery era, families were often broken up and slaves could own minimal personal property. During Jim Crow, white citizens passed laws preventing wealth accumulation and used the threat or actuality of violence to destroy that wealth which had accumulated.[6] Even well-meaning observers have asserted over many decades that if the Black community was able to accumulate more wealth, they would then be able to demand greater economic and political power. But without economic and political power, it is difficult to accumulate more wealth.

Instead, white people repeatedly adopted explicit policies removing African Americans from positions of economic opportunity. For example, consider one of Woodrow Wilson's first executive orders after he assumed the presidency in 1913, which removed Black Americans from management positions throughout the federal government and thereby took away opportunities for a good paycheck and stable employment.[7] Likewise, as part of the passage of Social Security and related programs in the 1930s, Southern senators worked as a bloc to ensure that jobs which Black workers disproportionately held—most notably in agricultural labor and domestic service—did not qualify for these benefits.[8] By preventing access to opportunities that white people of similar circumstances had, these kinds of actions took wealth from Black Americans in relative terms.

The post–World War II environment provided another opportunity for a dramatic expansion of government social provisions in the form of veterans' benefits. Federal programs for returning veterans such as the G.I. Bill promised economic independence to millions of Americans by providing subsidies to pursue higher education and purchase their own homes in newly constructed neighborhoods across the country. As policy scholar Suzanne Mettler has found, the social and political fabric that was created by this expansion of government aid allowed many of the recipients to experience an element of class mobility.[9] Unfortunately, as with many of the more far-reaching social aid programs of the New Deal, Black veterans were often excluded from fully accessing either of these important benefits through a combination of segregated schools—which prevented access even to those Black students who might have afforded them—and institutional policies against financing home purchases that would lead to interracial neighborhoods. While social benefits helped white beneficiaries see themselves as mainstream, those people of color who were able to access them were generally reminded instead of their overall exclusion from public life. As Mettler explains, "Whereas an overwhelmingly positive experience of government in a string of affirmative encounters led white veterans to conventional politics, the G.I. Bill's status as an exception to the rule in the experience of black veterans impelled them toward [political] involvement that challenged the system."[10]

While this systematic and pervasive blocking of Black opportunity had many aspects, there were three especially important areas of economic activity in which white and other Americans were in the aggregate able to develop intergenerational wealth while Black Americans were not. These were the accumulation of land for farming, the purchase of quality housing, and access to banking. Crucially, while Black access to all three of these resources—as with all discriminatory outcomes during this period—was in part limited by violence or the threat of violence, that violence by itself was not the explanatory factor. Instead, racist policies executed by both private businesses and governments at both the state and federal levels were the scaffolding which made it possible to construct these outcomes.

Land

When Russian Emperor Alexander II pronounced in 1861 that the serfs on private lands and estates of his empire would receive freedom from their feudal bonds, the accompanying manifesto provided that many serfs would be able to acquire some small grant of land that they could buy in payments over time from their previous noble overseers.[11] This minimalist policy of land reform was intended to provide for better social control of the newly free serfs, and while inconsistently implemented, it did delay widespread social unrest for decades. By contrast, when Abraham Lincoln declared enslaved persons located in the Confederate states to be free when he issued the Emancipation Proclamation on January 1, 1863, this grant of freedom did not come with any form of land reform. This was despite a burgeoning political movement—and some limited initiatives such as Sherman's Special Field Order 15—to do exactly that. Instead, postwar American leaders such as Andrew Johnson rejected calls to rebuild the social and economic order of the South by providing formerly enslaved African Americans "forty acres and a mule," instead returning much of the land and political dominance to former Confederate soldiers and officials.[12]

Pushing back against the overly lenient vision of Reconstruction put forward by Johnson, Radical Republicans in Congress created a set of laws addressing the "freedmen," which included a guarantee of civil rights as well as a vision of providing education and economic resources to them. The Freedmen's Bureau was created to help oversee this distribution, though its practical authority to enact this vision of economic support was limited by political realities and gridlocked government.[13] The failure of any large form of land redistribution after the Civil War consequently kept economic power—and, eventually, political power—primarily in white hands. While federal troops remained in states across the South, a pretense of equality continued where freed slaves could enjoy political rights. Once those troops left after the Compromise of 1877, this pretense largely evaporated. The reassertion of white power after 1877 led not merely to a locking in place but a retreat to worse conditions for Black Americans across the South. Those few who had gained either economic stability or political voice often lost it through legal manipulations or sheer violence and terror.[14]

One of the primary vehicles for this backsliding were the sharecropping contracts which white landowners could often coerce farmers with little wealth—both white and Black—to enter into. Sharecropping was especially oppressive for Black people, however, not just because of the sheer economic exploitation between individual plantation owners and their workers, but the degree to which the legal system targeted African Americans without work or who were otherwise perceived as "vagrants." Black workers were often completely prevented from traveling or exposed to such odious forms of legal scrutiny while doing so as to intimidate all but the most courageous from leaving their current living and working arrangements across the American South.[15]

Many of the social challenges faced by America today rest in that failure to ensure that freed slaves received some form of economic security since many of our contemporary disparities in social conditions stem from the racial wealth gap that stayed open due to that failure. Indeed, much of the reason that the War on Drugs has been so effective in targeting Americans of color is because economic and housing policies have relegated these citizens to isolated neighborhoods with little chance to build or sustain wealth, encouraging many to subsist by pursuing unregulated economic opportunities—including, but by no means limited to, the sale of controlled substances—that expose them to legal scrutiny.

Housing

The major disruption to the prevailing economic arrangements of the post-Reconstruction South came not from legal reform but from the economic needs of World Wars I and II, when defense production encouraged industry officials to recruit Black workers from the South to work in factories elsewhere, particularly major cities in the Midwest (such as Detroit and Chicago) and the Northeast (such as Philadelphia and New York).[16] However, Black people who moved out of the South during the Great Migration often traded one form of economic exploitation for another in the form of the housing market. In many places where Black families moved after World War II, federal policy made housing subsidies and insurance unavailable, leaving them with either low-quality housing that would not last as long as what white people could buy, worse financing options that made it difficult for Black home buyers to afford their payments and build equity, or both.[17]

In his 2017 book *The Color of Law*, housing policy scholar Richard Rothstein describes the interconnected reasons that the wealth gap often persists across generations in the kinds of neighborhoods that these conditions help to produce:

> The consequences of being exposed to neighborhood poverty are greater than the consequences of being poor itself. Children who grow up in poor neighborhoods have few adult role models who have been educationally and occupationally successful. Their ability to do well in school is compromised from stress that can result from exposure to violence. They have few, if any, summer job opportunities. Libraries and bookstores are less accessible. There are fewer primary care physicians. Fresh food is harder to get. Airborne pollutants are more present, leading to greater school absence from respiratory illness. The concentration of many disadvantaged children in the same classroom deprives each child of the special attention needed to be successful. All these challenges are added to those from which poor children suffer in any neighborhood—instability and stress resulting from parental unemployment, fewer literacy experiences when parents are poorly educated, more overcrowded living arrangements that offer few quiet corners to study, and less adequate health care, all of which

contribute to worse average school performance and, as a result, less occupational success as adults.[18]

Even if this kind of embedded inequity was not the avowed purpose of government housing policy throughout much of the twentieth century, it was certainly its outcome.

Rothstein's central argument is that much of the so-called "de facto" discrimination that government officials, judges, and scholars accept as merely automatic or market driven is built on top of a twentieth-century economic system where federal, state, and local officials worked together to build, implement, and enforce a system of racial segregation that both created and sustained "whites-only" areas and relegated non-white people to less desirable and more crowded urban locations from which policymakers could more easily divert resources.[19] Meanwhile, African Americans who sought to participate in the American economy after being released from centuries of relegation in slavery and feudal sharecropping regimes were denied the opportunity to build wealth and provide the kinds of class mobility that were often taken for granted by white families.

Rothstein meticulously documents the degree of direction that the federal government provided in the first half of the twentieth century to segregate government-subsidized and/or government-insured housing. In many cases, this housing replaced neighborhoods that had previously been integrated—if only by economic necessity when relatively recent white immigrants for whom the full benefits of whiteness had not yet accrued lived near Black people.[20] In nearly all cases, local and state officials as well as market participants involved with the housing industry—including developers, insurers, bankers, and real estate agents—worked in concert to sustain this segregation. Penalties for stepping out of this system were nearly always enforced on Black individuals, as well as sometimes on white people who sought to help break down these systems, even if only on an individual or community level.[21]

These barriers are perhaps best illustrated by the historical practice of real estate agents and government officials to classify neighborhoods that had large numbers of residents of color as dangerous and of little economic value. The practice became known as "redlining" due to the color-coded risk maps which federal housing programs began issuing in the New Deal to guide decisions such as which neighborhoods had properties that would be suitable for mortgage loans and homeowners' insurance. Those deemed least desirable or highest risk were colored red, keeping owners or potential owners of properties in these areas—often the only places where Black people could buy homes—from government subsidies or even commercial financial instruments to support homeownership. These red lines placed on a map in the early twentieth century would in many cases become the racial dividing lines of twenty-first-century America, and the legacy of this market control made most efforts to desegregate schools in cities across America in the 1970s and ’80s nearly impossible without extensive busing of students across neighborhoods, an effort that proved politically toxic. Today these neighborhoods of color are often still racially, socially, and economically isolated from the rest of the country, with their residents living a life outside of the larger city and isolated from their white and more economically successful neighbors.[22]

More recently, a newer generation of African American home buyers were targeted and victimized by financial institutions offering subprime mortgages. This campaign involved economic narratives that civic and community leaders encouraged about finding empowerment through homeownership and responsible personal finance, which often led individuals in Black communities to access loans with unaffordable terms or those which were unduly complicated and hard to fulfill. The motivation here was often not as directly racially exclusive as it had been previously—in many cases, simple avarice and greed operated as powerful reasons for the many individuals who participated in the marketing of these mortgages without any concern for their impacts.[23]

Even if not overtly racist, such practices have a cumulative and cyclical effect on neighborhood wealth that is similar to how Rothstein describes the mobility challenges faced by children who grow up in such places. As legal scholar Mehrsa Baradaran describes:

> Urban decline pushed businesses out of the ghetto, which led to further urban decline. As businesses moved to the suburbs where land was cheaper and business costs lower, the ghetto suffered from both high prices and general deterioration. In the economic trap of the ghetto, small retailers sold inferior products at higher prices because they had lower sales volumes, lower profits, and higher costs. Because suburban retailers had an economically diverse set of customers and higher sales volume, their costs were lower. The economy of the black inner city was a unique vortex of negative forces that further compounded poverty.[24]

What is noteworthy about this mechanism is that it is race-neutral, apart from the initial conditions that led Black people to live in such circumstances. Once the system was in place, it became largely self-reinforcing regardless of overt or even conscious intent.

Even when predominantly Black communities break out of these cycles, it is as often because they cease to be predominantly Black communities as residents are displaced during gentrification. Still, many historically Black urban areas are still in strong need of investment and access to the economic resources available outside of their neighborhoods because these areas are for practical purposes still segregated today. For example, recent research into personal walking tracker habits has shown that residents of minority neighborhoods are less likely to leave their communities for school, work, or leisure.[25] Even those Black residents who do manage to buy property often face added barriers in keeping their homes, as recent court cases around inaccurate home appraisals and increased tax foreclosures in minority communities in cities such as Chicago and Detroit demonstrate.[26]

Banking

One of the main outcomes of this disparate access to quality housing on manageable terms is that building wealth individually has often been difficult, if not impossible, for Black Americans. There has consequently been a system of barriers put in front of African Americans who might otherwise be able to provide an opportunity for their peers who are interested in opening businesses that serve the broader public—and, in the process, build a degree of intergenerational wealth that could threaten the power of white individuals or power structures. Among the most important of these systemic impediments is the difficulty Black people have faced in creating or utilizing banks and lending institutions. The banks that Black people have created often face higher regulatory costs, have had fewer opportunities to avail themselves of government-credit financing provided by various federal initiatives over the twentieth century, and have not benefited from bailouts in the same way that other financial institutions have.[27]

Beginning after the Civil War, many African Americans looked to build on their modest economic status by creating banks which could lend to other Black people in support of their business ventures. The first such effort was the Freedman's Bank, begun in 1865 with a charter from the US Congress. This bank was an economic and political project of both white abolitionists and Black activists, including Frederick Douglass. However, this bank lasted less than a decade, partly due to the general economic downturn of the Panic of 1873, but also as the result of a combination of poor investments and outright fraud executed by the bank's white managers.[28]

Similar results occurred throughout the decades that followed—as the cliché goes, "When Wall Street catches a cold, Harlem gets pneumonia." Future economic crashes also resulted in systemic defaults in banks owned by African Americans, while white banking institutions mostly survived to live another day. One outcome is that few Black-owned banks have survived to the present, which has contributed to the fact that much of the African American community is still either underbanked or completely unbanked.[29] One prominent example of a Black bank that strove to defy this stereotype, the Binga State Bank founded in early twentieth-century Chicago, managed to survive for some time and even took over white-owned institutions when they failed.

However, even this bank later failed while its founder, Jesse Binga, served time in prison for supposedly defrauding depositors, even though Binga was not accused of doing anything different than what many of his contemporary white bankers regularly did.[30]

The Great Depression and its devastating bank runs led to increased federal oversight of banking, more government backing for banks to prevent their failure, and the creation of federal deposit insurance laws that have largely made bank runs a nonexistent issue today.[31] Most historically Black banking institutions had failed before any of this, but even the ones that hadn't were not able to grow anywhere near the size of the conglomerate banks that dominate the sector today. This is because a major source of wealth for many of today's big financial institutions came from the regulation of the housing sector and the provision of federal mortgage financing and insurance which allowed banks to engage with a new and growing customer base. African Americans were explicitly excluded from many of these subsidies, depriving Black-owned banks of one way this major customer base might otherwise have used their services.[32] Thus Black banks could not easily establish a solid base in the mortgage industry, keeping them smaller and less integrated in the financial sector as a whole.

This outcome was not inevitable. In fact, before the homogenization of white identity which began in the years after World War II, many ethnically European immigrants also had economic and social infrastructure aimed at their own communities, including banks. These banks opened because traditional banks would not serve customers that weren't "creditworthy," a determination that only applied to most of the historical "melting pot" identities. Beginning in the early nineteenth century and leading into the early twentieth century, this included Irish, Italian, Polish, and many other immigrant communities. People outside of their nominal communities never shunned these banks in the same way that they often shunned Black banks, and as such, many of these banks continued to grow and integrate into the financial sector.[33] Increased assets and formal regulation of operations have allowed some of these banks to become today's market behemoths.

Consider two examples. M&F is one of the few still existing historically Black banks, operating out of Durham, North Carolina, since 1907. Today M&F has eight branches and a modest footprint in North Carolina's urban communities. Meanwhile, only a few years before M&F's founding, the Bank of Italy was created to serve its local community in San Francisco. Within a few years, the Bank of Italy became the Bank of America, a huge company today worth billions of dollars and operating over five hundred branches in the United States. While each bank was established to serve an ethnic community in a local area, only one was able to achieve the status of a bank operating on a nationwide scale. There are a number of reasons for this—access to federal deposit insurance and financing opportunities, exposure to a wider customer base, and the relative poverty in their surrounding communities.[34]

THE PROMISE AND LIMIT OF BLACK RESISTANCE

Even as it has developed for more than a century, the federal and state governments have largely stood aside from the problem of the racial wealth gap, offering little in the way of concentrated aid or even recognition of a clear problem. Meanwhile, Black Americans have been left to struggle and find their way out of this problem, despite often having little direct power to independently change the economic and political structures—to say nothing of the individual actions of corporations and fellow citizens—that both gave rise to and have perpetuated it. The African American response to this pervasive discrimination and exclusion has ranged from hopeful activism for acceptance and integration to angry denunciation, sometimes even inspiring calls for separatism. At other times, these motivations have converged in contrasting ways. This range is exemplified by two prominent Black activists who began their careers at the turn of the twentieth century—Booker T. Washington and W. E. B. Du Bois.

Washington is perhaps best known for the ideas associated with his "Atlanta Compromise," which sought to respond to the post-Reconstruction Jim Crow crackdown with an appeal to Black Americans to "turn the other cheek." The idea was that by not asking for political rotes such as the vote and instead seeking to better themselves through education, good works, and self-supporting business ventures, white people would eventually recognize the humanity of their fellow citizens.[35] As the violence that white Americans perpetrated on the African American community in response to the latter's momentary successes laid bare, this respect was not forthcoming. Such violence, which shattered the faith of many members of the Black middle class, included a violent coup in 1898 in North Carolina against elected leaders supported by a political coalition of poor white and Black voters, as well as race riots against Black communities in cities like Atlanta (in 1906) and Tulsa (in 1921).[36] An alternative group of activists led by Du Bois elected to take a more direct path toward advocating for the political and legal extension of civil rights, a strategy that attracted countless adherents, especially after Washington's death in 1915. This group formed the National Association for the Advancement of Colored People (NAACP) in 1909, whose legal arm was responsible for nearly all of the court victories that began to dismantle Jim Crow in the coming decades, most famously *Brown v. Board of Education*'s prohibition on racial segregation in schools.

Yet despite the progress and promise of such efforts to dismantle legal segregation, the parallel force of the long-established racial wealth gap combined with market dynamics to perpetuate severe inequality. Long before scholars such as Rothstein and Baradaran laid plain the intersecting economic and legal factors that make it more difficult for individual African Americans to accrue wealth—and therefore, in the aggregate, for majority Black communities to do so—civil rights leaders such as Malcolm X and Martin Luther King Jr. vocally described them. As Malcolm X explained in his last public appearance before his assassination in 1965:

> In Harlem, for instance, all of the stores are owned by white people, all of the buildings are owned by white people. Black people are just there, paying rent, buying the groceries. But they don't own the stores, clothing stores, food stores, any kind of stores; don't even own the homes that they live in. This is all owned by outsiders. And then these run down apartment dwellings, the Black man in Harlem pays more money for it than the man down in the rich Park Avenue section. It costs us more money to live in the slum, than it costs them to live down on Park Avenue. Black people in Harlem know this. And the white merchants charge us more money for food in Harlem—and it's the cheap food, it's the worst food; and we have to pay more money for it than the man has to pay for it downtown. So Black people know that they're being exploited and that their blood is being sucked and they see no way out of it.[37]

Meanwhile, although Martin Luther King Jr. took up the mantle of fighting for political rights that Du Bois had pursued at the start of his activist career, while often tempering his most prominent speeches with hopeful appeals to the better nature of white Americans in ways reminiscent of Booker T. Washington, his economic analysis was often not much different from that which Malcolm X sketched out. When King led the March on Washington in 1963, it was not just to demand civil liberties, such as equal access to public accommodations and the right to vote, but also economic and social rights that would provide people of color with the full participation in his Beloved Community. Civil rights leaders were insistent in their messaging throughout the 1960s about the need for economic justice as well as political and legal rights. While King's "I Have a Dream" speech is often today discussed in terms of its aspirations for the social recognition of equality, the economic themes of King's message in that speech are also clear. As he makes clear in his third paragraph: "In a sense, we've come to our nation's capital to cash a check. When the architects of our Republic wrote the magnificent words of the Constitution and the Declaration of Independence, they were signing a promissory note to which every American was to fall heir. . . . Instead of honoring this sacred obligation, America has given the Negro people . . . a check which has come back marked 'insufficient funds.' But we refuse to believe that the bank of justice is bankrupt."[38]

The march for "Jobs and Freedom"—a phrase which was part of its official title—that King led to Washington was thus intended to promote a broader economic reform package that addressed many of the deprivations that the children and grandchildren of former slaves had endured. In the years after King's "Dream" speech, he continued to reinforce this economic messaging. Lyndon Johnson's War on Poverty may have addressed some of the broader conversations about economic inequality, but little of the aid was directed toward African American communities to help them close the wealth gap with their white fellow citizens. After the initial legislative successes of the Civil Rights Movement—such as the 1964 Civil Rights Bill and the following year's Voting Rights Act—that provided (in most cases) for civil liberties, King's activism focused on economic justice and antipoverty measures.[39] These calls were less successful. They serve now as a reminder of the unfinished progress of King's dream.

After the federal civil rights legislation, the social and moral pressure on policymakers largely faltered, and those economic programs that Johnson was able to enact as part of his Great Society program led to a political backlash and cutbacks within a few short years, leaving many of the most ambitious promises of King's dream unfulfilled.[40] By the end of the 1960s, despite the many gains in formal civil liberties, Black Americans still faced entrenched racism on both a personal and a policy level, leading to continued residential segregation (especially in urban areas), an enduring (if somewhat diminished) wealth gap with white Americans, and numerous barriers to the economic and social opportunities that might help to further close that gap. Some of this frustration appeared evident in mass protests such as those which followed King's assassination in 1968, but it is worth remembering that the marches and even occasional violence of this late Civil Rights Movement era were happening in parallel with similar activities being undertaken by partisans of many other social movements of the era, especially those associated with opposition to the Vietnam War, specifically, and the New Left more generally. Of course, 1968 was also the same year that police clashed with protesters outside of the Democratic National Convention in Chicago. Two years later, National Guardsmen would kill four students and wound nine others on the campus of Kent State.[41]

THE NEW JIM CROW AND BLACK CAPITALISM

In response to the specific problems of Black poverty, Richard Nixon—later followed by both Ronald Reagan and George H. W. Bush—embraced a "black capitalism" model which emphasized self-help and stories of Black entrepreneurship, while providing little in the way of tangible aid to people in these communities.[42] Nixon described it in grandiose terms: "Instead of government jobs and government housing and government welfare, let government use its tax and credit policies [to power] the greatest engine of progress ever developed in the history of man: American private enterprise."[43] Many African Americans responded to this snub by either disengaging from politics or even embracing separatism—this kind of policy expression contributed to the rise of groups like the Black Panthers, as well as the rejection of capitalism itself by many activists.[44]

Neither approach could do little to combat the creation and sustenance of poor Black urban neighborhoods during the last third of the twentieth century, however. These communities were ignored, extracted from, or even simply bulldozed to make way for highway expansions or as part of blight-removal projects (both helpfully financed by the federal government, but with money distributed by local officials).[45] Such neighborhoods often acted less like a funnel and more like a sieve for Black wealth, where both residents and merchants paid higher prices on lower profit margins with little of the economic and social stimulus given to white communities. As with water fountains and schoolhouses in the Jim Crow South, the financial subsidies and benefits given to communities were both separate and unequal. Some of the practices and methods of support that white Americans did genuinely provide for communities of color, such as government deposits for Black banks, actually served to undermine the financial strength of these institutions by limiting their lending power because of restrictions on how this capital could contribute to the bank's lending portfolio.[46] While the separatists could instead seek to create Black pride and promote ownership and self-betterment (in a sort of callback to Booker T. Washington), they were still often trapped in poor neighborhoods that simply did not have the political power enjoyed by other demographic groups.

Many of these urban ghettos, created by explicitly segregationist policies, housed communities where law enforcement would eventually concentrate resources during the War on Drugs. In many of these majority Black urban communities, residents survived by engaging with the informal economy, doing jobs such as driving unregulated taxis, running unlicensed businesses, and producing and selling drugs. The drug trade was a pathway to wealth and status for some residents, a way to achieve some form of the rags-to-riches narrative that is crucial to the American experience. The trade of different drugs, including cocaine, heroin, and cannabis, made Black people the owners of capital and provided the opportunity to employ members of the community and spread their wealth to others.[47] These informal markets became the focus of a substantially higher degree of criminal enforcement than that faced by bootleggers during Prohibition, however. In the case of cannabis, that has been replaced in many places with a form of regulatory capture at the hands of the state.

THE ANTI-DRUG ABUSE ACT AND THE RACIALIZED ESCALATION OF ENFORCEMENT

Following the passage of the Controlled Substances Act (CSA), public concern around crime and social disorder in general was heightened in the later 1970s and '80s.[48] While the reasons for this were varied—including social dislocation related to deindustrialization, a deep and enduring economic downturn for much of the period, and continued racially coded tension stemming from both the achievements and failures of the Civil Rights Movement—public concern was also focused on drug use, in part because of its relation to a large number of veterans who came home from Vietnam with PTSD (post-traumatic stress disorder) and other war injuries. One outcome of this concern was a genuine movement to promote addiction and treatment policies as alternatives to policing and incarceration.[49] Ultimately, however, these efforts were coopted by elected officials to embrace criminal approaches to addiction by expanding the criminal code and the ranks of the imprisoned at a monumental scale.

This shift toward heavily emphasizing policing, enforcing, and incarceration as a way to curb drug use was in part influenced by a belief in what social scientists Gary Becker and Kevin Murphy would later term the "rational theory of addiction" in 1988.[50] The idea was that it is possible to reduce the prevalence of "deviant" behaviors, including drug use, by increasing the personal costs to the people or community engaging in that behavior. Government leaders therefore directed police to use highly visible tactics while also sharply increasing the criminal penalties for violating the law in an attempt to create a widespread expectation that use or sales of drugs would have harsh consequences. By seeking to impose additional constraints on both demand and supply, policymakers believed that few people would be tempted to use drugs. In other words, individuals were expected to make "rational" decisions to control their own drug use. Even if this approach can be effective in curbing *some* drug use—evidence suggests that criminal prohibition does lead to some reductions[51]—it is not a solution to end *all* drug use. This is because drug use, and especially addiction, is more complex than perfect rational models can duplicate. The reasons why people use drugs, as well as their choice of drugs to use, are informed by social and economic conditions and not simply their own internal compasses.[52]

At the federal level, this general view is evident in policies from both Republican and Democratic presidential administrations and Congresses from Nixon onward, with only slight changes to the veneer depending on the preferences of the political party and the public mood. While there was a brief period during the Jimmy Carter administration when legalization advocates hoped to make progress on decriminalization of cannabis, public concern about rising rates of cannabis use that developed toward the end of Carter's presidency made this decriminalization effort impossible to sustain.[53] Within only a few short years, the election of Ronald Reagan, who called cannabis the "most dangerous drug" during the campaign in which he unseated Carter,[54] heralded the end of this brief and little noticed period of liberalization. Parent activists across the country who were motivated by the perception that cannabis use was prevalent and sanctioned, particularly in the growth of stores that sold cannabis paraphernalia, also helped to bring this about. While some of the earliest groups in this parents' movement were worried mostly about the appeal of this paraphernalia to children and sought to limit public displays rather than take on cannabis use more generally, this movement was ultimately captured by more conservative activists and coopted by the Reagan administration.[55]

This regressive approach to cannabis was executed largely by the police, courts, and prisons. In 1981, there were approximately 22,000 inmates in federal custody; by the time President Clinton left office two decades later, this number had swelled to over 100,000 inmates.[56] Policymakers reformed state criminal codes to add drug offenses and provide for more extensive criminal penalties for trafficking during the same years, leading to growth in incarceration in state facilitates that mirrored the trends at the federal level.[57] While state prisons held less than a quarter of a million individuals at the beginning of the 1980s, by the end of the 1990s around 1.5 million Americans were held in state prisons and at least another half million were held in local ones.[58] The percentage of African Americans in jails and prisons today is nearly three times their share of the general population, largely a legacy of disproportionate approaches to criminal justice that were compounded by this period of increasingly mass incarceration.[59] The War on Drugs has been portrayed as having been fought on behalf of children of all races, but the evidence demonstrates that it was more often fought by politicians on behalf of white parents concerned about the "other" and against youth of color who were made to represent that "other," despite plentiful evidence that Americans of all races used and sold drugs.[60] In Massachusetts, for example, a report from the state chapter of the American Civil Liberties Union (ACLU) found that Black residents were arrested for cannabis possession at a per capita rate that was roughly four times greater than white people in 2008—the state voted in that fall's election to decriminalize the possession of small amounts of cannabis—and for sales at a per capita rate that was roughly six times greater, despite similar rates of use.[61] Where drug laws have been loosened, sympathetic white youth were intended as the beneficiary; where they have been tightened, concerns about Black or Latino youth prevailed.

While arrests for cannabis use were clearly racialized during these years of escalating enforcement, the experience of Black Americans with "crack" cocaine demonstrates the racial character of the War on Drugs more starkly than any other topic. In 1986, Congress passed the Anti-Drug Abuse Act, which among other things imposed a sentencing disparity between those arrested with so-called crack cocaine (mostly Black users) and those who used powder cocaine (mostly white users). The two forms of cocaine were identical in addictiveness, harm, and other aspects, but users of crack could be sentenced to the same term in jail as someone convicted of possessing more than ten times as much powder cocaine by weight.[62] Less than ten years after the passage of the Anti-Drug Abuse Act, the federal Sentencing Commission acknowledged the disparity (though they had no power to change the law).[63] It took more than two decades after this for Congress to pass 2010's Fair Sentencing Act in order to reverse the worst of the disparity. It took nearly another decade after that for Congress to make this change retroactive to many of the over 1,600 offenders who were not able to obtain relief at first.[64]

While the enforcement of other drug crimes involved regularly applying some of the harsher sentences, enforcement of cannabis laws generally had a softer touch on each individual—but they touched so many more people that their effects were felt at a broader level. Despite federal promises that drug enforcement was targeted toward major traffickers and had been built to deter these individuals with ever-increasing amounts of harsh sentences, a large portion of overall arrests during the three decades after the passage of the Controlled Substances Act were cannabis arrests, many of which did not result in actual charges. In 1982, over 70 percent of drug arrests nationally were cannabis related, although this proportion decreased somewhat during the 1980s as more political attention and federal resources were paid to the heroin and cocaine epidemics. For about a decade beginning in 1987, the proportion of cannabis arrests was less than heroin and cocaine, but by 1995, the dominance of cannabis in the nation's drug arrests had reasserted itself. Between 1990 and 2002, the number of cannabis arrests more than doubled nationally, while arrests for other drugs in the same period increased only by 10 percent. During that same period, youth cannabis use increased, prices fell slightly, potency went up, and the proportion of youth that stated cannabis was easy to access for them went as high as 87 percent.[65]

A different kind of enforcement disparity also appears in police encounter research. For example, consider that African American drivers are far more likely to be pulled over for stops during the day, when law enforcement is better able to see the race of the driver. For those pulled over, Black drivers are the most likely to be searched, despite the fact that levels of drug use are roughly consistent across racial demographics. Perhaps as a result of how many Black drivers are searched for no reason that could objectively lead one to suspect a crime, the overall *rate* of capture for drug crimes as a result of these stops is actually higher for white drivers.[66]

While these inequities in searches and arrests were no doubt harmful in and of themselves, the sentencing crackdowns of the 1990s that "tough on crime" politicians imposed at both the federal and state levels served to compound their damage. This movement included the adoption of three strikes laws for many felonies—including drug possession and sales—which meant that even those convicted of low-level possession offenses could end up with lengthy sentences.[67] Mandatory minimums adopted for drug crimes similarly took away judges' discretion to assess the actual social damage that a defendant's crime had caused.[68] In both cases, a police system that targeted people of color at disproportionate rates consequently meant that people of color would be more likely to get dragged into the criminal justice system for extended periods of time—and if they did make it out of incarceration, to bear the burden of having been convicted of a felony.

As Alexander argues in *The New Jim Crow*, the true power of the criminal justice system is additive in precisely this way.[69] It is small differences at each step of the justice process that both unknowingly and knowingly create the racial disparities in the prison population. Alexander explains how deliberate government policies have created a zone of exclusion for urban poor minority communities:

> What happens to [the urban poor] does not directly affect—and is scarcely noticed by—the privileged beyond the ghetto's invisible walls. Thus it is here, in the poverty-stricken, racially segregated ghettos, where the War on Poverty has been abandoned and factories have disappeared, that the drug war has been waged with the greatest ferocity. SWAT teams are deployed here; buy-and-bust operations are concentrated here; drug raids of apartment buildings occur here; stop-and-frisk operations occur on the streets here. Black and brown youth are the primary targets. It is not uncommon for a young black teenager living in a ghetto community to be stopped, interrogated, and frisked numerous times in the course of a month, or even a single week, often by paramilitary units.[70]

The public health research is clear that these interactions with law enforcement will negatively affect one's overall life course—including the ability to achieve educational goals, find steady employment, begin a family, participate in parenthood, and become an involved citizen. It will also frequently have clear health outcomes. For example, exposure to the criminal justice system drastically increases stress, which is directly linked to many chronic health problems such as heart disease and exposure to communicable conditions that result in early death.[71]

While Alexander's discussion concerns the criminal justice system in its entirety, we can zoom into the cannabis statistics and see these exact kinds of racial lines. Beginning in 2013, the ACLU released a series of reports titled *The War on Marijuana in Black and White*. Their central findings concern the prevalence of racial disparities in arrests, with Black people nearly four times as likely compared to whites to be arrested for marijuana possession from 2001 to 2009. Capturing the breadth in addition to the depth of the racial disparities, the ACLU reports also found that over 95 percent of the counties examined had arrests of Black people for cannabis possession higher than those of white people. Consider that African Americans are just as likely to use cannabis as white people, and it becomes clear that there is a racial directionality in the data.[72]

Fighting the Culture War on Drugs

There is a cultural aspect to these disparities that goes beyond the numbers. Consider that Black Americans spent the last half century seeing many examples of their "success" be media representations of drug dealers and gang leaders, who are alternately celebrated as cool and hip by a multiracial coalition of younger adults (including white people) while being seen as disorderly and dangerous by more conservative and rural voters (sometimes their parents or other older family members). Meanwhile, they themselves or a close family member or a friend have likely been arrested, profiled, or discriminated against, sometimes for the same drug use as that portrayed in popular culture. With drug use both condemned and celebrated, many community members have chosen sides in this debate, splintering a community that has collectively been negatively affected by the disproportionate policing of the War on Drugs.

While Black populations both individually and collectively bear the legal consequence for drug use and abuse, it is conversely true that white Americans suffer few consequences for cannabis use. The decriminalization movement of the 1970s was stopped dead in its tracks by reports of drug use by senior White House adviser Peter Bourne, who was eventually forced to step down from his post but otherwise faced few career consequences.[73] The largely white and middle-class parents' movement that emerged in response to the increases in cannabis use of the late 1970s helped build political support for decades of tough on crime policies that drove the mass incarceration of Americans of color but did little to alleviate any harms from drug use in those same urban communities of color, let alone show concern for the ill effects of heavy policing. While Nancy Reagan had proudly embraced the War on Drugs during her effort to capture an issue that would connect with voters, her initial efforts focused on white campaigns with almost entirely white faces.[74] Even the First Lady's signature phrase—"Just Say No"—was actually the genesis of Black activists in Oakland, including Joann Brand, who struggled to gain national recognition after Reagan highlighted the local campaign. Brand eventually lost control of the foundation she had established to coordinate activism on this issue, to corporate behemoth Procter & Gamble, who used the brand to sell cake mix and paper towels.[75]

The stigma of perceived cannabis use is both legal and cultural and continues to impact Americans today. While African Americans bore and continue to bear a disproportionate burden of the criminalization of cannabis, the legal and regulatory regime that condemned THC brought along with it a cache of cultural baggage and activists of any race who favor liberalization and have continuously dealt with that stigma for the last several decades. Certainly, the cultural association between race and problematic drug use has been sustained by decades of television and movies, as well as the occasional Black celebrity who is identified with the substance.

These stigmas persist beyond race, however, especially in official contexts. Even now, possession of a release from a doctor to purchase cannabis on the legal medical market will in many states disqualify the recipient from purchasing firearms or holding a government security clearance.[76] Early in the Biden administration, dozens of newly minted staffers were asked to leave their positions even after being encouraged to be forthright about past cannabis use.[77] Elon Musk's famous dalliance with a joint on the Joe Rogan podcast led to the frequent and pervasive auditing of SpaceX's employees to comply with NASA's drug use policies.[78] In years past, cannabis use would regularly result in evictions or interventions from family court, and convictions for even simple possession often led to the loss of all federal financial aid for young college students.[79] The cruelty of this response was in no way proportionate to the actual harms of cannabis use.

Even as more and more states legalize cannabis, the cultural stereotypes around perceived cannabis use continue to attract commentary, most often from those on the right. While voters on both sides of the political spectrum have voted for and against cannabis—in 2016, legal cannabis was adopted with 53 percent of the vote in Massachusetts while Clinton was winning the state with over 60 percent; four years later in South Dakota, a legal cannabis measure was adopted by voters with 54 percent of the vote while Donald Trump won that state with over 61 percent of the vote.[80] There are Trump voters today who actively use and promote cannabis, while there are liberal voters who are concerned about cannabis addiction and health risks. Even still, the cultural concern about cannabis use—somewhat separately from the question of whether it should be legal—is certainly more concentrated on the right.[81]

Apart from illuminating the contours of these dynamics, Michelle Alexander also argues against the work of many legal reform efforts led by groups such as the NAACP, noting that few of them questioned the political and legal regime that she argues is responsible for criminalizing an endless stream of Black and brown boys from the inner cities. Alexander points to what she believes are many of the difficult discussions about drug use that were ongoing in minority communities—with some still in favor of heavy policing and others for complete liberalization—but argues that these discussions occurred in the shadow of the criminal justice system that was designed to systematically disempower Black communities and could only be understood as a reflection of that context.[82] Speaking about the paradox of shame that many in Black communities experience when one of their family members is forcibly exposed to the criminal justice system, Alexander notes that

> a war has been declared on them, and they have been rounded up for engaging in precisely the same crimes that go largely ignored in middle and upper-class white communities—possession and sale of illegal drugs. . . . [And] because the drug war has been raging for decades now, the parents of children coming of age today were targets of the drug war as well. As a result, many fathers are in prison, and those who are "free" bear the prison label. They are often unable to provide for, or meaningfully contribute to, a family. Any wonder, then, that many youth embrace their stigmatized identity as a means of survival in this new caste system? Should we be shocked when they turn to gangs or fellow inmates for support when no viable family support structure exists?[83]

Roughly a decade after Alexander published her book, the murders of George Floyd and Breonna Taylor—among many others—demonstrated the necessity of focusing on systemic barriers that hinder Black Americans' equality and even safety regardless of the actions they take as individuals. Floyd was a semi-notable rapper who was criminalized by his experiences with law enforcement, serving various terms in prison, including for drug offenses. Yet his experience with exclusion from the system contrasts with Taylor's youthful engagement with the system. Taylor was a twenty-six-year-old emergency medical technician who was shot while police were trying to serve an arrest warrant based on false pretenses. The shootout that killed Taylor occurred when her boyfriend, who was legally armed and legitimately thought his house was being broken into, provoked a hail of police bullets by daring to defend himself.

The fact that both of these individuals ended up dead at the hands of police demonstrates the perceived impotence of either Booker T. Washington's brand of deference or W. E. B. Du Bois's pursuit of civil and legal equality for Black Americans. Indeed, media from the last several decades demonstrates widespread resignation about this futility. For example, comedian Chris Rock released a satirical video in the 1990s detailing how African Americans could avoid an "ass-kicking" at the hands of the police, purporting to give the viewer various forms of advice on how to prevent exposure to police violence, before conceding that following all of these recommendations only meant that you would "probably not" be exposed to a beating.[84]

Since Alexander's publication of *The New Jim Crow* in 2010, scholars and activists have used her words and central argument as part of a powerful rallying cry for a more universalist campaign of criminal justice and sentencing reform, though other scholars have questioned some of her claims about the origins of the War on Drugs, as well as the role that drug crime plays in the larger issue of mass incarceration.[85] A major theme that Alexander concludes her book with is a rising call for action to reform criminal justice systems and move away from carceral solutions and toward rehabilitation and reinvestment. Most significantly, Alexander warns that freeing people from prison and closing prisons is not enough to achieve real racial justice and end the New Jim Crow. She argues that relying on half measures is certain to result in a hollow victory that satisfies none and is vulnerable to political realignment and reinvention.[86]

One of the more notable examples of Alexander's central argument comes when she considers the long-asked question, "Where are the Black men?" Media personalities, political leaders, and other commenters have long remarked on the perceived invisibility of Black men, often in a patronizing or paternalistic voice. Prominent African Americans themselves have fallen into this trap, with leaders like Oprah and Barack Obama addressing this in different ways. Alexander argues that this mental trap is part of the New Jim Crow, with white society's deliberate indifference to the targeting of Black men instead resulting in a wave of self-criticism that divides communities of color and continues to harm the social fabric of families.[87]

THE REGULATION OF GAMBLING—A CAUTIONARY TALE

That the course of cannabis policy after the brief moment in the late 1960s and early 1970s when the initial regulatory structure proscribing its use fell away would be one of retrenchment and criminalization rather than regulated liberalization was hardly inevitable. Nowhere is this better suggested than by a comparison with how forms of gambling that had been widely prohibited before the same late 1960s and early '70s moment instead became heavily regulated and taxed but nevertheless widely legal.

Even before the threat of drug enforcement inspired a wave of criminalization across communities with large numbers of racial minorities, the enforcement of laws against gambling had served a similar purpose and produced a similar outcome. The informal gambling industry—exemplified in majority Black neighborhoods by the games of "policy" and "numbers"—enjoyed tacit approval by large urban political machines and the law enforcement that often served these interests. The small-scale suppliers of gambling operations were often Black owned and operated, providing crucial jobs and economic opportunity for low-income areas of large northern cities like New York and Chicago. When during the mid-twentieth century police agencies came to crack down on gambling crime, law enforcement efforts were often directed entirely at communities of color, producing racial disparities in the arrest statistics that display a striking familiarity to those in cannabis enforcement discussed in this book.[88]

The expansion of criminal due process rights in the 1960s directly undermined many of the existing law enforcement strategies for using the criminal code to regulate gambling, however. Many police forces used pure harassment strategies against the gamblers they arrested, searching and arresting them over and over again without warrants, knowing that the evidence and the detention would not hold up in court.[89] When police in Ohio arrested an African American woman named Mapp in the early 1960s due to the gambling paraphernalia found in her home, those initial charges were thrown out in favor of an obscenity prosecution that she eventually appealed to the Supreme Court, creating today's *Mapp v. Ohio* precedent, which deems evidence that law enforcement acquired illegally inadmissible in court.[90]

The crisis of confidence that hit law enforcement's pursuit of gambling was not informed by a drive to protect the economic interests of Black operators, however. Rather, it was an outgrowth of widespread concern for the respect of the law in an era when gambling prosecutions were clearly undermining public institutions by fostering corruption. Both the Chicago Police Department and New York Police Department engaged in widespread official protection rackets of gambling operations in exchange for bribes, and the public reaction to this corruption was to scrutinize Black communities where this kind of economic activity had played a key role in providing jobs and opportunities for economic growth across low-income minority neighborhoods.[91]

Likewise, when policymakers began to develop solutions to this issue, protection of the economic fortunes of poor urban workers of color was not the priority. Instead, early state lottery adopters, including New York and Illinois, cited the need for additional funding when measures were enacted through their legislatures in the 1970s. Even as those early state lotteries failed to displace established gambling operations in New York City, this was mostly a failure of vision on the part of legislators and their need to learn how to effectively market games of chance.[92] Later states would fix these policy design challenges by wholesale copying of methods from earlier illegal providers, resulting in the popular lottery games that are today played across state lines, such as Powerball and Mega Millions.[93] The expansion of state lotteries in the ensuing years would end the careers of "policy" and "numbers" operators in Black communities and expand penetration of gambling opportunities from a mostly urban clientele to rural areas across the country.[94]

Historian Matthew Vaz describes the political failure to consider the specific effects on communities of color that accompanied the legalization of lottery gambling:

> Appeals for racial justice, demands for economic self-determination, and claims of local prerogative in gambling practices all fell short in an atmosphere of racial backlash, economic retrenchment and heightened calls for stricter enforcement of the law. While gambling was once the lifeblood of emergent black politics and business in the North, in the aftermath of the consolidation of public lotteries, the resultant framework left black communities with no substantial connection to gambling beyond the role of lottery consumers. After several decades of conflict and debate, the question was settled. The urban poor were subjected to gambling as taxation, with little access to the profits and jobs from taxed gambling.[95]

The expansion of regulated casino gambling today, along with consideration of other types of legalized gambling such as sports betting, shows how this capture of the gambling market by state operators has largely given way to the even more regressive control exercised by private legalized operators. The number of options for those who wish to risk their money is ever increasing, taking market share away from state lotteries and regulated casinos and giving that revenue to large firms such as FanDuel and DraftKings. A 2021 study using data from West Virginia makes this clear, demonstrating that as increased opportunities to wager on sports became available, state lottery and slots revenue decreased, resulting in the loss of tens of millions of dollars for the state government.[96]

Showing that it has historically been possible to transition from an illicit market that was racially stigmatized to a ubiquitous legal one might be a source of hope for cannabis liberalization proponents. Yet this brief history of how it actually happened—with informally organized Black gambling rings coopted by state and then private actors that ultimately continued to harm Black communities, just in a different way—holds an important lesson for the importance of keeping social equity considerations at the forefront of the legal cannabis space. For one thing, police tactics against gambling operations later transferred to narcotics control efforts, limiting any sense of freedom that the legalization of gambling may have engendered. Meanwhile, the promise that legalization might hold as a potential economic opportunity for communities of color turned out to be a mirage, as states like Illinois embraced a government-run monopoly model to compete with informal operators, who were already being targeted by both gangs and police.

As chapter 3 will explore, the economic potential of cannabis legalization—and who is in line to benefit from this potential—is still in flux, while some legalization activists have begun to pivot from the earlier narratives regarding regulation and tax revenues to make an argument that cannabis legalization represents an opportunity to build ownership and generational wealth for Black Americans like Akele Parnell. The path toward this potential is still hazy, though, and many obstacles remain.

NOTES

1. *Green Market Report*, "Black History Month Spotlight: Akele Parnell," February 10, 2022, https://www.greenmarketreport.com/black-history-month-spotlight-akele-parnell/.
2. Kate Linebaugh and Ryan Knutson, "The Highs and Lows of Diversifying the Cannabis Industry," podcast, 17:30, in *The Journal*, co-produced by the *Wall Street Journal* and Gimlet Media, December 20, 2022, https://www.wsj.com/podcasts/the-journal/the-highs-and-lows-of-diversifying-the-cannabis-industry/0dde3849-c4c3-44db-99a2-9f0225f8283f.
3. Linebaugh and Knutson, "Highs and Lows."
4. Ellora Derenoncourt et al., "The Wealth of Two Nations: The US Racial Wealth Gap, 1860–2020," NBER Working Paper 30101, National Bureau of Economic Research, June 2022, 10–11, https://doi.org/10.3386/w30101.
5. Derenoncourt et al., "Wealth of Two Nations," 14.
6. William A. Darity Jr. and A. Kirsten Mullen, *From Here to Equality: Reparations for Black Americans in the Twenty-First Century* (Chapel Hill: University of North Carolina Press, 2020), 200–203.
7. Judson MacLaury, "The Federal Government and Negro Workers Under President Woodrow Wilson," paper presented at annual meeting of the Society for History in the Federal Government, Washington, DC, March 16, 2000, https://www.dol.gov/general/aboutdol/history/shfgpr00.
8. Mehrsa Baradaran, *The Color of Money: Black Banks and the Racial Wealth Gap* (Cambridge, MA: Harvard University Press, 2017), 101; and Darity and Mullen, *Here to Equality*, 247. See also Mary Poole, *The Segregated Origins of Social Security: African Americans and the Welfare State* (Chapel Hill: University of North Carolina Press, 2006).

9. Suzanne Mettler, *Soldiers to Citizens: The G.I. Bill and the Making of the Greatest Generation* (New York: Oxford University Press, 2005).
10. Mettler, *Soldiers to Citizens*, 141.
11. Darity and Mullen, *Here to Equality*, 9–10.
12. Darity and Mullen, *Here to Equality*, 207–13.
13. John M. Bickers, "The Power to Do What Manifestly Must Be Done: Congress, the Freedmen's Bureau, and Constitutional Imagination," *Roger Williams University Law Review* 12, no. 1 (2006): 86–89.
14. Baradaran, *Color of Money*, 19–22.
15. Richard Rothstein, *The Color of Law: A Forgotten History of How Our Government Segregated America* (New York: Liveright, 2017).
16. Baradaran, *Color of Money*, 68–70.
17. Rothstein, *Color of Law*.
18. Rothstein, *Color of Law*.
19. Rothstein, *Color of Law*.
20. Michael Omi and Howard Winant, *Racial Formation in the United States*, 3rd ed. (New York: Routledge, 2015).
21. Rothstein, *Color of Law*.
22. Qi Wang et al., "Urban Mobility and Neighborhood Isolation in America's 50 Largest Cities," *PNAS* 115, no. 30 (2018): 7739–40, https://www.pnas.org/doi/10.1073/pnas.1802537115.
23. Sarah Burd-Sharps and Rebecca Rasch, *Impact of the US Housing Crisis on the Racial Wealth Gap Across Generations* (New York: Social Science Research Council, 2015). See also Baradaran, *Color of Money*, 255–60.
24. Baradaran, *Color of Money*, 114.
25. Wang et al., "Urban Mobility," 7740.
26. Freddie Mac, "Racial and Ethnic Valuation Gaps in Home Purchase Appraisals," Research Note, September 20, 2021, https://www.freddiemac.com/research/insight/20210920-home-appraisals; Hugo Balta, "Racial Bias in Home Appraisals," *Chicago Reporter*, March 25, 2022, https://www.chicagoreporter.com/racial-bias-in-home-appraisals/; and Kirk Pinho, "Black Homeowners in Metro Detroit Face Greatest Home Value Disparity in Nation," *Crain's Detroit Business*, January 17, 2021, https://www.crainsdetroit.com/real-estate/black-homeowners-metro-detroit-face-greatest-home-value-disparity-nation.
27. Baradaran, *Color of Money*, 229, 265.
28. Baradaran, *Color of Money*, 29–32; and US Office of the Comptroller of the Currency, "The Freedman's Savings Bank: Good Intentions Were Not Enough; A Noble Experiment Goes Awry," https://www.occ.treas.gov/about/who-we-are/history/1863-1865/1863-1865-freedmans-savings-bank.html.
29. Baradaran, *Color of Money*, 109.
30. Emily Peck, "The Rise and Fall of a Black Banking Icon," Axios.com, February 28, 2022, https://www.axios.com/2022/02/28/the-rise-and-fall-of-a-black-banking-icon; and Baradaran, *Color of Money*, 71–74.
31. Baradaran, *Color of Money*, 75.
32. Baradaran, *Color of Money*, 105–10.

33. Baradaran, *Color of Money*, 126.

34. Baradaran, *Color of Money*, 6–8.

35. Baradaran, *Color of Money*, 301; and Derrick P. Aldridge, "Atlanta Compromise Speech," in *New Georgia Encyclopedia*, last edited October 1, 2020, https://www.georgiaencyclopedia.org/articles/history-archaeology/atlanta-compromise-speech/.

36. For North Carolina, see Doris Marie Provine, *Unequal Under Law: Race in the War on Drugs* (Chicago: University of Chicago Press, 2007), 53–54; and Darity and Mullen, *Here to Equality*, 216. For Tulsa, see Darity and Mullen, 18–22; Baradaran, *Color of Money*, 59–63; and Oklahoma Commission to Study the Tulsa Race Riot of 1921, *Final Report*, February 28, 2001, https://www.okhistory.org/research/forms/freport.pdf. For Atlanta, see Clifford Kuhn and Gregory Mixon, "Atlanta Race Massacre of 1906," in *New Georgia Encyclopedia*, last edited November 14, 2002, https://www.georgiaencyclopedia.org/articles/history-archaeology/atlanta-race-massacre-of-1906/.

37. Malcolm X, "Speech at Ford Auditorium (1965)," BlackPast.org, July 26, 2010, https://www.blackpast.org/african-american-history/speeches-african-american-history/1965-malcolm-x-speech-ford-auditorium/.

38. Martin Luther King, Jr. Research and Education Institute, Stanford University, "Freedom's Ring," accessed December 13, 2022, https://freedomsring.stanford.edu/?view=Speech.

39. Baradaran, *Color of Money*, 140; and Martin Luther King, Jr. Research and Education Institute, Stanford University, "Poor People's Campaign," in *Martin Luther King, Jr. Encyclopedia*, https://kinginstitute.stanford.edu/encyclopedia/poor-peoples-campaign.

40. Baradaran, *Color of Money*, 151–52.

41. Todd Gitlin, *The Sixties: Years of Hope, Days of Rage*, rev. ed. (New York: Bantam, 1993).

42. Baradaran, *Color of Money*, 179.

43. Mehrsa Baradaran, "The Real Roots of 'Black Capitalism,'" *New York Times*, March 31, 2019, https://www.nytimes.com/2019/03/31/opinion/nixon-capitalism-blacks.html.

44. Baradaran, *Color of Money*, 161–62.

45. Rothstein, *Color of Law*; and Brent Cebul, "Tearing Down Black America," *Boston Review*, July 22, 2020, https://www.bostonreview.net/articles/brent-cebul-tearing-down-black-america/.

46. See Baradaran, *Color of Money*, 203; and Gregory N. Price, "The Cost of Government Deposits for Black-Owned Commercial Banks," *Review of Black Political Economy* 23, no. 1 (1994): 23–24, https://doi.org/10.1007/BF02895738.

47. Alyssa Stryker, *Rethinking the "Drug Dealer"* (New York: Drug Policy Alliance, 2019), 36–44, https://drugpolicy.org/sites/default/files/dpa-rethinking-the-drug-dealer_0.pdf; and Mary E. Pattillo, "Sweet Mothers and Gangbangers: Managing Crime in a Black Middle-Class Neighborhood," *Social Forces* 76, no. 3 (1998): 747–74, https://www.jstor.org/stable/3005693.

48. Provine, *Unequal Under Law*, 95–98.

49. Provine, *Unequal Under Law*, 94–95; and Martin A. Lee, *Smoke Signals: A Social History of Marijuana—Medical, Recreational, and Scientific* (New York: Scribner, 2012), 134–35.

50. Gary S. Becker and Kevin M. Murphy, "A Theory of Rational Addiction," *Journal of Political Economy* 96, no. 4 (1988): 675–700, https://www.jstor.org/stable/1830469.

51. Ilyana Kuziemko and Steven D. Levitt, "An Empirical Analysis of Imprisoning Drug Offenders," NBER Working Paper 8489, National Bureau of Economic Research, September 2001, https://www.nber.org/papers/w8489.

52. Ole Rogeberg, "Taking Absurd Theories Seriously: Economics and the Case of Rational Addiction Theories," *Philosophy of Science* 71, no. 3 (2004): 263–65, https://doi.org/10.1086/421535.

53. Emily Dufton, *Grass Roots: The Rise and Fall and Rise of Marijuana in America* (New York: Basic Books, 2017), 101–5.

54. akchuk, "Ronald Reagan: 'Marijuana . . . Is Probably the Most Dangerous Drug,'" YouTube video, September 4, 2014, https://www.youtube.com/watch?v=VxHBx6H-xFo&ab_channel=akchuk.

55. Dufton, *Grass Roots*, 158–64.

56. Sentencing Project, "Growth in Mass Incarceration: Prison Population Over Time," accessed December 14, 2022, https://www.sentencingproject.org/research/.

57. Sentencing Project, "Growth in Mass Incarceration."

58. Mike Wessler, "Updated Charts Provide Insights on Racial Disparities, Correctional Control, Jail Suicides, and More," blog post, Prison Policy Initiative, May 19, 2022, https://www.prisonpolicy.org/blog/2022/05/19/updated_charts/.

59. Ashley Nellis, *The Color of Justice: Racial and Ethnic Disparities in State Prisons* (Washington, DC: Sentencing Project, 2021), 20, https://www.sentencingproject.org/app/uploads/2022/08/The-Color-of-Justice-Racial-and-Ethnic-Disparity-in-State-Prisons.pdf.

60. Matthew D. Lassiter, "Impossible Criminals: The Suburban Imperatives of America's War on Drugs," *Journal of American History* 102, no. 1 (2015): 126–40.

61. Jon B. Gettman, Emily Whitfield, and Matthew Allen, *The War on Marijuana in Black and White: A Massachusetts Update* (Boston: ACLU Foundation of Massachusetts, 2016), 6, 8, https://www.aclum.org/sites/default/files/tr-report-10-2016-final-with-cover.pdf.

62. Provine, *Unequal Under Law*, 109.

63. Provine, *Unequal Under Law*, 137–39.

64. *Concepcion v. United States*, 597 U.S. ___ (2022), https://www.supremecourt.gov/opinions/21pdf/20-1650_new_4gci.pdf.

65. Ryan S. King and Marc Mauer, "The War on Marijuana: The Transformation of the War on Drugs in the 1990s," *Harm Reduction Journal* 3 (2006): 1–17, https://doi.org/10.1186/1477-7517-3-6.

66. Emma Pierson et al., "A Large-Scale Analysis of Racial Disparities in Police Stops Across the United States," *Nature Human Behaviour* 4, no. 7 (2020): 737–39, https://www.nature.com/articles/s41562-020-0858-1.

67. Apoorva Joshi, "Explainer: Three Strikes Laws and Their Effects," blog post, Interrogating Justice, July 23, 2021, https://interrogatingjustice.org/mandatory-minimums/three-strikes-laws-and-effects/.

68. Jonathan P. Caulkins, "Are Mandatory Minimum Drug Sentences Cost-Effective?" Research brief RB-6003, RAND Corporation, 1997, https://www.rand.org/pubs/research_briefs/RB6003.html.

69. Michelle Alexander, *The New Jim Crow: Mass Incarceration in the Age of Colorblindness* (New York: New Press, 2010), 59–61.

70. Alexander, *New Jim Crow*, 122.

71. Ram Sundaresh et al., "Exposure to the US Criminal Legal System and Well-Being: A 2018 Cross-Sectional Study," *American Journal of Public Health* 110, no. S1 (2020): S116–22, https://doi.org/10.2105/AJPH.2019.305414; and Michael H. Esposito et al., "The Consequences of Contact with the Criminal Justice System for Health in the Transition to Adulthood," *Longitudinal and Life Course Studies* 8, no. 1 (2017): 57–74, https://doi.org/10.14301%2Fllcs.v8i1.405.

72. Ezekiel Edwards, Will Bunting, and Lynda Garcia, *The War on Marijuana in Black and White: Billions of Dollars Wasted on Racially Biased Arrests* (New York: ACLU, 2013), 17–22, https://www.aclu.org/report/report-war-marijuana-black-and-white; and Ezekiel Edwards et al., *A Tale of Two Countries: Racially Targeted Arrests in the Era of Marijuana Reform* (New York: ACLU, 2020), 7–10, https://www.aclu.org/report/tale-two-countries-racially-targeted-arrests-era-marijuana-reform.

73. Dufton, *Grass Roots*, 120–22.

74. Dufton, *Grass Roots*, 171.

75. Dufton, *Grass Roots*, 182–85.

76. On firearms, see Helen K. Sudhoff, *Blowing Smoke at the Second Amendment* (Los Angeles, CA: Reason Foundation, 2021), https://reason.org/wp-content/uploads/blowing-smoke-at-the-second-amendment.pdf; on security clearances, see US Secret Service, "Our Drug Policy," https://www.secretservice.gov/careers/drug-policy; on cannabis and the military, see Anthony Kuhn, "3 Consequences of Using Marijuana After Your State 'Legalizes,'" *Military Times*, April 14, 2021, https://www.militarytimes.com/opinion/commentary/2021/04/14/3-consequences-of-using-marijuana-after-your-state-legalizes/.

77. Chris Roberts, "Biden White House Admits Firing Staffers for Marijuana, But Still Employs Some Past Pot Users," *Forbes*, March 19, 2021, https://www.forbes.com/sites/chrisroberts/2021/03/19/biden-white-house-blasted-for-punishing-staffers-for-using-marijuana/?sh=6975ecd631a8.

78. Jacqueline Feldscher, "NASA Paid SpaceX for Safety Review After Musk Smoked Pot," *Politico*, October 16, 2019, https://www.politico.com/news/2019/10/16/nasa-musk-weed-048099.

79. On eviction, see Alexander, *New Jim Crow*, 57; and Lee, *Smoke Signals*, 322. On federal student aid, see Drug Policy Alliance, "Federal Student Aid Access," https://drugpolicy.org/issues/federal-student-aid-access; and Lee, *Smoke Signals*, 235.

80. On Massachusetts, see Ballotpedia, "Presidential Election in Massachusetts, 2016," https://ballotpedia.org/Presidential_election_in_Massachusetts,_2016, and "Massachusetts Marijuana Legalization, Question 4 (2016)," https://ballotpedia.org

/Massachusetts_Marijuana_Legalization,_Question_4_(2016). On South Dakota, see Ballotpedia, "Presidential Election in South Dakota, 2020," https://ballotpedia.org/Presidential_election_in_South_Dakota,_2020, and "South Dakota Constitutional Amendment A, Marijuana Legalization Initiative (2020)," https://ballotpedia.org/South_Dakota_Constitutional_Amendment_A,_Marijuana_Legalization_Initiative_(2020).

81. Arek Sarkissian, "Trump Doesn't Inhale, But the Cannabis Industry Is Betting His Supporters Do," *Politico*, October 8, 2019, https://www.politico.com/states/florida/story/2019/10/08/trump-doesnt-inhale-but-cannabis-is-betting-his-supporters-do-1221139; and Jeffrey M. Jones, "Marijuana Views Linked to Ideology, Religiosity, Age," Gallup, November 15, 2022, https://news.gallup.com/poll/405086/marijuana-views-linked-ideology-religiosity-age.aspx.

82. Alexander, *New Jim Crow*, 175–76.

83. Alexander, *New Jim Crow*, 167.

84. Clip available at InsaneNutter, "Chris Rock—How Not to Get Your Ass Kicked by the Police!" YouTube video, February 2, 2007, https://www.youtube.com/watch?v=uj0mtxXEGE8&ab_channel=InsaneNutter.

85. For an example of a critical take on Alexander, see John F. Pfaff, *Locked In: The True Causes of Mass Incarceration and How to Achieve Real Reform* (New York: Basic, 2017).

86. Alexander, *New Jim Crow*.

87. Alexander, *New Jim Crow*, 163–64.

88. Matthew Vaz, *Running the Numbers: Race, Police, and the History of Urban Gambling* (Chicago: University of Chicago Press, 2020), 109.

89. Vaz, *Running the Numbers*, 56.

90. Vaz, *Running the Numbers*, 110–11.

91. Vaz, *Running the Numbers*, 120.

92. Vaz, *Running the Numbers*, 127–31.

93. Vaz, *Running the Numbers*, 144–47.

94. Vaz, *Running the Numbers*, 153–55.

95. Vaz, *Running the Numbers*, 163–64.

96. Brad R. Humphreys, "Legalized Sports Betting, VLT Gambling, and State Gambling Revenues: Evidence from West Virginia," *Eastern Economic Journal* 47 (2021): 27, https://doi.org/10.1057/s41302-020-00178-0.

Chapter 3

Cannabis Legalization

A New Paradigm of Control?

Several decades after Congress passed the Controlled Substances Act (CSA) in 1970, state and local governments began to step back and reconsider the War on Drugs as a matter of policy. One early inspiration was the AIDS epidemic in the early 1980s, which helped to spur a major cultural change in narratives surrounding cannabis use when it became a common palliative cure for many individuals diagnosed with AIDS, a recognition of its capacity to reduce pain and improve appetite. This movement centered in San Francisco and was perhaps best personified by Mary Jane Rathbun—otherwise known as "Brownie Mary"—who distributed dozens of cannabis brownies per day to AIDS sufferers during the 1980s. Brownie Mary was arrested and subjected to police surveillance, but later went on to lead a successful citywide initiative to decriminalize cannabis for medicinal purposes in the early 1990s.[1] This policy victory anticipated the later 1996 statewide campaign to decriminalize cannabis in California, a political effort bitterly opposed by both federal leaders and statewide elected officials such as California's governor and attorney general—Pete Wilson and Dan Lungren—as well as three former US presidents. In that later contest, in which Rathbun played a key role along with fellow cannabis activist Dennis Peron, liberalization won out again.[2]

This political victory led to the relatively swift adoption of medical cannabis in several other states via both ballot initiative and state legislation.[3] Supporters of liberalization still had a number of logistical challenges in determining how to set up a legal supply network for the demand that existed. Nevertheless, the additional legal protection provided by these new legal state markets gave a shield for both patients and (some) providers and limited the scope of crackdowns by federal officials.

Despite these early successes, a significant strategic debate about how to move forward emerged in the movement for cannabis liberalization. Traditional activists had often been introduced to cannabis through the 1960s free use movement and generally saw the ability to grow and use cannabis as an inherent right. They were especially well represented by state and national groups under the National Organization for the Reform of Marijuana Laws (NORML) umbrella. NORML activists and their compatriots often argued that cannabis should not be heavily regulated by states or the federal government and rejected most forms of enhanced legal scrutiny for use, sales, and transfer.[4] They also were aware that the previous movement for cannabis liberalization during the 1970s had been defeated in part because of a political reaction to increased youth use, however, and so these activists were also committed to ensuring that legalization proposals would address and limit youth use.[5]

This movement split into two factions, however, when senior leaders of NORML left the group in 1995 to create the Marijuana Policy Project (MPP), which would come to represent a differing vision for legalization.[6] These activists sought to create a broad coalition in favor of legalization that acknowledged that many voters would want and even expect strict legal regulations in exchange for liberalization. This gradualist approach came to inform many of the ballot initiative and legislative campaigns to come, with advocates often promising that the proposed liberalization would involve strict limits on how cannabis could legally be bought and sold in a licensed system and that any other sale or use would come with criminal penalties.[7] In this vision, liberalization would actually solidify the control regime rather than remove it.

While early liberalization efforts were focused on medicinal uses only, a similar narrative developed to inform the movement to legalize recreational cannabis beginning in the mid-2000s. After voters rejected a 2006 ballot initiative in Colorado that would have legalized cannabis by simply removing it from the list of prohibited substances[8]—an approach that the more traditional NORML activists would prefer—Colorado's cannabis activists retooled their messaging to appeal to swing voters. This shift in strategy culminated in the successful passage of the state's Amendment 64 in 2012[9] (an event which will be discussed in more detail in chapter 4), the same year that Washington state voters approved a similar measure. After these twin victories, the modern movement for the legalization of recreational cannabis achieved a political realignment with few precedents in American history—one that saw state after state approve recreational legalization in a matter of years. While this was not the first time that drug use more generally or cannabis use specifically was liberalized, the relative speed and remarkable durability of these changes despite significant opportunities for defeat and denial have given many drug policy reformers hope about the potential for further progress.

The success of legalization efforts in Colorado and Washington was a surprising footnote to the election cycle that saw President Barack Obama reelected by a healthy margin and the political status quo on the federal level otherwise reinforced. Just two years earlier, a concerted effort by the US Department of Justice and the political establishment in California had beaten back a ballot referendum that would have legalized cannabis in that state.[10] While this initiative had several political flaws, it was the first time in decades that voters in any state had been invited to broadly challenge drug criminalization by creating a consumer market. The close result in California's 2010 initiative arguably presaged the success of legalization in Colorado and Washington just two years later.

The political strategy behind this legal shift involved an alliance between counterculture anti-government activists (mostly on the left) and a group of elites that were dissatisfied with the focus and scope of drug criminalization. Their new language and narrative proposed that cannabis regulations could be similar to those governing alcohol. While many Americans expressed some amount of doubt about alcohol as well, the new messaging nevertheless served as a familiar frame of reference for voters who were uncertain about what legal cannabis would look like.[11] Within several years, national polling showed a decisive majority in favor of legalization.[12] In turn, those early victories encouraged campaigners who successfully achieved legalization in a slew of other states that quickly followed. Indeed, every two years since then, millions more Americans have gained the legal right to possess and use cannabis for recreational purposes (though there have also been a few setbacks, such as a failed attempt in Arizona in 2016). The changing nature of the legalization discussion in such a short time is perhaps best illustrated by the fact that nearly all Americans now live in a state with medical access to cannabis.[13]

THE CASE FOR LEGAL CANNABIS AS REPARATIONS

In 2014, writer and activist Ta-Nehisi Coates published an essay in the *Atlantic* calling for a broad reexamination of reparations for American slavery, Jim Crow, and related instances of systemically supported racism, an idea that had long been the subject of high school college debate sessions and the odd academic event.[14] These previous debates had often framed the idea of reparations as a compulsory monetary payment to Black Americans made on behalf of white Americans. This simplified framing has been subjected to a great deal of criticism, much of it suggesting a mismatch between this model and the complex nature of race relations over the past two decades, with many recent immigrants to the United States seeing little to no benefit from the legacy of slavery and the population of Black Americans who might stand to benefit from these payments undergoing its own demographic and social changes, including the continued migration of "undeserving" people from Africa and Caribbean nations like Haiti.

Coates's work quickly became a hit and helped propel him to both increased attention and scrutiny. He later testified in front of Congress in favor of Representative John Conyers's long-dormant proposal for a national commission to study the idea of reparations. The article was later named the "Top Work of Journalism of the Decade" by a panel of judges at New York University,[15] and has been referred to in both popular media and scholarly debates ever since. Conversely, Coates has also achieved a minor anti-celebrity status amongst those on the right who regularly seek to target leftist thought.

Reparations are not a new concept here in the United States, however, even going beyond the example of German reparations to Israel after World War II that Coates noted. After the United States forcibly detained over 120,000 Japanese Americans during World War II, Congress quickly set up a "War Claims Act" which sought to recompense internees for the property that they were forced to abandon when removed from their homes and businesses. Due to gaps in both individual and institutional records, few payments were made and many former detainees suffered years of personal and financial ruin from their experiences.[16] Recognizing this, Congress passed a series of initiatives in the later half of the twentieth century to address Japanese American internees' continued claims, culminating in payments of $20,000 for each eligible person. The subject of who might benefit from these payments, as well as whether the payments were justified at all, was controversial, both among the Japanese American community and the broader public. Along with monetary payments, President George H. W. Bush issued a formal apology to Japanese Americans in 1991 on the fiftieth anniversary of the attacks on Pearl Harbor.[17]

This model of reparations is informative for the discussion of social equity in the context of cannabis decriminalization because it points to the difficulty of getting such measures approved as well as determining who should benefit from them. This ineffective initial movement for Japanese American internment reparations took decades to obtain even formal recognition from President Gerald Ford in 1976 in the form of an executive statement, and the passage of congressional legislation to set aside the money took over a decade longer.[18] In the years after World War II, few Japanese Americans discussed their experience of internment, especially with white people who might deny or minimize their experiences. Only after the creation of the "Redress" movement—inspired by the Black Civil Rights Movement of the 1960s—spurred a public discussion and campaign for official recognition of the internment program did serious progress get made toward a formal apology and monetary reparations.[19]

Reparations also face challenges in terms of determining the appropriate scale of proposed relief. For many of those Japanese Americans who experienced internment, few had the capacity or information to precisely assess the cost of three years of isolation as well as the lost property, earnings, opportunities, and connections that entailed. The hurried transfer of those detained often left little time to collect records and protect assets, and many lost their houses and other property. Even with an initial claims process held right after the war, very few eligible claimants were able to collect money.[20] By 1991, the total loss of these communities surely amounted to more than $20,000 per person, and in the end that figure was a political compromise between those who did not believe that the United States should pay anything and those who advocated for a more wholesale reparations program. Many Japanese Americans took satisfaction that a law was passed and some relief was given, though no amount of money would address the profound pain and exclusion they experienced.[21]

The historical legacy and present condition of Black Americans today is subject to great political debate, and there is little consensus among the broader public about racial matters that might permit discussion of reparations. In a 2021 poll, three in five respondents opposed reparations, including over a third of voters who supported President Biden in 2020. Black Americans strongly supported reparations, and white Americans opposed them with a slightly smaller margin, with Latinos and Asian Americans more evenly divided. When those opposed to reparations were asked why they opposed them, nearly half stated that they didn't believe the recipients were deserving, and other respondents also addressed the logistical and equity issues around distribution of payments. For those who were supportive of reparations, many respondents chose reasons that connected past inequality with continuing social conditions impacting minority communities.[22]

While Coates did not mention drug policy, mass incarceration, or cannabis—his essay focuses on the impact of housing policy on racial wealth gaps—the argument for critically examining reparations holds true for the context of cannabis legalization, especially in light of the Japanese internment example. Exact numbers are difficult to find, but it is certain that millions of Americans alive today have suffered some direct harm due to drug criminalization, even if we just look at cannabis. (For more on this, see chapter 2 and especially the case studies in chapters 4–9.) Much like Coates does in his article, we can clearly see a moral case for doing something for those impacted by criminalization, even though direct payments might be difficult and politically unfeasible.

Social equity cannabis policies are precisely these kinds of attempts to "do something" to repair the damages of criminalization. While it is perhaps too early to tell whether the recent wave of decriminalization activities related to cannabis are the start of a new era in US drug policy—for cannabis by itself or more broadly—it is precisely this moment's novelty that offers the potential to embed social equity policies from the beginning and perhaps, in this instance, forestall a repeat of the decades of suffering and lost opportunity faced by interned Japanese Americans confronting a flawed initial government response to their own form of injustice.

The Value of Reparations Today

The political campaign for reparations for Black Americans as we know it today and discussions over the logistical reality of following through on them have long and contentious histories which cultural historian Kirsten Mullen and economist William Darity cogently present in their 2018 book *From Here to Equality*. Among other issues, Darity and Mullen summarize decades of estimates for what the total potential cost of reparations payments to African Americans might be, both collectively and individually.

To determine one of the first estimates of the value of reparations in 1983, economic historians Roger L. Ransom and Richard Sutch approximated the difference in the value produced by enslaved Africans over the historical period of bondage against the value that was provided to these slaves in the form of food and other support, a method that suggests a lower bound of these estimates at $16.8 billion to $33.6 billion, depending on the inflation rate used to carry forward those amounts into 2022 numbers. Alternatively, political scientist Thomas Craemer has provided an estimate of reparations by calculating the value of hours exploited from enslaved workers during the period of American independence, arriving at potential values in excess of $18 trillion in 2022 currency. These upper-bound estimates—if paid individually to the forty million Black Americans alive today—would provide hundreds of thousands of dollars to each man, woman, and child who continues to live with the legacy of slavery and discrimination. Needless to say, a program of this scale and reach would be both historically unprecedented and also searingly contentious in America's racial and cultural context.

Conversely, the capacity of a fully legal and regulated cannabis market to provide tax revenue for social programs—whether in the form of direct reparations payments or any other social programs that ballot initiative organizers or elected officials may promise to voters—is relatively modest. Grand View Research, a market research firm that studies the legal cannabis industry, estimates that the industry's 2021 revenue was worth approximately $10.8 billion, with a potential compound growth of more than 14 percent per year, leading to perhaps as much as $40 billion in industry revenue by 2030.[23] Another research firm predicted a market value as large as $72 billion by 2030, if additional states act to legalize in the coming years.[24] This possible expansion would add to growth in states where it is already legal and create soaring profits for the industry as well as swelling tax revenue for state governments, which collected $3.7 billion in licensing fees, sales tax, and other revenue from the cannabis industry in 2021.[25] This industry also supported an increasing number of jobs, with nearly a half million Americans working in the sector that year.[26] While these numbers may sound large in and of themselves, the legal alcohol industry claimed as recently as 2018 to create two million jobs and as much as $122 billion in economic impact with taxes raised at every level from the municipal to the federal.[27]

While presumably the revenue from legal cannabis might be sufficient to meet the lower bounds of some of the reparations claims that Darity and Mullen examine, the entire productive capacity of the industry would have to be harnessed for decades to meet some of the higher-bound estimates. However, it would be a red herring to consider the potential of cannabis to fully meet any just reparations program's needs. Just as cannabis has been only one aspect of the War on Drugs, and just as the War on Drugs was only one part of a larger system of oppression that individuals and communities of color have faced in the last century, allocation of tax revenue derived from legal cannabis sales might play an important part in the discussion over legalization and reparations today without needing to bear the entire burden necessary to proceed.

The city of Evanston, Illinois, made this connection more explicitly with a reparations program started in 2021, which will be examined in chapter 7. For the moment, simply consider that any program of reparations should prioritize addressing the racial wealth gap. As Darity and Mullen suggest, "the racial wealth gap . . . [is] the most robust indicator of the cumulative economic effects of white supremacy in the United States . . . since today's differential in wealth captures the cumulative effects of racism on living black descendants of American slavery."[28] Whatever else legal cannabis might do for society, taxes and other fees related to its production, distribution, and consumption could at least provide a start toward confronting this problem.

CANNABIS TODAY

The Legal Market

The increased pace of cannabis legalization has led to a surge of sophistication in the products and services that the industry is capable of offering. Legacy market cannabis was often grown indoors in suboptimal conditions or grown outside with little regard for quality. Potency could be low, while fake or diluted products were common. With legalization, regulated providers have specialized. A visit to today's recreational cannabis dispensary is a clinical experience, with well-lit stores and a "menu" of products that include not just flower cannabis, but a wide variety of edibles, oils, and vaping products. Some of these edible products are not just the brownies of past years, but also carbonated beverages, ice cream, pills, and fruit chews. A variety of products straddle the line between recreational and clinical, with promises to cure sleep issues, anxiety, and lethargy.[29]

It is unclear from the existing data how much of the regulated market supply for cannabis is serving demand that existed before legalization and how much of the demand is induced by the combination of social permissibility and increased availability, both outcomes of legality. Data from market researcher BDSA suggests that nearly half of adults in legal states had consumed cannabis within the last six months and another quarter would be interested in doing so.[30] This implies that large market expansions will continue in further years, driving additional money into tax coffers. Cannabis hardly has the economic might of the alcohol industry or the social acceptability of the craft beer or wine industries, but it usually no longer incites the kind of moral panic seen in previous iterations of the War on Drugs.

Most notably, few political groups (even those on the religious right) focus on the impacts of cannabis anymore. While the Catholic Church, in particular, opposed some earlier legalization ballot measures,[31] there was never a concerted national effort against legalization among social conservatives at large. Smart Approaches to Marijuana (SAM), a group created by former Congressman Patrick Kennedy in 2013, has instead become the leading voice in opposition to many cannabis legalization efforts across the country. SAM notably does not claim to outright oppose legalization and instead focuses its rhetorical ammunition against "Big Marijuana" and in favor of increased protections against high-potency cannabis. While much of SAM's messaging continues to align with traditional "drug-free" campaigns, even within the group there has been a clear shift away from prohibitionist rhetoric.[32] SAM has also seen less policy success in recent years as more states legalize cannabis.

Whatever one thinks of its overall ideology, SAM's criticism of industry consolidation and big-market players does include some convincing points. Even though cannabis businesses face federal legal restrictions that make it difficult for them to operate across state lines (more on this below), the expansion of the legal market into larger states such as California and those on the East Coast has nevertheless fueled the growth of so-called multi-state operators (MSOs). The largest of these, Curaleaf, reported its 2021 revenue at $1.2 billion.[33] That company has used cash offers to expand its footprint to at least a dozen states, buying out competitors and often engaging in market-disrupting behavior.[34] Curaleaf and many of its larger competitors, including Trulieve, Green Thumb, Cresco, and Columbia, have encountered growing pains over the first years of regulated cannabis. But although many continue to post losses, their year-over-year revenue increases have continued to soar. Curaleaf's 2021 revenue was more than double 2020's, a pace consistent with other market leaders.[35]

As we will see in the following chapters, MSOs are often complicated actors to engage with when pursuing social equity efforts in the legal market. While their increased legal revenue and consolidation create a collective interest that speaks to the growing power of the cannabis industry, their vision of this industry is inherently exclusive, as their business plans rely on efficiencies of scale that come from market dominance. MSOs also benefit from the long wait times and high costs associated with opening up a legal cannabis business, as prospective business owners burn up much of their capital while waiting for regulatory approval and have little left once their doors open. Once there, larger operators are able to invest desperately needed operating capital in exchange for exploitative or extractive contracts, leaving the original owner with little income or wealth.[36]

Another reason the large, established companies have an inherent advantage over newer entrants is that opening and running a legal cannabis business is an expensive and difficult endeavor. It requires expertise in the science of growing and harvesting the plant itself—which few Americans had any experience of doing at scale before liberalization began. In most places, it also means navigating an entirely new market with a unique regulatory apparatus. Almost by definition, then, there are very few people with a skill-set that precisely matches what is needed in any given state. While many businesses have to operate under some sort of regulatory regime in which compliance entails a certain amount of expense, cannabis businesses are in a largely unique position due to the novelty of the regulatory structure and its cannabis-specific aspects. One particularly costly example of this has to do with the fact that the current regulatory regime for cannabis is seldom built around the dangers of the drug itself, instead responding to political pressure to appear to be curtailing youth use. All market participants must therefore comply with burdensome regulations and documentation, but new, smaller operators are far less likely to be able to afford the increased compliance costs because they can't just pass these costs onto customers in brand new markets that still involve plenty of sellers in the unregulated market, who don't face these conditions.[37]

Cannabis operators are also exposed to higher costs compared to many other businesses as a result of how they are uniquely taxed. For nearly all legal industries, businesses may deduct the expenses associated with normal operations from their legally recognized revenue on both the state and federal levels. This ensures that taxes are being paid on the profits of the business rather than the gross revenue. Often lawmakers are especially generous toward business owners, allowing for a wide range of activities to count as part of their operations, whether those be health insurance costs for employees or the jet-buying decisions of top executives. However, federal tax law explicitly treats all business expenses related to what the federal government considers to be the illegal drug trade—even those of state-licensed cannabis businesses—as nondeductible, turning the usual generosity into a peevish miserliness.[38] This disparate treatment is often reflected in state tax laws as well, even in states that have decriminalized cannabis. While some states such as California, Michigan, and Massachusetts have recently allowed state-licensed businesses to deduct their expenses on state returns,[39] the federal prohibition still operates as a drag. Advocates of social equity policies have often been the loudest in pointing out this inequity, as it hurts the bottom line of Black-owned cannabis businesses the most.[40]

Leaving the Legacy Market

The legacy supply for cannabis is divided into two large buckets. The first is composed of a small number of larger operators who offer experiences similar to, if not quite equivalent to, the regulated market. Some of these operate as autonomous delivery networks or are connected to merchants on the edge of legality who offer cannabis-adjacent products. Many so-called "head shops" or "bong shops," stores where shoppers can obtain the ornate glass sculptures used by many to smoke flower cannabis, also offer a combination of cannabis flower and edibles to consumers savvy enough to know the secret path to entry.[41]

Many cannabis consumers are also able to obtain their product from a wider group of "social supply" participants, who are users who also sell a small quantity of cannabis, in part to finance their own consumption. This group—much larger in the number of individuals involved, but each of whom is involved in a very small volume of trade—comprises the second bucket.[42] It is this social supply which often most concerns policymakers, who see it as the vehicle for youth initiation of drug consumption.[43] Policy efforts to target this social supply have often proved frustrating and unsuccessful, however. Cannabis legalization itself was portrayed by advocates as a vehicle for controlling youth access to cannabis after the failures of the prohibition model; and while youth consumption has not noticeably spiked in most states that have legalized cannabis, legalization has also not led to a decrease, given the strength of the legacy market.[44]

The advent of legalization has therefore at most diverted some business from legacy providers, who often continue to be competitive on the basis of lower prices, different product offerings, established customer relationships and habits, and other factors. But even in instances where illicit providers would like to transition to running a legal business, the precise terms of legalization have often made these efforts prohibitively difficult. In the case of African Americans, those terms have frequently combined with the persistent negative economic effects of both the Jim Crow and New Jim Crow eras to make it all but impossible.

Today, the legacy market for cannabis has come to represent a portion of the community wealth for Black communities. Very little of the wealth in this market is funneled through the formal economy—few drug sellers deposit their earnings with a bank and file a yearly return with the IRS. Even if this does protect the wealth from confiscation by law enforcement, it also limits the capacity to engage in more protected and predictable wealth growth tools available to those in the formal economy. Nor does the wealth benefit institutions in Black communities such as local banks and the businesses they lend to, preventing these operators and their money from achieving full integration into today's capitalist economy.

The major challenge encountered by many cannabis market regulators today is not the unknowns of cannabis itself—despite its illegality at the federal level and in many state contexts, research on its health and social effects has been extensive. Rather, the question is how to ensure that people who participated in the cannabis market when the only choice was to do so illicitly now join the ranks of regulated providers. It is still tempting to many state legislators and policymakers to fall back on the mechanisms of criminal enforcement to ensure this transition. In fact, many activists have observed cannabis regulators entering discussions with law enforcement with the goal of providing a negative incentive for unlicensed sellers of cannabis.

This is the worst response to the continued existence of the illicit market.

While sellers may not join the regulated market out of inertia or due to the slightly higher profit margins that can be had in the illicit arena, the more likely reason why many legacy providers may not move toward legality is that they face insurmountable financial barriers to do so. Possession of liquid assets, such as savings accounts, real estate, and other forms of wealth that can easily be converted into cash, allows someone in any business to quickly adapt to changing circumstances in ways that someone without these resources cannot. Liquid wealth is particularly important in the formation of cannabis businesses, however, because they involve a federally illegal substance. Bank and credit card companies like Visa and Mastercard view cannabis-related transactions as highly risky and therefore refuse to conduct them or do so only at an inflated cost.[45] The federal government itself will not provide small business loans for cannabis companies,[46] and most institutional investors have given cannabis companies a wide berth (with the partial exception of MSOs in more recent years). As a result, most American cannabis businesses operate on an exclusively cash basis. Legal operators need access to cash and other liquid assets to maintain day-to-day operations where entrepreneurs in other fields might be able to easily rely on credit to manage their cashflow. Many state regulators, acknowledging this reality, require that licensees have access to liquid assets as a benchmark of viability.[47]

As chapters 1 and 2 established, however, Black people in general have faced both a historical and ongoing deficit in access to this sort of individual and community capital, compared to white Americans. Many cannabis entrepreneurs have used their own 401Ks or borrowed against the real estate that they own in order to finance their entry into the market, picking up similar "angel" investments from family and friends in their network.[48] Because of the racial wealth gap, those entrepreneurs are nearly always white.[49] Many Black businesses in other industries have opened in the face of the same challenges, with government or small community banks often providing small loans—but of course, these are rarely options when the planned business involves cannabis. This is especially true for banks that operate in predominantly Black neighborhoods, which are generally exposed to higher risks than otherwise comparable institutions.[50]

Even if you can manage to get a cannabis business off the ground, the challenges of operating in an all-cash environment lead to additional costs. Cannabis businesses have to pay extensive bank fees for handling large cash deposits, as well as transaction costs to get cash to and from a bank safely and without theft.[51] Like all businesses, cannabis producers and dispensaries must pay rent, employees, for services to maintain day-to-day operations, and for product to put on the shelf. Without access to traditional lending, cash businesses are less likely to survive and are more likely to require large infusions of capital to maintain operations. In areas of the country where concentrated poverty is high and generational wealth is low, Black Americans will certainly struggle to create and sustain businesses in an industry with these disadvantages.

Legalization of possessing and using cannabis products and state regulation of the trade of producing and selling them under these conditions are inevitably going to fall the wrong way on communities of color in the aggregate because of the decades of structural inequities in accumulated wealth that they have inherited. The persistence of deploying law enforcement to minority communities where the legacy market is still quite strong simply makes things worse. Taken together, the legal market has become in many places a tool for the powerful to slowly squeeze and eventually displace the existing supplier market for cannabis, rather than a brave new world where everyone has a chance at going legitimate. Legal regulated cannabis markets don't just fail to benefit those in minority communities; in jurisdictions where few legacy market participants have integrated into the regulated market, law enforcement operations that target non-licensed operators often serve to directly decrease Black wealth.

Regulating Legal Cannabis

The political successes of the early legalization movement rested almost entirely on emphasizing a future of strong regulation in order to rebut narratives that legal cannabis would pose a threat to children. This is especially clear when looking at the legalization campaigns in Colorado (see chapter 4) and Massachusetts (see chapter 6). The history of this opposition narrative goes back decades. It was, for example, the impetus for the parents' movement which began in the late 1970s as a response to increased youth use of cannabis and the perceived ubiquity of cannabis paraphernalia (briefly discussed in chapter 2). The quick reaction of politicians who took up the cause of the parents' movement in turn provided a clear lesson to advocates for legalization.

Jon Gettman, a drug policy reformer who served as the head of NORML for part of the 1980s, was himself a seller of cannabis paraphernalia during that earlier period. He spoke to the failures of the earlier decriminalization movement and the market it created: "The problem with the freewheeling paraphernalia market was that . . . [m]uch like sex is used to sell cars, we were, in retrospect, using drugs to sell knick-knacks." This "exploitation of drugs was offensive to some, especially to parents trying to keep their kids away from any drug use, illegal or otherwise." With the benefit of hindsight, Gettman decided that "it is time for marijuana consumers, the merchants of tobacco accessories, parents' groups, and antidrug crusaders to put aside our differences and work together on the issue on which we all seem to agree—keeping drugs out of the hands of kids."[52]

The nature of youth regulations specifically will be further explored in later chapters, but Gettman's concern about what he called "pandering to an illegal interest" in drugs has proved salient in modern discussions about cannabis legalization, though often at the price of skepticism and even criticism from those in the cannabis industry itself.[53] Policymakers who want to ensure a robust legal market need to consider the unique situation that cannabis businesses face and be careful not to impose an overall set of burdens that push the price of legal cannabis so high that purchasers seek legacy suppliers or drop out of the market entirely. These largely hidden costs mean that a nominal sales tax figure that seems reasonable for another business like a liquor store may be ill-suited to enabling a cannabis supplier to stay in business. This issue has come up wherever legalization has been discussed, but some of the most comprehensive research and policy action has come from the United States' northern neighbor, Canada.

In contrast to the United States, Canada has boldly moved forward with cannabis legalization at the federal level. After Canadian Prime Minister Justin Trudeau was first elected in 2015, he worked to implement his campaign promise of legal cannabis, ultimately succeeding in 2018. Canada's federal government let the rules for sales be set on the provincial level (akin to an American state), allowing for wide variety in implementation guidelines.[54] The unequivocal nature of the federal policy shift nevertheless provided a pathway for even those skeptical of cannabis to have a voice in controlling its regulatory future, as well as a clear mandate to limit the legacy market as a vehicle for maximizing governmental revenue streams. As a result, the Canadian market is a unique venue to see the impact of pricing, taxes, and the future of a legacy market in a comparative setting.

Canada's experience demonstrates that there is a model for a national regulatory structure that will give discretion to lower levels of government, though given the relative population size of Canada and the less concentrated effects of criminalization on communities of color there, the legalization of cannabis at the federal level in the United States would still represent a new era in the cannabis market. Likely the most important lesson from Canada for the United States is that the legacy market is still an important player for consumers even in the context of full legalization[55]—as such, policymakers in Canada are continuing to pay close attention to the effect of taxes on pricing and market behavior, and it would be useful for American policymakers to keep a close eye on the outcomes of those experiments.

Cannabis, like alcohol and tobacco and many other substances, certainly has negative social externalities—behaviors, health conditions, and outcomes that impact those who are not a direct party to the sale and consumption of cannabis. Legalization has certainly led to an increase in impaired driving, for example, with some scholars pointing to a particular rise in fatalities from drivers who had consumed both alcohol and cannabis.[56] Legalization has also led to increases in calls to poison control hotlines and visits to the emergency room for cases of minor consumption and over-ingestion.[57]

A more complicated but potentially still negative outcome is that increased consumption among the younger generation has also changed the labor market—employers (such as Amazon) now regularly waive drug tests in as many positions as they can.[58] Employers must balance the needs of their workforce with the population they recruit from, with older moral sentiments about cannabis and those who use it falling away and being replaced with a more savvy relativism. Even the military has adopted this approach, as recruiting has bottomed out in recent years—increases in waivers for past cannabis use have closely followed this downturn.[59] It is too early to tell whether or not such waivers have affected military readiness or the bottom lines of companies, but there is at least a potential cost to them that must be evaluated.

As these and other broad-based effects of cannabis legalization become clearer, market regulators will eventually reach a theoretical point at which the negative outcomes of increased consumption of cannabis might outweigh the revenue benefits for the state, giving some support for using prices to control consumption.[60] When policymakers seek to set regulatory policy for a substance like cannabis in a way that redresses these drawbacks while maintaining its social benefits, one tool they look to is to try to "price in" the costs of these negative social externalities into the price that consumers pay for the product that is causing them. Economists call the use of taxation to help set a market price in which the social costs are taken into account a "Pigouvian tax" (after the economist credited with popularizing the idea). Such a tax works by raising revenue that can be used to offset damages—through running campaigns to prevent intoxicated driving, for example—as well as by suppressing consumption to reduce the incidence of such outcomes. With cannabis legalization often portrayed as a "cash cow" for state governments, however, the tax rate is frequently set higher than the market "clearing" price, resulting in a mismatch between the quantity demanded by consumers and the price set by the regulated market.

The legacy supply of cannabis is well positioned to fill this gap, and the continued strength of these informal channels has bedeviled policymakers from the United States and Canada in recent years. Legalization in Canada did noticeably decrease the size of the legacy market by as much as a third in its first year, but significant numbers of Canadians still report acquiring cannabis through a legacy provider.[61] Some of the most significant factors in establishing who moves to the legal market and who does not are price and convenience, however, indicating that many state legal markets in the United States will struggle to reduce the legacy market until cannabis stores are widely available.

I will discuss many experiences of regulators trying to understand and set prices in the case studies I cover later in this book. In few American states have government regulators been completely successful in curbing legacy market operations, however, and in many legal states the legacy suppliers still meet much of the market demand for cannabis. As already discussed, the price of legal cannabis is informed by a combination of taxes, regulatory difficulty, and the factors of production, and legacy market prices benefit from a clear advantage in avoiding the first two. The problem from a social equity standpoint is that many social equity operators—who are by definition drawn from communities where they are disproportionately likely to be disadvantaged when it comes to access to wealth, financing, and the like—require higher initial and sustained prices to pay back their investors and keep their businesses running. Conversely, many MSOs and white-financed cannabis businesses are able to sustain operations past the initial "green boom" phase of legal cannabis, where the legal market price crashes as supply outstrips demand. After the surge, consumers are less willing to pay higher prices for the novelty of legal supply and might either wait for lower prices or return to legacy market suppliers.

In order to help encourage illicit market participants to come into the regulated market, then, policymakers need to demonstrate to legacy sellers that moving their economic activities to the legal market serves both their own best interest and the interest of their communities, providing jobs and tax revenue that directly helps them and those they identify with. This assurance will ring hollow, however, unless participants feel like they are able to survive as operators in this legal market, which means that policymakers must seriously consider ways to lower current financial and regulatory barriers to entry and encourage market conditions that will enable a legal cannabis business to sustain itself in the short-term and then grow over time.

Evaluating Legalization's Outcomes—A Mixed Bag

Despite its political victories, the movement for legalization has often made bold promises that remain unfulfilled. Advocates in many states claimed that legalization would help reduce youth access to cannabis and other harder drugs by segmenting and regulating the markets for cannabis. Instead, the data on youth use of cannabis has remained relatively level in many states, while both increasing and decreasing in others in the wake of recreational legalization.[62] Youth use of cannabis, as well as tobacco, has been more noticeably impacted by the growing gray market of loosely regulated vaping products.[63] The challenges of this were made clear in late 2019 when a national epidemic of breathing issues affected regular users of vaping tobacco and cannabis across the United States. This epidemic was related to the use of vitamin E acetate, a common additive to gray-market vaping oils.[64]

On a more positive note, legalization has undoubtedly succeeded in reducing the total number of people, including those of color, who are subjected to criminal justice involvement as a result of cannabis possession or sale. Even though those who are arrested for crimes related to cannabis in fully recreationally legal states are still highly disproportionately people of color, there are still far fewer absolute numbers of arrests than existed under the earlier prohibition regime.[65] If we accept this basic standard, then cannabis legalization has achieved some policy success. Still, this would be akin to celebrating that you only got stabbed today with two inches of the four-inch knife that stabbed you yesterday. You still got stabbed.

In this same way, communities of color can hardly celebrate the end of criminalization after being brutalized for decades as part of a largely unsuccessful policy experiment aimed at answering whether ever-increasing amounts of funding and militarized law enforcement could successfully decrease the availability of drugs sold on the street. Research on that exact question has demonstrated that increased funding for law enforcement and the public presence and recognition of enforcement operations have little relationship to the street price of drugs and the economic incentives that motivate participants in the illegal market for drugs, whether for cannabis or any other substance in question.[66] Given that authorities were targeting minority communities for substances such as crack and heroin for decades while entirely legal and regulated drugs such as Oxycontin were then left to wreak havoc in largely white rural communities demonstrates the clear futility of the War on Drugs. Meanwhile, hit TV shows such as *Breaking Bad* and *The Wire* have reinforced the perception of the systemic inability of the state to disrupt the supply in drug markets, which are always quick to recover in order to meet ever-consistent demand. Studies looking at the comparative usage rate between different substances, whether illegal or not, often find that the differences are best explained by a combination of access, economics, and social trends—not criminal enforcement.[67]

In the wake of this overwhelming evidence of both how people actually act and indeed how they perceive the legal structures that have supported the War on Drugs for decades, legalizing the recreational possession and sale of cannabis and taking away the criminal enforcement of cannabis laws are obvious steps to take toward acknowledging the wrongs of criminalization. Yet it is only one such step in adopting the sort of radical yet simple solutions that scholars such as Michelle Alexander suggest would both serve to change the dynamics around legalization and give communities of color the power to thrive and be resilient. For example, even in absence of later convictions, prior convictions for cannabis possession and trafficking continue to haunt millions of Americans. The lasting effects can be extensive—the American Bar Association's National Inventory of the Collateral Consequences of Conviction assembles over 44,000 separate consequences from all criminal convictions identified in federal and state law.[68] They also can be far from trivial. A criminal record for a drug crime can make it difficult to get an education, hold a job, maintain a relationship with one's children, and participate in civic life (most importantly by voting). A felony conviction can also seriously impact access to housing—including state-funded group homes for drug treatment and medical issues.[69]

The progress on relieving this burden has been mixed at best, as many states that have created paths to eliminate or expunge past convictions have made the process to do so difficult, often requiring the convicted individual to hire a lawyer or follow a multistep process. In California, nearly 120,000 residents had gotten relief between 2018 and early 2022, but over 30,000 were still seeking it through the courts. State lawmakers had sent over $16 million in dedicated funding to California courts in order to address the backlog, but the pandemic and other logistical issues got in the way.[70] Similarly, Illinois legislators provided for the statewide expungement of cannabis offenses in their 2019 legalization law, but local agencies have until 2025 to comply with the law, leaving many individuals uncertain about their status.[71]

While far more Americans have criminal records than remain in jail for cannabis convictions, the number is likely non-trivial even if it is difficult to estimate. The Last Prisoner Project (LPP), a justice-oriented nonprofit founded by noted cannabis activist Steve DeAngelo, suggests in its advocacy materials that the number is 40,000 inmates.[72] While there is some discussion about whether this figure accounts for more recent decreases in enforcement as additional states have legalized, it is likely that there are a fair number of people still inside jails and prisons across the country regardless.[73] LPP's advocacy work for those still caught up in the criminal justice system has focused more directly on individual cases of imprisonment rather than systemic issues, but these individual cases nevertheless highlight the high systemic barriers to justice that are still in place. In one representative instance, former Michigan inmate Maurice Shumate was released in early 2022 after serving six years in jail for manufacturing and transferring less than five kilograms of cannabis. While his original sentence was fifteen years, LPP and some of its affiliated activists were able to pressure the Michigan Parole Board to grant him clemency.[74] LPP has also raised over a million dollars to help citizens returning from jail and prison.[75] While at least some progress is being made to ensure that sometime soon no more Americans will have their freedom taken away for participating in the cannabis market, these individual stories of continued criminalization speak to the enduring nature of cannabis prohibition and the kinds of issues that social equity activists must continue to address.

SOCIAL EQUITY—A TIPPING POINT

The remainder of this book is intended to help readers understand the diversity of cannabis equity programs. The core argument that I make is that many of the existing programs do not completely fulfill a reparative goal, for many of the reasons raised in this chapter, and that further work is needed for cannabis legalization to have a broad impact on communities of color impacted by the War on Drugs. Dividing this discussion into case studies of different state experiences, which we can then compare, lets us see the importance of context and the actions of particular stakeholders in determining the success or failure of a specific program. The perceived failure of a program can salt the ground for future policy innovation, while perceived success is at least a baseline for future activism.

So far, the vast majority of social equity policies adopted across the country in those states where equity has been addressed through legislation can be classified more generally as licensing priority or exclusion systems. These programs often promise to give those negatively affected by the War on Drugs—or even more narrowly by cannabis arrests and convictions—an opportunity to participate in the legal regulated market, with some states giving additional credit for this history in a point system to determine who gains access, other states providing particular license types exclusively for properly classified social equity applicants, and still others seeking to provide some sort of financing for those looking to open a business. By my count, as of the writing of this book (2023), at least eight states—Massachusetts, Illinois, New Jersey, New York, Colorado, Connecticut, California, and Pennsylvania—have some sort of statewide social equity program, while many other local jurisdictions have provided for one in their area.

Another major category of assistance that is provided to those targeted by criminalization involves training and technical assistance. This is a traditional tool of equity initiatives aimed at establishing minority businesses or banks.[76] These programs often do address a real need for information, connections, and assistance, but they do not address the equally real wealth and capital access gaps that Black Americans face, particularly those who grew up in traditionally majority-minority urban neighborhoods. Massachusetts was one of the first states to offer a more comprehensive and deliberately planned program beginning in 2017, as will be discussed in chapter 6, though in some other states, municipalities and other jurisdictions had offered smaller mentorship programs.[77]

These programs have provoked some controversy within the smaller world of social equity activism because while this kind of partnership often jointly benefits both the mentor and the mentee, the mentor is better positioned to take advantage of the gains, and thus many mentees do not see the kind of boost they had anticipated. Partly as a result of this feedback, the years after Massachusetts launched its social equity technical assistance program have seen several other states and cities implement different versions of this approach, with mixed results in generating new cannabis businesses. It is much too early to declare these programs failures, though, as both licensing and financing take a great deal of time, not enough of which has passed in most cases.

The last major type of equity design is also very recent, and so it is premature to judge it for policy success. First adopted by Illinois in 2019, it attempts to directly correct for the racial wealth gap by providing business loans for social equity applicants.[78] Since then, other states such as New York,

Washington, and Massachusetts have also adopted a similar mechanism. As of the writing of this book, many of the loans have not been dispersed, so it is difficult to understand who the final recipients may be and what outcomes will result. Of particular note, however, is that these programs have been directly tied to the collection of cannabis revenue, with states such as New York setting aside percentages of collected revenue into a trust fund for these purposes.[79] The intentionality of this design is clear, and regardless of the specific programs' outcomes, it sets a good precedent for the importance of trying to establish more direct conduits for the social benefits of legalization to reach individuals and communities that were most affected by criminalization.

Despite their wide variety, most of these social equity programs share one common design attribute which is a crucial flaw that significantly limits their effectiveness and breadth: when examining the eligibility requirements for each program, one can see that they are often framed around personal economic indicators such as income, residence in particular areas, or conviction of a cannabis offense in the past. For example, the Massachusetts Cannabis Control Commission's Social Equity Program requires that applicants have less than 400 percent of the area median income and reside in an Area of Disproportionate Impact. These formally designated areas are themselves chosen based on a combination of economic variables and criminal justice statistics. A careful reader might now notice the flaw: despite being intended to address decades of systemic discrimination and disempowerment based on race, these programs do not actually account for race in distributing their benefits. In Massachusetts, these benefits are currently rather modest—primarily licensing preference and technical assistance—though legislative leaders have also more recently provided further benefits, such as loans to social equity cannabis businesses that are financed by dedicated cannabis tax revenue, modeled on New York's system.[80]

Why do these programs adopt this defensive crouch? It comes not from a lack of vision on the part of those designing such programs, but rather from a combination of legal and political limitations. The legal limitations come primarily from the most recent Roberts-era Supreme Court decisions on the role of race in crafting social policy. This philosophy is best exemplified by Roberts himself in one of those decisions, *Parents Involved* (2007), which limited the use of racial preferences in an educational context on the basis that the best "way to stop discrimination on the basis of race is to stop discriminating on the basis of race."[81] While this attitude may be rather simply stated and have a particular clarity to it, it ignores the long institutional history of legalized color lines that have solidified economic and political power toward primarily wealthier white communities and away from communities of color.

There is also a political reality to these decisions. Explicit racial quotas of the type that conservatives have long complained about have simply become unfeasible, even among politically liberal circles that accept many of the basic ideas about the link between racial preference and economic status in America.[82] It is impossible for advocates of social equity in cannabis programs to quickly change either the jurisprudential or political context in which these programs operate, so this program design feature is understandable, even if it is unfortunate.

The difficulty of not being able to easily incorporate racial considerations explicitly into programs designed to redress the problems of racism highlights one of the gaps between the rhetoric of many social equity activists in the cannabis space and the reality of what might be achieved. As well-intentioned and passionate as these calls are, it is difficult to see these social equity programs playing any significant part in addressing the large systemic gaps created by racist policies and practices. This is partly a question of scale—even as the national cannabis market continues to expand, the revenue brought in by legal cannabis sales is extremely small compared to the larger pool of government revenue and spending. Encouraging ownership of cannabis businesses by racial minorities toward a goal of building wealth is certainly a laudable pursuit, but ultimately the legal cannabis market will not build the kind of community wealth that was taken away from Black communities by decades of underinvestment and overpolicing.

Paradoxically, this suggests that the inability to target cannabis social equity programs in racial terms might not be as devastating an outcome as it might at first seem. For one thing, it reminds us that there must be more to social equity pursuits than just entrepreneurship programs, a lesson well illustrated by considering the importance of expunging past convictions—a policy that by its very nature is race neutral and yet can often make a bigger difference for Black and brown people who are affected by it than for their white counterparts. Similarly, policies that try to lower the need to operate a cannabis business on an all-cash basis will almost inevitably do a great deal to help those who have the least access to cash.

Meanwhile, discussions around the motivations for providing social equity programs and their particular attributes have significant value for promoting justice, however, when connections can be made to possible areas for social equity policies that could simultaneously be made in other industries where Black individuals and communities are left out. Consider a recent report from the *Boston Globe* that discusses liquor licenses in the city. Whiter neighborhoods have higher access to eateries serving alcohol, while only 2 percent of license holders are Black in a city with an overall Black population that is ten times greater.[83] While focusing efforts on equity in one industry is in a sense more easily achieved, racial justice requires this larger lens that looks across industries. When we see the dynamics in the regulated alcohol industry, the historical racial color lines remain clear, with Black Americans overrepresented in customer-facing and entry-level positions such as bussers and waitstaff and underrepresented in senior management and ownership.[84] A program that explicitly recognizes racial barriers to cannabis business ownership would do little to solve this problem, but one that encourages cross-industry organization or even heightened enforcement of existing labor and civil rights laws might improve conditions at a social level that cannabis equity policies by themselves might not.

The reality is that by most standards, social equity programs in legal cannabis markets simply will not have the reach or breadth to satisfy calls for reparations while also suffering from the same access and institutional barriers that many economic development programs experience. However, I will argue in the rest of this book for an alternative framing that would celebrate the diversity in many of the programs that exist today, while providing the impetus to grow the legal regulated market in areas where the illicit market is still strong. Both communities of color and individuals of color stand to benefit from increased participation in the regulated market, and by working with entrepreneurs of color, cannabis regulators can create opportunities for wealth generation amongst, while also generating tax revenue to help develop. the communities that they live in. This will only be achieved by acknowledging and building on the racial legacy of cannabis criminalization while understanding that cannabis is a drug that will continue to be used across lines of color, class, and perspective.

NOTES

1. Martin A. Lee, *Smoke Signals: A Social History of Marijuana—Medical, Recreational, and Scientific* (New York: Scribner, 2012), 228–29.
2. Lee, *Smoke Signals*, 246–51.
3. For an overview of medical cannabis legalization, see National Conference of State Legislatures, "State Medical Cannabis Laws," updated September 12, 2022, https://www.ncsl.org/health/state-medical-cannabis-laws.
4. Joe Bonni, "You Down with MPP?" *Boston Weekly Dig*, February 11, 2003, reprint available at http://www.mapinc.org/drugnews/v03/n237/a06.html?127.
5. Emily Dufton, *Grass Roots: The Rise and Fall and Rise of Marijuana in America* (New York: Basic Books, 2017), 202.
6. Bonni, "You Down with MPP?"
7. Marijuana Policy Project, "Our History," https://www.mpp.org/about/history/.
8. Lee, *Smoke Signals*, 401.
9. Emily Crick, Mark Cooke, and Dave Bewley-Taylor, "Selling Cannabis Regulation: Learning from Ballot Initiatives in the United States in 2012," Policy Brief 6,

Global Drug Policy Observatory, November 2014, 19–21, https://www.swansea.ac.uk/media/Selling-Cannabis-Regulation.pdf.

10. J. Andrew Sinclair, Jaclyn R. Kimble, and R. Michael Alvarez, "Why Did Proposition 19 Fail?" in *Something's in the Air: Race, Crime, and the Legalization of Marijuana*, ed. Katherine Tate, James Lance Taylor, and Mark Q. Sawyer, 54–64 (New York: Routledge, 2014).

11. Crick, Cooke, and Bewley-Taylor, "Selling Cannabis Regulation," 17.

12. Jeffrey M. Jones, "Marijuana Views Linked to Ideology, Religiosity, Age," Gallup, November 15, 2022, https://news.gallup.com/poll/405086/marijuana-views-linked-ideology-religiosity-age.aspx.

13. National Conference of State Legislatures, "State Medical Cannabis Laws" and "Deep Dive: Marijuana," https://www.ncsl.org/bookstore/state-legislatures-magazine/marijuana-deep-dive.aspx.

14. Ta-Nehisi Coates, "The Case for Reparations," *The Atlantic*, June 2014, https://www.theatlantic.com/magazine/archive/2014/06/the-case-for-reparations/361631/.

15. Arthur L. Carter Journalism Institute, New York University, "Ta-Nehisi Coates' 'The Case for Reparations' Named Top Work of Journalism of the Last Decade," news release, October 14, 2020, https://www.nyu.edu/about/news-publications/news/2020/october/ta-nehisi-coates---the-case-for-reparations--named-top-work-of-j.html.

16. Daniel Shoag and Nicholas Carollo, "The Causal Effect of Place: Evidence from Japanese-American Internment," working paper, January 2020, 30–31, https://scholar.harvard.edu/shoag/publications/long-run-causal-impact-place-evidence-income-and-mobility-effects-japanese.

17. Isabella Rosario, "The Unlikely Story Behind Japanese Americans' Campaign for Reparations," CodeSwitch, *NPR*, March 24, 2020, https://www.npr.org/sections/codeswitch/2020/03/24/820181127/the-unlikely-story-behind-japanese-americans-campaign-for-reparations; and National Museum of American History, "Redress Payments," https://americanhistory.si.edu/righting-wrong-japanese-americans-and-world-war-ii/redress-payments.

18. Gerald R. Ford Presidential Library and Museum, "President Gerald R. Ford's Proclamation 4417,"https://www.fordlibrarymuseum.gov/library/speeches/760111p.htm.

19. Rosario, "Unlikely Story."

20. Rosario, "Unlikely Story."

21. Greg Robinson, "The Paradox of Reparations: Japanese Americans and African Americans at the Crossroads of Alliance and Conflict," in *Minority Relations: Intergroup Conflict and Cooperation*, ed. Greg Robinson and Robert S. Chang, 159–88 (Oxford: University Press of Mississippi, 2016).

22. Kiana Cox and Khadijah Edwards, "3. Reparations for Slavery," Pew Research Center, August 30, 2022, https://www.pewresearch.org/race-ethnicity/2022/08/30/black-americans-views-on-reparations-for-slavery/.

23. Grand View Research, "Report Summary: Legal Marijuana Market Size, Share and Trends Analysis Report by Product Type (Flower, Oil and Tinctures), by Application (Medical, Adult Use), by Region (North America, Europe, APAC, LATAM,

Africa), and Segment Forecasts, 2023–2030," https://www.grandviewresearch.com/industry-analysis/legal-marijuana-market.

24. New Frontier Data, "New Frontier Data Projects Annual US Cannabis Sales to More than Double to $72B by 2030," news release, March 23, 2022, https://www.globenewswire.com/en/news-release/2022/03/23/2408755/0/en/New-Frontier-Data-Projects-Annual-U-S-Cannabis-Sales-to-More-Than-Double-to-72B-by-2030.html.

25. Marijuana Policy Project, "Cannabis Tax Revenue in States that Regulate Cannabis for Adult Use," last updated April 5, 2022, https://www.mpp.org/issues/legalization/cannabis-tax-revenue-states-regulate-cannabis-adult-use/.

26. Bruce Barcott and Beau Whitney, *Jobs Report 2022*, with Max Savage Levenson and Chris Kudialis (Seattle, WA: Leafly, 2002), 4, https://leafly-cms-production.imgix.net/wp-content/uploads/2022/02/22132544/LeaflyJobsReport2022.pdf.

27. American Beverage Licensees, "America's Beer, Wine and Spirits Retailers Create 2.03 Million Jobs and $122.63 Billion in Direct Economic Impact," news release, October 23, 2018, https://ablusa.org/americas-beer-wine-spirits-retailers-create-2-03-million-jobs-122-63-billion-in-direct-economic-impact/.

28. William A. Darity Jr. and A. Kirsten Mullen, *From Here to Equality: Reparations for Black Americans in the Twenty-First Century* (Chapel Hill: University of North Carolina Press, 2020), 263.

29. Stephanie Watson, "Medical Marijuana FAQ," WebMD.com, December 18, 2021, https://www.webmd.com/a-to-z-guides/medical-marijuana-faq.

30. BDSA, "Cannabis by the Numbers," slide deck, Beer Marketer's Insights conference, May 12, 2022, 3, https://bdsa.com/wp-content/uploads/2022/05/BDSA_Cannabis-by-the-Numbers_Beer-Marketers-Insights-Presentation_May-2022-1.pdf.

31. Emma Green, "Why the Catholic Church Is Leading the Fight Against Legal Pot in Massachusetts," *The Atlantic*, November 1, 2016, https://www.theatlantic.com/politics/archive/2016/11/boston-archdiocese-marijuana-legalization/505997/; and Clemente Lisi, "Recreational Marijuana Legalization Becomes New Front in the Culture Wars Following Midterms," *Religion Unplugged*, November 11, 2022, https://religionunplugged.com/news/2022/11/10/2022-midterm-elections-catholic-bishops-increasingly-vocal-against-recreational-marijuana-use-fall-short-following-passage-in-missouri-and-maryland.

32. For example, see Smart Approaches to Marijuana (SAM), "How Legalizing Marijuana Affects Your Health and Safety (extended)," YouTube video, October 19, 2022, https://www.youtube.com/watch?app=desktop&v=lko7ufmgYag&ab_channel=SmartApproachestoMarijuana%28SAM%29.

33. CompaniesMarketCap.com, "Curaleaf," Revenue History for Curaleaf, https://companiesmarketcap.com/curaleaf/revenue/.

34. *MJBizDaily*, "Curaleaf Finalizes Grassroots Deal, Grows Marijuana Footprint to 23 States," March 18, 2022, https://mjbizdaily.com/curaleaf-finalizes-grassroots-acquisition-grows-marijuana-footprint-to-23-states/.

35. CompaniesMarketCap.com, "Curaleaf."

36. Matt Hawkins, "Marijuana Investing: The Pros and Cons of MSOs," *Kiplinger*, last updated September 22, 2021, https://www.kiplinger.com/investing/stocks/marijuana-stocks/603477/marijuana-investing-the-pros-and-cons-of-msos.

37. Simplifya.com, "A Simple Way to Estimate Cost of Compliance," blog post, December 1, 2021, https://www.simplifya.com/simple-way-to-estimate-cost-of-compliance/.

38. Congressional Research Service, "The Application of Internal Revenue Code Section 280E to Marijuana Businesses: Selected Legal Issues," report no. R46709, March 10, 2021, https://crsreports.congress.gov/product/pdf/R/R46709.

39. On Massachusetts, see Wolf & Company, P.C., "Massachusetts Passes Income Tax Relief for Cannabis Business," blog post,https://www.wolfandco.com/resources/alerts/massachusetts-income-tax-relief-cannabis-businesses/; on other states, see Wolters Kluwer, "Do States Allow Income Tax Deductions for Marijuana Business Expenses?" blog post, September 15, 2021, https://www.wolterskluwer.com/en/expert-insights/do-states-allow-income-tax-deductions-for-marijuana-business-expenses.

40. For example, see Jelena Grove, "What Is the 280e Tax Code and How Is It a Liability for Social Equity Licensees in 2020?" *This Is Our Dream* (blog), accessed December 15, 2022, https://thisisourdream.com/what-is-the-280e-tax-code-and-how-is-it-a-liability-for-social-equity-licensees-in-2020/.

41. Ed Hersh, "Smoke Shops, Convenience Stores, and an Open Secret," *West Side Rag*, June 6, 2022, https://www.westsiderag.com/2022/06/06/smoke-shops-convenience-stores-and-an-open-secret.

42. Andrew D. Hathaway et al., "'It's Really No Big Deal': The Role of Social Supply Networks in Normalizing Use of Cannabis by Students at Canadian Universities," *Deviant Behavior* 39, no. 12 (2018): 1672–80, https://doi.org/10.1080/01639625.2017.1411047.

43. Matthew Taylor and Gary R. Potter, "From 'Social Supply' to 'Real Dealing': Drift, Friendship, and Trust in Drug-Dealing Careers," *Journal of Drug Issues* 43, no. 4 (2013): 392–406, https://doi.org/10.1177/0022042612474974.

44. Youth use will be discussed throughout the book; see especially chapters 4 and 9.

45. Lindsay Konsko, "Why You Can't Always Buy Marijuana with a Credit Card," blog post, NerdWallet.com, January 18, 2014, https://www.nerdwallet.com/article/credit-cards/buy-marijuana-credit-card.

46. Justia.com, "Financing a Cannabis Business," last reviewed September 2022, https://www.justia.com/cannabis-law/financing-a-cannabis-business/.

47. For example, see Cannabis Regulatory Agency, State of Michigan, "What Are the Capitalization Requirements for Each Type of License?" https://www.michigan.gov/cra/faq/licensing-list/apps-new/what-are-the-capitalization-requirements-for-each-type-of-license; and Associated Press, "Want to Grow Arkansas Medical Marijuana? Here's How Much You'll Need to Pay Annually," *The Cannabist*, January 5, 2017, https://www.thecannabist.co/2017/01/05/arkansas-medical-marijuana-grow-fee-2/70668/.

48. Mark Calvey, "Angel Investors Are High on Legal Marijuana's Opportunities," *San Francisco Business Times*, August 15, 2014, https://www.bizjournals.com/sanfrancisco/blog/2014/08/marijuana-cannabis-pot-angel-investing-startups.html.

49. Katharine Neill Harris and William Martin, "Persistent Inequities in Cannabis Policy," *Judges' Journal* 60, no. 1 (2021): 9–13, https://www.bakerinstitute.org/sites/default/files/2021-02/import/inequities-in-cannabis-policy-2021.pdf.

50. Mehrsa Baradaran, *The Color of Money: Black Banks and the Racial Wealth Gap* (Cambridge, MA: Harvard University Press, 2017), 272–73; and Beth Healy, "OneUnited Moves to Foreclose on Historic Church," *Boston Globe*, February 29, 2012, https://www.bostonglobe.com/business/2012/02/29/oneunited-bank-taking-steps-foreclose-charles-street-african-methodist-episcopal-church/TXwcVjuDZlCv4m1MA8B6NM/story.html.

51. Shariq Khan, "US Pot Sellers Stash Cash as Banks Leave Them High and Dry," Reuters, May 24, 2021, https://www.reuters.com/world/us/us-pot-sellers-stash-cash-banks-leave-them-high-dry-2021-05-24/.

52. Dufton, *Grass Roots*, 202.

53. Will Yakowicz, "Weed vs. Greed: How America Botched Legalizing Pot," *Forbes*, August 2, 2022, https://www.forbes.com/sites/willyakowicz/2022/08/02/how-america-botched-legalizing-cannabis-berner-cookies-kim-rivers-trulieve-steve-deangelo/?sh=70693b874489.

54. Malcolm G. Bird, "Legalized Cannabis in Canada: Federalism, Policy, and Politics," in *High Time: The Legalization and Regulation of Cannabis in Canada*, ed. Andrew Potter and Daniel Weinstock, 22–34 (Montreal: McGill-Queen's University Press, 2019).

55. Colin D'Mello, "Cannabis Customers Have Been Complaining Ontario's Pot Is 'Too Dry,'" *CTV News*, December 7, 2020, https://toronto.ctvnews.ca/cannabis-customers-have-been-complaining-ontario-s-pot-is-too-dry-1.5220170.

56. See generally Sarah B. Windle et al., "Impaired Driving and Legalization of Recreational Cannabis," *Canadian Medical Association Journal* 193, no. 14 (2021): E481–85, https://doi.org/10.1503/cmaj.191032; Tyler J. Lane and Wayne Hall, "Traffic Fatalities within US States that Have Legalized Recreational Cannabis Sales and Their Neighbours," *Addiction* 114, no. 5 (2019): 847–56, https://doi.org/10.1111/add.14536; and Julian Santaella-Tenorio et al., "Association of Recreational Cannabis Laws in Colorado and Washington State with Changes in Traffic Fatalities, 2005–2017," *JAMA Internal Medicine* 180, no. 8 (2020): 1061–68, https://doi.org/10.1001/jamainternmed.2020.1757.

57. See Yuyan Shi and Di Liang, "The Association Between Recreational Cannabis Commercialization and Cannabis Exposures Reported to the US National Poison Data System," *Addiction* 115, no. 10 (2020): 1890–99, https://doi.org/10.1111/add.15019; Jonathan M. Davis et al., "Public Health Effects of Medical Marijuana Legalization in Colorado," *American Journal of Preventive Medicine* 50, no. 3 (2016): 373–79, https://doi.org/10.1016/j.amepre.2015.06.034; and George Sam Wang et al., "Marijuana and Acute Health Care Contacts in Colorado," *Preventive Medicine* 104 (2017): 24–30, https://doi.org/10.1016/j.ypmed.2017.03.022.

58. Bill Chappell, "Amazon Will Stop Testing Job Seekers for Marijuana and Now Backs Legalizing Weed," *NPR*, June 2, 2021, https://www.npr.org/2021/06/02/1002409858/amazon-wont-test-jobseekers-for-marijuana; and Gavin Butler, "Companies Are Getting Rid of Drug Tests Because They Can't Find Enough Workers,"

Vice, September 17, 2021, https://www.vice.com/en/article/y3d7kx/companies-employers-drug-tests-labour-shortage.

59. Beth J. Asch et al., *An Empirical Assessment of the US Army's Enlistment Waiver Policies: An Examination in Light of Emerging Societal Trends in Behavioral Health and the Legalization of Marijuana* (Santa Monica, CA: RAND Corporation, 2021), 39, https://www.rand.org/pubs/research_reports/RR4431.html.

60. Rosalie Liccardo Pacula and Russell Lundberg, "Why Changes in Price Matter When Thinking About Marijuana Policy: A Review of the Literature on the Elasticity of Demand," *Public Health Reviews* 35 (2013), https://doi.org/10.1007/BF03391701.

61. Kieran Delamont, "Legacy to Legal Brands Are Taking Over the Cannabis Industry," blog post, Leafly.ca, last updated February 10, 2022, https://www.leafly.ca/news/canada/once-illegal-brands-are-taking-over-the-legal-cannabis-market; Syed Mahamad and David Hammond, "Retail Price and Availability of Illicit Cannabis in Canada," *Addictive Behaviors* 90 (2019): 402–8, https://doi.org/10.1016/j.addbeh.2018.12.001; and Jason Childs and George Hartner, "Displacing the Illicit Cannabis Market: Challenges and Trade-Offs," in *The High North: Cannabis in Canada*, ed. Andrew D. Hathaway and Clayton James Smith McCann, 73–96 (Vancouver, BC: UBC Press, 2022).

62. See generally Rebekah Levine Coley et al., "Recreational Marijuana Legalization and Adolescent Use of Marijuana, Tobacco, and Alcohol," *Journal of Adolescent Health* 69, no. 1 (2021): 41–49, https://doi.org/10.1016/j.jadohealth.2020.10.019; and Steven Davenport, Jonathan P. Caulkins, and Mark A.R. Kleiman, "Controlling Underage Access to Legal Cannabis," *Case Western Reserve Law Review* 65, no. 3 (2015): 541–66, https://scholarlycommons.law.case.edu/cgi/viewcontent.cgi?article=1041&context=caselrev.

63. Katherine M. Keyes et al., "Frequency of Adolescent Cannabis Smoking and Vaping in the United States: Trends, Disparities and Concurrent Substance Use, 2017–19," *Addiction* 117, no. 8 (2022): 2316–24, https://doi.org/10.1111/add.15912.

64. US Federal Drug Administration, "Think E-Cigs Can't Harm Teens' Health?" content current as of June 29, 2022, https://www.fda.gov/tobacco-products/public-health-education/think-e-cigs-cant-harm-teens-health; and Jayne O'Donnell and David Robinson, "People Are Vaping a Deadly Substance Along with THC: Why Isn't Vitamin E Acetate Illegal?" *USA Today*, updated November 25, 2019, https://www.usatoday.com/story/news/health/2019/11/15/vitamin-e-acetate-deadly-thc-vape-additive-no-regulations-cdc/2569828001/.

65. Caislin L. Firth et al., "Did Marijuana Legalization in Washington State Reduce Racial Disparities in Adult Marijuana Arrests?" *Substance Use &* Misuse 54, no. 9 (2019): 1582–87, https://doi.org/10.1080/10826084.2019.1593007; and Brynn E. Sheehan, Richard A. Grucza, and Andrew D. Plunk, "Association of Racial Disparity of Cannabis Possession Arrests Among Adults and Youths with Statewide Cannabis Decriminalization and Legalization," *JAMA Health Forum* 2, no. 10 (2021), https://doi:org/10.1001/jamahealthforum.2021.3435.

66. See generally Jonathan P. Caulkins and Peter Reuter, "How Drug Enforcement Affects Drug Prices," *Crime and Justice* 39, no. 1 (2010): 213–71, https://www.jstor.org/stable/10.1086/652386; Peter Reuter and Mark A. R. Kleiman, "Risks

and Prices: An Economic Analysis of Drug Enforcement," *Crime and Justice* 7 (1986): 289–340, https://www.jstor.org/stable/1147520; and Peter Reuter, ed., *Understanding the Demand for Illegal Drugs* (Washington, DC: National Academies Press, 2010), https://nap.nationalacademies.org/read/12976/chapter/4#32.

67. Adam Gelb et al., "More Imprisonment Does Not Reduce State Drug Problems," issue brief, Pew Charitable Trusts, March 8, 2018, https://www.pewtrusts.org/en/research-and-analysis/issue-briefs/2018/03/more-imprisonment-does-not-reduce-state-drug-problems; and Global Commission on Drug Policy, *Enforcement of Drug Laws: Refocusing on Organized Crime Elites* (Geneva, Switzerland: Global Commission on Drug Policy, 2020), https://www.globalcommissionondrugs.org/wp-content/uploads/2020/06/2020report_EN_web_100620.pdf.

68. American Bar Association, *Collateral Consequences of Criminal Convictions: Judicial Bench Book* (Chicago, IL: American Bar Association, March 2018), 5–7, https://www.ojp.gov/pdffiles1/nij/grants/251583.pdf.

69. American Bar Association, *Collateral Consequences*, 5–7.

70. A. J. Herrington, "California Bill Filed to Accelerate Cannabis Conviction Expungements," *High Times*, January 27, 2022, https://hightimes.com/news/california-bill-filed-to-accelerate-cannabis-conviction-expungements/.

71. Renée Cooper, "Thousands Still Eligible for Record Expungement Two Years After Illinois Legalizes Recreational Marijuana," WCIA.com, September 16, 2021, https://www.wcia.com/news/target3/thousands-still-eligible-for-record-expungement-two-years-after-illinois-legalizes-recreational-marijuana/.

72. Last Prisoner Project, "Exactly How Many People Are Locked Up for Weed?" accessed December 16, 2022, https://www.lastprisonerproject.org/cannabis-prisoner-scale.

73. Last Prisoner Project, "Exactly How Many People"; see also Jeffrey Robinson, *Who's* Really *In Prison for Marijuana?* (Washington, DC: Office of National Drug Control Policy, 2005), https://www.ojp.gov/sites/g/files/xyckuh241/files/media/document/whos_in_prison_for_marij.pdf.

74. Mariah Daley, "Maurice Shumate Released From 15-Year-Sentence," blog post, Last Prisoner Project, February 23, 2022, https://www.lastprisonerproject.org/maurice-shumate-released-from-15-year-sentence.

75. Last Prisoner Project, *2021 Annual Report* (Denver, CO: Last Prisoner Project, 2021), 11, https://irp.cdn-website.com/08efa45c/files/uploaded/Annual%20Report%202021%20%282%29.pdf.

76. Baradaran, *Color of Money*, 183.

77. For more, see chapter 6.

78. For more, see chapter 7.

79. For more, see chapter 8.

80. For more on social equity policies in Massachusetts, see chapter 6.

81. *Parents Involved in Community Schools v. Seattle School District No. 1*, 551 U.S. 701 (2007).

82. Stephen F. Smith, "Clarence X? The Black Nationalist Behind Justice Thomas's Constitutionalism," *New York University Journal of Law & Liberty* 4 (2009): 611.

83. Danny McDonald, "The Whiter the Boston Neighborhood, the Easier It Can Be to Find a Restaurant with a License to Serve Booze, Report Shows," *Boston Globe*, June 20, 2022.

84. Zippia.com, "Restaurant Owner Demographics and Statistics in the US," last updated September 9, 2022, https://www.zippia.com/restaurant-owner-jobs/demographics/; Sergey Chernenko and David S. Scharfstein, "Racial Disparities in the Paycheck Protection Program," NBER Working Paper 29748, National Bureau of Economic Research, February 2022, https://doi.org/10.3386/w29748; and Restaurant Opportunities Centers United, *Ending Jim Crow in America's Restaurants: Racial and Gender Segregation in the Restaurant Industry* (New York: ROC United, 2015), 25–27, https://laborcenter.berkeley.edu/pdf/2015/racial-gender-occupational-segregation.pdf.

Chapter 4

Colorado

Legalization Without Equity

Colorado has an unfortunate legacy in the history of cannabis criminalization: it is the state where the first two individuals were arrested after the 1937 Marihuana Tax Act ushered in the federal prohibition of cannabis. Cannabis activists have in recent decades frequently memorialized these two men—Samuel Caldwell and Moses Baca—as liberalization efforts have piled victory on top of victory. Caldwell is often highlighted, though Baca was in fact the first to be arrested.[1]

After a decade of arrests for petty crimes since entering the United States from Mexico in 1929, Baca was apprehended in the middle of the night when police found him with a quarter of an ounce of cannabis. Law enforcement records had highlighted Baca's Mexican heritage throughout his years of arrests, and national news made sure to note this and added more lurid details involving possible use of a gun. Caldwell had previously been arrested for bootlegging and, despite the products he was accused of selling, was known not to be a cannabis user himself. A contemporary of both men reported that local police had warned Caldwell to avoid Mexicans for fear of being associated with cannabis.[2] The arrests of Baca and Caldwell marked the beginning of Harry Anslinger's power to enforce federal restrictions against cannabis use, an occasion so important to Anslinger that he took a personal interest in their cases, taking a two-day train ride from Washington, DC, to draw national attention to the occasion.[3] Their arrests also anticipated the racialized associations that Americans—and law enforcement in particular—would make between cannabis and criminality in the decades that followed.

More than Colorado's notoriety in the historical record of cannabis criminalization, however, its status as one of the first two states to legalize recreational use makes it the ideal focus of the first case study in this book. As seen below, Colorado's approach to legalization set the initial terms of debate over the status of cannabis in the United States in ways that are still apparent today. Yet while those terms were in part a response to the state's long history of criminalization, they were also born from a reaction to California's first-in-the-nation legalization of medical marijuana in the mid-1990s and the lessons—and intentional contrasts with—that Colorado's legalization advocates and early entrepreneurs learned from that state's experience. So while the history of Baca, Caldwell, and the many state residents that followed them into the net of law enforcement is key to understanding how cannabis legalization came to take the form that it did in Colorado, so too is a basic knowledge of how its fellow traveler to the west came to develop a market for medical marijuana.

For many of those in the Golden State who used cannabis—both in the decades before legalization and its early medical-only years—access to the substance was as much a moral right (especially for those who depended on it as a medical necessity) as a desire. That access was also secured in the face of resistance at every level of government. Though the lush climate of much of California is ideal for growing cannabis, the enforcement actions of the federal Drug Enforcement Administration had created an environment where it often required a righteous zeal to maintain a going concern. This was as true for the "buyers clubs" and cooperatives that popped up in cities like Oakland, San Francisco, and Los Angeles with the beginning of the AIDS crisis as it was for the rural farming communities of the Emerald Triangle counties of Northern California, where growing cannabis has been an economic reality and moral crusade for decades.[4]

Even before California voted to decriminalize medical cannabis in 1996, the state's movement had begun to train an army of disciples on these truths. Oaksterdam University, founded in Oakland in 2007 by a partnership of veterans of the underground market, gave participants the opportunity to learn the finer points of growing and preparing cannabis for consumption from those with industry experience.[5] These veterans—such as movement leader Dennis Peron—also had another important message for participants: pot is not for profit.[6] While that might have been a fundamental truth to Peron, the students of this cannabis school lacked the same doctrinal faith, and it was they who would go beyond California to other jurisdictions such as Colorado where growing cannabis was not as easy or established, and which had different cultural contexts for cannabis use.[7] These California exports include Wanda James and Scott Durrah, a power couple that later helped to highlight emerging racial disparities in ownership after founding an edibles dispensary in Denver.[8] Another was Dan Rogers, who has consulted in the industry and launched companies in developing markets such as Florida but first joined the medical cannabis industry as an owner in Colorado.[9]

Despite the spiritual and practical importance that California held for such pioneering cannabis figures, its unique local history made it a less-than-ideal model for how legalization activists in other states might campaign for reforms and set up a legal market. State and local officials in California had long remained hands off when it came to the cannabis industry, either seeking to respect the will of California voters or to acknowledge the political reality that cannabis use was a red line for many of their constituents, though these same officials also sought to tread carefully with outright endorsement of the trade for fear of federal backlash.[10] Thus the concept of formalized regulation and cooperation with tax authorities was alien to many in California.

Though Colorado shares some of its cultural heritage with other western states such as California, including a legacy of working-class Mexican immigrant farm laborers who brought "marihuana" across the border, cannabis faced a different historical and environmental context in the Mile High State.[11] As a western state with a relatively high educational attainment and a vibrant political culture on both sides of the aisle, Colorado and the ballot initiative campaigns it hosts regularly make national news and serve as a proving grounds of sorts for activist groups, otherwise ignored by policymakers, that seek to have their narratives considered by the average voter. Although California also has a long history of prominent ballot propositions, it was difficult to craft a cohesive campaign message for cannabis in that state and likewise too expensive to continue the fight for legalized cannabis after California successfully created a medical market and then later voted down a recreational use measure, so many activists moved to more fertile fields elsewhere.[12] Given time to develop within the state's own particular political and cultural situation and the comparative ease of placing a ballot initiative before voters there, Colorado proved to be an attractive alternative.

Responding to their own local context and history—in particular a voting population that skews more conservative than in California—Colorado's legalization activists made the creation of a highly regulated and taxable market a centerpiece of their campaign. With the passage of Amendment 64 by voters in 2012, Colorado became one of the first two states to legalize and regulate recreational cannabis in the United States, and so it, rather than California, became a clear beacon for many Americans seeking to figure out what legalization should look like (for better or for worse). Indeed, the approach that Colorado activists took represented a larger political innovation in regulatory policymaking that sought to tie legalization of controversial substances and behaviors to the benefits of licensing and regulation. Previous efforts to use this model across the nation in other areas such as gambling, prostitution, and even drugs had met with mixed results, but proponents in Colorado learned from a previous failed legalization initiative in the state how to build a relationship with voters that eventually led to success.

Building on years of activism undertaken by a broad coalition of organizers, Amendment 64's adoption served as a clear signal that the movement to revisit the criminalization of cannabis had reached maturity and that voters were likely to favorably respond to a legalization campaign that took fears of possible negative outcomes seriously. After implementation, however, Colorado came to represent the lack of diversity in ownership within the cannabis industry, as many of the companies and individuals who were successful in its early green boom were all white and in most cases had little past experience or connection to cannabis organizing.[13] The state also initially crafted rules that made it nearly impossible for previously convicted individuals to join the market, only recently revising their regulations in an attempt to draw legacy suppliers into the legal market.[14] Given Colorado's inspirational role for other states, it is worth considering precisely what worked in terms of crafting a winning campaign and what hasn't worked in terms of translating the system that the campaign envisioned into a realized market. This chapter will therefore offer a brief history of both the era of criminalization and the early cannabis legalization movement in Colorado, as well as a critique of the market that has developed there in the years since legalization passed.

CANNABIS CRIMINALIZATION IN COLORADO

Colorado first adopted a form of criminalized regulation of cannabis in 1917 when the state legislature passed a law making cannabis possession subject to a $100 fine and a month in jail.[15] Western states, including Colorado, had been among the first to criminalize cannabis after migrants in search of economic opportunities from Mexico brought the substance across the border.[16] Six years later, a news story from Denver highlighted this connection, reporting on the arrest of "Tony Planta," whom it implied had been selling cannabis to local high school students. The news story noted the spread of the plant from Mexico and also stated that cannabis was difficult to control because federal legislation such as the Harrison Act had yet to touch on it.[17]

In fact, for many Mexican farm laborers, cannabis functioned as both an herbal remedy for conditions such as rheumatism as well as a method to supplement their low wages. Many of these immigrants had first come to the United States to work in labor-intensive sugar beet farms.[18] Even as Mexican laborers filled this function, however, the existing social and legal regime prevented many of them from making a transition to ownership, which in turn made them easier to exploit, keeping their wages lower. For these vulnerable workers, cannabis represented both herbal wellness and an economic freedom that they were not able to socially or legally possess. However, even as stories of cannabis use spread in the broader media, the few opportunities for racial commingling in Colorado meant that actual use and its economic impacts were still largely confined to the migrant population in these early decades.[19]

Despite this reality, state lawmakers were apparently inspired to further crack down on the perceived trend of Mexican immigrants corrupting local youth by making a second offense of growing or selling cannabis a felony in 1929. A local chaplain quoted in a news story from that year explained that "if a prison term faces growers and sellers of this narcotic weed, they are going to give up its use faster than [be]fore. . . . It is a dangerous drug, especially since it becomes available to children and forms a habit so quickly."[20] Local newspapers also did not hesitate to reinforce the connection to Mexican immigrants well into the 1930s, when Anslinger's campaign for the Marihuana Tax Act was in full swing. For example, the editor of the *Alamoosa Daily Courier* wrote to federal officials in 1936 to say: "I wish I could show you what a small marihuana cigaret [*sic*] can do to one of our degenerate Spanish-speaking residents. That's why our problem is so great; the greatest percentage of our population is composed of Spanish-speaking persons, most of whom are low mentally, because of social and racial conditions."[21] Amidst this fear and xenophobia, Mexicans nevertheless continued to be a significant part of the illegal cannabis industry in Colorado—the 1956 arrest of former beet farmer Manual Hernandez from Mead, who had been supplementing his beet farming with cannabis that he sold to an increasingly diverse local market, represents but a small slice of the larger contributions that Mexican immigrants made to the Colorado cannabis industry.[22]

The effects of the campaign to link cannabis with negative health and moral outcomes would last decades, as a 1967 research report on "dangerous drugs" produced for the Colorado state legislature demonstrates. During the thirty years following Moses Baca's and Samuel Caldwell's arrests in 1937, cannabis was regarded by the state of Colorado as a narcotic, classified alongside many other substances that created a physical dependency. This 1967 report described the overall approach of drug regulation, highlighting the dangers of addiction and violent crime created by these substances. However, even this report's authors seemed to doubt cannabis's classification in Colorado law, calling the effects of the drug "complicated." They also openly mused about the potential consequences for legalizing cannabis, though the report did not offer a specific timeline for doing so, as it indicated that further research on the health impacts and addictive potential of cannabis would be needed.[23] By 1973, several state legislators introduced a bill to fully legalize the sale and possession of cannabis, though this effort did not succeed. Instead, acting on the initiative of local Denver-area prosecutors who began to deprioritize cannabis prosecutions, the legislature in 1975 downgraded some of the penalties given to individuals arrested for cannabis possession to include only fines rather than jail terms, though harsher penalties were retained for transactions involving minors.[24]

Despite the legislature's partial decriminalization of cannabis in the 1970s, Colorado state and local law enforcement made at least 210,000 arrests for the substance in the years between 1986 (when there were 4,076 arrests) and 2010 (10,493 arrests), with at least half of those arrests occurring in the last decade of that period—outstripping the rate of population growth and indicating a rise in the likelihood of getting arrested in the years before full legalization was adopted.[25] Possession of less than an ounce of cannabis still held some consequences—those cited would be charged with a "petty offense" and issued a summons that required them to show up in court on the threat of being charged with failure to appear, which was itself a more serious misdemeanor offense that carried a potential punishment of six months in jail.[26] During this time, many jurisdictions in Colorado also adopted cannabis possession prohibitions at the local level, codes that often mirrored or even provided for enhanced penalties beyond those found in state law. Judges had discretion about whether to charge individuals under state or local codes.[27]

In the 1970s and '80s, arrest records were held in courthouse records rooms, where they were generally inaccessible except for people conducting the most dedicated and thorough background checks. But as such records began to be computerized and became accessible through a wider array of official sources, more and more Coloradans had a reason to be concerned about whether a past arrest would impact their job search, application to college, or something similar.[28] Although Colorado does not have a large Black population, possession arrests—and most likely their consequences—still demonstrated a pervasive racial bias: from 2001 to 2010, Black individuals were arrested at least three times as often as white people. Hispanic individuals were likewise arrested one-and-a-half times as often as white people. All of this despite data demonstrating that white Coloradans actually used cannabis at higher rates during this period.[29]

In 2012, the year voters in the state opted to legalize cannabis, police in Colorado arrested 13,225 individuals for cannabis offenses, with more than four in five of those for possession crimes. By 2019, several years after legalization, the number of arrests had fallen to 4,290.[30] This larger shift can obscure some interesting details, however. One of these is that felonies charged for some sort of cannabis offense, which in the years immediately before legalization were in excess of 2,000 per year, fell only modestly in the years immediately after legalization and were back at similar levels to those from the pre-legalization era within five years. Well over two-thirds of these charges are dismissed every year, indicating some form of deferred judgment or other leniency. This trend survived the legalization of cannabis in 2012.[31] The more granular data also shows that the decline in post-legalization cannabis arrests occurred only in specific contexts, with nearly all of the citations from cannabis use on roads and other public locations falling off, while enforcement in elementary and secondary schools as well as institutions of higher education remained steady.[32] Racial disparities continued to show up in the arrest statistics as well, though by 2019 state data showed that the gap between white and Black individuals had narrowed somewhat—Black people were now only twice as likely to face arrest.[33]

THE DISPENSARY MODEL OF CANNABIS ACCESS

Even as Colorado arrested people for cannabis possession in growing numbers in the late 1990s, cracks in the regime began to appear. Colorado voters weighed in twice in favor of medical cannabis. First, a 1998 initiative was approved by voters, but the secretary of state refused to count the victory after courts identified issues with the ballot petitions.[34] Two years later, voters again opted to create a legal right for medical patients to consume and thus possess small amounts of cannabis. Much like California's similar initiative from four years earlier, the mechanism behind this was rather simple: prospective patients or registered caregivers were provided a defense from criminal prohibitions on cannabis if they possessed less than two ounces of cannabis or six plants. Additionally, doctors were provided a system for recommending medical cannabis to their patients under regulation from the state medical board. One of the major challenges that soon impacted patients looking to use this right was an inability to legally purchase the cannabis, however, as dispensaries were almost completely unregulated and still subject to legal harassment from federal officials. State and local officials influenced by those opposed to cannabis use also often sought to limit their operations.[35]

Colorado's efforts, along with those of additional states that legalized the medical use of cannabis during the George W. Bush administration, also ran straight into a federal enforcement regime that was not at all interested in scaling down. Both Bush's first attorney general, John Ashcroft, and the administration's "drug czar," John Walters, expressed a desire to renew the War on Drugs.[36] This included surveilling and focusing on states with medical cannabis laws while also continuing the Clinton's administration's efforts to influence state ballot initiative elections. Escalating relative to Clinton, the Bush administration pursued criminal charges against dispensaries, rather than civil complaints.[37] Many of the larger enforcement actions that the Bush administration carried out centered on California, where federal officials sought to pressure dispensaries with raids and criminal charges while also warning local officials and those who sought to do business with cannabis establishments, such as landlords, that they were exposing themselves to lawsuits and other enforcement actions.[38] While the Supreme Court granted legal cover to these efforts in *Gonzalez v. Raich* (2005),[39] federal efforts were never enough to pose a real challenge to medical cannabis in California or elsewhere.

Cannabis advocacy in Colorado took another turn when two University of Colorado students died from alcohol poisoning in 2004, which helped to inspire Safer Alternatives For Enjoyable Recreation (SAFER), a campaign led by a young activist named Mason Tvert and sponsored in part by the Marijuana Policy Project. Tvert pointed out that that cannabis is a safer intoxicant than alcohol and advocated for legal penalties that matched this reality.[40] Tvert had personal experience with this incongruity—as an eighteen-year-old he once ended up in the emergency room when he drank too much alcohol. As he recalled, "I almost drank myself to death. But no one ever asked who sold me, an 18-year-old, a lethal amount of alcohol."[41] Conversely, being arrested with a small amount of cannabis snagged Tvert and his friends in one of America's many jurisdictional drug task force operations.

Tvert's campaign inspired some off-campus activism when SAFER sponsored a local initiative in the City of Denver to decriminalize cannabis, which passed in fall 2005.[42] Despite the fact that city officials, led by then-mayor John Hickenlooper (later Colorado's governor and a US senator), vowed that this measure would not stop local enforcement of cannabis possession laws, it was clear that the message which Tvert and other activists promoted had reached voters.[43] After their success in Denver, Tvert and his colleagues at SAFER continued their activism—often with a flair for drama. At one point, Tvert challenged Hickenlooper, the owner of a chain of breweries, to a contest of consuming alcohol versus cannabis to see which individual might experience harmful effects first.[44]

This framing of comparative impacts continued to inform legalization narratives for years to come, especially when SAFER proposed a statewide initiative to expand on local efforts such as those in Denver. Advocates first tried their hand at liberalizing state cannabis laws in 2006 with a statewide ballot initiative, Initiative 44, that would have removed criminal penalties for the possession of up to an ounce of cannabis. Promoters framed this straightforward decriminalization as an effort to allow residents to have the personal choice to consume cannabis if they should want to.[45] The title of the committee that submitted the initiative to the ballot indicated the messaging that activists would come to use for years: the Alcohol-Marijuana Equalization Initiative Committee.[46]

SAFER spent a fraction of the amount of money on the campaign compared to Initiative 44's opponents—including the local Catholic Church and national advocacy group Focus on the Family—and many statewide officials opposed the initiative, including newly elected Governor Bill Ritter.[47] Voters themselves proved unready for decriminalization and rejected Initiative 44 with over 58 percent of the vote.[48] Among the notable lessons that the activists who worked in this space learned was the importance of regulation—simple legalization measures without a vision for how cannabis access would be regulated were unpopular for voters and would likely be rejected.[49]

A major theme of the opposition in 2006 was the threat that legalized cannabis could pose to families and children in particular, exemplified by group names such as "Guarding Our Children Against Marijuana." The language that appeared first in the guidance issued to voters likewise noted that "marijuana use may lead a person to use or possess other illegal drugs. Under Amendment 44 overall drug use in the state may rise, and legalizing the possession of marijuana will increase not only the availability and acceptability of marijuana, but also the likelihood that minors will have access to the drug. Colorado does not want to become a magnet for illicit drug users."[50]

This theme of potential danger would be carried forward into attempts to reform Colorado's medical cannabis market, which state officials had tried and failed to set limits on in 2007.[51] Over the next four years, cannabis dispensaries in Denver and the state as a whole grew exponentially, and many of them came to embrace the regulatory model that state officials created in part to respond to political pressure on this issue but also to maximize revenues.[52] This control regime was designed to ensure that federal officials would look the other way if and when states like Colorado continued to move forward on liberalization, accepting as a given that federal officials would closely examine the integrity of such a market, as well as outcomes around youth use.[53]

By 2009, residents of Denver's South Broadway district watched as the area became home to a cannabis haven sometimes called "Broadsterdam" or the "Green Mile,"[54] populated in part by an exodus of entrepreneurs from California seeking to make their mark. Soon enough, Denver alone would have well over one hundred dispensaries and began earning its reputation as the "Mile High City" in a new way.[55] A state lawmaker described the rush: "This reminds me of 1899 in Cripple Creek, Colorado, when somebody struck gold. Every 49er in the country is making it for Denver to open a medical marijuana dispensary."[56]

Though Governor Ritter had opposed legal cannabis as a candidate, the threat of budget shortfalls by the end of his first and only term in office led him to sign a set of laws in 2010 to impose a strict set of controls that would create a regulated network of dispensaries for medical patients to access, while expanding the state's system for registering patients; in exchange, the cash-strapped state would reap added tax revenue.[57] A large portion of existing operators in Denver did not have the willingness or capacity to cooperate with expanded regulation, however, closing their doors instead.[58] Combined with the partial relaxation of federal enforcement during the early Obama administration, these changes began to develop into the state's regulated cannabis industry.

Colorado's differing experience with its initial medical marijuana market compared to California's was to a large degree an effect of the latter's position as the first to act. California preferred to keep the nascent medical market at arm's length—with informally organized collectives and largely unofficial connections with local officials—for fear that direct government actions to support it would run afoul of federal law enforcement and place state officials in legal jeopardy. That loose regulation in turn defined an early cannabis market in California that saw a wide variety of production and distribution mechanisms, as well as—because there was no tax burden to meet—overall lower costs. With California's example largely dispelling worries of severe risk from federal enforcement, however, Colorado's medical market evolved with a profit mindset for both operators and state officials, who like Ritter openly sought to maximize the revenues that the new industry could bring to state coffers.

This distinction in Colorado's early medical market has had a cascading series of effects for the nature of cannabis production and use in the state that are still felt today, in large part because it set the immediate terms of debate for recreational legalization in the state far more directly than anything that was happening in California by that point. Along with its imperative to protect public health, the tax incentive meant that Colorado gained an interest in enforcing strict rules to control supply, which has led to mandates that security cameras closely monitor nearly all areas of the physical spaces where cannabis is handled, long retention times to discourage stealing, and audits to make sure that product is not getting diverted into the unregulated market.[59] This strict scrutiny also brought production indoors, where cannabis could be grown more precisely than in the largely outdoor and less standardized growing environments of California. This in turn cultivated a focus on increasing potency, changing the nature of the end product for many users. Among other outcomes, this indoor growing has also served to drastically increase the carbon footprint of the industry, an issue that regulators in many western states are only now beginning to address.[60]

AMENDMENT 64

It was not until 2012 that activists in Colorado were willing to try a recreational legalization measure again. Voters in California had sent a potentially foreboding signal for legalization with the 2010 rejection of their own ballot measure. Even though activists and others had warned of flaws in the design of that initiative, many legalization supporters were disheartened by the setback. Federal officials from the Obama Justice Department had weighed in during the 2010 California vote to warn residents that federal enforcement of laws pertaining to cannabis would not stop, a move that some argued had a chilling effect for late voters deciding how to cast their ballot.[61] Still, legalization advocates believed that passage in some state was only a matter of time.

On their second try in less than a decade, the proponents of 2012's Amendment 64 took a sharply different approach to policy design than that seen in 2006's Initiative 44. Mason Tvert, the longtime cannabis activist in the state who had created SAFER, became the campaign director for the committee in support of Amendment 64; it would come to be called the Campaign to Regulate Marijuana Like Alcohol. He extended and developed the comparative messaging linking the prospect of cannabis legalization to existing regulatory models for alcohol.[62] Later initiatives in support of legalization in other states would copy this approach, even as significant differences persisted among legalization supporters concerning the best regulatory model for cannabis use. The messaging linking alcohol regulation to the prospect of legal, regulated cannabis sales was intended to provide persuadable voters in Colorado and the other states that were considering legal cannabis that year—Oregon and Washington—with a vision of what regulation would look like, as well as how tax money collected from this system would be spent. Polling research had looked at previous efforts to legalize and identified those voting blocs that might be persuadable with the right message. This evidence suggested that women aged thirty to fifty were particularly willing to support legalization under the right circumstances, but they had a number of concerns that might animate them to oppose a ballot measure depending on its precise contents.[63] As such, many activists targeted these voters, looking to find an angle that would bring more of them to their side.

Unlike six years earlier, the supporters of legalization were successful in outspending their opposition, though most mainstream politicians, including now-governor Hickenlooper, continued to oppose legalization.[64] Reflecting the target demographic that the legalization supporters—organized as Sensible Colorado for the 2012 campaign—had identified as open to changing their minds, many of the campaign's supporting narratives involved allied law enforcement officials discussing how the reform measure would allow them to address different types of crime, divert money from the illicit market, and provide additional tax revenue to schools. Brian Vicente, codirector of the campaign, summarized the rationale behind this strategy: "we also ran with the 'marijuana is safer than alcohol' message . . . about the relative harms of marijuana versus alcohol and why one is criminal and why one is not," even though it did not poll quite as well. More centrally, however, "we did know that our target demographic by and large was 30–50 year old women and . . . that tying money, marijuana tax money, to school construction did well amongst women. . . . Other than that our messages were fairly broad . . . [with] the law enforcement resources and the tax revenues being the primary ones that measurably did impact on people."[65]

Polling prior to the election in the three states with legalization initiatives revealed that voters overall were supportive of legalization as a concept. As was true of the prime target demographic that Vicente identified, however, many other voters had unanswered questions regarding implementation that would preclude their support when it came time to vote.[66] Compared to the framework that was put before voters in previous legalization efforts, the additional regulatory ballot measure language that Colorado supporters developed along with their counterparts in Washington state allowed both of these campaigns to develop specific narratives that helped voters understand what legalization would look like, as well as to refute opposition narratives concerning potential increases in rates of impaired driving and youth use. Ads that emphasized the relative safety of cannabis use as compared to other illegal activities that might attract law enforcement attention reinforced this messaging. For example, a spot that quoted a variety of citizen speakers included one who suggested that "we can all do something to make our schools better and our communities safer. Why should we let criminals profit from illegal marijuana sales when that money could be going to upgrade and improve our schools? $40 million annually in tax revenue. Our schools need that, so I'm voting yes."[67]

This approach was part of a strategy of allaying the fears of those who might otherwise agree with local and state law enforcement officials who were opposed to the measure, such as Boulder County Attorney Ken Buck and Colorado Attorney General John Suthers, who referred to the general uncertainty of legalized cannabis and its impact on youth use to explain their opposition.[68] A notable shift from the earlier measure was the US Justice Department's noninterference, which came as the effort to reelect Barack Obama sought to mobilize youth voters.[69] The silence from federal officials, as well as a less-unified or engaged opposition compared to 2006, allowed legalization supporters to outraise opponents in Colorado,[70] ensuring that the messaging of the Campaign to Regulate Marijuana Like Alcohol had considerable reach.

Even as legalization supporters were looking to hone their arguments on regulation and tax issues to appeal to their target demographic of women aged thirty to fifty, they also needed to ensure that the core parts of the reform coalition who had other interests, including younger voters and the medical cannabis community, remained engaged in the campaign. The previous legalization effort in California had received resistance from medical cannabis supporters, while efforts in Washington state in 2012 were opposed by some who believed that the regulatory system proposed there was in fact too restrictive.[71]

One way that Colorado's supporters tried to avoid these problems was by including ballot language which did not have rules restricting youth driving as strict as those in Oregon's measure.[72] The hope was that this would help keep them from turning off youth voters who were broadly supportive of legalization. A notable dissenter from those who generally supported legalization was the editorial board of the *Denver Post*, which argued that the measure should not be embedded into the state constitution because it would take flexibility away from lawmakers who would later need to adjust details of implementation.[73] (This challenge would later prove not to be an obstacle, as voters eagerly embraced the taxes that legalization brought.) Despite these and other concerns, Amendment 64 passed in Colorado with over 55 percent of the vote in the 2012 election, while Washington state voters also acted to pass their own measure, though voters in Oregon rejected the reform measure there.[74] Polling in Washington and Colorado indicated that support for the measure had increased in the final months among women aged thirty to fifty, suggesting that the regulation messaging had indeed made a difference in building support for legalization.[75]

Recognizing the shift, Governor Hickenlooper announced in December 2012 that he would appoint a task force of state officials and other individuals to determine how Colorado should implement Amendment 64. Members of this task force included a range of political leaders and state officials, as well as representatives from the Amendment 64 campaign, the medical marijuana industry, consumers, the public defenders' offices, and employees of private businesses, and they committed themselves to avoiding relitigating the campaign and instead designing the best system for consumers and citizens. This task force comprised five working groups and heard testimony from experts and members of the public, eventually issuing fifty-seven recommendations to the governor by May 2013. They included creating parallel markets for both medical and recreational cannabis, changing criminal laws to adjust for the new legal reality, and creating rules for home cultivation of cannabis. The commission also recommended a system of regulatory reporting, which the legislature embraced by commissioning a series of reports on the progress of legalization—these reports have come to be cited thousands of times as additional states looked to Colorado as a beacon for what legalization might look like elsewhere.[76]

One of the specific recommendations that the governor's commission made and the legislature adopted was a special state excise tax on cannabis. Amendment 64 had included a 15 percent excise tax, though how this tax would be implemented was not clearly defined in the final text of the amendment, and there were fears that the revenue from these taxes would not be enough to even fund the regulation costs that the state would incur, much less the $40 million that Amendment 64's supporters had promised schools. Tax policy quickly became central to understanding the future of the recreational cannabis market's success, as one observer explains:

> Try to think of another industry that has supported attacks on itself. But then again, try to think of another industry that has embraced 500 pages of regulations on itself to the question that we need to ask ourselves is, are we taxing it too high? Are we taxing it too low? It's kind of the Goldilocks principle. If we tax it too high, [supply] goes back into the black market, people buy it cheaper, but it ends up in the hands of kids and criminals. Again, if we tax it too low, we can't do the seed to sale tracking, we can't do some of the other things that we'd like to do with those taxes to make sure that kids aren't using and criminals aren't profiting from this money's flowing now into hundreds of brand new entrepreneurial startup businesses. And for every dollar that's spent in business that's multiplied throughout the local economy.[77]

As a result of these sorts of considerations, one of the first things state legislators did when addressing the task force's recommendations was to refer a statute to voters to approve a law that would authorize the excise tax envisioned in the amendment, as well as an additional 10 percent sales tax on all retail transactions.[78] This was required due to the state's famously tax-shy political culture, manifested in a 1992 constitutional amendment known as the Taxpayer Bill of Rights (TABOR), which limited state spending increases to an inflation-adjusted yearly raise, with any surpluses required to be returned in the form of a check to taxpayers.[79]

The referendum authorizing these taxes was Proposition AA, and in a reflection of Colorado voters' general inclination toward tax resistance, the debate for this amendment developed not as a continuation of the previous year's discussion regarding the efficacy and practicality of legalizing cannabis, but as one about the state's ongoing dedication to limiting the size and scope of government. This shift in focus was demonstrated when many Republicans in the state legislature voted against referring Proposition AA to the ballot.[80] During fall 2013, opponents of the measure organized "free joint" events throughout the state in a fit of pique to protest the added taxes proposed by legislators.

Attorney and co-organizer of an event in Boulder, Rob Corry, who styled himself the "Robin Hood" of pot, described how anti-tax events tried to paint a picture of two sides in the debate: "The free joint giveaway was a resounding success; people are now talking about the largest tax increase in Colorado history, when before this was a 'stealth' campaign from the pro-tax side." Suggesting the complicated politics of cannabis in Colorado, Corry described the anti-tax protest as "a people-centric, positive, energetic event, where the thousands of people present all had smiles on their faces," while an event in favor of Proposition AA "was a handful of politicians in the shadow of the Bastille. We peddled happiness (for free), they peddled fear (with a price)."[81] Nevertheless, Proposition AA was resoundingly endorsed by over two-thirds of Colorado voters who turned out that year, along with a slew of additional local tax initiatives aimed at the growing industry.[82]

The debate over Proposition AA and the other task force recommendations makes clear that Colorado policymakers and the activists who were pressuring them in these early days were simply not thinking of social equity in the way that it has developed as an issue subsequently. The task force and the legislation that was adopted in the year after legalization focused almost exclusively on questions of taxes, market structure, and regulatory issues.[83] Part of this was surely a bandwidth issue—given Colorado's pole position in the development of recreational cannabis markets, elected leaders were simply overwhelmed with the volume of suggestions from both legalization supporters and opponents, as well as the lack of models on which to base any of their decisions.

This lack of attention to social equity may also have simply been one of salience: Coloradans, similar to residents in the other early adopter states such as Oregon, Washington, and Alaska, are disproportionately white compared to the rest of the country[84] and likewise lack large urban centers with concentrated communities of color such as those found in Chicago and New York City. Drug policy scholar Douglas Berman explains the effect that this demographic situation had on decisions about what to focus on when developing the legal market in Colorado and similar states: that although "we were starting to see from very much the bottom up the grassroots efforts . . . [and] continuing talk about the need to do something about the war on drugs generally, but, you know, the war on marijuana in particular. . . . at the same time, it was quite disconcerting that, particularly in Colorado and Washington, I think, not surprisingly, particularly white states, that social equity, any kind of equity was sort of left out of the conversation." Berman suggests why: "The fear was, I think, that focusing on the harms of prohibition, the past and all the racial inequalities would alienate or at least, make nervous the soccer mom voters or the other folks that was thought to be needed to build a coalition toward reform."[85]

DISCUSSING EQUITY IN POST-LEGALIZATION COLORADO

Despite fears that the federal government would prevent Colorado from implementing the outline of Amendment 64, the Justice Department's so-called Cole Memo (named after the Justice Department official who wrote it) announced in 2013 a policy of nonintervention in states with legal cannabis programs.[86] While many cannabis activists nationwide hailed Colorado's example, the new legal recreational market was actively hostile to many legacy market suppliers and participants. The state's Marijuana Enforcement Division (MED) was required to turn down applications from those who had convictions that would impeach their "good moral character," a distinction that would haunt applications for the first years of legalization in the state. This provision has been loosened recently,[87] but even the knowledge of this rule's past existence has served to discourage people of color from building businesses and acquiring the capital needed to transform their legacy market experience into economic opportunities.[88]

Outside of Colorado, social equity activists have largely looked at the state's legalized market as a missed opportunity for legacy participants, except for those few who had been able to surmount the early scrutiny given to license applicants and had access to the kind of capital that was required to operate in the industry.[89] However, as social equity considerations became an activist focus elsewhere, the tools developed in other states and local areas eventually influenced a movement for such considerations in Colorado. One issue was that Colorado initially did little to address people with previous cannabis convictions. By 2018, there were still as many as forty people serving prison time for nonviolent cannabis criminal offenses in Colorado jails and prisons.[90] While in office, Governor Hickenlooper only acted to pardon or commute the sentences of a limited number of these by the end of his term,[91] leaving much of the work of removing past convictions to his successor in office, current governor Jared Polis.

Unlike Hickenlooper, Polis had supported Amendment 64 and he openly courted the state's legal cannabis industry during his 2018 campaign for governor, hiring a campaign coordinator to direct outreach to it and working with dispensaries on voter messaging.[92] After enduring his Republican opponent's charges that he was promoting the use of drugs, Polis embraced his friendly relationship with the industry upon taking office, signing a range of measures that his predecessor—whom many in the cannabis industry viewed as a reluctant ally—had previously vetoed. By the time Polis was overwhelmingly reelected in 2022, he felt able to hold a celebration with SAFER's legalization activist Tvert, where the two were pictured holding a commemorative check representing the $2.2 billion in revenue that the industry had brought to the state's residents.[93]

Jason Singer, who was one of the few state representatives to support Amendment 64 when it was on the ballot, used that event as a moment to take stock about the political evolution that Colorado had engaged in to get to this point. He opined that "I don't think we would have been the shining example of success for the country, and possibly even the world, without everyone being willing to do a little give and a little take." The key for Singer was how Colorado's approach brought together multiple stakeholders: "law enforcement and drug and alcohol counselors and medical marijuana patients and veterans and dispensary owners all sat down and basically agreed to a certain set of values and policies. We're seeing the fruits of our labor now."[94] This analysis suggests the difficulty of introducing what might have been contentious social equity measures on the ground floor of legalization efforts, as well as what might be required to advance the movement in that direction.

Much like with cannabis legalization itself, the City of Denver has served as a local leader in the state for efforts to adopt social equity measures. In 2019, Denver's mayor, Michael Hancock, announced the "Turn Over a New Leaf" program, which provided clinic events where those with previous convictions in the city's courts could come and have their previous records dismissed with no financial cost to them. In partnership with advocacy groups and cannabis industry participants, five clinics were offered in the first year of the program, during which applicants could get free transportation and childcare while meeting with a city attorney who would help process the expungement applications.[95] Coming on the heels of this initiative, the state legislature has also acted twice to make it easier for the governor to grant pardons to those previously convicted of cannabis possession. In 2020, legislators removed paperwork requirements for pardon requests for possession offenses involving less than one ounce of cannabis.[96] The year after that, they fully legalized the possession of less than two ounces of cannabis in state statutes and likewise streamlined the pardon process for individuals who had been convicted of possession of these larger amounts,[97] potentially giving as many as 4,000 additional people an opportunity to move forward in life without these criminal charges on their records.[98]

Denver has also developed a plan to provide license exclusivity to social equity applicants—a strategy first conceptualized and crafted in Massachusetts, as will be discussed in chapter 6—particularly for those types of market services that have lower barriers to entry, such as delivery. In 2022, Denver's city council rewrote many local cannabis regulations with an eye toward greater equity, and the programs since announced include giving new delivery operators a three-year exclusivity period and lowering fees and other regulatory barriers that would prevent operators from sustaining their investment or justify their remaining in the unregulated legacy market.[99] The City of Aurora also announced a similar exclusivity program.[100] Building on these successes, the state has also recently announced a range of policies—including additional licenses and special funding for social equity participants—intended to catch Colorado up with the best practices of other states that have legalized cannabis. This is in part a response to the national debate around social equity policies that has evolved since Amendment 64 and the emerging scrutiny of Colorado's cannabis industry, particularly related to who owns licenses.[101] In 2018, the state MED released data that showed that white people controlled at least 79 percent of cannabis licenses, though by 2022 updated ownership statistics claimed that the state had met a goal of ensuring that at least 15 percent of owners were considered racial minorities.[102]

Wanda James has become a notable symbol of these limited opportunities available to Coloradans of color in the legalized cannabis space. She has a history of Colorado political activism, and along with her husband, Scott Durrah, has been a serial entrepreneur, including as founders of an edibles dispensary in Denver called Simply Pure.[103] James's entry into the cannabis industry was motivated in part by her brother's arrest at seventeen in the state of Texas for cannabis possession, which led to him spending over a decade in the criminal justice system.[104] James has often been featured as one of the first African Americans to own a dispensary in Colorado, yet her experience over the first several years navigating the recreational market was the exception that proved the rule, as few owners of color were able to jump through the various hurdles that confronted them in the years immediately after the state established the recreational market.[105]

Much like her earlier forebears in the cannabis movement, James has combined her personal business efforts with a passion for advocating for greater opportunities for people of color to escape from the stigma of criminalization and join the legal industry, speaking publicly about her own story as well as working with policymakers to increase opportunities for equity nationwide.[106] James is emphatic about the political nature of cannabis work, stating simply that "if you are not in politics, you are not in cannabis." For her, the reasons for are partly practical: "If you don't know your city council member, how do you know what is going to happen in your city when these licenses come down?" But this engagement has also given James agency to shape her own business and the broader environment of the cannabis market. Because she is politically involved, James notes that "I get phone calls before a bill goes live, and the city council person, or the lobbyist for the city council person, asks me 'hey Wanda, take a look at this bill, is there anything that you need in this?'" As James further points out, she is hardly alone in this—it is exactly what large corporations such as MSOs make part of their standard business practice.[107]

Expanding from this lesson, another activist named Sarah Woodson founded Color of Cannabis, a Denver-based activist group that worked to develop regulations with the city that would eventually lead it to establish a city-funded mentorship program for those interested in entering the industry. Speaking of the challenges her participants face, Woodson explains that "folks just don't know how to enter the industry, especially if you are from communities that have been negatively impacted."[108] This insight, along with those that James expressed, suggests not just the continued relevancy of the kind of organic and locally focused organizing for justice that defined much of the early advocacy for legalization but its paramount importance as a counterweight to the increasing lobbying heft of large corporations and the complex red tape that a heavily regulated market entails.

TAX REVENUES AND SOCIAL BENEFITS

Colorado began to receive record tax revenues after legalization began, sparking a nationwide frenzy of interest from austerity-weary state officials across the country attracted by the prospect of providing similar revenue for their own budgets. Total collections of all forms of state tax revenue related to cannabis in Colorado from legalization until 2022 stood in excess of $2.3 billion, including over $300 million taken in during that year alone.[109] This was reduced somewhat from a pandemic-era high, but still amounted to approximately 1 percent of all total tax revenues for fiscal year 2022.[110] Cannabis tax revenues in both Colorado and the other early adopter state of Washington have demonstrated a strength and consistency in returns that have seen total revenues exceed other "sin" taxes such as those for alcohol and tobacco products.[111]

Cannabis tax revenue also helps local governments—for example, Denver has collected over $400 million in tax revenue thanks to recreational and medical sales since 2014, most recently projecting $85 million in collections for 2022. This money makes up a 5.1 percent share of all municipal revenues for that fiscal year, demonstrating how cannabis has changed the budget picture in communities across the state. Mimicking Denver's experience, the City of Aurora has also seen additional revenues totaling over $14 million in 2020 alone.[112] Resistance to the industry nevertheless persists in some places, such as Colorado Springs, where after years of reluctance to consider allowing local stores, voters ultimately rejected an initiative in 2022 that would have allowed local licenses and a special local excise tax.[113]

One of the frequently unappreciated bright spots for equity in Colorado is how the state has used the revenue it has collected from cannabis excise taxes. When the state legislature asked voters in 2013 to approve additional taxes on cannabis, it estimated revenue for the first two years of operation to be around $70 million per year.[114] Per Amendment 64's guidelines, the first revenues were to be deposited in a fund set aside for school construction grants—now known as the Building Excellent Schools Today Grant Program. This fund allows local school districts to apply for matching money from the state to replace aging infrastructure and lessen the burden on local taxpayers while providing students with more equitable opportunities.[115]

By 2015, however, the state had collected a surplus excise tax of $66 million, prompting legislators to place an additional measure on the ballot to ask voters for permission to make supplementary deposits to the school construction fund rather than refund the money back to taxpayers or cannabis licensees—this measure passed overwhelmingly.[116] By the 2021 budget year, after the legislature allowed the full amount of cannabis excise taxes to be dedicated to this fund, revenues were in excess of $97 million and have exceeded all the other types of tax revenues that are set aside in this fund, which include land taxes, lottery proceeds, and interest.[117] It is clear that the state has been able to fund a number of additional school building projects because of the additional revenue available from cannabis legalization.[118]

Local governments have also made good use of the additional revenue that legalized cannabis has brought. In 2022, Denver was projected to spend a total of $28.1 million across affordable housing, homelessness, youth violence, and immigration services, as well as an additional $5.7 million on grant and loan funding to small businesses in the city.[119] This revenue has also gone to a local effort known as "High Costs" to educate children aged twelve to eighteen on the use of cannabis, reaching approximately 81 percent of city youth.[120] This campaign differs in tone and messaging from previous national campaigns such as DARE (which will be discussed in chapter 9), and specifically suggests ways that teens can safely use, rather than completely avoid, cannabis.[121] In Aurora, cannabis taxes have funded homelessness services, including a twenty-four-hour center, and have been directed toward nonprofits that work to secure family housing.[122]

The broad popular support for taxing this new industry at a high rate to benefit socially desirable spending such as building schools is an enduring feature of cannabis policy in state after state. Defining precisely where the new revenue is going can serve as a key selling point for convincing political holdouts who still oppose legalization—whether voters or legislators—even if higher taxes will make the regulated market more costly for suppliers and potentially less diverse. Of course, the targeted spending areas have evolved in each state, and with the inclusion of states with greater shares of Black residents in the legal cannabis market, greater care has been taken lately to steer this money to programming that will benefit communities of color.

COLORADO'S NATIONAL LEGACY

The political promise of regulation and the recognition of a lost opportunity to create a diverse industry from the outset both emerged as central features in Colorado's status as the early model of cannabis legalization nationwide. Voters in the state (and beyond) embraced the central justification that Amendment 64 supporters advanced: a regulated market would be the best way to limit youth use and other perceived forms of harmful interactions with cannabis, while the money that the state might gain from legalization could be used to advance a variety of social causes, most importantly education. Crucially, participants in the already-regulated Colorado medical market embraced this effort, helping to ensure legalization would be a political success and that they would be able to access the consumers and additional revenue that the recreational market might bring. As drug policy scholar Douglas Berman explained in a panel event years later, "California, turn[ed] down the first full legalization initiative in 2010, in part because the medical industry said 'we don't like [how] this changes our business model and we're gonna vote against it.' Then Colorado [and] Washington figured out [they] had to include the medical industry first in line for the new [market]" to win over support.[123] Conversely, those who have had a more direct role in the illicit legacy market and bear the social consequences of that activity—especially criminal records—as well as those who don't have access to liquid forms of wealth, have largely been shut out from this development.

Colorado will always be seen as a trailblazer for legalization, a reputation certainly well deserved given both the state's early vote for medical cannabis in 2000 as well as the focused activism of a select group of individuals within Colorado that were committed to using the state's initiative power to chart a path forward toward reforming drug control laws both locally and nationally. Amendment 64's campaign and implementation fundamentally reset the national conversation around ending cannabis prohibition in a way that few activists dreamed possible, and the progress made in the decade after has demonstrated the importance of this early work in ensuring that legalization itself survived.

Colorado continues to be at the vanguard of national drug policy. In 2022, voters supported Proposition 122, making it one of the first states to decriminalize and establish limited access programs for psilocybin and other "magic mushroom" substances.[124] Still, by focusing on some of the more technical aspects of legalization such as tax rates, public safety, and youth access, the state's early conversations surrounding cannabis legalization by their nature ignored the social context around one of the strongest arguments often fielded in favor of legalization: its possible use as a tool for reparation of past injustice, particularly for people of color. Legalization supporters eventually came to strongly emphasize the scale of arrests that had been occurring across the country as a result of prohibition policies, as well as the clear racial disparities in these arrests that motivated the larger critique of the War on Drugs that many legalization activists kept in the back of their minds.

Even though Colorado's initial program did not include the suite of policies to advance social equity that later states have come to embrace, many equity-oriented cannabis activists might still rightfully define their work in Colorado as furthering social equity. This is most obviously because of practical outcomes such as expungements of criminal records, but it is also because they simply made it possible for activists—and, crucially, voters—in future states to see legalization as possible in the first place. Many social equity concepts, such as the importance of promoting economic opportunities for those affected by criminalization, were not widely considered until the basic question of whether a legal market could even be created was first answered.

Few activists in Colorado's early days had a specific idea of what a legal cannabis industry would look like, however, and so the economic consolidation that followed gave prohibition supporters a new target: "Big Cannabis." As will be seen in chapter 5, Ohio's Issue 3 campaign—combined with actions in other states that the medical cannabis market undertook—would demonstrate the power of entrenched market players to limit competition and dominate the emerging recreational space. In the process, it would show some of the important limits on the potential for sweeping social change that were present in Colorado's early approach to legalization and regulation. Even if voters had supported regulation as a vehicle for allaying fears about widespread cannabis use, such as potential youth use, these regulations could not be exploited for economic gain without popular backlash.

NOTES

1. Daniel Glick, "Marijuana Prohibition Began with These Arrests in 1937," Leafly.com, last updated July 28, 2020, https://www.leafly.com/news/politics/drug-war-prisoners-1-2-true-story-moses-sam-two-denver-drifters-became-cannabis-pioneers.
2. Glick, "Marijuana Prohibition Began."
3. *Minneapolis Journal*, "Finish War Ordered on Marihuana," October 17, 1937, reproduced in Glick, "Marijuana Prohibition."
4. Nikki and Swami, "The Hardscrabble Origins of California's Fabled 'Emerald Triangle' (Part II)," *Merry Jane*, August 29, 2017, https://merryjane.com/culture/the-hardscrabble-origins-of-californias-fabled-emerald-triangle-part-ii; and Ashley Manta, "Remembering the San Francisco Cannabis Buyers Club, the Nation's First Dispensary," Leafly.com, last updated July 28, 2020, https://www.leafly.com/news/lifestyle/san-francisco-cannabis-buyers-club-nations-first-american-dispensary.
5. Oaksterdam University, "Trusted Leaders in Cannabis Education and Certification," https://oaksterdamuniversity.com/about/.
6. Peter Hecht, *Weed Land: Inside America's Marijuana Epicenter and How Pot Went Legit* (Berkeley: University of California Press, 2014), 156.
7. Hecht, *Weed Land*, 156.

8. Hecht, *Weed Land*, 161.

9. Dan Rogers, "Rogers Financial," https://dancannabis.com/.

10. For examples in Oakland and Los Angeles, see Hecht, *Weed Land*, 21, 87–88.

11. Nick Johnson, *Grass Roots: A History of Cannabis in the American West* (Corvallis: Oregon State University Press, 2017), 69–73.

12. Miriam Pawel, "California Ballot Initiatives Are Powerful: The Powerful Have Noticed," *New York Times*, November 5, 2018, https://www.nytimes.com/2018/11/05/opinion/california-ballot-initiatives-direct-democracy.html.

13. Bart Schaneman, "Minority Cannabis Ownership Negligible in Colorado, But New Social Equity Law Aims to Spur Progress," *MJBizDaily*, updated December 17, 2021, https://mjbizdaily.com/minority-cannabis-ownership-negligible-in-colorado-but-new-law-aims-to-spur-progress/.

14. Mark David Evans, *The Consequences of Conviction: Sanctions Beyond the Sentence Under Colorado Law* (Denver: Office of the Colorado State Public Defender, 2019), 78, https://www.coloradodefenders.us/wp-content/uploads/2019/12/Consequences-of-Conviction-2019-Edition-1.pdf.

15. William Breathes, "Colorado Cannabis Time Capsule, 1929: Legislators Make Sale and Cultivation a Felony," *Westword*, December 21, 2012, https://www.westword.com/news/colorado-cannabis-time-capsule-1929-legislators-make-sale-and-cultivation-a-felony-5856142.

16. Richard J. Bonnie and Charles H. Whitebread, *The Marihuana Conviction: A History of Marihuana Prohibition in the United States* (Charlottesville: University of Virginia Press, 1974), 39.

17. William Breathes, "Colorado Cannabis Time Capsule, 1923: 'Mexican Dope Ring Operating in Denver,'" *Westword*, June 20, 2014, https://www.westword.com/news/cannabis-time-capsule-1923-mexican-dope-ring-operating-in-denver-5902872.

18. Johnson, *Grass Roots*, 73–74.

19. Johnson, *Grass Roots*, 77–79.

20. Breathes, "Time Capsule, 1929."

21. Bonnie and Whitebread, *Marihuana Conviction*, 101.

22. Johnson, *Grass Roots*, 69.

23. Colorado Legislative Council, *Dangerous Drugs and Drug Abuse Control*, Research Publication No. 127, December 1967, 8–23, http://hermes.cde.state.co.us/drupal/islandora/object/co:2584/datastream/OBJ/view.

24. National Governors' Conference Center for Policy Research and Analysis, *Marijuana: A Study of State Policies and Penalties* (Washington, DC: National Institute of Law Enforcement and Criminal Justice, November 1977), 186–201, https://www.ojp.gov/pdffiles1/Digitization/43880NCJRS.pdf.

25. Harry G. Levine, Jon B. Gettman, and Loren Siegel, *210,000 Marijuana Possession Arrests in Colorado, 1986–2010* (New York: Marijuana Arrest Research Project, 2012), 4, http://marijuana-arrests.com/docs/210,000-Marijuana-Arrests-In-Colorado.pdf. Colorado population figures available at Colorado Department of Local Affairs, "Regional Data Lookup," https://coloradodemography.github.io/population/data/regional-data-lookup/.

26. Levine, Gettman, and Siegel, *210,000 Marijuana Possession Arrests*, 4.

27. Michael Roberts, "Marijuana: $1K Fine, Year in Jail for Possession Possible But Unlikely, Says Lakewood PD," *Westword*, September 7, 2012, https://www.westword.com/news/marijuana-1k-fine-year-in-jail-for-possession-possible-but-unlikely-says-lakewood-pd-5842109.

28. Levine, Gettman, and Siegel, *210,000 Marijuana Possession Arrests*, 5.

29. Levine, Gettman, and Siegel, *210,000 Marijuana Possession Arrests*, 6.

30. Jack K. Reed, *Impacts of Marijuana Legalization in Colorado* (Denver: Colorado Division of Criminal Justice, July 2021), 25, https://cdpsdocs.state.co.us/ors/docs/reports/2021-SB13-283_Rpt.pdf.

31. Reed, *Impacts*, 30.

32. Reed, *Impacts*, 27.

33. Reed, Impacts, 23.

34. Jeralyn Merritt, "Shaky Path for Colorado's Marijuana Ballot Initiative," *5280*, January 20, 2005, https://www.5280.com/shaky-path-for-colorados-marijuana-ballot-initiative/.

35. Sensible Colorado, "History of Colorado's Medical Marijuana Laws," 2013, http://sensiblecolorado.org/history-of-co-medical-marijuana-laws/#.

36. Hecht, *Weed Land*, 69.

37. California NORML, "Jury Acquits Eugene Davidovich/DA Re-Targets Lambert," blog post, March 28, 2010, https://www.canorml.org/jury-acquits-eugene-davidovichda-re-targets-lambert/.

38. See *Gonzalez v. Raich*, 545 U.S. 1 (2005).

39. *Gonzalez v. Raich* represents the Supreme Court's unwillingness to establish limitations on Congress's interstate commerce clause, favoring the supremacy of federal (criminal) regulation despite state efforts to permit some basic form of control over the market. This will be explored in chapter 9.

40. Martin A. Lee, *Smoke Signals: A Social History of Marijuana—Medical, Recreational, and Scientific* (New York: Scribner, 2012), 401.

41. Caleb Hannan, "The Don Draper of Pot," *Politico*, December 3, 2013, https://www.politico.com/magazine/story/2013/12/the-don-draper-of-pot-mason-tvert-100609/.

42. Patrick O'Driscoll, "Denver Votes to Legalize Marijuana Possession," *USA Today*, November 3, 2005, http://usatoday30.usatoday.com/news/nation/2005-11-03-pot_x.htm.

43. Alan Gathright, "Pot Vote Prompts Worldwide Attention," *Rocky Mountain News* (Denver, CO), November 4, 2005, reprinted in "US CO: Pot Vots Prompts Worldwide Attention," Media Awareness Project, http://www.mapinc.org/drugnews/v05/n1726/a03.html?1332.

44. Hannan, "Don Draper of Pot."

45. Safer Colorado, "Press Room," November 10, 2006, archived at http://web.archive.org/web/20061110033754/http://safercolorado.org/safer-doc.

46. Jason Bane, "Smoking Weed 'Makes Denver SAFER!'" *5280*, October 13, 2005, https://www.5280.com/smoking-weed-makes-denver-safer/.

47. Ballotpedia, "Colorado Marijuana Possession, Initiative 44 (2006)," https://ballotpedia.org/Colorado_Marijuana_Possession,_Initiative_44_(2006).

48. Colorado Office of the Secretary of State, *Official Publication of the Abstract of Votes Cast for the 2005 Coordinated, 2006 Primary, 2006 General*, 144, https://www.sos.state.co.us/pubs/elections/Results/Abstract/pdf/2000-2099/2006AbsractBook.pdf.

49. Hannan, "Don Draper of Pot."

50. Legislative Council of the Colorado General Assembly, *Analysis of the 2006 Ballot Proposals*, Research Publication No. 554, September 14, 2006, 14–15, https://myctbl.cde.state.co.us/sites/default/files/pdf/blue-book/BlueBook2006.pdf.

51. Sensible Colorado, "History of Colorado's Medical Marijuana Laws."

52. Hecht, *Weed Land*, 161–63.

53. Hecht, *Weed Land*, 166.

54. Hecht, *Weed Land*, 161–63.

55. Joel Warner, "Dismantling Denver's 'Pot Capital' Misnomer," *Westword*, January 6, 2010, https://www.westword.com/news/dismantling-denvers-pot-capital-misnomer-5825956.

56. Hecht, *Weed Land*, 188.

57. Lee, *Smoke Signals*, 374; and Jeffrey Wolf, "New Medical Marijuana Rules Pass, Ritter Says He'll Sign It," *9News*, May 11, 2010, https://www.9news.com/article/news/local/politics/new-medical-marijuana-rules-pass-ritter-says-hell-sign-it/73-338221418.

58. Hecht, *Weed Land*, 167–68.

59. Hecht, *Weed Land*, 199.

60. Johnson, *Grass Roots*, 170–79.

61. Melissa R. Michelson and Joe Tafoya, "The Latino Politics of Proposition 19: Criminal Justice and Immigration," in *Something's in the Air: Race, Crime, and the Legalization of Marijuana*, ed. Katherine Tate, James Lance Taylor, and Mark Q. Sawyer, 115–25 (New York: Routledge, 2013).

62. Emily Crick, Mark Cooke, and Dave Bewley-Taylor, "Selling Cannabis Regulation: Learning from Ballot Initiatives in the United States in 2012," Policy Brief 6, Global Drug Policy Observatory, November 2014, 5, https://www.swansea.ac.uk/media/Selling-Cannabis-Regulation.pdf.

63. Crick, Cooke, and Bewley-Taylor, "Selling Cannabis Regulation," 13–14.

64. Ballotpedia, "Colorado Marijuana Legalization Initiative, Amendment 64 (2012)," https://ballotpedia.org/Colorado_Marijuana_Legalization_Initiative,_Amendment_64_(2012).

65. Crick, Cooke, and Bewley-Taylor, "Selling Cannabis Regulation," 9.

66. Ballotpedia, "Colorado Marijuana Legalization Initiative, Amendment 64 (2012)."

67. Colorado Marijuana Initiative 2012, "What If? Latino Voices for Amendment 64," YouTube video, October 31, 2012, https://www.youtube.com/watch?v=8KycY5QuI0Y&ab_channel=ColoradoMarijuanaInitiative2012.

68. Crick, Cooke, and Bewley-Taylor, "Selling Cannabis Regulation," 12.

69. Crick, Cooke, and Bewley-Taylor, "Selling Cannabis Regulation," 11.

70. Ballotpedia, "Colorado Marijuana Legalization Initiative, Amendment 64 (2012)."

71. Crick, Cooke, and Bewley-Taylor, "Selling Cannabis Regulation," 13.
72. Crick, Cooke, and Bewley-Taylor, "Selling Cannabis Regulation," 13.
73. *Denver Post*, "Amendment 64 Is the Wrong Way to Legalize Marijuana," editorial, October 12, 2012, https://www.denverpost.com/2012/10/12/editorial-amendment-64-is-the-wrong-way-to-legalize-marijuana/.
74. Crick, Cooke, and Bewley-Taylor, "Selling Cannabis Regulation," 13–19.
75. Crick, Cooke, and Bewley-Taylor, "Selling Cannabis Regulation," 13–19.
76. Amendment 64 Implementation Task Force, *Task Force Report on the Implementation of Amendment 64: Regulation of Marijuana in Colorado*, Denver, CO, March 13, 2013, 10–13, https://fliphtml5.com/gnse/nzgj.
77. History Colorado, "Growing Reason," Vimeo video, April 1, 2019, https://vimeo.com/317484359.
78. Prop AA, "Prop AA Update with Rick Ridder—Sept. 27, 2013," YouTube video, September 27, 2013, https://www.youtube.com/watch?v=nUc9lQzjpJ8&ab_channel=PropAA.
79. Prop AA, "Prop AA Update."
80. Ballotpedia, "Colorado Proposition AA, Taxes on the Sale of Marijuana (2013)," https://ballotpedia.org/Colorado_Proposition_AA,_Taxes_on_the_Sale_of_Marijuana_(2013).
81. Michael Roberts, "Marijuana: Attorney Rob Corry on Today's Joint Rally in Boulder," *Westword*, September 23, 2013, https://www.westword.com/news/marijuana-attorney-rob-corry-on-todays-free-joint-rally-in-boulder-5821177?storyPage=2.
82. Marijuana Policy Project, "Colorado Passes Proposition AA Tax Measure," blog post, November 8, 2013, https://blog.mpp.org/tax-and-regulate/colorado-passes-proposition-aa-tax-measure/.
83. Amendment 64 Implementation Task Force, *Regulation of Marijuana in Colorado*, 15–16.
84. Population demographics, including race, are available from the US Census Bureau at https://data.census.gov/.
85. The Ohio State University Moritz College of Law, "Social Equity 2.0: Expanding Horizons," YouTube video, December 13, 2021, https://www.youtube.com/watch?v=SHz_qQ-TcGQ&ab_channel=TheOhioStateUniversityMoritzCollegeofLaw.
86. James M. Cole, "Memorandum to All United States Attorneys," August 29, 2013, https://www.justice.gov/iso/opa/resources/3052013829132756857467.pdf.
87. Joey Bunch, "Polis Signs Social Equity Bill for Colorado Marijuana Industry," *Colorado Politics*, updated November 8, 2021, https://www.coloradopolitics.com/legislature/polis-signs-social-equity-bill-for-colorado-marijuana-industry/article_a93b9574-ba5b-11ea-bb74-8b1553a52c63.html.
88. Chandra Thomas Whitfield, "Capitalizing on Cannabis: Meet Colorado's Black 'Potrepreneurs,'" *NBC News*, April 20, 2015, https://www.nbcnews.com/news/nbcblk/capitalizing-cannabis-meet-colorados-black-potrepreneurs-n344556.
89. Michael B. Hancock, "Mayor Hancock Reflects on 10 Years of Legalized Recreational Marijuana in the Mile High City," YouTube video, April 20, 2022, https://www.youtube.com/watch?v=JXUsjraDyow&ab_channel=MichaelB.Hancock.

90. John Frank, "Colorado Governor Is Considering the Release of Nearly 40 Inmates with Marijuana Convictions," *Denver Post*, February 6, 2018, https://www.denverpost.com/2018/02/06/colorado-governor-marijuana-commutation/.

91. Nic Garcia, "Hickenlooper Pardons 26 Coloradans for Theft, Drug and Other Convictions," *Denver Post*, updated January 25, 2019, https://www.denverpost.com/2018/08/23/hickenlooper-pardons-26-coloradans/.

92. John Frank, "It Wasn't Just Cash: How Texting Cannabis Voters and Tech Outreach Strategies Lifted Jared Polis to Victory," *Colorado Sun*, November 8, 2018, https://coloradosun.com/2018/11/08/how-jared-polis-won/.

93. John Frank, "Meet America's First Pot Governor, Colorado's Jared Polis," *Colorado Sun*, January 7, 2019, https://coloradosun.com/2019/01/07/americas-first-marijuana-governor-colorado-jared-polis/.

94. Savannah Mehrtens, "Colorado Officials, Cannabis Industry Leaders Celebrate 10th Anniversary of Amendment 64," *Denver Gazette*, updated December 29, 2022, https://denvergazette.com/news/marijuana/colorado-officials-cannabis-industry-leaders-celebrate-10th-anniversary-of-amendment-64/article_4a888cf0-4a71-11ed-84ad-57fdab26121d.html.

95. Ashley Kilroy, *Turn Over a New Leaf: Report* (Denver, CO: [Denver Department of Excise and Licenses], September 4, 2019), https://www.denvergov.org/files/assets/public/marijuana-info/documents/tonl_report.pdf.

96. Colorado General Assembly, "HB20–1424: Social Equity Licenses in Regulated Marijuana," Bill Summary, https://leg.colorado.gov/bills/HB20-1424.

97. Colorado General Assembly, "An Act Concerning Certain Criminal Marijuana Offenses," HB 21–1090, https://cbi.colorado.gov/sites/cbi/files/documents/HB%2021-1090%2C%20concerning%20certain%20MJ%20offenses_final%20act.pdf.

98. Colorado Bureau of Investigation, Department of Public Safety, "Marijuana Pardons," https://cbi.colorado.gov/sections/biometric-identification-and-records-unit/marijuana-pardons.

99. Joe Rubino, "Denver Tweaks Marijuana Delivery Rules as Businesses Struggle to Get Off the Ground," *Denver Post*, September 19, 2022, https://www.denverpost.com/2022/09/19/denver-marijuana-delivery-licenses-regulations-cannabis-social-equity/.

100. City of Aurora (CO), "Retail Marijuana Delivery and Social Equity," https://www.auroragov.org/business_services/marijuana_and_hemp_licensing/retail_marijuana_delivery_and_social_equity.

101. Colorado Department of Revenue, Specialized Business Group, "Social Equity: Equity, Diversity and Inclusion is a Priority for the State of Colorado," https://sbg.colorado.gov/med/social-equity.

102. Colorado Department of Revenue, Specialized Business Group, "MED Licensee Demographic Information," https://sbg.colorado.gov/med/MED-licensee-demographic-information.

103. Michael Roberts, "Marijuana: Wanda James on Closure of Edible Business, MMJ Banking, Obama and More," *Westword*, October 10, 2012, https://www.westword.com/news/marijuana-wanda-james-on-closure-of-edibles-business-mmj-banking-obama-and-more-5830735.

104. *CNBC*, "For Wanda James Being in the Cannabis Industry Isn't About Making Money; It's About Social Justice," January 22, 2021, https://www.cnbc.com/video/2021/01/22/for-wanda-james-being-in-the-cannabis-industry-is-about-social-justice.html.

105. Whitfield, "Capitalizing on Cannabis."

106. Mona Zhang, "The *High Times* Interview: Wanda James," *High Times*, June 24, 2016, https://hightimes.com/business/the-high-times-interview-wanda-james/.

107. APB Speakers, "Pot, Power and Politics—Wanda James," YouTube video, January 3, 2022, https://www.youtube.com/watch?v=ZqU0JCNXFq8&ab_channel=APBSpeakers.

108. Noel Brennan, "A Look at Diversity in the Cannabis Industry on 420," *9News*, April 20, 2022, https://www.9news.com/article/news/local/diversity-in-cannabis-industry-420/73-b5116cbe-7797-4553-8f59-64a031eacca4.

109. Colorado Department of Revenue, "Marijuana Tax Reports," https://cdor.colorado.gov/data-and-reports/marijuana-data/marijuana-tax-reports.

110. Colorado General Assembly, "Explore the Colorado State Budget," https://leg.colorado.gov/explorebudget/.

111. Richard C. Auxier and Nikhita Airi, *The Pros and Cons of Cannabis Taxes* (Washington, DC: Tax Policy Center, September 28, 2022), 12, https://www.taxpolicycenter.org/publications/pros-and-cons-cannabis-taxes/full.

112. City of Aurora (CO), *Financial Performance Report: Fourth Quarter, 2020*, 1, https://cdn5-hosted.civiclive.com/UserFiles/Servers/Server_1881137/File/Business%20Services/Marijuana%20Regulations/2020%20Q4%20MJ.pdf.

113. Ballotpedia, "Colorado Springs, Colorado, Ballot Question 300, Allow for Retail Marijuana Establishments Initiative (November 2022)," https://ballotpedia.org/Colorado_Springs,_Colorado,_Ballot_Question_300,_Allow_for_Retail_Marijuana_Establishments_Initiative_(November_2022).

114. Colorado Legislative Council, "Proposition AA: Retail Marijuana Taxes," Fiscal Impact Statement, September 24, 2013, https://www.leg.state.co.us/LCS/Initiative%20Referendum/1314initrefr.nsf/b74b3fc5d676cdc987257ad8005bce6a/e3e37fa33a36873887257b6c0077ac93/$FILE/Retail%20Marijuana%20Taxes_FN.pdf.

115. Colorado Department of Education, "BEST Grant Program," https://www.cde.state.co.us/capitalconstruction/best.

116. Bente Birkeland, "With Proposition BB, Colorado Votes on Marijuana Tax Money—Again," *KUNC*, October 20, 2015, https://www.kunc.org/politics/2015-10-20/with-proposition-bb-colorado-votes-on-marijuana-tax-money-again#stream/0.

117. Andy Stine, *Building Excellent Schools Today (BEST) Annual Report* (Denver: Colorado Department of Education, February 2022), 27, https://www.cde.state.co.us/capitalconstruction/bestfy21legislativereport.

118. Colorado Department of Education, "Marijuana Tax Revenue and Education," updated November 2, 2022, https://www.cde.state.co.us/communications/2021marijuanarevenue.

119. City of Denver (CO), *The Denver Collaborative Approach: Leading the Way in Municipal Marijuana Management* (Denver: City of Denver, 2022), 14, https:

//www.denvergov.org/files/assets/public/business-licensing/documents/marijuana-annual-report-2022.pdf.

120. City of Denver (CO), *Denver Collaborative Approach*, 21.

121. iNSIGHTS Lab, *2019 High Costs Campaign Evaluation: Denver Teens Survey, November–December 2019* (iNSIGHTS Lab, 2020), https://www.thehighcosts.com/wp-content/uploads/2020/02/HighCosts_2019Post-CampaignSurvey_Results.pdf.

122. Jon Murray, "Cautious Approach on Marijuana Legalization Has Reaped Millions to Help Aurora's Homeless," *Denver Post*, updated December 30, 2018, https://www.denverpost.com/2018/12/28/aurora-marijuana-taxes-benefits-homeless/.

123. The Ohio State University Moritz College of Law, "Cannabis on the Ballot: Lessons Learned from the Marijuana Reform Movement," YouTube video, October 27, 2022, https://www.youtube.com/watch?v=R8FQ8gHvoPM&ab_channel=TheOhioStateUniversityMoritzCollegeofLaw.

124. Ballotpedia, "Colorado Proposition 122, Decriminalization and Regulated Access Program for Certain Psychedelic Plants and Fungi Initiative (2022)," https://ballotpedia.org/Colorado_Proposition_122,_Decriminalization_and_Regulated_Access_Program_for_Certain_Psychedelic_Plants_and_Fungi_Initiative_(2022).

Chapter 5

Ohio

Equity Without Legalization

In 1970, during the height of social activism against the war in Vietnam, protests rocked college campuses as students resisted the draft and the actions of the Nixon administration, including the illegal American bombing of Cambodia. The deployment of National Guard troops by state leaders in a bid to control the situation often made things worse. Instead of control, the volatile environment sometimes led to violence—including in Ohio on May 4, 1970, when Guardsmen opened fire on a crowd of students at Kent State University who were protesting the war, killing four, wounding nine others, and provoking a national outcry and multiple investigations. Local prosecutor Ronald Kane responded by ordering the college to shut down for the remainder of the semester.[1]

After law enforcement had an opportunity to search students' dorms and residences several days later, Kane appeared at a press conference where he proudly displayed the fruits of these searches—including marijuana, firearms, and other "contraband" that highlighted the subversive element that the protesting students supposedly represented. Even though the students and the local ACLU objected to the constitutionality of the searches and their relevance to the shooting investigation, the flaunting of cannabis as a supposed symptom of social disorder was an oft-used tactic of law-and-order politicians of the era, including Richard Nixon himself.[2] The day after the shooting, several Kent State students met with presidential advisor John Ehrlichman, who later helped Nixon craft the federal prohibition regime under the Controlled Substances Act, announced six months later.[3]

Thirty-five years after the Kent State shootings, Ohio voters considered Issue 3, otherwise known as the "Ohio Marijuana Legalization Initiative." This measure, very different from the voter-passed legalization in other states that had come before it, envisioned giving the exclusive right to cultivate cannabis for Ohio consumers to a group of ten limited liability companies

(LLCs), many of which were owned by celebrities or wealthy business leaders.[4] Among them was an LLC involving several descendants of the Taft family, Ohio political royalty that over the past century has included a US president, a powerful US senator and, more recently, Bob Taft III, the governor of Ohio from 1999 to 2007 (who himself was opposed to Issue 3).[5] In exchange for this monopoly power, the ten license holders agreed to allow workers at their vertically integrated facilities to unionize, while also committing to ensure that these workers were diverse and that there were opportunities for those previously involved with the legacy market to move into the legal one.[6] Much like Colorado's legalization measure, this initiative was submitted to the voters as a constitutional amendment, which the organizers hoped would prevent state legislators from modifying or otherwise invalidating the legalization plan.[7] Unlike Colorado's measure, Ohio's Issue 3 proved unpopular with voters and went on to a dismal result, uniting many cannabis users and prohibitionists in opposition.[8]

Among other reasons why Issue 3 both received national attention in fall 2015 and ultimately failed was the supporting campaign's official mascot, nicknamed "Buddie"—a green cannabis "bud" with ample muscles, dressed in a white superhero uniform, that toured the state over the course of the campaign, visiting college campuses and other popular locations. Buddie received a torrent of criticism from the opposition, mostly over fears that this mascot would lead to a larger normalization of cannabis use. At the same time, even many supporters of legalization in a general sense felt that the mascot and the messaging of the larger campaign reflected a corporatization of the discussion, with some calling for an end to the use of Buddie, whom they compared to tobacco's Joe Camel.[9]

Issue 3's proponents intended Buddie to be a symbol that would motivate youth voters and help drive excitement about the fall campaign, but instead this effort served as another example of the dissonance between advocacy for the regulatory model that Issue 3 had articulated and the wishes of many of the grassroots cannabis activists across the state, who abhorred the monopoly provisions as directly antithetical to the message of taking a liberal approach to cannabis. For initiative organizer Ian James, these critiques were empty platitudes that did not recognize the challenges in working to legalize cannabis in a conservative state such as Ohio without the support of national groups such as NORML and MPP, which had generally focused on more liberal places like Colorado. As James put it, "Unless you find a way for the national groups to participate and spend the millions of dollars necessary to win, then you're not going to have the funding necessary for this. It is a very, very large, complex state."[10] Notable in both James's point and the larger discussion around Buddie is that comparatively little of the debate about Issue 3 or the reasons for its failure had to do with the fears of cannabis-related social disorder that had pervaded similar campaigns just a generation or two earlier.

Ohio is a curious state to include as a case study in a book about cannabis social equity, given that only medical cannabis has been legalized in the state at the time of writing. Yet the specifics of why Issue 3 failed helped to shape the debate around market consolidation and the prospects for social equity in the market for recreational sales, in turn influencing future cannabis activism and legislation in other states. It demonstrated that the cultural messaging around cannabis had changed drastically even since the Amendment 64 campaign that happened only three years earlier in Colorado, having reached relatively widespread acceptance among elites and society at large. As Tamar Todd, a leader in the movement to promote cannabis legalization ballot initiatives throughout the United States, reflected: "And then that Ohio initiative came across, and everyone said, 'Holy smokes, I don't support this legalization initiative. I've been working on legalization my entire life—who is going to get all the money from this new industry? [Issue 3] is not fair.'" For Todd, the implications for future campaigns were clear: "Suddenly, everyone's saying I only support a certain kind of legalization initiative, and then has to meet these other elements."[11]

Including a consideration of Ohio in this book alongside more obvious choices such as Colorado also speaks to the experience of many states that do not yet have recreational legalization but do have an active medical market. Notably, Ohio's medical market has incorporated racial equity provisions in awarding licenses. These racial preferences have proved legally controversial, later being struck down by a Franklin County judge, a decision that remains controlling after the two appellant parties withdrew their appeal in 2021.[12] This case, along with similar litigation in other states, demonstrates the legal challenges that may accompany complex licensing criteria that seek to identify communities and individuals most impacted by the War on Drugs for the purpose of providing them with market preferences or even exclusive access. Such litigation has served to identify some of the administrative and technical challenges inherent in this process while also delaying the issuance of licenses to those who might otherwise benefit from those provisions.

In the end, Ohio clearly demonstrated an emerging divide in the cannabis legalization movement between the profit motive and the larger philosophical arguments that have long energized a large body of activists. If Colorado had shown that some cannabis suppliers were willing to embrace regulation as a cost of being able to participate in a legal industry, Ohio made clear that voters were not willing to sacrifice principles of competition and social equity in favor of legalization itself or the perceived threat that unregulated cannabis could pose to youth. This helped push future legalization campaigns to incorporate principles of social justice that explicitly embraced racial justice goals and an attention to including communities that had been impacted by criminalization. As the larger national campaign for legalization expanded to more racially diverse states, members of these communities would also participate in and make claims on the movement for legalization, contesting the original focus on regulation and tax revenue as the primary arguments for reform.

CANNABIS CRIMINALIZATION IN OHIO

Ohio legislators did not criminalize cannabis until the end of the 1920s, declining to address it when they created the state's first larger drug control scheme in 1923, later opting to create legal prohibitions on cannabis in 1927.[13] Then in 1931, Ohio adopted the Uniform Narcotic Drug Act that many other states were in the process of considering at the time (discussed in chapter 1). Ohio's narcotic control laws were further tightened two decades later in 1955 in response to an advisory commission led by the state's attorney general.[14] This change enhanced sentences for state narcotics offenses in line with the Boggs Act that had recently passed Congress (mentioned in chapter 1).[15]

As part of a wave of state legislatures revisiting their work in the 1960s as the federal narcotics regulatory scheme underwent increasing legal scrutiny, Ohio officials took notice of cultural and political pressure to reexamine their earlier drug policy choices—most prominently, the question of whether cannabis was a narcotic. Just as Colorado's legislature had questioned the inclusion of the non-narcotic cannabis in its narcotics regulatory scheme in 1967, Ohio's Legislative Service Commission issued a similar report in the same year that was more explicit about the nature of the public conversation occurring around cannabis use at this time. For example, it describes research by Richard Goldstein which purported to show that half of college students would try cannabis by graduation (although this estimate was met with some skepticism). Usage was undoubtedly common, however, with university officials agreeing that at least 10 to 15 percent of college students would use cannabis during their four years of study. Likewise, the report notes that "the designation of marihuana as an illegal drug has not served as a deterrent. Certainly, the attractiveness of forbidden activities and the questioning of taboos have long been recognized as a part of the college experience."[16]

This report, and the similar investigation by Colorado's legislature, make clear that by the mid-1960s much of the public remained uncertain about how to approach cannabis while also being largely unaware of any medicinal uses. It is notable that legalization of cannabis was not proposed as an option. This report seems to have had an impact, however, as Ohio's legislature moved only three years later to reclassify cannabis as a hallucinogen. Then in 1975, the state conformed its regulatory approach to the guidelines of the federal Controlled Substances Act. Although the federal law reclassified cannabis to remove it from the list of narcotics, it retained penalties for its manufacture, distribution, and possession. Several years later, the Ohio legislature authorized a limited-term therapeutic use program through the state Department of Health.[17] Despite this brief window of liberalization, most states—including Ohio—declined to craft new legislation or regulations that would establish legal access to cannabis in the midst of political headwinds in the late 1970s, leaving therapeutic measures like this in the dust heap.[18]

In the decades after this step, most actions that the Ohio legislature took on drug law in general and cannabis specifically served to increase penalties for criminal offenses. Between 1981 and 2006, legislators adopted at least twelve different measures enhancing or creating new criminal penalties regarding cannabis.[19] In 1997, the legislature acted, seemingly in direct opposition to California's medical use ballot initiative that passed a year earlier, to strike a "medical purposes" affirmative defense for use that had been allowed under state law but was largely defunct.[20] This was part of a more general trend in state law, with the number of drug felonies on the books increasing from 50 to 197 between 1974 and 2020, while the overall number of felonies grew from 146 to 752 during the same period.[21] As one activist pointed out when describing the state Legislative Service Commission's report on this subject: "it showed a couple of things that I can't say were surprising, other than the sheer volume."[22]

Only after 2011 did the legislature break a thirty-year streak of pursuing tougher restrictions on cannabis by acting to relax or revise some of these penalties in the other direction, first by decriminalizing possession of small amounts of cannabis.[23] Even this step has seemed to many to be too late and too little, as many legislators continue to be loyal to punitive approaches to drug control. The effects of this decriminalization were not equally felt, however, as many Ohio residents live in cities or municipalities which have the authority to establish higher consequences for cannabis possession and other offenses beyond those found in state law.[24] As Gary Daniels, chief lobbyist for the Ohio ACLU, summarized in 2022: "We [in Ohio] still subscribe to this idea that drug problems are best handled and perhaps exclusively handled through cops, courts, and cages. The idea that we should be trying something different seems to be rather an alien concept among many legislators at the Statehouse. Indeed, today, drug possession remains the number-one reason why people end up in an Ohio prison, and drug trafficking remains the number-two reason why people end up in an Ohio prison."[25]

ENFORCEMENT OUTCOMES

Given that legal developments around cannabis criminalization in Ohio have largely followed national trends, it's unsurprising that statistics describing cannabis use and arrests in the state have likewise been consistent with those describing most of the United States. An April 2001 "Threat Assessment" from the National Drug Intelligence Center gives a clear indication that law enforcement in Ohio viewed cannabis as the most abused illicit drug that they would encounter, and the bulk of drug arrests and enforcement activity was targeted toward cannabis. This report further describes the retail market for cannabis, pointing to both organized crime and independent groups as largely controlling the trade. It is clear, though, that market participants were racially diverse and likely presented Black residents of the geographic communities described within the report with some opportunities for economic and social advancement.[26]

Similarly, a summary of arrests for cannabis that criminologist John Gettman produced provides another view of the influence of cannabis on Ohio's drug enforcement regime. In 2007, Ohio law enforcement made 23,335 arrests for cannabis; using estimates of regular cannabis users in the state from demographic studies, this would indicate that the average cannabis user had a one in fifty chance of being arrested in that year.[27] Note that possession arrests made up the bulk of these arrests: only 8 percent of them were for selling cannabis. Overall, cannabis arrests made up just under half of drug arrests in the state that year—and approximately 6 percent of all arrests for any reason—requiring hundreds of millions of dollars in spending to support this expensive approach to law enforcement.[28] When compared to admissions for drug treatment, the disproportionate scale of cannabis enforcement seems even more out of sync with its impact on society. In 2007, little more than one in five admissions for drug treatment services in the state were for cannabis use, with over half of these being court referred. Meanwhile, there were nearly twice as many admissions for alcohol—a completely legal substance.[29]

A report issued by the ACLU of Cuyahoga County—which includes Cleveland and is one of the state's largest counties, with over a tenth of Ohio's population—demonstrates once again how the War on Drugs has had a disproportionate impact on communities of color. For instance, the county's percentage of Black residents is nearly double that of the state as a whole. Depressingly but unsurprisingly, Cuyahoga's share of the state prison population is also approximately double its share of the state's overall population.[30] The racial disparities in drug enforcement in Cleveland have long been a known fact. For example, a 2003 report by a grand jury empaneled in the county led by Pastor Marvin McMickle notes a number of troubling practices related to drug enforcement and referrals to the criminal justice system that drove this trend.[31] One of these is the strategy of charging offenders caught with cocaine pipes with felony indictments—which would involve serious life consequences for the defendants if they were convicted. Many of these charges were based solely on the possession of very small amounts of cocaine itself. When the grand jury and county judges questioned this practice, local prosecutors fought back against efforts to limit drug prosecutions based on this fact.[32] Little changed in the years after these initial concerns, however, with the ACLU report noting that the bulk of the county's drug arrests originate from Cleveland's predominantly African American east side.[33]

While the above details are certainly suggestive, consistent data about cannabis arrests and prosecutions that can be objectively interpreted—as with most attempts to collect criminal justice statistics on the state and local levels—is at times difficult to find in Ohio. This is part of a broader reality for the period prior to when the first states elected to legalize cannabis in 2012. Because it was an early entrant to the market, Colorado benefited from a series of deliberate data collection exercises and reporting procedures directed by the legislature with an intent to understand the impact of legalization. For places with improved data, much of the scholarship on cannabis policy has consistently highlighted racial and social disparities in arrest rates. Given that legalization has not yet moved forward in Ohio, data there is sparser and perhaps more subjective.

This lack of clear information has in turn muddied the debate between groups such as the ACLU and NORML that advocate for greater liberalization of drug laws, and individuals representing law enforcement and public health who want to maintain the stricter control regime now in place. Much of the data on cannabis arrests in recent decades has come from activists who are fighting against criminalization—these groups have been effective in highlighting the scale of drug enforcement using statistics like the total number of arrests, as well as the racial disparities in those arrests. The challenge in this data often comes when trying to understand how cannabis arrests influence the criminal justice system as a whole, however. Certainly data found by Gettman and the ACLU of Cuyahoga County serve to illustrate how much substance regulation as a whole plays into criminal justice, though it is difficult to compare the kind of enforcement activities and time spent on a cannabis arrest with that of more serious crimes, such as murder or sexual assault, or even other forms of nonviolent crime, such as fraud or possession of underage pornography.

Gettman's estimate that cannabis offenses represent 6 percent of all arrests in Ohio would indicate that Ohio taxpayers spent approximately $400 million on cannabis enforcement in that year,[34] though this kind of analysis is often criticized as insufficient by law enforcement given that few of these individuals spent much, if any, time in prison.[35] The contradiction in these enforcement patterns—heavy numbers of arrests combined with light penalties—instead speaks to incentives for law enforcement to obtain additional funding to supplement operations, such as federal Byrne Justice Assistance Grants, which often went to drug task forces across the country in order to supplement staffing and equipment costs.[36]

ISSUE 3

While the push to put cannabis legalization on the ballot in Ohio gained a great deal of steam after Colorado and Washington voted to legalize in late 2012, the origin of what would become Issue 3 had its roots in policy developments that were already underway inside Ohio before those outside initiatives were in the headlines. A key player was Ian James, an Ohio political consultant and activist who had lengthy experience in state politics dating from when he worked on his first political campaign just after college in 1990.[37] James was featured by *Ohio Magazine* as one of the state's brightest political strategists, a reputation he earned when nearly two decades later he worked on a statewide ballot initiative known as the Casino Approval and Tax Distribution Amendment, later listed on the 2009 ballot as Amendment 3.[38]

Ohio voters had previously rejected a series of initiatives that sought to legalize casino gambling in the state, handing advocates defeats in 1996, 2006, and 2008. For 2009's Amendment 3, its drafters—including James—wrote in exclusivity provisions that benefited the prime contributors to the legalization effort: JACK Entertainment and Penn National Gaming.[39] The campaign was narrowly successful, winning approval with 53 percent of the vote, though it had been met with a chorus of editorials and elected officials who criticized the monopoly provision, arguing that voters should not write monopolies into the state constitution despite any of the promised economic benefits casino legalization might bring.[40] With immense profits in sight for the financial sponsors, Amendment 3 brought out tens of millions of dollars in spending on both sides, though supporters were at a decided advantage with the backing of the interested companies.[41]

James followed his 2009 victory by working with a small medical cannabis advocacy organization known as the Ohio Rights Group, which by mid-2013 was interested in developing a medical cannabis legalization initiative in the state for 2015.[42] James would later decide that the Ohio Rights Group proposal was not ambitious enough and instead opted to seek full legalization, leaning on the same model which had been successful for casino gambling. James recruited Chris Stock, a lawyer who had previously worked for the state attorney general's office, to draft the ballot language, while venture capitalist and fundraiser Jimmy Gould helped gather a group of interested investors in the legalized cannabis market.[43] Gould himself invested in the effort (and would later join the state's medical market) while he recruited a series of wealthy individuals to start their own ventures. Spanning the private equity and sports worlds of the state, they included a pain specialist, a football player, a basketball star, a singer, and a descendant of native son William Howard Taft.[44] The funders would later contribute nearly $36 million to the effort to enshrine their monopoly on the legal cannabis market in Ohio.[45]

As part of their pitch to Ohio voters, the drafters and intended beneficiaries of the law organized themselves into a group that came to be called ResponsibleOhio. James's vision for this effort is apparent in a campaign prospectus that his consulting firm issued in summer 2014, in which it is also clear that he had successfully assembled a strong range of political, development, and legal talent to his side, among them Jeremy Bird, a former staffer on Barack Obama's two successful campaigns for Ohio's electoral votes in 2008 and 2012.[46] The prospectus is aimed squarely at potential funders and emphasizes the business opportunity that joining the effort would present to them: "Strategic planning begins with the basics: *identifying Principal Funders who understand and appreciate the 'return on investment'* of legalized and regulated marijuana and who, in 2014, are prepared to spend $250,000 on campaign set-up" and millions more on actions such as "ballot language drafting and testing," signature gathering, and "a campaign to identify and mobilize majority voter support." Lest the profit motive be missed, it added, "*Our goal with this business opportunity is to uniquely position Principal Funders for a growth market* in Ohio where annual sales are expected to exceed $1 Billion dollars."[47]

By the time the campaign was formally announced in late 2014, James had split from his original partnership with Ohio Rights Group, whose separate medical cannabis initiative failed to achieve anywhere near the required number of signatures to get on the ballot.[48] Conversely, buoyed by the millions of dollars in investment from the funders that ResponsibleOhio recruited, Issue 3 was able to collect twice the number of required signatures to place its language before voters in 2015.[49] Much like the earlier 2009 casino amendment, Issue 3 tied the awarded licenses to specific plots of land owned by the intended recipients of operator's licenses, ensuring that only these preapproved LLCs would be allowed into the legal market should the language be approved by voters. As elaborated by a task force that ResponsibleOhio helped to organize, led by then-Hamilton County prosecutor (and future state Supreme Court Justice) Joe Deters and an assemblage of other state and local officials in June 2015, this structure was advantageous because the limited number of "tier one" growing facilities that Issue 3 authorized would create an artificial scarcity that would increase their value while also making regulation of those facilities easier.[50]

ResponsibleOhio's proposal included the creation of a state regulated agency, the Ohio Marijuana Control Commission, to be overseen by a seven-member board that included a citizen with experience in the marijuana industry as well as a member of the general public. The sponsors of the initiative would be set up as suppliers in this new market, with all dispensaries as well as product manufacturers mandated to buy from one of these ten suppliers. The political calculations in Issue 3's text were curious and in some ways contradictory, with concessions to both cannabis activists—in the form of a home grow allowance that would have permitted individuals to have four flowering plants—as well as concerned parents, for which the language prohibited dispensaries from being located within 1,000 feet of schools, churches, libraries, or playgrounds. Municipalities were given a strong opt-out provision, and revenue from taxation of the market participants was earmarked for local governments.[51]

In electing to give preference to a small group of well-financed and positioned providers, James's decision to pursue a monopoly advantage does not appear all that distinct from how some government officials in states such as Illinois and Massachusetts might have preferred to build the recreational market. Ohio's Issue 3 was notable, however, for attempting to do what no other state had previously done: skip legalization of the medical use of cannabis in favor of moving straight to recreational use. Issue 3 would also establish a medical system, but Ohio voters and elected officials had no previous experience with cannabis regulation, arguably making voters more susceptible to narratives during the 2015 campaign that legalization could lead to an unregulated market that could cause increases in harmful use, especially in youth. Still, James was certain that the necessary funds to build the political coalition for the ballot measure and provide a counterbalance to opponents' narratives would be in excess of any fundraising that grassroots supporters could provide. The ballot initiative prospectus that he drew up included planning for an eighteen-month period after the measure was to pass to ensure that the implementation would maintain the favorable position for the principal funders.[52]

ResponsibleOhio's messaging is notable as it more explicitly incorporated a racial critique to the War on Drugs than earlier legalization campaigns in other states. This messaging was hardly surprising; when discussing public safety issues, the task force report that ResponsibleOhio commissioned relies largely on the ACLU's earlier published research into racial disparities in cannabis arrests.[53] The report also discusses the collateral consequences of convictions, highlighting narratives about how the impact of criminalization has disproportionately taken economic stability and opportunities from communities of color. For example, it notes that Ohio is one of many states where a misdemeanor arrest for cannabis possession can serve to bar an individual from public housing, and convictions can result in reporting to boards of professional licensure for a variety of occupations.[54] Quoting from an earlier report on these collateral consequences, the task force highlighted that "if, as recognized in beginning in the 1970s, marijuana offenses are considered less of an affront to civil society than violent crimes such as murder, rape or kidnapping, or even less an affront than other drug offenses, our study shows that this consideration is rarely found in any of the collateral sanctions."[55]

In the end, however, much of this narrative did not make it into the campaign's final messaging despite being available to Issue 3's supporters. Although a video posted to the campaign's website in August 2015 includes a discussion of "social justice,"[56] various press releases and other campaign communications indicate a move away from more explicitly emphasizing these themes.[57] This hesitation was likely explained by activist Kyle Strickland, who said that "we shouldn't be talking about race because as soon as the conversation focuses on race, it polarizes certain political players and actually makes it harder to have a reform conversation than if we talk and center the discourse on other issues."[58] The narratives that the supporting campaign highlighted instead focuse on regulation and the economic benefits of legalization, with statements such as: "Issue 3 establishes an industry that will create tens of thousands of jobs in Ohio. It permits, regulates, and taxes marijuana sales by licensed growers and retailers . . . [and] the initial ten-license limit is consistent with recommended best practices, and avoids problems other states with more grow sites have encountered in maintaining quality, ensuring safety, tracking product and collecting taxes."[59]

Meanwhile, opponents of legalization continued to focus on the potential threat of increased youth use in ads such as this: "Issue 3 legalizes marijuana-infused products like candy and cookies, which often have dangerously high levels of THC, and are highly tempting to children, including very young children. High limits on personal possession of marijuana will result in broad exposure of our children and underage high school and college students to marijuana. Issue 3 allows 1,159 retail marijuana stores—that's more locations than Starbucks or McDonalds, and nearly three times the number of state liquor stores."[60] Once the campaign was launched and the measure's language was released, the proposal to create a constitutionally protected monopoly proved deeply controversial, both among cannabis legalization supporters and Ohio voters and legislators in general—and the opposition campaign swiftly added that angle to its criticism. An official representing the opposing group Drug Free Action Alliance cut straight to the chase right after Issue 3's language was released: "if you put the creators of the *Sopranos* and *Breaking Bad* in the same room they couldn't come up with a plot this far fetched. Perhaps the details will help clarify things but right now it sounds like 10 wannabe drug lords are going to ask Ohio voters to constitutionally protect their cartels and turf."[61]

After it became clear that ResponsibleOhio organizers had gotten enough petition signatures to get Issue 3 on the ballot, Ohio legislators responded by drafting a separate proposed constitutional amendment, submitted to the voters as Issue 2.[62] This legislatively referred initiative would prohibit future constitutional amendments from creating market monopolies, which if passed would render Issue 3 moot because any constitutional amendments that voters passed would be enacted in the order they were seen on the ballot. As an added measure, Issue 2's language also directly prevented Issue 3 from taking effect, with the expectation that if voters passed both initiatives, a future vote or clarification from the state Supreme Court would be necessary to sort out the apparent conflict. This anti-monopoly proposal proved no less controversial for cannabis legalization supporters and voters in the state than did Issue 3. Many civil liberties groups remained neutral on or even opposed Issue 3, even as there was anger and opposition to the legislatively referred Issue 2. For example, the Ohio Green Party opposed both Issue 2 and Issue 3, decrying the monopoly structure of Issue 3 while also blasting the legislature for compromising the ballot initiative process and limiting citizen rights to petition on other topics such as health care and the environment.[63]

In the end, despite some polling indicating that the measure had a chance at passing, Issue 3 was defeated by nearly two-thirds of the vote. Meanwhile, Issue 2—the legislative response to Issue 3: the "Initiated Monopolies Amendment," which ResponsibleOhio campaigned against—passed narrowly with 51 percent of the vote.[64] This amendment, while serving as a poison pill by the legislature for Issue 3, also set a larger constitutional bar for monopolies embedded in popular initiatives. Despite some legalization activists' fears that a defeat of a flawed measure would signify a setback for legalization more broadly, the quirks of Issue 3 made it much more difficult to turn its defeat into a broader statement about cannabis—or about messages of equity in connection with legalization. Instead, many social equity activists quickly looked forward to 2016, when the prospect of additional states voting on legalization would provide a much clearer verdict on the messaging around police overreach in the War on Drugs.

EQUITY IN THE MEDICAL MARKET

The next few years would demonstrate the high stakes of the fight for equity, even in a state where cannabis was not recreationally legal. While the state's voters had rejected the flawed cannabis legalization measure presented to them in 2015, the state nevertheless moved forward with establishing a medical cannabis program. Before Issue 3 reached the Ohio ballot in 2015, longtime state senator Bob Hagan had introduced a cannabis reform bill in every session of the legislature since 1997.[65] Surely not by coincidence, Ohio legislators displayed a sudden interest in the legal status of cannabis in 2016, as the public discussion around the ballot initiative had demonstrated a strong public interest in some form of reform. National advocacy groups also believed the time was ripe for another reform push, with the Marijuana Policy Project signaling an intent to put a medical initiative on the Ohio ballot as soon as the following year.[66] This legislative push culminated in House Bill 523, which passed and was signed into law in 2016, the year following Issue 3's defeat.[67]

This medical cannabis law created only a shadow of the broad regulated market envisioned by the ballot measure, however. H. B. 523 limited retail storefronts across the state to only forty locations, while Issue 3 would have allowed for over a thousand.[68] One of the sponsors of this legislation, then-state representative Steven Huffman, later noted the uncertainty that drove this early effort: "We listened to a lot of people on the committee, [including representatives] from the children's hospitals, labor unions, medical marijuana industry, medical industry, pharmacy, law enforcement addiction, and had a bunch of hearings. . . . [But at] the time, we didn't know what we didn't know, [and so] we made it very restrictive."[69]

Despite the relatively conservative approach to creating Ohio's medical market that such limits indicate, state lawmakers made one particularly progressive decision in order to respond to the equity discussion raised during the ballot campaign: they created a mandate in state law for minority inclusion in the new businesses that medical legalization ushered into existence. The mandate required that the state Department of Commerce award 15 percent of the licenses for cultivators, processors, and testing laboratories to economically disadvantaged groups, including African Americans, Native Americans, Hispanics, and Asian Americans. Using the law passed by the Ohio legislature, the commerce department developed a scoring system to evaluate applications for different licenses, though this scoring system itself did not include a mechanism to ensure diversity. Instead, the department developed a secondary process to award licenses to minority applicants to meet its mandate.[70] The principle of priority licensing for equity applicants has since become a goal for many activists, though the resulting court case challenging this measure demonstrates the profound challenges these laws must meet in order to be sustained by the courts.

When the Department of Commerce elected to issue two of the twelve initial medical cannabis licenses to Parma Wellness Center and Harvest Grows over competitor Greenleaf Gardens in 2017, Greenleaf challenged the mandate in court in a case that would eventually be known as *Pharmacann Ohio, LLC v. Ohio Department of Commerce*.[71] Both Parma Wellness and Harvest Grows had scored lower than Greenleaf Gardens on the department's scoring system. Because Parma Wellness and Harvest Grows qualified as being owned by a minority according to the legislature's definition, however, they were awarded licenses when the department used its secondary pathway to skip applicants with higher scores—such as Greenleaf—until it got to those who would meet the legislation's ownership diversity goals.[72]

Such explicit set-asides are sometimes used to help ensure diversity in government vendor searches and contracting, though both state and federal precedents demand the application of the so-called "strict scrutiny" standard when race is one of the criteria used to privilege certain applicants. The government agency faces a high (though hardly impossible) burden to demonstrate that the consideration of race fits a "compelling government interest," and a court will often examine whether the government agency contemplated any methods that could achieve the same interest without using race. Evidence of past racial discrimination can be used to sustain programs such as this, but courts are still skeptical of these set-asides and will usually demand that the policy drafters explain how they had access to this evidence and used it to craft a narrowly tailored measure that explicitly seeks to address this past disparity.[73]

In its case filed in Ohio's Franklin County late in 2017, Greenleaf Gardens sued in order to receive the license that the use of the commerce department's primary race-neutral scoring system would have given it, asserting that the racial set-asides mandated by law were invalid under the state constitution. Greenleaf's attorneys argued that the state legislature had not adequately met its burden when calling for a racial set-aside for medical cannabis licensing.[74] After a year's worth of proceedings, Judge Charles Schneider issued a summary judgment in favor of Greenleaf, holding that the statute was flawed and that the Ohio Legislature had not met its constitutional burden when crafting the legislative language.[75] Though the decision was initially appealed, the appellants eventually withdrew their cases and the decision remains standing today.

One significant issue raised in the Greenleaf litigation is the nature of the evidence given to support the existence of previous discrimination. The case files brought together the main sources influencing debate on the status of the medical use of cannabis while also showing the limited information on equity policies that Ohio legislators used when crafting H.B. 523. These exhibits include national reports on the racially disparate nature of cannabis enforcement, some specific research on state drug policies and enforcement, as well as all of the testimony and information considered by the legislature's research and drafting staff.[76] But while the state submitted a number of exhibits to demonstrate this history of discrimination, little evidence suggests that legislators actively considered it, and as such, Judge Schneider declined to consider this "post-enactment" justification. The court did consider the evidence of past marijuana arrests that the legislature had access to, finding that these studies did not provide the legislature with the supporting proof needed to sustain a finding of discrimination. The decision also compared the Ohio measure's language with that found in those of other states. Judge Schneider noted that no other state explicitly awards licenses on racial grounds, even if other licensing programs might award additional points for diverse ownership.[77]

The evidentiary record in the *Pharmacann* case shows that legislators focused much more on the economic details of the market that they were trying to set up, particularly on limiting its scope to tightly control supply and prevent diversion. The few exhibits that deal with equity centered around a set of articles collected from California regarding the incomplete implementation of city-level social equity licensing programs in Los Angeles and San Diego.[78] Also included in these exhibits are a series of reports on minority business enterprise plans, beginning with one that the state of Ohio produced in 2001 and including additional reports from Cincinnati and Cleveland. These reports highlight many of the common challenges in ensuring that government contracting funds and other resources reach an equitable share of the population, including outright racism and sexism, barriers created by public agency managers, perceptions of the "good old boy" network that excludes new participants, and barriers in gaining the necessary funding, including late payments by the state or primary contractors on the bids.[79] Few of these challenges would be unfamiliar to entrepreneurs of color working to get into the cannabis sector. Yet the *Pharmacann* case's summary judgment makes it difficult to imagine future racial set-asides in cannabis licensure or related areas—particularly those operating on a statewide basis—being able to withstand legal scrutiny. Especially with the conservative turn in US Supreme Court precedent on policies such as affirmative action, lower courts will likely be highly skeptical of licensing programs that specify quotas without specific evidence that supports the rationale and design of those preferences.

To this day, Ohio's approach in H. B. 523 also restricts the ability of people with previous cannabis convictions to enter the industry, despite additional educational and professional opportunities to expand the workforce in this growing field. Tasha Rountree, a registered caregiver and patient in Ohio, observed in a 2022 panel on the state's medical cannabis law that this restriction needlessly forces people into illegal activity who would just as easily—and might even prefer to—perform similar work in a legal and regulated context. As Rountree suggested, "What we need is an inclusive way to get people who used to sell weed or drugs into a legal market. They already know the market. We just need a way to give them a clean record so that they can participate in a legal arena. If this comes again with training, that is why we have schools like Grassroots University or the Cleveland Cannabis College, because we can teach you how to cultivate [and] what the rules and the regulations [are which will allow] more people who will participate in a legal arena versus an illegal arena."[80]

While Rountree's point echoes one which has been heard elsewhere in this book and highlights a barrier faced by many people around the United States, in making it she also alluded to some local efforts to build wealth for communities of color. Cleveland has hosted a Cannabis College, which has had over seven hundred graduates who have gone on to participate in Ohio's medical market or those nearby, such as in Michigan and Pennsylvania.[81] The school has partnered with former NBA basketball player Al Harrington, who has set a goal for his company, Viola, to help establish one hundred Black millionaires in the cannabis industry. Harrington explained that he wants "to bring awareness" to the idea that "the war on drugs was aimed towards [the Black] community, and they used cannabis as pretty much the main drug to continue to lock us up." For Harrington, mechanisms that continue to disproportionately keep Black people out of new legal markets perpetuate this injustice. As he puts it: "All this money being made now, we're not represented; we're not there. I feel like we pioneered this industry."[82]

A later twist that emerged with one of the litigants in the *PharmaCann* case demonstrates additional challenges for building equity among the cannabis industry's investors and owners. Harvest Grows—one of the two companies that received the licenses that prompted Greenleaf to challenge Ohio's diversity mandate—eventually received three licenses for growing and selling cannabis in the state of Ohio. By early 2019, however, Ohio had put a pause on these licenses after questions emerged about the ownership structure of Harvest Grows and its relationship with the larger national company sharing its name. As part of Harvest's application for its equity license, the company was required to certify that at least 51 percent of the company was owned by a racial minority. These documents list the owner of a local construction business, Ariana Kirkpatrick, as Harvest Grow's owner, though the paperwork also lists Steve White, the CEO of parent company Harvest Health, as an interested party in the license. State regulators questioned whether Kirkpatrick was in fact the beneficial owner when internal company documents showed that White was in fact Harvest Grow's CEO.[83] Harvest Health also faced questions about ownership and licensing in Pennsylvania's medical cannabis market after documents filed with that state showed the company with interests in as many as seven dispensary applications.[84]

A little more than a year later, in early 2020, regulators and Harvest announced that they had reached a settlement that would allow the company to keep its licenses. Under its terms, Harvest did not admit to misleading regulators, but did agree to pay the state Pharmacy Board $500,000 and ensure that Kirkpatrick retained ownership of the Ohio licenses for at least eighteen months.[85] Kirkpatrick would come to be the face of Harvest Health across Ohio, receiving accolades as an equity icon for the burgeoning cannabis industry.[86] Regulators have not taken any further action against Harvest's licenses in Ohio, but in little more than a year the national company was bought out by cannabis conglomerate Trulieve, now the fourth-largest cannabis company according to market data from *MJBizDaily*.[87]

The challenge of understanding who owns cannabis companies and who benefits from the wealth that is generated from them speaks to the nature of capital markets and the desire to utilize any avenue that represents a potential advantage, no matter the cost or propriety. The Harvest Health case is only one of several examples of wealthy cannabis companies working with local individuals to obscure ownership and evade regulatory oversight.[88] While regulators have a number of reasons to be interested in the ownership of cannabis licenses, the concern around social equity is foundational. If larger companies are working with social equity applicants to acquire beneficial licensing preferences, this misuse will remove genuine opportunities for those with legacy market experience or any other qualifying characteristic to enter the legal market. It also contributes to a larger consolidation within the industry and reduces the effectiveness of regulatory oversight aimed at preventing youth diversion and other public health concerns.

THE FUTURE OF CANNABIS IN OHIO

As mentioned before, Ohio voters still have not had an opportunity to revisit the topic of cannabis legalization, nor has the state legislature or other elected officials (conservative Republicans have recently held nearly all statewide offices) shown interest in changing the status quo of cannabis policy. This is despite northern neighbor Michigan's 2018 legalization,[89] as well as debates in other surrounding states, such as New York and Pennsylvania, which share similar demographics, particularly in the more rural areas of each state. Still, Ohio voters clearly support some form of legalization and activists sought to place a legalization initiative before voters in 2022, though the measure did not gain enough signatures before a deadline to make the ballot. After litigation by campaign organizers, Ohio legislators agreed on a path to place a legalization measure on the 2023 November ballot, giving Ohio voters the opportunity to once again consider the legal status of cannabis.[90]

At the same time, Ohio's effort to legalize cannabis under the control of a market monopoly reflects, despite its failure, the strong interest in investment opportunities and further market consolidation in the industry as it encounters remarkable growth. Many companies that have participated in Ohio's medical market are also invested in licensed businesses across the country,[91] and this highly lucrative oligopoly has spread as additional states have taken steps to liberalize access to cannabis within their borders. Ohio's experience also speaks to the potential consequences stemming from the paucity of data about or insight into successful regulatory regimes. These blind spots persist in many places even after Colorado and Washington struck the first blows against prohibition in 2012. While both of those states had experience with rudimentary medical cannabis regimes, Ohio had none of this experience—leaving its experience with the gambling industry as an obvious but ultimately flawed model to follow instead. Both supporters and opponents of legal cannabis revolted at the prospect of the kind of market consolidation that Issue 3's monopoly structure would have entailed.

Given this lack of direct experience, ResponsibleOhio's campaign is notable in that its messaging nevertheless reflected a larger shift in legalization campaign messaging toward highlighting the impacts of criminalization, particularly in communities of color. While Issue 3's promoters only addressed this in a somewhat oblique way, even the bare acknowledgment of this history provided an avenue for voices representing these communities to participate in the discussion. The importance of this shift was felt almost immediately with H. B. 523's social equity provisions. Although these failed to withstand challenge in court, the fact that the record demonstrates that the Ohio legislature included these provisions as an afterthought and with little tangible examples of equity policies that might work better suggests a possible path that states could take to avoid such failures in the future. The remainder of the case studies in this book will examine this effort to build a set of sustainable policies for regulators to consider when looking to address the historical impacts of criminalization and to extend these policies to other jurisdictions, including the federal government.

Lastly, Issue 3 also provides a negative example that helped mobilize many cannabis activists against the commercialization of cannabis, a threat that Jason Ortiz, a longtime cannabis activist who would later play a key role in legalization in Connecticut, highlighted when he looked back on the campaign. As Ortiz recalled, Issue 3 "would have given a percentage of the industry to very random people—Nicholas Lachey from 98 Degrees was like one of the prominent owners that was going to get his name written into the state constitution." Ortiz's reaction was typical among pro-legalization advocates who nevertheless disliked Issue 3's structure: "I remember [thinking] . . . this is not the legalization I was fighting for in college." For Ortiz, this discouragement translated directly into further action when he "asked [fellow activist Shaleen Title] where can we find better policy? Can we, you know, start to shift this conversation into a positive space? And she recommended that I join [a group called] Minority Cannabis Business Association, so that we could draft a law together and actually bring people of color to stakeholders to the table to explain exactly what it is that we want . . . [in order] to have a unifying language to express that in states throughout the country."[92] In a roundabout way, then, Ohio helped groups like this produce a model that could be exported elsewhere.

The new ballot initiative effort that Ohio voters will consider in 2023 reflects these developments in messaging and content that have occurred both in Ohio and in the larger movement for legalization in the eight years since Issue 3 failed. The text of the bill would dedicate 36 percent of the expected revenue from legalization to a "social equity and jobs" fund, which would support efforts to address the impacts of criminalization more broadly. Beyond simply abandoning the strict limits on licensing that the last plan would have included, the new initiative would also help those previously convicted of cannabis offenses gain opportunities in the market, for whom the proposed law dedicates fifty licenses.[93]

Ultimately, Ohio's 2015 ballot initiative had only scratched the surface of what has become a broader national conversation about who would benefit from legalization. While the policy landscape in states with any form of legalized cannabis before 2015 was characterized by tight regulation with a focus on avoiding either federal intervention and/or a popular backlash from perceived negative outcomes, legalization campaigns in future states—whether driven by the ballot initiative process or the legislature—would feature the racial legacy of criminalization more prominently while incorporating demands for equity access into the economic potential of legalization. Activists in Massachusetts, for example, were paying close attention to events in Ohio and consciously rejected efforts to give any advantage to larger suppliers even if it would cost their campaign politically and financially.[94]

As the next three chapters of this book will demonstrate, social equity has quickly developed into a rallying cry for legalization more broadly. It has thus effectively become a political requirement in most states that they must address social equity when considering legalization—or, as in places like Colorado, reforms to their extant regulatory regimes—if their new approach has any chance of moving forward.

NOTES

1. Associated Press, "Kent State Massacre: 50 Years Since Four Students Were Killed by the National Guard," *MarketWatch*, May 4, 2020, https://www.marketwatch

.com/story/kent-state-massacre-50-years-since-four-student-were-killed-by-the-national-guard-2020-05-04.

2. Margaret Ann Garmon, ed., "Legal Chronology May 5, 1970–January 4, 1979," Special Collections and Archives, Kent State University Libraries, https://www.library.kent.edu/special-collections-and-archives/legal-chronology-may-5-1970-january-4-1979.

3. Garmon, "Legal Chronology."

4. Marijuana Policies of Ohio Taskforce, *Marijuana and Ohio: Past, Present, Potential*, June 2015, 8.

5. Lewis Wallace, "Issue 3 Divided Taft Family," *WOSU*, November 5, 2015, https://news.wosu.org/news/2015-11-05/issue-3-divided-taft-family.

6. Marijuana Policies of Ohio Taskforce, *Marijuana and Ohio*, 2.

7. Sean Klammer, "Responsible Ohio: Successes, Failures, and the Future of Adult Marijuana Use in Ohio," *Ohio State Law Journal Furthermore* 79 (2018): 144.

8. Ballotpedia, "Ohio Marijuana Legalization Initiative, Issue 3 (2015)," https://ballotpedia.org/Ohio_Marijuana_Legalization_Initiative,_Issue_3_(2015).

9. Sam Tracy, "Stop Using a Superhero Mascot to Campaign for Marijuana Legalization in Ohio," petition, Change.org, 2015, https://www.change.org/p/yeson3ohio-stop-using-a-superhero-mascot-to-campaign-for-legalization-nomarijuanamascots.

10. Nushin Rashidian, "Is Responsible Ohio's Mascot Buddie 'The Joe Camel of Marijuana'?" *The Guardian*, October 21, 2015, https://www.theguardian.com/us-news/2015/oct/21/buddie-responsible-ohio-mascot-joe-camel-big-business.

11. The Ohio State University Moritz College of Law, "Cannabis on the Ballot: Lessons Learned from the Marijuana Reform Movement," YouTube video, October 27, 2022, https://www.youtube.com/watch?v=R8FQ8gHvoPM&ab_channel=TheOhioStateUniversityMoritzCollegeofLaw.

12. Journal Entry of Dismissal in *Pharmacann Ohio, LLC v. Ohio Department of Commerce*, 18AP-954 Ohio 10th App. (2021), https://fcdcfcjs.co.franklin.oh.us/CaseInformationOnline/imageLinkProcessor.pdf?coords=jBX5qMK4lyzo%2BekULz0dG%2FPnKFt5rM1jzkpv9Cg1HwK5UNdcMYcw3LOixQ1V%2B%2FxBsMQA8qS7T3IcqJhLxpFWcoLzP42a2e1sxt5SK%2FVPOe6kR77%2F0%2FXR%2FGv6vMBqbqzLY%2FdRgx2LUw%2BlBLFbEqBp2VJfrirf60f2woi7R8A5Ig0%3D.

13. Ohio Criminal Sentencing Commission, "History of Marijuana Laws in Ohio," 1, in Sara Andrews to Ohio Criminal Sentencing Commission Members and Advisory Committee, "Re: History of Marijuana Laws in Ohio and Supplemental Interesting Reports," memo, October 19, 2015, https://www.supremecourt.ohio.gov/Boards/Sentencing/resources/general/historyMarijuana.pdf.

14. Ohio Criminal Sentencing Commission, "History of Marijuana Laws in Ohio," 1.

15. Richard J. Bonnie and Charles H. Whitebread, *The Marihuana Conviction: A History of Marihuana Prohibition in the United States* (Charlottesville: University of Virginia Press, 1974), 215.

16. Ohio Legislative Service Commission, *Drug Abuse Control*, Staff Research Report No. 86, Columbus, Ohio, March 1967, 42, available in Andrews to Ohio Criminal Sentencing Commission.

17. Ohio Criminal Sentencing Commission, "History of Marijuana Laws in Ohio," 2.

18. Emily Dufton, *Grass Roots: The Rise and Fall and Rise of Marijuana in America* (New York: Basic Books, 2017), 211–12.

19. Ohio Criminal Sentencing Commission, "History of Marijuana Laws in Ohio," 2–4.

20. Ohio General Assembly, "An Act to Amend Section 2925.11 of the Revised Code to Eliminate the 'Medical Purposes' Affirmative Defense to the Offense of Possession of Marihuana," S. B. 2, 122nd General Assembly, http://archives.legislature.state.oh.us/bills.cfm?ID=122_SB_2.

21. The Ohio State University Moritz College of Law, "Where Do We Go from Here? Criminal Justice Reform in Ohio," YouTube video, January 6, 2022, https://youtu.be/2pzRVbzL1qs.

22. Ohio State University, "Where Do We Go from Here?"

23. Ohio General Assembly, "An Act to Amend Sections 109.42 . . . 5149.311 of the Revised Code and to Amend Section 3 of Am. Sub. H.B. 130 of the 127th General Assembly," Am. Sub. H. B. No. 86, 129th General Assembly, http://archives.legislature.state.oh.us/BillText129/129_HB_86_EN_N.pdf.

24. Marijuana Policies of Ohio Taskforce, *Marijuana and Ohio*, 75.

25. The Ohio State University Moritz College of Law, "Making the Case for Data-Driven Sentencing Reform in Ohio," YouTube video, May 25, 2022, https://youtu.be/cFcGRkUvrr8.

26. National Drug Intelligence Center, "Marijuana," *Ohio Drug Threat Assessment*, April 2001, https://www.justice.gov/archive/ndic/pubs/659/marijuan.htm.

27. Jon Gettman, *Marijuana in Ohio: Arrests, Usage, and Related Data*, Bulletin of Cannabis Reform, October 19 2009, 1–3, available as Exhibit 0E321-F20 in *Pharmacann Ohio, LLC v. Jacqueline T. Williams, et al.*, 17 CV 10962, Franklin County (OH) Court of Common Pleas, https://fcdcfcjs.co.franklin.oh.us/CaseInformationOnline/imageLinkProcessor.pdf?coords=RWTMrj%2FpXxxnvWeMIaP4Fc2M8tS8n7OK18L2LAK%2BiysF86xAMuDIBcjYaYUvJUapNloEODZbWuwCd5MOuQuE702oCENELdfn7Rv1AWy5piytM5NaDeKtThbRI6M%2BHShT9fNy%2FUzzRDbzCxI7IFkWTXgkHDwDVXVM%2F7FSqxLQtqU%3D.

28. Gettman, *Marijuana in Ohio*, 1.

29. Gettman, *Marijuana in Ohio*, 8.

30. ACLU of Ohio, *Overcharging, Overspending, Overlooking: Cuyahoga County's Costly War on Drugs* (Cleveland: ACLU of Ohio, 2011), 4.

31. Phyllis L. Crocker, "Appointed But (Nearly) Prevented from Serving: My Experiences as a Grand Jury Foreperson," *Ohio State Journal of Criminal Law* 2 (2004): 291–98, https://kb.osu.edu/bitstream/handle/1811/72870/OSJCL_V2N1_289.pdf.

32. Mona Lynch, *Selective Enforcement of Drug Laws in Cuyahoga County, Ohio: A Report on the Racial Effects of Geographic Disparities in Arrest Patterns*,

report, Citizens for a Safe and Fair Cleveland, 2008, 12–14, http://realneo.us/system/files/DrugArrestsCuyahoga.pdf.

33. ACLU of Ohio, *Overcharging, Overspending, Overlooking*, 2.

34. Gettman, *Marijuana in Ohio*, 3.

35. Jeffrey Robinson, *Who's* Really *in Prison for Marijuana?* (Washington, DC: Office of National Drug Control Policy, 2005), https://www.ojp.gov/sites/g/files/xyckuh241/files/media/document/whos_in_prison_for_marij.pdf.

36. Drug Policy Alliance, *Federal Byrne Grants: Drug War Funds Available for Drug Treatment* (New York: Drug Policy Alliance, September 2010), https://drugpolicy.org/sites/default/files/FactSheet_ByrneJAG_Sept.%202010.pdf.

37. Tom Hodson, "Ian James: Personal Passion for Marriage Equality," *WOUB*, June 18, 2013, https://woub.org/2013/06/18/ian-james-personal-passion-marriage-equality/.

38. Hodson, "Ian James."

39. Klammer, "Responsible Ohio," 141.

40. Ballotpedia, "Ohio Marijuana Legalization Initiative, Issue 3 (2015)," https://ballotpedia.org/Ohio_Marijuana_Legalization_Initiative,_Issue_3_(2015).

41. Ballotpedia, "Ohio Casino Approval and Tax Distribution, Amendment 3 (2009)," https://ballotpedia.org/Ohio_Casino_Approval_and_Tax_Distribution,_Amendment_3_(2009).

42. Klammer, "Responsible Ohio," 142.

43. Klammer, "Responsible Ohio," 143.

44. Ballotpedia, "Ohio Marijuana Legalization Initiative, Issue 3 (2015)."

45. Klammer, "Responsible Ohio," 143.

46. The Strategy Network, LLC, *Prospectus 2015: Ohio Marijuana Legalization and Regulation* (Columbus, OH: Strategy Network, 2014), 4, archived at https://www.documentcloud.org/documents/2096463-ro-prospectus.html.

47. Strategy Network, *Prospectus 2015*, 4. Emphases added.

48. Mark Naymik and Brent Larkin, "Campaign to Legalize Marijuana Use in Ohio Quietly Underway and Borrows Page from Casino Campaign," Cleveland.com, December 18, 2014, archived at https://perma.cc/5WL9-QCT5.

49. Klammer, "Responsible Ohio," 144.

50. Marijuana Policies of Ohio Taskforce, *Marijuana and Ohio*, 8.

51. Full text of Issue 3 is available from the Ohio Secretary of State's Office at "Issue 3: Grants a Monopoly for the Commercial Production and Sale of Marijuana for Recreational and Medicinal Purposes," 2015, https://www.ohiosos.gov/globalassets/ballotboard/2015/3-language.pdf.

52. Strategy Network, *Prospectus 2015*, 42.

53. Marijuana Policies of Ohio Taskforce, *Marijuana and Ohio*, 69–81.

54. Marijuana Policies of Ohio Taskforce, *Marijuana and Ohio*, 72–76.

55. Marijuana Policies of Ohio Taskforce, *Marijuana and Ohio*, 78.

56. ResponsibleOhio, "Legalizing Ohio: An Introduction," YouTube video, August 6, 2015, https://www.youtube.com/watch?v=bCOwAIvQM9Y; screenshot archived at https://web.archive.org/web/20151203172122/https://www.youtube.com/watch?v=bCOwAIvQM9Y.

57. YesOn3Ohio.com, "Last Chance to Make History," accessed November 3, 2015, archived at https://web.archive.org/web/20151103173155/http://yeson3ohio.com/.

58. Ohio State University, "Where Do We Go from Here?"

59. Barbara Gould et al., "Vote Yes on Issue 3," Ohio Secretary of State, 2015, https://www.sos.state.oh.us/globalassets/ballotboard/2015/3-for.pdf.

60. Eric Burkland et al., "Official Argument Against Issue 3," August 17, 2015, Ohio Secretary of State, https://www.sos.state.oh.us/globalassets/ballotboard/2015/3-against.pdf.

61. Alan Johnson, "Group Aims for 2015 Ballot Issue to Legalize Marijuana," *Columbus* (OH) *Dispatch*, December 19, 2014, archived at https://perma.cc/M69K-5RGF?type=image.

62. Keith Faber et al., "Vote YES on Issue 2: Protect Our Constitution from Monopoly Interests," Ohio Secretary of State, 2015, https://www.sos.state.oh.us/globalassets/ballotboard/2015/2-for.pdf.

63. Jackie Borchardt, "Libertarians, Green Party Oppose ResponsibleOhio's Marijuana Legalization Plan," Cleveland.com, May 29, 2015, https://www.cleveland.com/open/2015/05/libertarians_green_party_oppos.html; and Ballotpedia, "Ohio Initiated Monopolies Amendment, Issue 2 (2015)," note 15, https://ballotpedia.org/Ohio_Initiated_Monopolies_Amendment,_Issue_2_(2015)#cite_note-green-15.

64. Ohio Secretary of State, "2015 Official Election Results," https://www.ohiosos.gov/elections/election-results-and-data/2015-official-elections-results/.

65. Jo Ingles, "Longtime Lawmaker Who Sponsored Med Pot Bills Reacts to House Passed Plan," *Statehouse News Bureau*, May 11, 2016, https://www.statenews.org/government-politics/2016-05-11/longtime-lawmaker-who-sponsored-med-pot-bills-reacts-to-house-passed-plan.

66. Jessie Balmert, "Marijuana Policy Project Drops Ohio Medical Marijuana Initiative," *Cincinnati* (OH) *Enquirer*, May 28, 2016, https://www.cincinnati.com/story/news/politics/2016/05/28/marijuana-policy-project-drops-ohio-medical-marijuana-initiative/85083418/.

67. Ohio House of Representatives, Republican Newsroom, "Medical Marijuana Legislation Passes Ohio House," May 10, 2016, https://ohiohouse.gov/news/republican/medical-marijuana-legislation-passes-ohio-house-77939.

68. Klammer, "Responsible Ohio," 155.

69. The Ohio State University Moritz College of Law, "Ohio Cannabis Reform in Focus: Medical Marijuana," YouTube video, April 14, 2022, https://www.youtube.com/watch?v=6nJ3YwddjyE&ab_channel=TheOhioStateUniversityMoritzCollegeofLaw.

70. "Defendant Harvest Grows, LLC's Brief in Opposition," in *Pharmacann Ohio, LLC v. Jacqueline T. Williams, et al.*, 17 CV 10962, Franklin County (OH) Court of Common Pleas, September 14, 2018, 3–6, https://fcdcfcjs.co.franklin.oh.us/CaseInformationOnline/imageLinkProcessor.pdf?coords=iwFK2JLKokC9bTKnDIhvqy%2FdIhlAJt0e52Z9FEjXDo%2B12Z1myqYs9btFX%2BnYnXsia8lqfJySIi6L%2FwAXZQaqT1gsg%2FvlfxQ%2B8Ny7jSgUoHX5av

dupg4rp9LsX8eoz7T0YkcCPGVSRI2gQSKL8yloZZTk6BsAxRJ6k0YipD4M0Kw%3D.

71. *Pharmacann Ohio, LLC v. Ohio Department of Commerce*, 17 CV 10962, Franklin County (OH) Court of Common Pleas (2018), 2–4, https://fcdcfcjs.co.franklin.oh.us/CaseInformationOnline/imageLinkProcessor.pdf?coords=FVu%2F%2FDLIvfuxMC7HxgEcx%2Bn4GY33YqowI40W0qo4RynoIV3M3h6Ho4Ri9cmOYUBjoNR7eZOWk0cZsBi4xl9oNa3Wi4Tos2XAGucl%2BrYogNKgr%2BjEKk4CQmCNk5IUpWyAEkVdSt146bbgwhB00S%2F4wUc%2B7zk4tUetgQFJ%2BcHqLzw%3D.

72. "Defendant Harvest Grows, LLC's Brief in Opposition," 3–6.

73. *Pharmacann Ohio, LLC v. Ohio Department of Commerce*, 5–7.

74. Jackie Borchardt, "Ohio Medical Marijuana: 'Racial Quota' for Grow Licenses Ruled Unconstitutional," *Cincinnati* (OH) *Enquirer*, November 16, 2018, https://www.cincinnati.com/story/news/2018/11/16/ohio-medical-marijuana-court-finds-racial-quota-unconstitutional/2023545002/.

75. Borchardt, "Ohio Medical Marijuana."

76. Records for case no. 17 CV 010962 are available via the Franklin County Clerk of Court's website at https://fcdcfcjs.co.franklin.oh.us/CaseInformationOnline/caseSearch?7oZ5BTzAMXQc39QqOAVT.

77. *Pharmacann Ohio, LLC v. Ohio Department of Commerce*, 20–21.

78. *Pharmacann Ohio, LLC v. Ohio Department of Commerce*, 15–17.

79. "Defendant Harvest Grows, LLC's Brief in Opposition," 13–15.

80. Ohio State University, "Ohio Cannabis Reform in Focus: Medical Marijuana."

81. Sean McDonnell, "Cleveland School of Cannabis Starts Online Program for Home Growers of Marijuana," Cleveland.com, August 17, 2022, https://www.cleveland.com/business/2022/08/cleveland-school-of-cannabis-starts-online-program-for-home-growers-of-marijuana.html.

82. Jabari Young, "Former NBA Forward Al Harrington Wants to Make 100 Black Individuals Millionaires Through the Cannabis Business," *CNBC*, updated June 15, 2020, https://www.cnbc.com/2020/06/13/al-harrington-wants-to-make-100-black-people-millionaires-with-cannabis.html.

83. Sam Wood, "Harvest, the Big Marijuana Company on the Ropes in Pennsylvania, Accused of Misleading Ohio Regulators," *Philadelphia Inquirer*, July 31, 2019, https://www.inquirer.com/business/weed/harvest-health-cannabis-marijuana-pennsylvania-ohio-20190731.html.

84. Wood, "Harvest."

85. Andrew J. Tobias, "After Paying $500k in Settlement, Medical Marijuana Company Can Open Three Ohio Dispensaries," Cleveland.com, March 6, 2020, https://www.cleveland.com/open/2020/03/after-paying-500k-in-settlement-medical-marijuana-company-can-open-three-ohio-dispensaries.html.

86. Shanique Yates, "Meet the Only Black Woman Licensed to Grow, Dispense and Sell Cannabis in the State of Ohio," *AfroTech*, October 12, 2021, https://afrotech.com/first-black-cannabis-dispensary-owner-ohio.

87. David Abbott, "Trulieve Amazing: Trulieve Deal to Acquire Harvest Finalized, Creating Nationwide Cannabis Empire," *Tucson Weekly*, October 23, 2021, https:

//www.tucsonweekly.com/tucson/trulieve-amazing-trulieve-deal-to-acquire-harvest-finalized-creating-nationwide-cannabis-empire/Content?oid=31459407.

88. Jolene Hansen, “The Making of an MSO,” *Cannabis Business Times*, July 2022, https://www.cannabisbusinesstimes.com/article/standard-wellness-ohio-multistate-operator-cannabis-jared-maloof/.

89. Chastity Pratt and Alexandra Schmidt, “Michigan Approves Recreational Marijuana: What You Need to Know,” *Bridge Michigan*, November 6, 2018, https://www.bridgemi.com/michigan-government/michigan-approves-recreational-marijuana-what-you-need-know.

90. Maeve Walsh and Natalie Fahmy, “How Marijuana Could Become Legal in Ohio in 2023,” *NBC4i*, updated January 24, 2023, https://www.nbc4i.com/news/local-news/how-marijuana-could-become-legal-in-ohio-in-2023/.

91. Cynthia Fernandez, “Top Ranked Ohio Dispensary Applicants Largely Out-of-State MSOs,” *Grown In*, February 9, 2022, https://grownin.com/2022/02/09/top-ranked-ohio-dispensary-applicants-largely-out-of-state-msos/.

92. The Ohio State University Moritz College of Law, “Social Equity 2.0: Lessons from Recent State Developments,” YouTube video, December 13, 2021, https://www.youtube.com/watch?v=OAUYY6YpIZY.

93. Regulate Marijuana Like Alcohol, “Initiative Text,” 2021, https://justlikealcohol.com/initiative-text/.

94. Jeffrey Moyer, “Implementing Social Equity: Opportunities and Challenges from Marijuana Legalization in Massachusetts,” in *Stoneover: The Observed Lessons and Unanswered Questions of Cannabis Legalization*, ed. Nikolay Anguelov and Jeffrey Moyer (Lanham, MD: Lexington Books, 2022), 90–92.

Chapter 6

Massachusetts

A Vision for Social Equity

On September 21, 2016—little more than a month before voters in the state would go to the ballot box to decide whether to legalize recreational use of cannabis—Massachusetts State Police and National Guard officers, supplemented by a helicopter and multiple vehicles, swarmed the property of eighty-one-year-old Margaret Holcomb. A resident of the western Massachusetts town of Amherst, Holcomb was not home at the time, but officers still got what they were looking for: a single cannabis plant set aside in a raspberry patch, which Ms. Holcomb grew to help with pain from arthritis and glaucoma. Police went to several other households in the area as part of a larger effort by state law enforcement—funded by federal grants—to crack down on cannabis growing in "plain view" of a helicopter flying over residential property. Police made no arrests as part of this curtain-closing effort at criminalization, but the confiscations rattled local residents and led to speculation that these actions were part of a misguided attempt to draw attention to cannabis in the minds of voters ahead of the fall election. As local attorney and activist Michael Cutler put it, "We're seeing the last throes of police hostility to the changing laws. They're taking the position that if it's in plain view, it's somehow illegal."[1]

Only a few days later, cannabis activist and lawyer Shanel Lindsay stood outside the gold dome of the Massachusetts State House in downtown Boston and told her own story about being targeted for cannabis use even after the state had passed a decriminalization law:

> What should have been a normal traffic stop—the officer said I turned right on red when there was a sign—turned very sinister once he saw a small amount of cannabis in my open purse. The police officer ordered me out of my car, began to search my vehicle even though I told him no. After digging through my personal belongings, he found a small jar of cannabis and slapped the cuffs

> on me and threw me in the back of a police cruiser. I was sitting there terrified, watching my car get impounded, and as we are driving down to the station, I'm pleading with him and asking why he is arresting me and bringing me down to the courthouse. They told me that I was going to be brought down to the courthouse and arraigned, the same courthouse I had appeared in many times before [as a lawyer], but this time it was going to be as a criminal.[2]

Lindsay later was able to convince officers to weigh the cannabis they found on her, which was under the personal possession allowance provided by the decriminalization measure.[3] This permitted her to be released, but for many people of color without the legal training and social status she was able to leverage that day, these all-too-common stories have tragic—and permanent—consequences.

In my effort to understand and document the activism that inspires and pushes Americans of different backgrounds to organize for social equity in cannabis, I have been fortunate to bear witness to quite a lot of this work and even to participate myself as a resident of Massachusetts over the last several years. Still, as someone who is not native to the communities where much of the discriminatory enforcement and economic exclusion has been concentrated, I have been fortunate to have the opportunity to hear many locals share their experiences. As part of my research for this book, for example, I worked with the Big Hope Project—an organization led by a pair of brothers, social worker David Jean-Jacques and legacy market participant Harry Jean-Jacques. Harry's initial efforts to join the legalized cannabis market in Massachusetts were stymied by his criminal record,[4] and so the brothers instead founded Big Hope, where they worked to build collective success for individuals who had experience with cannabis criminalization.[5]

With the help of David and Harry, I was able to speak with a focus group of entrepreneurs looking to begin cannabis businesses in Massachusetts, often building on their work in the legacy market. The identifying characteristic they all shared was a personal experience with the War on Drugs. This focus group confirmed many of the things I have written about in this book and underlined the importance of making sure that stories such as theirs are part of the ongoing discussion around the economic opportunities that cannabis legalization should represent for communities of color.

For example, one such participant described a pernicious aspect of the criminalization era, noting that the police would "use marijuana as the excuse to get to other things." If arrested for cannabis, "you might get something on your record, but you don't get time [in prison] for that. But you are gonna get time for the gun [or] cocaine" that the police might also find as part of a search after the cannabis arrest. "So marijuana was . . . a way to get, you know, the thugs and stuff like that, because if they were smoking weed, and it was illegal, but they most likely had guns [or other illicit items then] . . . it wasn't about cannabis. . . . If you take that excuse away, what excuse do you have now to pull us over?"[6] Such views matter not only because of the insight they give into how criminalization used to work, but also because of the cautionary stance social equity activists should take to prevent whatever good they can achieve through one measure from simply being canceled out by another.

Even with the success of legalization in removing criminal penalties, the expanded focus on social equity did not open up opportunities for entrepreneurs with this activist's profile. While ballot organizers in Ohio had incorporated themes of social equity into their campaign narratives in 2015, the experience in Massachusetts just one year later involved a broader vision of equity that also entailed a much more complicated regulatory implementation. This experience helped to bring to light a number of additional challenges with social equity policies beyond those raised in Colorado's recreational market or Ohio's medical one, most of which have yet to be resolved to this day.

The Question 4 ballot measure and the campaign that accompanied it promised Massachusetts voters both additional money flowing into state coffers from legal cannabis sales as well as a solution for decades of criminalization that had brought down police enforcement on communities such as Brockton and Fall River or the Roxbury and Dorchester neighborhoods of Boston. Among other things, Question 4 established the Cannabis Control Commission, which spent its first years looking to understand the best way to regulate and diversify a growing industry while engaging with and providing opportunities to those from whom criminalization took so much. This chapter will look at some of these programs and examine their potential—and potential drawbacks—as well as highlight the continued importance of action at every level of government to reinforce and strengthen equity programs.

CANNABIS CRIMINALIZATION IN MASSACHUSETTS

Boston's Racial Dynamics

A combination of progressive ideals and hostility to people of color has marked much of Boston's history. This duality has been apparent in many areas of life, but it has been especially visible in infrastructure projects because of their tendency to reflect an idealistic vision of technocratic improvement for the future even as they physically disrupt people's real-world lives and environments in the present—often in quite unequal ways. Starting with the "Central Artery" project in the 1950s, Boston welcomed what was sold as a highway that would make moving around the city much easier. Its actual impact was much different: construction of the highway required the destruction of historical neighborhoods that were almost entirely inhabited by lower-income families. Much of this housing was also racially integrated—albeit because poor white and Black residents had few other options, not because they actively chose to live near each other.[7] When people who had been living in the now-razed neighborhoods found new housing, it tended to be in far more segregated areas than before—in part because public housing projects in the city were typically segregated and in part because practices such as redlining made it appreciably more difficult for Bostonians of color to find quality housing compared to their white counterparts.[8] By clearing these neighborhoods in the name of one kind of progress, then, Boston thus furthered the regressive racial segregation of its population. When courts ordered busing programs in the 1970s to integrate Boston schools in response to these conditions, they were met with often violent racial unrest.[9]

Little of this past would be obvious to today's visitor to Boston, however, as the much-reviled aboveground highway was eventually moved underground during Boston's "Big Dig" project, while the clashes over busing in the early 1970s have faded from view. Instead, they'd see the Rose Kennedy Greenway, the easily connected yet largely gentrified neighborhoods that abut the modern Orange Line, and the highly mobile young professional population that gives the city's politics its reputation for progressiveness.[10] Nevertheless, the scars of these mid-century moments still remain in the racial and cultural makeup of the city, such as the continued residential segregation and poverty that impacts neighborhoods like Roxbury and Dorchester.[11]

And those most directly affected by this past certainly do still see it. At least among Black people, Boston is known for being uniquely unwelcoming to Americans of color. A *Boston Globe* Spotlight report from 2018, for example, featured a poll of African Americans nationally in which 54 percent of respondents found Boston unwelcoming, far more than the next most unwelcoming city of Charlotte (at 38 percent).[12] Boston has always had a relatively small Black population compared to many large northeastern cities, and the city never developed a Black middle-class neighborhood like those seen in other major urban areas. The communities of color that did develop have also rarely seen their residents reach the higher echelons of business or politics. Boston's first Black mayor only took office in 2021, and even then it was because city council president Kim Janey succeeded departing mayor Marty Walsh when he left office early to take a job in the Biden administration. However, Janey was ultimately defeated—along with fellow Black city councilor Andrea Campbell—in the 2021 mayoral election by now-mayor Michelle Wu. Janey and Campbell combined to split much of the votes from historically Black communities, leading to a shut-out in the fall run-off election.[13]

Criminalization

Massachusetts first effectively criminalized the possession of cannabis in 1911 when the legislature authorized the search and seizure of cannabis and other substances such as morphine and opium, providing for a fine or six months in jail if anyone holding these was not a pharmacist or medical professional.[14] Three years later, the legislature further prohibited the production or transfer of cannabis and other regulated substances outside of medical provision, while also enhancing sentences for prohibited activities.[15] This push came at the same time that other eastern states, including Maine and New York, were increasing restrictions on access to various substances commonly known as patent medicines. It is notable, however, that this increased regulation was not apparently accompanied by widespread media attention to cannabis use or an association with crime or other social problems.[16] The fact that the laws and the medical literature in Massachusetts and surrounding states such as New York used the terms often favored by the era's medical authorities—"cannabis indica" and "hasheesh"[17]—rather than that commonly used to associate cannabis use with its Mexican roots in the American southwest, "marihuana," suggests instead that they viewed cannabis regulation primarily as a medical measure rather than a social control one.

The development in Massachusetts of either cannabis legislation specifically or narcotics legislation more generally is hard to track in the immediate period following this point, but what is clearly evident is that legislators were continually adding details and enhancing penalties in the decades that followed. According to a law review article from 1961, the state was one of the few which had not passed the Uniform Narcotic Drug Act, but it also notes that the Massachusetts laws were in some ways more strict than this national standard.[18] Though the legislature did not seem to reconsider the penalties or classification of cannabis during the 1960s, a Supreme Judicial Court (the state's highest court of appeal) decision shows its jurists grappling with similar questions about the nature of cannabis that policymakers and litigants in many other states were posing at roughly the same time.

In *Commonwealth v. Leis* (1967), the court was faced with a challenge stating that the legislature had not appropriately considered scientific evidence when classifying cannabis as a narcotic, violating the challengers' due process rights under the state constitution. The court considered many of the same health questions that had been posed in Colorado, Ohio, and elsewhere in the 1960s, especially regarding the likelihood that cannabis could cause psychotic breaks in some users. Nevertheless, it held that the legislature had appropriately used its regulatory power to prohibit cannabis, finding that the classification of cannabis as "mind-altering" was supported by evidence and thus fit the definition of a narcotic that the legislature had adopted. As a result, the decision rejected the due process claim that the petitioners had brought.[19]

With this question settled, cannabis remained criminalized in Massachusetts in the years that followed. By the turn of the twenty-first century, the state was consistently arresting thousands of people per year for various cannabis offenses, with a gradual increase in both possession and trafficking charges over the first decade of the 2000s. In 2008—the year that voters elected to decriminalize possession of less than an ounce of cannabis—state and local law enforcement reported at least 5,595 arrests for possession and 1,038 arrests for either sales or manufacturing. A later analysis revealed that not all arrests were consistently reported by local law enforcement, indicating that these figures might be an undercount. After this year, possession arrests declined sharply to less than 15 percent of the previous total, while the level of more serious charges remained consistent.[20]

The arrest records of the Boston Police Department demonstrate clear racial disparities in cannabis enforcement. Examining the nearly 25,000 cannabis-related arrests that city police made from 2000–2018, over two-thirds involved a Black resident—despite the fact that Black people comprise slightly less than a quarter of the city's population.[21] These arrests were concentrated in the primarily Black neighborhoods of Dorchester and Mattapan and imposed a heavy cost on residents. One participant in the regulatory process in Massachusetts described this impact to me with a theoretical example:

> Guys working at the hotel downtown, they go to Boston English High School. They have to take care of the family, go work a full day until midnight. And they leave and they have a joint in their pocket to help them relax and here comes a [police officer] and snags them off the street, presto, [they] got a record [which] kept them from securing housing [or] employment. And if [they] went to college [they wouldn't be able to study] health education or any of the sciences [if they] had a criminal record.[22]

Decriminalization

In the early twentieth century, Massachusetts was an important contributor to the creation of a mechanism that laid the groundwork for cannabis legalization itself—the ballot initiative. As part of the progressive political movement that swept the country in the first decades of the last century, many state constitutions adopted this political tool, which remains a key element of

American political culture to this day. Initiatives can be used by the powerless as well as the powerful; they can challenge the existing political order as well as attempt to solidify it.

In Massachusetts, the creation of the initiative power was part of a larger constitutional reordering that represented a political renegotiating of the status quo from the state's traditional power centers in Anglican town meetings across the state to the immigrant and largely Catholic newer populations.[23] The "initiative and petition" power that the state's 1917–1918 constitutional convention introduced allowed voters to deliver a petition to the state government to change, amend, or negate laws passed by the legislature. As in other states that passed similar measures during this period, this gave citizens a unique degree of direct democratic control over the local and state agencies of government—although in Massachusetts, the legislature itself retained the power to amend or even cancel voter-passed initiatives. Unlike in Colorado and Ohio, voters in Massachusetts also did not have the power to initiate constitutional amendments themselves, which limited the capacity for activist groups to lock in their desired policy changes. While many of the warnings that people voiced at the time regarding the challenges that direct democracy would present did prove prescient—especially the ease with which the ballot initiative might be coopted by powerful forces to solidify their power[24]—it has also demonstrated its continuing utility as a method to accomplish social and political reform.

Cannabis legalization is strong evidence of this utility, as already seen in this book's earlier chapter on Colorado, as well as the long string of other successful cannabis ballot measures stretching back to California's medical initiative in the mid-1990s. In Massachusetts, where the legacies of alcohol prohibition and Puritan culture are still prevalent outside the I-495 belt around Boston, challenges to the existing order of cannabis criminalization had long fallen on deaf ears. Still, just because the Commonwealth's Beacon Hill power elites wished otherwise didn't mean that the residents of the state as a whole didn't desire change. This was clearly demonstrated in the 2008 ballot initiative that decriminalized cannabis in the Commonwealth.

This initiative loosened criminal sanctions on cannabis sale and possession, most notably by lessening the offense of possession to an ordinance violation with a $100 fine, which would be non-arrestable and would not show up on any offender's permanent record.[25] Several states had already hosted decriminalization ballot measures by this point with mixed success—voters had rejected earlier efforts in Washington state, Oregon, and Alaska, but in 2002, voters in Arizona had approved modest reductions in penalties. Even this approach was a concession to avoid the perception that the initiative would "legalize" cannabis, a conversation that neither Massachusetts nor any other state at that point was ready to have.

One indication of this is that the state's otherwise progressive governor Deval Patrick opposed decriminalization, as did the editorial board of the *Boston Globe*.[26] Despite this elite signaling, along with efforts by much of the law enforcement community and some of their close colleagues in the public health sector to campaign against it, the initiative proved nearly as popular as President Barack Obama's first election, garnering over 62 percent of the vote in 2008.[27] The durability of the popular movement to challenge the existing order of criminalization would then be demonstrated four years later when a similar effort to legalize the medical use of cannabis easily passed.[28]

If the twin successes in 2008 and 2012 suggested that the majority of Massachusetts voters were already skeptical of the War on Drugs–style criminalized approach to cannabis regulation that had long ruled the day, a major 2011 scandal likely cemented those beliefs and perhaps extended their influence. That year brought to the public eye the actions of two chemists in state police labs, Sonja Farak and Annie Dookhan, who were later convicted of tampering with and ingesting lab samples from tens of thousands of drug evidence exhibits to feed their own addictions.[29] As bad as their crimes were, the state's response to them demonstrates a shocking institutional indifference to the real-life impacts of drug prosecutions on low-income communities, as law enforcement and prosecutors moved to make it difficult for those impacted to resolve their convictions.[30]

An investigation by the state Supreme Judicial Court later ordered Attorney General Maura Healey's office to work with local prosecutors to identify and dismiss cases against tens of thousands of Massachusetts residents who had collectively served untold years in prison as a result of Farak's and Dookhan's actions.[31] The class action case that forced these dismissals was brought by Nicole Westcott, a central Massachusetts woman who, while dealing with addiction, experienced criminal stigmatization and the threat of jail in response to charges that resulted in probation. During the ensuing litigation against the state, Westcott described her experience: "I turned my life around, despite—not because of—the way the state punished me for suffering from an addiction. In 2014, at the very same time I was trying to turn my life around, the state was withholding evidence that could have helped me. I just want them to be held accountable just as I was held accountable."[32]

A later Netflix documentary about the case, *How to Fix a Drug Scandal* (2020), demonstrates compelling evidence of denial and official protection that have typified the retreat from the War on Drugs.[33] By 2022, over 61,000 convictions had been vacated by the state's highest court, while the state had agreed to pay $14 million to a class of 31,000 claimants who were impacted by this fraud; this was in addition to the nearly $30 million the state has spent to investigate the cases.[34] Massachusetts eventually closed the drug lab where both Farak and Dookhan had worked, but the questions raised by their misconduct could possibly impact a larger universe of up to 250,000 drug convictions. Reformist prosecutor Rachael Rollins supported the effort to dismiss all of these convictions during her time as Suffolk County district attorney, and court cases remain ongoing in the attempt to uncover the totality of this grave miscarriage of justice.[35]

The larger scandal and the cases that were eventually dismissed as a result of it have overshadowed the larger challenge that Massachusetts has experienced with expungements, however. Legislators working on cannabis reform declined to address expungement in the wake of the voter-passed cannabis law in 2017 (discussed below), instead folding this effort into a larger criminal justice reform package that passed in 2018.[36] These reforms have largely been panned as failures, however, as the criteria for expungement was highly limited and the burden of obtaining the relevant records, preparing the paperwork, and submitting an application for judicial review fell on those with previous eligible convictions. In the first six months after the law became effective in early 2019, the state received 2,186 petitions for relief, of which only 352 were approved by judges. Only 17 of these expungements were related to cannabis offenses, a tiny fraction of the tens of thousands of charges that should be eligible for relief.[37] Further reforms announced in 2022 as part of the legislative revision of the state's cannabis law made it easier to receive relief for cannabis convictions by removing the requirement for judicial discretion to grant expungement, though legislators still declined to embrace an automatic expungement process as seen in other states such as Illinois and New York.[38]

ENVISIONING SOCIAL EQUITY IN QUESTION 4

The campaign to legalize recreational adult possession and sales of cannabis in Massachusetts that came in 2016 was different than the earlier ballot initiatives. Building on recent successes in Colorado and Washington, the movement for cannabis legalization was still in its early days, with public attention focused on headlines out of Denver as the nation's first pot shops opened their doors in 2014. This felt very real to many of the younger students and professionals who lived in and around Boston, and a campaign to bring this policy change to as many states as possible quickly emerged. Starting in 2015, two rivaling ballot initiative campaigns began to emerge that would try to create the structure of what legalization could look like in the Commonwealth. Each of these efforts had their origins in the larger split in the cannabis legalization movement previously discussed in chapter 3, though Massachusetts's specific experience diverged from how those divisions took hold elsewhere in ways that would greatly influence future efforts to legalize cannabis.

MassNORML, the state branch of the older and more libertarian-flavored national cannabis advocacy group which for many years has organized events on the Boston Common—most notably every year on April 20—was the center of one of those efforts. The other was organized by the Marijuana Policy Project, the group which had split from NORML over disputes about philosophy and strategy, and which had earlier helped organize initiatives on legalization in other states, including Colorado's 2012 effort. This second group of organizers also included participants in the emerging market for medical cannabis. For a short period of time, legalization advocates worried that both initiatives would fight for ballot access, possibly confusing voters and imperiling final passage of either. The initiative organizers later reached a compromise, however, with both efforts largely combined into what became Question 4 on the 2016 ballot, which leaned away from the more libertarian impulses of some advocates.

Cannabis equity activist Shaleen Title, a member of the ballot initiative drafting committee, took the lead internally—and later in public during the ballot campaign that followed—in pressing the case that cannabis legalization should be a vehicle for social and economic equity in the communities where cannabis criminalization had traditionally been a vehicle for state oppression and exclusion.[39] Recognition and discussion of this reality had largely been sidelined in the legalization movement until then, with the exception of the failed 2015 Ohio Issue 3 campaign discussed in chapter 5. While on the drafting committee for Question 4, however, Title (and others) advocated for greater market access for those previously criminalized, and against licensing priorities for those in the medical cannabis industry—stances which notably led some medical participants in the drafting process to leave the effort and remain neutral or even oppose Question 4.[40] These opponents claimed that the measure would undermine the regulatory system they had complied with and pointed to Question 4's relaxed approach to local regulation as well as the allowance for home-grown cannabis.[41] Title largely won the day, however, and was later appointed to the Cannabis Control Commission, where she ended up serving for over four years as a champion for social equity policies, an effort in which she often found herself on the losing end of 4–1 votes when she felt that the commission wasn't living up to Question 4's promises of improved consumer access and social equity.[42]

The polarization in the Question 4 drafting committee room reflected a larger divide that had emerged in Massachusetts and other jurisdictions between the established medical cannabis industry and the expanded network of potential providers who hoped to supply recreational customers. One participant explained, however, that the conflict was a side effect of what was ultimately a useful process: "The real benefit was having everybody in the same room, so that all of the activists, everybody who supported reform, could see where the tension was, and see the perspectives from the other side, of stakeholders. . . . It helped everybody understand the constraints we were under, with what we could do under the law, and not do with a single piece of legislation."[43]

In Massachusetts, the ballot measure to legalize the medical use of cannabis in 2012 had been narrowly drafted to license a select group of well-resourced individuals to provide patients with the cannabis they needed. Under this law, the state Department of Public Health had jurisdiction to regulate the market, which resulted in a licensing process that was slower and lacked the transparency that many activists had hoped for. Additionally, providers were required to be nonprofits that were vertically integrated, meaning that they had to both produce and sell their product, a requirement that vastly increased the capital investments and excluded participation from anyone who might have the "taint" of having previous participation with the legacy market.[44]

The result of this earlier policy design choice was that many medical providers had different perspectives concerning the best way to establish a market compared to the larger cannabis community, both in Massachusetts and elsewhere—perspectives which coincided with their own incentives to maintain market share. For example, existing medical providers often argued that they should have preferences or even exclusivity in emerging recreational markets because their expertise and infrastructure would guarantee that recreational consumers would have access to cannabis when recreational sales began, while also ensuring compliance with the highly regulated environment and reducing potential youth use and exposure.[45] In other states such as Illinois, regulators went a step further and sought to exclude individuals from growing small amounts of cannabis at home; in cases where such exclusions weren't included in legalization ballot measures, medical providers actively opposed recreational legalization.[46]

Protecting existing markets has even sometimes driven non-cannabis suppliers to oppose legalization. For example, Insys Therapeutics—best known for the conviction of a number of its top executives in a fraud case related to selling an addictive opioid[47]—contributed $500,000 in 2016 to a group opposing cannabis legalization in Arizona, admitting in investor filings that the competition from legal sales of cannabis might hurt its efforts to sell a synthetic THC product known as Syndros that it developed to treat loss of appetite and nausea.[48] The political and economic interests of medical providers, cannabis patients, and those who wanted to have recreational access to the substance clearly diverged on such questions, a split that would become fully apparent in Massachusetts after legalization passed.

The movement for social equity in cannabis is of course much larger than Shaleen Title's efforts—she was often joined on the drafting committee of Question 4 by Shanel Lindsay and many other members who all had some personal or professional experience with the failures of drug prohibition. The campaign for Question 4 in 2016 also represented a coalition of interests, including advocates for racial and social justice, medical cannabis providers who wanted to expand to a new market, young professionals in and around the state's urban cores who wanted to enact a vision of the tolerance seen in states like Colorado, and voters who simply recognized the large toll that the War on Drugs and the hypocrisy of the efforts to implement it had placed on many thousands of lives—especially the lives of people of color.[49] Even still, the campaign's messaging often reflected the consistent themes of regulation and taxes found in previous states' efforts, as seen in one pre-election advertisement: "I was a Boston PD cop and now as a professor, I believe Yes on 4 is a smart choice to protect families. . . . [It] requires strict product packaging and bans advertising directed towards kids. Question 4 bans consuming marijuana in public. It will tax and regulate marijuana for adults 21 and over, bringing millions in revenue for schools or law enforcement."[50]

Despite examples such as this, a notable part of the campaign for Question 4 also centered on racial disparities in cannabis enforcement. For example, a pre-election report from the Massachusetts ACLU showed that Black residents were at least four times as likely as white residents to be arrested for cannabis possession, despite usage rates that were relatively equivalent across racial groups.[51] Previous campaigns had discussed cannabis arrests in a general way, but supporters of Question 4 highlighted the linkage to specific communities and engaged in more explicit discussion of the racial disparities in enforcement—such as Shanel Lindsay's story, as recounted in the opening to this chapter—rather than pushing them aside. As one campaign official explained, this focus augmented earlier strategies rather than replacing them: "Our overall message was the failure of prohibition. Part of that message was the problem that prohibition had caused certain communities [to be] disproportionately impact[ed]. That was not our lead message [but] it was always a component of our messaging."[52]

Question 4 also attracted a broad coalition against it, including a special committee of the state legislature that issued a report opposing legalization, and a nearly universal slate of opposition by statewide elected officials, including both governor Charlie Baker and Boston mayor Marty Walsh.[53] One of the more notable objections that the opposition raised was the threat that ubiquitous cannabis stores might pose in local neighborhoods, a message brought home in one memorable ad that showed a mom with her daughter walking past sweets in store windows—implied to be cannabis edibles—before being surprised to see her son come out of a dispensary. The narrator darkly warns: "Question 4 would allow thousands of pot shops and marijuana operators throughout Massachusetts neighborhoods like yours. Shops that sell pot edibles that look like candy with high-potency marijuana. In pro-pot states, incidents of drugged driving and fatal car accidents are up. More dispensaries than McDonalds and Starbucks combined. Higher potency, dangerous drivers."[54] The larger conversation in Massachusetts often centered on the fears about youth use that ads like this brought up, despite the fact that social equity was raised as a secondary issue from time to time.

THE CANNABIS CONTROL COMMISSION

Question 4 did pass, but it showed a much narrower coalition in support of legalization—less than 54 percent of voters were in favor of it—than did previous cannabis liberalization efforts in the state.[55] This suggested that despite the measure's passage, the path to implementation would be a politically complex one. Significant doubts remained, including about how promises of social equity made during the initiative campaign would be realized and about how to find the right degree of local control that would allow the new industry to flourish. Minority communities in particular were skeptical of the promise of social equity and voted accordingly. In the city of Boston itself, the four wards in which Black residents make up an absolute majority and collectively represent more than half of the city's total Black population (centered in Roxbury and Dorchester) each voted for Question 4 at a lesser proportion than voters citywide did. In Ward 18, Question 4 passed with only 53 percent of the vote, with Black residents making up a slight majority of residents.[56]

After voters passed legalization in November 2016, previously ambivalent legislators opted to weigh in on the specifics of regulation, initially choosing to delay enactment of the voter-passed question and later amending the language in the summer of 2017.[57] This was exactly the fear of previous initiative organizers in Colorado and Ohio, where campaigns had proposed constitutional amendments in order to limit the jurisdiction legislators would have to potentially limit the ensuing market.[58] While the initial ballot measure had a three-member commission appointed by the state treasurer to oversee regulation and licensing, the expanded framework for implementation that legislators adopted increased the commission to five members and split appointment powers between a larger group of statewide office holders. One of these members (jointly appointed by the attorney general, treasurer, and governor) was mandated to have a background in "legal, policy and social justice issues related to a regulated industry."[59]

While the reforms enacted by the legislature—including expanded local control measures giving town and city officials more authority over zoning in their jurisdictions—were panned by many legalization supporters,[60] a small group of legislators was successful in adding language that enhanced the mandates governing the Cannabis Control Commission's (CCC) obligations to foster social equity in the new regulated market. These mandates first required a study of whether "there is evidence of discrimination or barriers to entry in the regulated marijuana industry." If the CCC found that there was, they had to "adopt diversity licensing goals that provide meaningful participation of communities disproportionately affected by cannabis prohibition and enforcement, including minority business enterprises, women business enterprises and veteran business enterprises." The CCC was also required to "develop training programs designed and implemented to achieve meaningful participation by minority persons, women, and veterans," which would cover things such as recruitment strategies and workforce training.[61] Although these guidelines could prove ephemeral depending on who was involved in running the CCC, social equity gained an important ally when former Question 4 drafter and legalization activist Shaleen Title was appointed to the "social equity" seat on the CCC.

Title faced a formidable task in establishing an accessible regulated market—the other four commissioners had all opposed Question 4 when it was on the ballot.[62] As the CCC first began drafting regulations for the recreational market in Massachusetts and then revised them over the first years of legalization, however, the vision for what social equity policies would entail became clear. Title and her fellow commissioners benefited from the fact that many of the state's political actors, including the legislature and the statewide elected officials responsible for appointing the CCC, gave the topic a wide berth. The legislature had also given the CCC a broad yet vague agenda to advance equity, meaning there was ample room for innovation. The CCC did not have unlimited budgetary authority—so they could not use cannabis tax revenue to fund incentives to help develop the market—but their open mandate allowed Title to propose a series of programmatic initiatives that sought to build opportunities for those who had experienced criminalization to enter the market. The other commissioners did not always agree with Title, but she sometimes found allies, including CCC Chair Steve Hoffman and fellow commissioner Britta McBride, who sought to enforce the letter of the equity regulations that they approved.

Speaking in early 2018, Title explained that one of the CCC's most important jobs was "to ensure disproportionately impacted communities have an opportunity to be part of [legalization]. In implementing that, we've been first focused on identifying those communities based on arrest rates and economic data, and second, how do we help provide a fair opportunity to people from those communities. So far we've been focused on community outreach and technical assistance with the application, including [keeping fees low]." She talked about the importance of flexibility, as well: "Because we are the first state to do this, it is very much expected that there will be tweaks that will need to be made."[63]

As Title observed, one of the CCC's main challenges in the effort to build social equity policies was to define what constituted an "area of disproportionate impact" as outlined by the legislature. Most people perceived that arrests for drugs—like many indicators of poverty and institutional neglect—were concentrated in communities of color, including both specific neighborhoods in Boston as well as towns and cities across the state. Still, determining the actual indicators that officials would use to designate these areas has proved difficult, because of both disagreements about what data is most relevant and systematic limitations in the data that is even available.

The CCC first sought to hire a researcher to confront this challenge in early 2018, eventually contracting with noted criminologist and cannabis activist Jon Gettman to help inform selection of the qualifying areas. Gettman's analysis combined census-derived economic indicators such as unemployment and poverty along with criminal justice statistics from the National Incident-Based Reporting System (NIBRS) and local police agencies to identify the towns where both poverty and criminalization were concentrated in order to determine which localities had been most impacted by the War on Drugs.[64] Ultimately, Gettman ranked locales across the state by six different indicators, developing a list that the CCC used to select twenty-nine towns and cities, along with specific census tracts in Boston, Springfield, Worcester, and Lowell.[65]

The selection of these specific areas has been the subject of a great deal of criticism. Notably, Gettman did not include a race category in his analysis, even though the CCC's equity program was specifically envisioned to help address racial disparities in arrests that had impacted individuals and communities of color. As such, while Gettman's analysis did bring in a wide array of both urban areas with residents of color, including Brockton, Chelsea, and Randolph, as well as many of the long-underinvested-in "Gateway" cities such as Fall River, Worcester, and Haverhill, some of the other places that were included did not have diverse populations, leading to concerns that the data sources examined by Gettman and accepted by the CCC were incomplete.[66] Towns such as Monson, a small locality near Springfield, and Spencer, located in Worcester County, had white populations of over 97 percent, meaning their residents of color numbered fewer than 300 each.[67] One notable absence in the CCC's initial selections was the city of Lawrence, which Gettman excluded from his analysis because the city's police force did not submit data to the NIBRS dataset.[68]

In 2021, the CCC revisited their initial designations. This effort began with a follow-up data search by a University of Massachusetts team, who replaced Gettman's six indicators with four indicators, which included poverty, drug arrests, and also the racial makeup of the community. This later effort classified the state's localities into tiers of impact, with many of the places that had previously been defined as areas of disproportionate impact falling out of the top ranking. This work was more thorough and clearly informed by the criticism of Gettman's approach. Although Lawrence still was not included in the final ranking due to the missing data issue, the study's accompanying narrative report clearly identified that rationale and the potential impact on the city. Likewise, the analysis's authors also excluded some municipalities that were predominantly seasonal or college towns, as many of the students who might have been represented in the arrest data would not be the intended target of this policy.[69]

Even as the dispute over the CCC's community designations took off, its plan to provide for social equity in the recreational market had taken shape by mid-2018. It centered on three distinct efforts. The two most public were the Social Equity Program, a technical assistance and business incubator program, and the Economic Empowerment (EE) license category, which the CCC developed to give an advantage to license applicants with certain characteristics. The eligibility criteria for each program are somewhat distinct, but both share a common theme: residence in towns and cities that are defined as racially diverse and lower income or having a personal connection with the War on Drugs (either individually or through a close family member).[70]

For participants, equity programs were supposed to be an opportunity for the state to redress previous policy harms. One EE applicant stated that "Social Equity to me means a sincere, concerted effort to correct wrongs in areas of past societal and systemic inequities in all areas of our lives, especially in regard to economic opportunities and the criminal justice system, by affording support for those who have been impacted by past inequities so that they receive the opportunities that those with more 'privilege' take for granted."[71] Others framed the equity program in terms of one that should provide economic opportunities to individuals as an essential step in promoting community development. As one participant put it: "In order for economic opportunity to reach more marginalized areas, equity and investment needs to be put in the hands of those who have lived in and serviced the community for many years. A minority-owned business is more likely to employ other at-risk classes and engage in initiatives that directly benefit the community and ensure that money invested in the neighborhood stays in the neighborhood and has the opportunity to lift the financial possibilities of many instead of just a select few."[72]

The first cohort of the Social Equity Program launched in 2018 and featured an array of programming that prepared participants for complying with regulations issued by the commission, understanding business practices like marketing and acquiring financing, and ensuring that they had a business plan. The CCC has since hosted an additional two cohorts of participants, bringing together individuals with experience in the legacy market with entrepreneurs who have not previously considered opening a cannabis business. Many participants appreciated the design of the materials and the effort put in by the organizers, but it became clear by the later iterations of the program that some key needs of participants, such as financing, were the most important for ensuring that those in the program would be successful once they started their businesses—and that efforts which did not address these needs would ultimately fall short.[73]

The CCC intended that many of the Social Equity Program participants, along with the broader universe of EE license applicants, would be able to successfully compete for licenses on an equal footing with other applicants, including those that had previously organized as vertically integrated nonprofits to comply with the state's medical market regulations. Putting its faith in the power of programmatic efforts to change the industry, the CCC chose not to provide specific license preferences in the early years of the market.[74] These hopes proved unrealistic, however, as most EE participants struggled to overcome the burden of regulatory compliance, obtain financing for their efforts, and win local government approval. The last two issues proved most challenging—while many EE licensees were able to get approval from the CCC itself, few were able to open their doors to customers even five years after legalization began.[75] The financial challenge was well known to advocates of the initial ballot initiative. As one explained: "A lot of kinds of people who are adversely impacted, they don't have the capital to open up a conservation facility. So how can we get these folks who may not be able to get private banking to attract private wealth to finance them?"[76]

The CCC's third effort to fulfill its social equity mandate garnered less attention than the first two programs, but it has been important in shaping the market. Under the CCC's required "Positive Impact Plans," all license applicants must discuss how their business contributes to social equity. Critics have derided the plans as often being rudimentary and lacking in substance. A 2019 review of them, for example, found that many lacked a basic understanding of social equity and measures for accountability. Only 21 percent of the examined plans met all five of the themes that CCC researchers identified as being essential.[77] During the first year of operation, however, the agency revisited the requirements for such plans during CCC meetings and issued additional guidance, while also warning a number of licensees that they needed to make their impact plans more detailed. In several instances, the CCC placed conditions on yearly license renewal approvals related to revising these plans.[78]

Despite its many shortcomings, the CCC has generally tried to implement policies that will advance social equity and has shown a willingness to revisit past missteps. This is partly due to the efforts of a small but persistent group of activists who believe that the recreational market should not be dominated by medical providers. These activists, as well as many prospective licensees, routinely showed up at CCC meetings in the early months of the agency's work. They included Grant Ellis, an advocate for medical patients who came to be known for his Facebook Live broadcasting of CCC meetings as well as his thorough social media posts about developments in the regulated market.[79] A number of other individuals and groups were vocal critics of agency decisions, often leading to boisterous and long public meetings and calls for accountability that forced the members of the CCC to carefully consider many of their decisions. These groups included MassNORML, which had originally advocated for a different approach to regulation, as well as the Massachusetts Recreational Consumer Council, which advocated both for consumers and for the inclusion of participants with legacy market experience.[80] Later groups of Social Equity Program participants banded together to collaborate on business incubators and collaborations, such as the Big Hope Project fellowship created by Harry and David Jean-Jacques.[81]

By 2022, the state legislature had also received pressure from industry participants, equity activists, and those at the CCC to revisit the initial legalization law in order to address a number of technical and substantive issues. State senator Sonia Chang Diaz led a joint committee of legislators who examined the industry, including the authority of the CCC to regulate the "host-community agreements" that industry participants were required to sign with local towns, as well as the gaps in social equity policy that the CCC was unable to address through programmatic efforts. Building on the efforts of states such as Illinois (see chapter 7), the Massachusetts legislature eventually created a Cannabis Social Equity Trust Fund consisting of 15 percent of the revenue that the state would receive from cannabis taxes, estimated to be $20 million annually. This money would be directed by a board appointed in early 2023, and it is yet unclear where any funds that are set aside will be spent.

CAMBRIDGE: BEYOND TECHNICAL ASSISTANCE

A critical test of the prospect for social equity in regulated cannabis markets emerged in the infancy of Massachusetts's licensing program. Many of the more progressive jurisdictions in the Commonwealth, including western localities like Northampton, had charged ahead when the CCC began issuing its first retail sales licenses.[82] When the initial rush of availability and excitement that came after the first stores opened in mid-2018 started to ebb, however, the full consequences of some of the choices that policymakers made when developing the legal framework for recreational cannabis became clear.

Cannabis licensing in many smaller towns and cities—as well as in some bigger and more progressive population centers in and around Boston—was locked in a struggle between cautious local officials and activists who wanted to ensure that the recreational market that emerged was fully accessible to social equity participants. Local officials were still sensitive to the concerns of their electorate, which was often different from and more conservative than the larger collective of voters that had approved Question 4. In cities like Boston, there were worries that the distance requirements that the voter-approved law had put into place would limit opportunities for equity applicants or force them to compete against each other for limited geographic space.[83] Such limited opportunities prompted one participant to express frustration about sometimes having to compete even against fellow equity license applicants: "We want to compete. We don't want to kill each other and slice each other's throats. We want to compete like the dispensaries are able to."[84]

Meanwhile, the small network of medical providers that dominated the market in Massachusetts had by 2017 organized itself into a group called the Commonwealth Dispensary Association. As mentioned earlier, many of the suppliers of medical cannabis had remained neutral on adult-use legalization in 2016, but they actively participated in policy efforts to shape the new market. Even as state officials did not give in to demands for market preference and exclusion, many medical cannabis businesses were finding more receptive audiences on the local level. State lawmakers had provided a license conversion option for medical providers, but the CCC showed no interest in creating any further preferences for medical companies, in no small part due to Commissioner Title's opposition to the idea. Lawmakers had elected to shift regulation of these companies from the Department of Public Health to the CCC, a process that would take years. Still, the relationships that medical providers had established on the local level would themselves prove a key asset in getting a head start to sell to recreational consumers, as many of the towns and cities that had already approved medical facilities granted local approval for conversion.[85]

The unpredictable consequences of Massachusetts lawmakers' decision to grant local authorities a great deal of discretion over the awarding of licenses and the ways in which local cannabis businesses could operate were also vividly illustrated by intense fights over Cambridge's implementation plan. In 2019, local officials there had begun the process of allowing recreational stores to open and determining the way in which the city would locate and regulate them. With a famously progressive population, elected officials did not face the kind of skepticism about legalization itself that led many communities to pass ordinances prohibiting cannabis establishments altogether. Still, passions in the city were high regarding what form the legal cannabis market would take in the city and neighboring area. Cambridge's three existing medical establishments—Revolutionary Clinics, Healthy Pharms, and Sira Naturals—hoped to get access to the lucrative recreational market estimated to be worth millions. Few would have thought this would be a difficult result. Initially, city councilors working to establish the criteria for the city's eight recreational licenses planned to give additional flexibility on location to state-certified social equity applicants, but they would have provided an opportunity for conversion for existing medical dispensaries as well.[86]

However, after some initial pushback from local activists advocating for a more robust approach to social equity, council members Quinton Zondervan and Sumbul Siddiqui developed a bolder plan that would set the stage for a bitter licensing battle. Instead of giving location preferences to the city's social equity applicants—a prospect that might have set many of these applicants in competition with each other and split the community members who were arguing for their inclusion—Cambridge would instead give these applicants market exclusivity for two years in order to become established and profitable.[87] This proposal was controversial among both members of the city council and local residents, but the loudest cry of opposition came from the city's medical cannabis providers. Nearly immediately, city officials were hit with a blaze of opposition from Revolutionary Clinics as well as a swell of participants at council meetings wearing white shirts that decried the equity proposal as a threat to the economic viability of the medical dispensaries in the city.[88]

The political pressure on city councilors was intense enough that some sought a compromise that would preserve the clinics' ability to apply for adult-use licenses while enhancing the economic viability of social equity operators. Councilor Denise Simmons led this effort, seeking to bring together social equity activists and medical dispensaries in order to avoid divisive political fights and costly litigation.[89] The medical dispensaries initially offered to create a nonprofit that would contribute $1 million to be split among the city's social equity applicants. After negotiations in which this financial offer was increased to as much as $7.5 million, these compromise efforts failed and Cambridge moved forward with the social equity exclusion period plan.[90]

The bitter political wrangling also erupted into the media, with proponents of the dispensaries' compromise sending out mailers to all local residents, while a supporter of the social equity exclusion period fired back by calling the compromise proposal a "slave amendment."[91] By late 2019, the council had adopted the original Zondervan and Siddiqui proposal and drawn a lawsuit from Revolutionary Clinic.[92] This lawsuit later failed to gain traction before the dispensary withdrew it, and the Commonwealth Dispensary Association later faced external criticism and internal blowback from their efforts to undermine social equity across the state with a similar lawsuit against the commission after exclusivity licensing was adopted for the delivery market.[93]

Legal exclusionary periods in favor of social equity cannabis businesses have since been adopted in other jurisdictions.[94] Cambridge's measure came alongside equity-focused licensing proposals from the cities of Somerville and Boston, each of which carved out a clear space for equity applicants in their licensing processes.[95] Likewise, the CCC built on the exclusivity precedent set by Cambridge by later limiting a new class of delivery licenses to only social equity applicants, which the commission felt would provide a leg up into the industry with a low-barrier business opportunity.[96]

Still, even as city officials in the Boston area carefully parsed the limits of their authority to favor social equity applicants, the drawbacks of this reliance on local jurisdictions to pursue social equity policies remain clear. Boston itself announced a small grant fund of up to $15,000 for potential business entrepreneurs to enter the cannabis market. But as activist Joe Gilmore, who has a long history of undertaking consumer advocacy work and has since served in city and state government roles advancing social equity policies, points out: "Many people have been denied, because of where they live doesn't fall under the census tracts identified by the Commission" as areas of disproportionate impact. Many of these "are historically black and brown areas . . . [but] we're seeing other areas that are more economically sound qualify for this social equity program."[97]

Even those social equity applicants who were interested in participating in the regulated market in Massachusetts have to navigate a thicket of institutional and political minefields to have any chance at success. And while the state offered some technical assistance to social equity applicants, the gaps in this program were clear even to CCC regulators, who quickly learned that this kind of help was a dead end for people who couldn't receive the financing needed to start their businesses in the first place. COVID-19 also posed a particular challenge to implementation of social equity efforts, with the pandemic freezing much of the CCC's licensing work for an extended period beginning in March 2020.[98] Many social equity applicants had already been waiting years for initial approval of their paperwork by CCC staff, even as they often faced immense challenges at the local level. Some applicants had given up even before the pandemic, having burned hundreds of thousands of dollars in capital on complicated business plans, rent for locations that went unused while they awaited regulatory approval, and living expenses while they worked full-time to get their businesses off the ground. These challenges were surely faced by many applicants regardless of social equity eligibility, but the fragile ecosystem of legacy market providers even interested in going "legit" was already small, and these delays have surely done no favors for this group.

THE CHALLENGES AHEAD

Social equity activists in Massachusetts have long been skeptical of state and local efforts to build equity in the recreational market, and there remains a deep well of cynicism about the prospects for long-term success in this area. Still, the landscape for equity shifted drastically in mid-2022 after the state legislature chose to revisit the legal regime it created five years earlier. Some of the pressure to do so came from public scrutiny about the "host-community" agreements outlined by the earlier law, which permitted municipalities to charge licensees in their borders with "impact fees" of up to 3 percent of gross revenues to offset the cost of additional public services and other negative outcomes.[99] Communities often lacked any evidence that these cannabis establishments imposed additional service costs, and legal scrutiny of these practices also heightened after Fall River's mayor was arrested and convicted of soliciting cash bribes for cannabis licenses.[100]

Social equity activists had also developed a list of priorities after having seen the CCC's initial social equity focus run aground against the racial wealth gap and local inertia, as well as having the opportunity to see alternative policies being implemented in states such as Illinois and New York (discussed in chapters 7 and 8, respectively) that seemed promising for Massachusetts as well. In one sign of the power of these examples, the legislature's Joint Committee on Cannabis proposed to devote as much as 20 percent of the cannabis excise tax revenue flowing into state coffers to a Social Equity Loan Fund that would give applicants the opportunity to level the playing field for getting startup capital. This legislation also solidified the CCC's authority to regulate host-community agreements and to limit impact fees, which could instead be harnessed in favor of social equity.[101]

Efforts to legalize cannabis through ballot initiatives had begun in Colorado as arguments that legalization could provide better control of cannabis through a regulatory system rather than a punitively oriented criminal justice one—while also providing extra revenue for state and local governments. While the revenue outcome has been wildly successful in many places, it is also worth considering how the regulated market has displaced legacy suppliers in states with the most mature markets. A July 2022 report from the CCC in partnership with David Hammond, a Canadian researcher who has studied competition between the legal and legacy markets, demonstrates that regulated suppliers have largely displaced the legacy market for much of the cannabis purchased in Massachusetts.

Using a sample of 4,683 cannabis consumers, the CCC estimated that 64 percent of all cannabis products were sourced from the regulated market in 2019 and 2020. More sophisticated product differentiation has allowed regulated suppliers to offer products such as tinctures, concentrates, and liquid drops, and these products are overwhelmingly purchased at dispensaries. These suppliers have less market share for simpler products, such as cannabis flower for smoking, but even there they account for roughly half of all sales. Unsurprisingly, users under twenty-one years old, who cannot legally purchase cannabis, reported being much more likely to use legacy market suppliers. Some of the other primary reasons consumers cited for using the legacy market were the price of product combined with the distance they would need to travel to purchase it.[102]

It is clear that the community of activists who first worked together to place legalization on the ballot in 2016 has influenced the early shape of cannabis legalization in Massachusetts, especially because so many of them have since agitated both inside and outside government to ensure that their vision of legalization would be realized. Despite the shortfalls, it is to their credit that space exists today in the Massachusetts industry for both the activist supporters of legalization as well as those who have been impacted by criminalization. Very few of these activists have had the same story and influence as Shaleen Title, though others have served on the Cannabis Advisory Board or spoken to legislators and state and local officials about their experiences and goals. That said, Title's time in office speaks to the mixed legacy of Massachusetts in the larger national conversation around social equity. While her work on the CCC to advance this agenda won her national recognition as a fierce advocate for equity in the market, the implementation of many of the CCC's efforts went unfulfilled by the time she left her position.

Still, even if Massachusetts has demonstrated the pitfalls of implementing social equity policies, it has also suggested the tremendous potential for pursuing them. The vision of equity was clearly laid out in both the campaign and the law, with the legislature later endorsing and expanding the enacted ballot initiative to explicitly mandate the new Cannabis Control Commission to pursue certain equity policies. Equity also got a very direct shot of adrenaline with the appointment of Shaleen Title as one of the five members of the CCC, which she and a growing coalition of activists have used to build toward greater wins at the local level both in Massachusetts and in other states that these earlier efforts served as a model for. While the ultimate success of social equity in Massachusetts is still uncertain, legislators in Illinois, New Jersey, New York, and Connecticut have all drawn on its policy example in an effort to continue to expand the ways in which cannabis legalization can serve as an opportunity for communities of color impacted by the War on Drugs. The fact that Massachusetts, among other later states to legalize, has started to serve in this exemplary role—and that its example explicitly embraces social equity—suggests just how far the discussion has evolved in the national coalition for cannabis legalization since Colorado's pioneering initiative created the first template.

NOTES

1. Scott Merzbach, "Raid! National Guard, State Police Descend on 81-Year-Old's Property to Seize Single Pot Plant," *Daily Hampshire* (MA) *Gazette*, September 30, 2016, https://www.gazettenet.com/MarijuanaRaid-HG-100116-5074664.

2. Massachusetts Marijuana Initiative 2016, "Yes on 4 Is a Vote for Social Justice," YouTube video, October 7, 2016, https://www.youtube.com/watch?v=HgVdADbtXhY&ab_channel=MassachusettsMarijuanaInitiative2016.

3. Massachusetts Marijuana Initiative 2016, "Yes on 4."

4. Big Hope Project, "Team," https://www.bighopeproject.org/team/harry-jean-jacques/.

5. Big Hope Project, "Our Mission," https://www.bighopeproject.org/our-mission/.

6. Big Hope fellow in discussion with the author, Dorchester, MA, December 14, 2022.

7. Mass Moments, "August 8, 1954: Central Artery Project Announced," https://www.massmoments.org/moment-details/central-artery-project-announced.html.

8. Stephanie Leydon, "How a Long-Ago Map Created Racial Boundaries That Still Define Boston," *GBH*, November 12, 2019, https://www.wgbh.org/news/local-news/2019/11/12/how-a-long-ago-map-created-racial-boundaries-that-still-define-boston; Harvard Chan-NIEHS Center for Environmental Health, "Racial Residential Segregation in Greater Boston," July 18, 2022, https://storymaps.arcgis.com/stories/bd15a5eb9eae49cda09bfa7368272f89; and Catherine Elton, "How Has Boston Gotten Away with Being Segregated for So Long?" *Boston*, December 8, 2020, https://www.bostonmagazine.com/news/2020/12/08/boston-segregation/.

9. Bruce Gellerman, "'It Was Like a War Zone': Busing in Boston," *WBUR*, September 5, 2014, https://www.wbur.org/news/2014/09/05/boston-busing-anniversary, and "Busing Left Deep Scars on Boston, Its Students," *WBUR*, September 5, 2014, https://www.wbur.org/news/2014/09/05/boston-busing-effects.

10. Eswaran Selvarajah, *Gentrification of Codman Square Neighborhood: Fact or Fiction?* with contr. by Vidhee Garg (Boston: Codman Square Neighborhood Development Corporation, July 31, 2014), https://www.csndc.com/wp-content/uploads/2020/10/Gentrification-Internal-Analysis-Eswaran-Final-July-25-2014.pdf.

11. David Scharfenberg, "Massachusetts' Public Schools Are Highly Segregated: It's Time We Treated That Like the Crisis It Is," *Boston Globe*, updated December 11, 2020, https://www.bostonglobe.com/2020/12/11/opinion/massachusetts-public-schools-are-highly-segregated-its-time-we-treated-that-like-crisis-it-is/.

12. Akilah Johnson, "Boston. Racism. Image. Reality," Spotlight, *Boston Globe*, December 10, 2017, https://apps.bostonglobe.com/spotlight/boston-racism-image-reality/series/image/.

13. Meghan E. Irons and Zoe Greenberg, "'It's a Shame': Some Black Residents See Lost Opportunity as Janey, Campbell Concede in Boston Mayoral Race," *Boston Globe*, updated September 14, 2021, https://www.bostonglobe.com/2021/09/14/metro/march-history-this-boston-mayoral-race-black-residents-pause-reflect/.

14. Massachusetts General Court, *Acts and Resolves Passed by the General Court of Massachusetts in the Year 1911* (Boston: Wright & Potter, 1911), 359, https://archive.org/details/actsresolvespass1911mass/page/n433/mode/2up?q=Cannabis.

15. Massachusetts General Court, *Acts and Resolves Passed by the General Court of Massachusetts in the Year 1914* (Boston: Wright & Potter, 1914), 704–5, https://archive.org/details/actsresolvespass1914mass/mode/2up?q=cannabis.

16. Author review of the *Boston Globe* archives.

17. For example, physician Victor Robinson published a short pamphlet in 1912, *An Essay on Hasheesh*, that circulated widely among medical professionals—particularly in the Northeast—with reviews of Robinson's text appearing in medical journals over the next few years referring to "cannabis indica" and "hasheesh" and noting the substance's origins in Asia. See Richard J. Bonnie and Charles H. Whitebread, *The Marihuana Conviction: A History of Marihuana Prohibition in the United States* (Charlottesville: University of Virginia Press, 1974), 48. See also "An Essay on Hasheesh. Including Observations and Experiments. By Victor Robinson," book review, *Medical Review of Reviews* (1912), http://doi.org/10.1056/nejm191208081670610; and "An Essay on Hasheesh," book review, *Nature* 91 (1913): 241, http://doi.org/10.1038/091241b0.

18. Donald J. Cantor, "The Criminal Law and the Narcotics Problem," *Journal of Criminal Law and Criminology* 51, no. 5 (1961): 518, https://scholarlycommons.law.northwestern.edu/cgi/viewcontent.cgi?article=4977&context=jclc.

19. *Commonwealth v. Leis*, 355 Mass. 189 (1969), https://casetext.com/case/commonwealth-v-leis.

20. Samantha M. Doonan and Julie K. Johnson, *A Baseline Review and Assessment of Cannabis Use and Public Safety: Part 2; 94C Violations and Social Equity; Literature Review and Preliminary Data in Massachusetts* (Boston: Massachusetts Cannabis Control Commission, April 2019), 20, https://mass-cannabis-control.com/wp-content/uploads/2019/04/1.-RR2-94C-Violations-FINAL.pdf.

21. Doonan and Johnson, *Baseline Review*, 53–54.

22. Quoted in Jeffrey Moyer, "Implementing Social Equity: Opportunities and Challenges from Marijuana Legalization in Massachusetts," in *Stoneover: The Observed Lessons and Unanswered Questions of Cannabis Legalization*, ed. Nikolay Anguelov and Jeffrey Moyer (Lanham, MD: Lexington Books, 2022), 86.

23. George H. Haynes, "How Massachusetts Adopted the Initiative and Referendum," *Political Science Quarterly* 34, no. 3 (1919): 454–75, https://www.jstor.org/stable/pdf/2141686.pdf.

24. Haynes, "How Massachusetts Adopted the Initiative," 473–74.

25. YesOnQuestion2.com, "Lt. Tom Nolan," YouTube video, October 21, 2008, https://www.youtube.com/watch?v=-00FVeU4_T8&ab_channel=YesOnQuestion2.

26. Ballotpedia, "Massachusetts Question 2, Change Marijuana Possession from Criminal to Civil Penalties Initiative (2008)," note 18, https://ballotpedia.org/Massachusetts_Question_2,_Change_Marijuana_Possession_from_Criminal_to_Civil_Penalties_Initiative_(2008)#cite_note-14.

27. Ballotpedia, "Massachusetts Question 2, Change Marijuana Possession from Criminal to Civil Penalties Initiative (2008)," https://ballotpedia.org/Massachusetts_Question_2,_Change_Marijuana_Possession_from_Criminal_to_Civil_Penalties_Initiative_(2008).

28. Ballotpedia, "Massachusetts Medical Marijuana Initiative, Question 3 (2012)," https://ballotpedia.org/Massachusetts_Medical_Marijuana_Initiative,_Question_3_(2012).

29. Massachusetts Office of the Inspector General, *Investigation of the Drug Laboratory at the William A. Hinton State Laboratory Institute, 2002–2012*, Boston, March 4, 2014, https://www.mass.gov/doc/investigation-of-the-drug-laboratory-at-the-william-a-hinton-state-laboratory-institute-2002-0/download; and Maggie Mulvihill and Jon Schuppe, "Epic Massachusetts Crime Lab Scandal May Involve Even Broader Wrongdoing, Judge Says," *NBC News*, September 22, 2022, https://www.nbcnews.com/news/us-news/massachusetts-crime-lab-drug-testing-scandal-rcna48940.

30. Dan Adams, "SJC Says Boston Judge Erred in Denying Marijuana Expungement," *Boston Globe*, September 8, 2022, https://www.bostonglobe.com/2022/09/08/marijuana/sjc-says-boston-judge-erred-denying-marijuana-expungement/.

31. Deborah Becker and Hafsa Quraishi, "Thousands to Split $14M in Mass. Drug Lab Scandal," *WBUR*, August 26, 2022, https://www.wbur.org/news/2022/08/26/massachusetts-drug-convictions-tampering-settlement-disbursement.

32. Karen Morales, "Thousands of Drug Cases to Be Dismissed by State DAs," *Bay State Banner* (Dorchester, MA), December 8, 2017, https://www.baystatebanner.com/2017/12/08/thousands-of-drug-cases-to-be-dismissed-by-state-das/.

33. Erin Lee Carr, dir., *How to Fix a Drug Scandal*, TV series (Jigsaw Productions, 2020).

34. Mulvihill and Schuppe, "Massachusetts Crime Lab Scandal."

35. Maggie Mulvihill, "Judge Declines Mass Dismissal of Cases from Tainted Drug Lab," *WBUR*, October 7, 2021, https://www.wbur.org/news/2021/10/07/dookhan-farak-drug-lab-tampering-dismissal-superior-court-ruling.

36. Will Brownsberger, "Criminal Justice Reform at a Glance," blog post, WillBrownsberger.com, May 6, 2018, https://willbrownsberger.com/criminal-justice-package-at-a-glance/.

37. Dan Adams, "'An Utter Failure': Law Meant to Clear Old Convictions, Including for Marijuana Possession, Helps Few," *Boston Globe*, November 28, 2021, https://www.bostonglobe.com/2021/11/28/marijuana/an-utter-failure-law-meant-clear-old-convictions-including-marijuana-possession-helps-few/.

38. Pauline Quirion, "Governor Bakers Signs Cannabis Social Equity Bill Making Expungement of Decriminalized Cases Easier," blog post, MassLegalServices,

August 12, 2022, https://www.masslegalservices.org/content/governor-baker-signs-cannabis-social-equity-bill-making-expungement-decriminalized-cases.

39. MRCC, "Weed Is Now Legal in MA | What Are The Rules? | Lawyers Tell Us How #WeedTalk Ep 1," YouTube video, March 9, 2017, https://www.youtube.com/watch?v=l65C3qPvr_U&t=39s&ab_channel=MRCC.

40. Jeffrey Moyer, "Innovation Through Popular Diffusion: Seeking Social Equity Through Cannabis Legalization in Massachusetts," Ph.D. diss., University of Massachusetts Boston, 2020, https://scholarworks.umb.edu/doctoral_dissertations/597/; and Joel Warner, "Meet the Unlikely Champions of Legalized Weed in Mass.," *Boston Globe Magazine*, October 18, 2016, https://www.bostonglobe.com/magazine/2016/10/18/why-marijuana-opposition-effective-liberal-mass/QAN3Chb4AxpXCQKFKJ1M5M/story.html.

41. Adam Vaccaro, "Medical Marijuana Lobbyist to Oppose Pot Legalization Push," Boston.com, January 21, 2016, https://www.boston.com/news/untagged/2016/01/21/medical-marijuana-lobbyist-to-oppose-pot-legalization-push.

42. Dan Adams, "Q&A with Outgoing Cannabis Commissioner Shaleen Title," *Boston Globe*, December 29, 2020, https://www.bostonglobe.com/2020/12/29/marijuana/qa-with-outgoing-cannabis-commissioner-shaleen-title/.

43. Quoted in Moyer, "Implementing Social Equity," 91.

44. Aukje K. Lamonica, Miriam Boeri, and Timothy Anderson, "Gaps in Medical Marijuana Policy Implementation: Real-Time Perspectives from Marijuana Dispensary Entrepreneurs, Health Care Professionals and Medical Marijuana Patients," *Drugs: Education, Prevention and Policy* 23, no. 5 (2016): 422–34, https://doi.org/10.3109/09687637.2016.1150963.

45. Lynette French, "We Support Patients' Rights to Grow Their Own Medicine," blog post, Surterra.com, December 13, 2022, https://www.surterra.com/blog/florida-homegrow.

46. French, "We Support Patients' Rights"; and Kris Krane, "Company-Led Ballot Initiatives May Be Good for the Cannabis Industry, But Are They Good Policy?" *Forbes*, September 19, 2019, https://www.forbes.com/sites/kriskrane/2019/09/19/company-led-ballot-initiatives-may-be-good-for-the-cannabis-industry-but-are-they-good-policy/?sh=4a57b8549195.

47. Tim McLaughlin, "Insys Founder Faces Stiff Prison Sentence, $100 Mln-Plus in Forfeiture," Reuters, January 23, 2020, https://www.reuters.com/article/insys-opioids/insys-founder-faces-stiff-prison-sentence-100-mln-plus-in-forfeiture-idUSL1N29R1A4.

48. Lee Fang, "Pharma Company Funding Anti-Pot Fight Worried About Losing Business, Filings Show," *The Intercept*, September 12, 2016, https://theintercept.com/2016/09/12/pharma-opioid-marijuana/.

49. Moyer, "Innovation Through Popular Diffusion."

50. Massachusetts Marijuana Initiative 2016, "Yes on 4—Families (:30)," YouTube video, October 25, 2016, https://www.youtube.com/watch?v=lCBqLr-2NTc&ab_channel=TheTelegraph.

51. Jon B. Gettman, Emily Whitfield, and Matthew Allen, *The War on Marijuana in Black and White: A Massachusetts Update* (Boston: ACLU Foundation

of Massachusetts, 2016), 6, 8, https://www.aclum.org/sites/default/files/tr-report-10-2016-final-with-cover.pdf.

52. Quoted in Moyer, "Implementing Social Equity," 92.

53. Ballotpedia, "Massachusetts Marijuana Legalization, Question 4 (2016)," https://ballotpedia.org/Massachusetts_Marijuana_Legalization,_Question_4_(2016).

54. Campaign for a Safe and Healthy MA, "Neighborhoods," YouTube video, October 18, 2016, https://www.youtube.com/watch?v=bjtmo2M3Exw&ab_channel=PBSNewsHour.

55. Ballotpedia, "Massachusetts Marijuana Legalization, Question 4 (2016)."

56. Mark Melnick and Nicoya Borella, *City of Boston: Race Distribution by Wards, 2010 Census Population* (Boston: Boston Redevelopment Authority, April 2011), https://www.bostonplans.org/getattachment/d1ba4403-b97e-4d6b-9561-9331fd0e4629; and Boston (City of), *City of Boston, State Election—November 8, 2016, Question 4: Marijuana*,Boston.gov, https://www.boston.gov/sites/default/files/embed/0/036_-_2016_-_11-08-16_-_question_4_-_marijuana.pdf.

57. Will Brownsberger, "The Marijuana Compromise," blog post, WillBrownsberger.com, July 16, 2017, https://willbrownsberger.com/the-marijuana-compromise/.

58. Moyer, "Innovation Through Popular Diffusion."

59. Massachusetts General Laws, *Cannabis Control Commission*, Part I, Title II, Chapter 10, Section 76, https://malegislature.gov/Laws/GeneralLaws/PartI/TitleII/Chapter10/Section76.

60. Sean J. Kealy, "Marijuana Legalization and the Role of the Massachusetts Legislature," *Boston University Law Review* 101 (2021): 1192–93, https://www.bu.edu/bulawreview/files/2021/07/KEALY.pdf.

61. General Court of Massachusetts, *An Act to Ensure Safe Access to Marijuana*, Bill H. 3818 (2017), https://malegislature.gov/Laws/SessionLaws/Acts/2017/Chapter55.

62. Colin A. Young, "Latest Appointee Ensures Question 4 Opponents Will Have Majority on Cannabis Commission," *WBUR*, September 1, 2017, https://www.wbur.org/news/2017/09/01/latest-appointee-ensures-question-4-opponents-will-have-majority-on-cannabis-commission.

63. Neighborhood View, "Neighborhood View: Shaleen Title on Regulating Cannabis, Racial Equity, Etc.," YouTube video, February 6, 2018, https://www.youtube.com/watch?v=wi8iazOkarE&ab_channel=NeighborhoodView.

64. Jon B. Gettman, *The Impact of Drug and Marijuana Arrests on Local Communities in Massachusetts* (Boston: Massachusetts Cannabis Control Commission, December 8, 2017), 3–5, https://masscannabiscontrol.com/wp-content/uploads/2017/12/Impact-of-Drug-and-Marijuana-Arrests-on-Local-Communities-in-Massachusetts.pdf.

65. Massachusetts Cannabis Control Commission, *Guidance for Identifying Areas of Disproportionate Impact* (Boston: Massachusetts Cannabis Control Commission, April 2018), https://mass-cannabis-control.com/wp-content/uploads/2018/04/Guidance-for-Identifying-Areas-of-Disproportionate-Impact.pdf.

66. Colin A. Young, "Lawrence Seeks Equity from State Cannabis Regulators," *Boston Business Journal*, October 15, 2021, https://www.bizjournals.com/boston/news/2021/10/15/lawrence-seeks-equity-status-from-state-cannabis-r.html.

67. Population demographics including race are available from the US Census Bureau at https://data.census.gov/.

68. Young, "Lawrence Seeks Equity."

69. Jennifer M. Whitehill et al., *Identifying Disproportionately Impacted Areas by Drug Prohibition in Massachusetts* (Worcester: Massachusetts Cannabis Control Commission, March 2021), 11–16, https://donahue.umass.edu/documents/MA_Cannabis_Control_Commission_Study_Report1_3-11-21_FINAL.pdf.

70. Massachusetts Cannabis Control Commission, *Guidance on Equity Programs* (Boston: Massachusetts Cannabis Control Commission, June 2020), https://masscannabiscontrol.com/wp-content/uploads/062020_Guidance_Equity.pdf.

71. Jessica R. Hamilton, Samantha M. Doonan, and Julie K. Johnson, *Special Report: A Baseline Review and Assessment of the Massachusetts Cannabis Industry's Required Positive Impact Plans* (Boston: Massachusetts Cannabis Control Commission, October 2019), 28, https://masscannabiscontrol.com/wp-content/uploads/2019/10/Special_Report_A_Baseline_Review_and_Assessment_of_the_Massachusetts_Cannabis-Industry%E2%80%99s_Required_Positive_Impact_Plans-Oct-2019.pdf.

72. Hamilton, Doonan, and Johnson, *Special Report*, 28.

73. Hamilton, Doonan, and Johnson, *Special Report*, 27.

74. Seth Richtsmeier, "Equity, Not Equality: How Massachusetts Is Ensuring a Diverse Cannabis Industry," blog post, Cannabis Creative, https://cannabiscreative.com/blog/equity-not-equality-how-massachusetts-is-ensuring-a-diverse-cannabis-industry/.

75. Jeanette DeForge, "State Cannabis Law Offers Licenses for Marginalized Populations But Few Apply, Experts Said in Holyoke Panel Discussion," *MassLive*, updated June 24, 2019, https://www.masslive.com/news/2019/06/state-cannabis-law-offers-licenses-for-marginalized-populations-but-few-apply-experts-said-in-holyoke-panel-discussion.html; and Alexander Lekhtman, "Frustrations Boil Over Massachusetts Cannabis Equity Delays," *Filter*, January 17, 2020, https://filtermag.org/massachusetts-cannabis-equity-protests/.

76. Quoted in Moyer, "Implementing Social Equity," 100.

77. Massachusetts Cannabis Control Commission, *Special Report*, 21–22.

78. Massachusetts Cannabis Control Commission, *Special Report*, appendix 4.

79. Shira Schoenberg, "Marijuana Trade Association Drops Delivery Lawsuit Amid Public Pressure," *CommonWealth*, January 25, 2021, https://commonwealthmagazine.org/drug-addiction/drugs/marijuana-trade-association-drops-delivery-lawsuit-amid-public-pressure/; Colin A. Young, "Task Force Would Target Illegal Marijuana Sellers," SouthCoastToday.com, December 18, 2019, https://www.southcoasttoday.com/story/news/2019/12/18/task-force-would-target-illegal/2059356007/; and Grant Smith Ellis, "About Grant Smith Ellis," Patreon, https://www.patreon.com/GrantSmithEllis.

80. Lekhtman, "Frustrations Boil Over."

81. Big Hope Project, "Programs," https://www.bighopeproject.org/programs/.

82. Mike Plaisance, "History Made with 1st Purchases of Recreational Marijuana in Northampton, Massachusetts," *MassLive*, November 20, 2018, https://www.masslive.com/news/2018/11/history_made_with_1st_purchase.html.

83. Seth Daniel, "How Buffer Zone Rules Are Impacting Cannabis Dispensaries in Some Boston Neighborhoods," *WBUR*, October 4, 2021, https://www.wbur.org/news/2021/10/04/blue-hill-avenue-marijuana-shops-buffer-zone.

84. Quoted in Moyer, "Implementing Social Equity," 102.

85. Max Bowen, "Is Pot Pie Shrinking? Advocates, Store Owners Assess Whether Cannabis Market Oversaturated," *Daily Hampshire* (MA) *Gazette*, December 30, 2022, https://www.gazettenet.com/The-shrinking-pot-pie-49299488.

86. Declan J. Knieriem, "Cambridge City Council Weighs Recreational Marijuana Legislation," *Harvard Crimson* (Cambridge, MA), June 30, 2019, https://www.thecrimson.com/article/2019/6/30/city-council-recreational-marijuana/.

87. Dan Adams, "Follow the Money in Fight Over Cambridge Pot Policy," *Boston Globe*, July 1, 2019, https://www.bostonglobe.com/news/marijuana/2019/07/01/follow-money-fight-over-cambridge-pot-policy/GORrl0PgO5J9jRSt1yYsYO/story.html.

88. Marc Levy, "Judge Has a New Rejection for Dispensary Lawsuit to Break Two-Year Head Start on Recreational Pot," CambridgeDay.com, October 10, 2020, https://www.cambridgeday.com/2020/10/10/judge-has-a-new-rejection-for-dispensary-lawsuit-to-break-two-year-head-start-on-recreational-pot/.

89. Knieriem, "Cambridge City Council."

90. Knieriem, "Cambridge City Council."

91. Nik DeCosta-Klipa, "How a Debate in Cambridge Over Recreational Marijuana Turned Ugly," Boston.com, September 26, 2019, https://www.boston.com/news/local-news/2019/09/26/cambridge-marijuana-debate/.

92. Jessica Bartlett, "Revolutionary Clinics Drops Lawsuit Over Cannabis License Restrictions in Cambridge," *Boston Business Journal*, January 28, 2021, https://www.bizjournals.com/boston/news/2021/01/28/revolutionary-clinics-drops-lawsuit-over-cannabis.html.

93. Levy, "Judge Has a New Rejection"; and Dan Adams, "Marijuana Trade Group Drops Lawsuit Against State After Backlash," *Boston Globe*, January 25, 2021, https://www.bostonglobe.com/2021/01/25/marijuana/dispensary-trade-group-drops-lawsuit-against-state-after-backlash/.

94. In Connecticut, see Minority Cannabis Business Association, "Legal Status," Connecticut Equity Project State Briefing, https://minoritycannabis.org/equitymap/connecticut/; in Denver, see Desiree Mathurin, "Denver's Trying to Make Cannabis Delivery a More Attractive Business—and Exclusive to Social Equity Licensees," Denverite.com, September 19, 2022, https://denverite.com/2022/09/19/denvers-trying-to-make-cannabis-delivery-a-more-attractive-business-and-exclusive-to-social-equity-licensees/.

95. For Somerville, see Joe Creason, "Economic Empowerment and Cannabis in Somerville," *Somerville* (MA) *Times*, September 1, 2021, https://www.thesomervilletimes.com/archives/110833; for Boston, see Boston (City of), "Boston Equity Program for Cannabis Businesses," Boston.gov, last updated February 17,

2023, https://www.boston.gov/departments/economic-development/cannabis-equity-program.

96. *Boston Business Journal*, “Cannabis Commission Backs Giving Minority Groups Exclusive Access to Delivery Licenses in Massachusetts,” *MassLive*, April 29, 2019, https://www.masslive.com/marijuana/2019/04/cannabis-commission-backs-giving-minority-groups-exclusive-access-to-delivery-licenses-in-massachusetts.html.

97. Grant Smith Ellis, “Episode 1: Shaleen Title and Joe Gilmore,” in *Cannabis Policy Watch*, produced by Cannabis Policy Watch, January 12, 2022, https://anchor.fm/grant-smith-ellis/episodes/Episode-1-Shaleen-Title-and-Joe-Gilmore-e1crrqe.

98. Practical Law Commercial Transactions, “Massachusetts Reopens Recreational Marijuana Businesses Following COVID-19 Closure,” May 20, 2020, https://content.next.westlaw.com/practical-law/document/I91d43d4599d911eabea3f0dc9fb69570/Legal-Update-Massachusetts-Reopens-Recreational-Marijuana-Businesses-Following-COVID-19-Closure?viewType=FullText&originationContext=document&transitionType=DocumentItem&ppcid=612fed1d39ef49d38d501caed192046d&contextData=(sc.Default).

99. Colin A. Young, “Cannabis Commission to Revisit Regulations Around Equity, Host Agreements in Massachusetts,” *New England Public Media*, September 20, 2022, https://www.nepm.org/regional-news/2022-09-20/cannabis-commission-to-revisit-regulations-around-equity-host-agreements-in-massachusetts.

100. Jo C. Goode et al., “‘Jaisel Was Dirty’: Marijuana Vendors Detail Bribes Demanded by Former Mayor Correia,” *Herald News* (Fall River, MA), May 5, 2021, https://www.heraldnews.com/story/news/courts/2021/05/05/live-updates-corruption-fraud-trial-former-fall-river-mayor-jasiel-correia-marijuana-extortion-bribe/4952528001/.

101. Dan Adams, “Sweeping Cannabis Bill Becomes Law, After Yearslong Effort on Reforms,” *Boston Globe*, August 11, 2022, https://www.bostonglobe.com/2022/08/11/marijuana/sweeping-cannabis-bill-becomes-law-after-yearslong-effort-reforms/.

102. Massachusetts Cannabis Control Commission, *Cannabis Use Trends in Massachusetts, Findings from the International Cannabis Policy Study, 2019 and 2020* (Boston: Massachusetts Cannabis Control Commission, July 2022), 67, https://masscannabiscontrol.com/wp-content/uploads/2022/09/International-Cannabis-Policy-Study-2019-2020.pdf.

Chapter 7

Illinois

Policy Design for Social Equity

On February 17, 2017, Chad Robertson and two of his friends were dropped off outside Chicago's Union Station on a layover during a bus trip from Memphis, Tennessee, to his home in Minneapolis. Seeking respite from the cold, the group tried to go inside the station while they waited for the next bus, but Amtrak Police Officer LaRoyce Tankson and other officers stopped Robertson and accused him of smoking cannabis. After a brief interaction in which an officer attempted to search his pockets, Robertson fled, at which point Tankson shot and killed him. Tankson later stated that he believed that Robertson had attempted to reach for a firearm, but after the shooting no firearms were found on Robertson's body or with his traveling companions.[1] Three years later, now-former officer Tankson was acquitted of first-degree murder charges.[2] This is of course another sad and predictable example of law enforcement enacting violence on a young man of color, and it is likewise an instance where the criminalization of cannabis led to an effective death penalty.

The previous three chapters of this book demonstrated the nearly exclusive role that interest groups and voters have held in the legalization of cannabis over the last several decades. Indeed, the ballot initiative itself was once described in the political science literature as the "gun behind the door,"[3] a mechanism to force popular representation in government where elected lawmakers might defer or decline action. The scholarship about the responsiveness of elected officials and the political system as a whole to ballot initiatives is mixed at best, though this is often a function of the complicated nature of initiatives themselves, which must be written by specific individuals and then put through an array of bureaucratic hoops, each of which introduces transaction costs and decreases the possibility of the popular voice being faithfully transmitted. Still, it is certain that the ballot initiative has served as a clear if rather blunt instrument to deliver citizens' verdicts on the criminalization of cannabis. The practical and political impact of these verdicts is respected by elected leaders, even if they would otherwise prefer to limit the opportunities for voters to weigh in. For example, the initiatives in Colorado and Massachusetts provided a clear signal that their state legislatures should create a regulatory system for cannabis. Although the failure of Ohio's initiative for the most part preserved the status quo, it arguably pushed legislators to quickly establish access to medical cannabis.

As a state where voters have no power to initiate legislation, however, Illinois is one of the first places where lawmakers took the driver's seat on cannabis legalization. By the later half of the 2010s, Illinois legislators were jumping at the opportunity to further liberalize cannabis markets, passing a law in 2016 to reduce penalties for those accused of cannabis possession from a misdemeanor to a small fine and then further expanding the state's medical cannabis program in 2018.[4] State senator Heather Steans and state representative Kelly Cassidy, both from Chicago, also proposed a legalization bill in 2017, though legislative leaders and then-governor Bruce Rauner posed insurmountable hurdles for that measure despite Illinois's noted liberal tilt.[5] When Rauner was defeated by billionaire venture capitalist J. B. Pritzker in 2018 on a platform that included a significant promise to legalize cannabis, however, elected leaders were fast to act.[6]

Their actions made Illinois the first state to legalize cannabis through the legislative process rather than by ballot initiative, and the first to pair legalization with a broader economic package that went beyond mere licensing in order to advance opportunities that might help communities of color. These policies, along with the fact that advocates for social equity were appointed as state officials responsible for administering cannabis regulations, helped advance the idea within the industry more generally that social equity policies were important for future expansion. As Danielle Perry—a Black woman appointed as the state's chief regulatory officer in 2021—explained, Illinois's approach to legalization is in some sense a next step in a longer evolution that has yet to be fully realized. As she put it, for early legalization states like Colorado, Washington, and Oregon, "equity wasn't even in the conversation. And I love those guys. . . . They have been great partners and friends to me, but I like to call that out. Because when you think about cannabis, now you get on the national regulators' calls. I'm the only Black person on the call. I mean, that says something about Illinois."[7]

Perry's celebration of the progress her state has achieved also suggests the distance there is yet to travel—both in Illinois and nationally—in terms of fully achieving social equity in cannabis. As this chapter will show, the legislative path to legalization holds great promise because it has the potential to create a far more robust set of policies and programs than ballot initiatives while also allowing more flexibility in how money stemming from the cannabis industry can be raised and directed. But it is not a panacea—the same legislators and government officials can be dictated by competing political concerns to those advanced by social equity advocates, while the legislative process does not intrinsically protect the state from market conditions such as inadequate supply or the pressures of unforeseen events such as the COVID-19 pandemic. Despite only a few years in existence, then, Illinois's experience provides a useful example of the considerations that future legislative bodies—at both the state and the federal levels—should examine when crafting their own legalization regimes.

CANNABIS CRIMINALIZATION IN ILLINOIS

Illinois farmers began growing hemp in the mid-nineteenth century,[8] but Illinois did not practically regulate the sale or possession of any substance until 1853, when the state legislature passed a law requiring the accurate labeling of all substances sold, with criminal penalties for violators.[9] Then in 1874, legislators further required that any substances that might be poisonous, such as arsenic, strychnine, or prussic acid (cyanide), be properly labeled as such. Responding to increasing fears about drug abuse, legislators also sought to control pharmacies through regulation beginning in 1881, passing a law that restricted the transfer of such substances as opium and morphine to those under the age of fifteen. This regulatory approach continued in 1903, when legislators sought to control the trafficking of cocaine through better recordkeeping requirements and enhanced penalties. It took until 1908 for state legislators to begin to consider prohibition for cocaine, and then only of sales to those whom the druggist believed to be addicted.[10]

While up to this point Illinois had anticipated the measures found in federal legislation such as the Pure Food and Drug Act, the passage of the Harrison Act in 1914 (see chapter 1) pushed Illinois to follow the federal lead by fully embracing criminal prohibition of some substances obtained without the prescription of a medical doctor or other authorized individual and by limiting pharmacists' ability to distribute opium or coca leaves, making it much more difficult to access them. Penalties for violating such prohibitions were initially discussed within the part of the legal code focused on regulating pharmacies, but in 1931 the state legislature formalized this legal structure and moved much of the language prohibiting possession or transfer of prohibited substances to the criminal code.[11]

Presaging this transformation and demonstrating the perceptions that influenced it, the *Chicago Tribune* in 1929 associated rising rates of cannabis use among "American" youth with the increased immigration of "Mexican laborers" while reporting on a failed effort by state legislators that year to regulate cannabis. This effort apparently failed when a state senator who also served as a Chicago druggist held the bill in committee.[12] The immigration of at least thirty thousand Mexicans to the Chicago area by 1929, however, was enough for law enforcement to take greater notice of cannabis use, which was interposed on top of tensions between ethnic communities in Chicago during this time. One scholar, quoting a number of participants in this context, found that white Chicagoans widely resented Mexicans, and their social, if not legal, status was similar to that of Black residents of the South in that era.[13]

The 1931 law, first called the "Narcotic Drug Control Law," referred to the federal Harrison Act and followed the general structure of the model law that the Uniform Law Commission later promoted (see chapter 1). It was notable for making many violations of its restrictions on substances such as opium, morphine, heroin, and codeine felonies, though at this earlier stage, cannabis was specifically excluded from Illinois's enhanced prohibition regime.[14] Cannabis was in fact not included in this larger narcotic schedule for over a decade, even as the legislature further acted in 1935 to fully adopt the Uniform Narcotic Drug Act, which extended legal restrictions on trafficking and possession from pharmacists and direct prescribers to individuals, hospitals, and manufacturers alike.[15] During this time, media representations of cannabis use, as well as more ideologically inclined publications—such as those produced by the Woman's Christian Temperance Union—indicated a concern that the cannabis use many perceived to be a mainstay of Mexican communities in Chicago was spreading to young people who "come from good homes."[16]

By 1945, the legislature sharply changed course, bringing cannabis into its regulatory scheme and even providing for additional penalties on cannabis specifically. Although that disparate treatment only lasted until 1949, cannabis still remained under the criminal eye of the state for decades to come.[17] These events in Illinois were highly influenced by federal trends, including the creation of the federal Bureau of Narcotics and the public advocacy of agency head Harry Anslinger, as well as the more general misclassification of cannabis as a narcotic. As discussed in previous chapters, this widespread and unfortunate legal fiction served both to imprison those who were caught violating the law for much longer periods than they might otherwise have served as well as to maintain a cloud of stigma around cannabis itself, making discussion of changing the classification politically difficult and strained.[18] This legal regime largely remained in place in Illinois for the next two decades, though the legislature did increase penalties at least twice during this period.[19]

Unlike state courts in Massachusetts and elsewhere, however, which had rejected arguments that the narcotic classification of cannabis ran afoul of constitutional protections of due process and equal protection, Illinois courts proved more open to these assertions. In *People v. McCabe* (1971), the Illinois Supreme Court held that an appellant being charged and sentenced to a mandatory minimum sentence of ten years in prison as a first-time offender was an equal protection violation and that the classification of cannabis as a narcotic drug by the legislature was "arbitrary."[20] This legal challenge came in the wake of the wave of changes to state laws that followed the passage of the federal Controlled Substances Act in 1970 and not long after the Illinois legislature acted to pass both a state-level Controlled Substances Act and a separate Cannabis Control Act. This separation reflected state leaders' acknowledgment that cannabis was not a narcotic as they had previously regulated it, refining the regulatory regime to respond to concerns that both drug control in general as well as cannabis control specifically had been unsuccessful responses to use and abuse.[21] Illinois is one of the first states to intentionally separate cannabis from its larger drug regulation law, as well as to provide that simple possession of cannabis without intent for sale would be a misdemeanor, which would be more easily purged from an individual's criminal record.[22]

Criminal Enforcement in Chicago

Just as Chicago's specific demographic changes helped to usher in state-level efforts at cannabis regulation, the local dynamics of the state's largest city helped to determine how enforcement of cannabis laws would affect millions of people in Illinois as criminalization was enacted over the course of the twentieth century. The political legacy of the city's larger-than-life dynastic Daley clan, whose members had a nearly ironclad fix on city politics beginning in 1955 and ending only in 2011, hovers over any recounting of criminal justice in Chicago. In particular, Richard J. Daley and his son, Richard M. Daley, each served as the city's mayor for more than four decades combined during that period—the troubled time between their two tenures saw a succession of five mayors over the course of fewer than thirteen years. During this interregnum the city did elect its first African American mayor—Harold Washington—but his tenure in office was overshadowed by the younger Daley's expected ascendency to the office.

The Daleys were consummate machine politicians, albeit ones who sought to represent their times, carefully combining themes of urban renewal and the representation of different interests across the city's racially and socially diverse spectrum with a recognition of power and how to wield it. Under Richard Daley Sr., city leaders were often focused on neighborhood concerns and resisting the kind of outmigration that impacted other urban cores of the era, such as Detroit. Much of this occurred at the expense of movement on civil rights, which the senior Daley was not a champion of. His son's service as mayor represented a more deliberate engagement with the city's minority neighborhoods, though this did little to help the economic mobility of people in these neighborhoods, particularly on the South Side, where many residents to this day struggle with economic and social exclusion.

The political and institutional tensions present in police enforcement against gambling prohibitions was a strong factor in the senior Daley's ascent to the mayoralty. During the 1950s, Chicago's police force was engaged in a high-profile campaign, led by then-mayor Martin H. Kennelly, to crack down on the policy game that was widespread in many minority neighborhoods.[23] While initially this effort had support across the color line as a matter of public morality and safety, Black political leaders such as congressman William L. Dawson would later come to condemn it, believing that law enforcement specifically targeted gambling operations in Black neighborhoods, sometimes as a cover for white organized crime to disrupt or supplant these activities.[24] The congressional Kefauver Committee had shone a light on the connection between urban organized crime and police corruption in 1950, and the inconsistent enforcement of gambling laws had led to scrutiny of police officers, particularly those who took bribes.[25]

The Kennelly administration backed the officers who resisted a requirement to disclose their outside income, and the campaign to reduce illicit gambling across the city—along with lingering racial tensions—had soured much of Chicago's political establishment on Kennelly by the 1955 mayoral election. In this race, the elder Daley ran against Kennelly, who, after being spurned by Democratic Party bosses when seeking their endorsement, ran a smear campaign against Daley insinuating that the city's Black voters were supporting him and would expect special consideration after the election.[26] Kennelly's supporters also made allegations that Congressman Dawson was involved in gambling and narcotics activities that occurred in Black neighborhoods, and that voters should not endorse the presumed yet nonexistent alliance between Dawson and Daley. This racial fearmongering was not enough to save Kennelly, who was opposed by many Black voters because of his earlier failure to ensure that the police protected efforts to integrate housing.[27] While many Black voters did end up supporting Daley, they received little practical benefit from the new administration. Congressman Dawson lost much of his political patronage power, and those Black residents involved in the unregulated gambling industry faced harassment by both white organized crime groups as well as the police.[28]

Both Chicago and Illinois at large continued to struggle with law enforcement corruption surrounding efforts to stamp out gambling, though the unregulated rings located in Black neighborhoods in Chicago lost much of their economic viability by the 1960s. Their fate was largely written by the

1970s, when efforts to establish a locally regulated "policy" game in the Illinois state legislature gave way instead to a state-run lottery that mimicked enough of the aspects of these games to establish popularity across the state.[29] Meanwhile, law enforcement in Chicago and throughout the rest of the state was increasingly focused on the perceived threat of drugs, frequently using the same tactics that they had perfected in pursuit of gambling to instead go after alleged drug offenders.

Richard Nixon himself underscored the importance of taking a tough stance on cannabis specifically to the senior Daley in a 1971 White House meeting, saying that "I'm against legalizing marijuana because, I know all the arguments about, well, marijuana is no worse than whiskey. . . . But the point is, once you cross that line, from the straight society to the drug society—marijuana, then speed, then it's LSD, then it's heroin, etc., then you're done."[30] Both Daleys held little sympathy for drug offenders and would happily go along with the national trend in increased drug enforcement that Nixon's opinion foreshadowed. Daley Jr. served for eight years as the prosecutor in charge of Cook County, where he was successful in ramping up felony drug prosecutions from just over 900 in 1979 to nearly five times that only six years later.[31] After becoming mayor in 1989, he only indicated interest in backing off cannabis enforcement in 2004, calling enforcement of criminal penalties on cannabis a waste of public resources.[32]

Much like in gambling enforcement, the War on Drugs presented an opportunity for corruption and police misconduct on a large scale. One example is the career of Chicago Police Sergeant Ronald Watts and a team of narcotics officers acting under his command. Watts was found to be responsible for over 200 false drug convictions resulting in hundreds of years of sentenced time. In the case that brought Watts to the attention of internal affairs, the police officer had demanded protection money from Chicago residents Ben Baker and Clarissa Glen and repeatedly arrested them beginning in July 2004 for narcotics offenses when they refused to pay. After a subsequent arrest in December 2005, Baker and Glen complained to authorities about Watts's actions, although it took over a decade and Watts himself being arrested as part of a federal drug sting for the city government to take any official notice of this corruption.[33]

Eventually, Watts was later arrested again by city police, and many of the convictions based on his police work were reversed. Many of his colleagues were also implicated in helping with the coverup over the years. An additional investigation by journalists at the *Intercept* told the story of two Chicago police officers who sought to uncover Watt's misconduct. Rather than being listened to and rewarded by their superiors, they were hounded and disparaged as "rats."[34] A lawyer involved in the effort to exonerate many of the individuals who had been convicted based on Watts's work outlined how the emphasis on harsh penalties in the War on Drugs framework enabled Watts to perpetrate these crimes: "Watts . . . would have drugs in his sleeve, and he would come up and say, this is yours, you're going to jail today." His leverage came from his ability to quickly put his targets in a position where their futures were seriously at risk—a direct result of how criminal penalties around drugs quickly elevated based on the amount you were found with. The lawyer explained that "we're talking about what's called [a] Class X amount of drugs . . . which save for murders are the most serious felony in the state of Illinois," which meant that Watts could easily set you on the path to "six to thirty year prison sentences."[35]

Watts's behavior was obviously criminal, but as in other states, even those law enforcement officers working squarely within the confines of the law left a devastating impact on residents of the state. Just as with the enforcement of gambling laws decades ago, what had begun as a moralistic desire to address addiction became an effort to economically control and limit communities of color. The legacy of criminalization has left these communities continually wounded, whether law enforcement had the pretext of gambling or narcotics to justify their actions. It was this kind of legacy that efforts to legalize met with in both Massachusetts and Illinois in their attempts to address long-standing tensions surrounding criminal justice issues.

LEGISLATING LEGALIZATION

Before Illinois, the primary vehicle for pursuing cannabis legalization in the United States was by popular referenda. While not always successful—as illustrated by Colorado's and Ohio's first attempts at decriminalization—this method has to this point at least been far *more* successful than legislative action. Yet given their constitutional limitations, ballot initiatives are often an imperfect vehicle for comprehensive social reform. In nearly all of the states that had previously hosted a cannabis ballot measure, notably Colorado,[36] laws proposed via the initiative process must remain confined to one "subject"—failure to do so can lead to legal challenges. Many of the first states that legalized cannabis via ballot initiative had some restrictions that would have precluded social equity efforts, particularly ones like Massachusetts that do not allow for appropriations in the initiative itself (although in Massachusetts the legislature is required to "appropriate such money as may be necessary to carry such law into effect"[37]).

The inclusion of social equity provisions—even conceptually—could have put the entire initiative open to legal challenge in states with these restrictions, and so drafters were limited in their ability to add many provisions that might address criminalization. Legislators themselves, however, have much greater plenary power to draft laws and can often directly appropriate tax revenue in a way that is difficult or impossible for initiatives to do. At the same time, legislators are politically accountable in a way that interest groups like the Marijuana Policy Project could never be. If MPP or any other group that organized legalization initiatives across the country failed to attract the political support to pass a law, or even managed to pass a poorly written initiative, then they would face nothing other than criticism, while at least in theory legislators' careers are on the line. Illinois's lack of any ballot initiative process at all meant that the legislative route was the only path forward for legalization in the state and, ultimately, the differing political payoffs in Illinois combined with policy drafters who were unbound by the limited reach of the ballot initiative to deliver a much different form of legalization than seen elsewhere.

Governor Pritzker's campaign promises to legalize cannabis gave state legislators a clear mandate to act on legalization after the 2018 election. By April of the following year, legislators in both houses of the state legislature had separately begun to discuss plans to legalize cannabis as well as comprehensively address many of the challenges this change would bring. This political environment gave new life to legalization bills that Chicago-area state representative Kelly Cassidy and state senator Heather Steans had first introduced during the 2017 legislative session and reintroduced again in 2019,[38] which supporters pursued on the basis of both their social equity impacts as well as the potential revenue enhancements for the state.[39]

The original bill prioritized criminal justice reform by offering expungements as part of the legalization process and providing a pathway for licenses for those with experience in the legacy market. As it worked its way through the legislature, the bill's authors kept these basic goals in place even as the bill changed in other ways. For example, the law tried to address some of the questions that those opposed to legalization had raised, such as clear rules to allow local municipalities to opt out of sales, as well as measures to allow employers to maintain drug-free workplaces, among others. One of the more notable compromises was the removal of home grow provisions, with this allowance only given to patients in the state's existing medical program rather than to residents at large.[40]

By the end of May 2019, the state senate had voted in favor of this modified version, passing a bill that Steans said aspired to be the "gold standard" of how social equity issues would be handled across the nation.[41] Within days, the state house also passed the legalization measure, putting the issue on the fast track for final passage. Pritzker signed the Cannabis Tax and Regulation Act (CTRA) into law on June 25, making Illinois the eleventh state to legalize cannabis for recreational use, with a target date for recreational sales to begin on January 1, 2020.[42] Soon after legalization passed, Pritzker appointed state senator Toi Hutchinson as his new "czar" of cannabis policy, who would supervise the work across several state agencies to ensure that legalization would both be effective and equitable. Speaking about her appointment, Hutchinson noted that she's "always said that equity should be the cornerstone of this new industry and I'm going to work every single day to ensure that those who have been disproportionately impacted by drug policies have the opportunity to start businesses and thrive here in Illinois."[43]

The CTRA proved to be a step forward for equity that yet remains elusive in many other states. Two main features distinguish the Illinois law from previous equity programs: a financial allotment from excise taxes to be spent on social equity programs, and its plan to help expunge previous cannabis convictions. By dedicating at least 25 percent of cannabis tax revenues for equity programs, Illinois lawmakers demonstrated their intent to make cannabis legalization a bridge toward helping communities of color that had previously been targeted in the War on Drugs. Despite this effort, the fact that a substantial majority of the bill's revenue would still help fill state coffers did not thrill all of those who came from communities of color. For example, state representative Curtis Tarver II criticized this provision in a way that echoed criticism of the previous transition from gambling enforcement to state-run lotteries: "We've had 50 damn years to work on the issue. Nobody saw fit to do it and then, all of a sudden when it's an opportunity to make money from the same things that have decimated our communities, all of a sudden it's about criminal justice reform. It's offensive."[44]

Practical issues have also served to somewhat undermine the CTRA's lofty goals. At the outset of the legal era, Illinois had to quickly confront multiple challenges in the market, including limited supply to meet demand.[45] Soon after this, the COVID-19 pandemic hit, causing licensing and regulatory delays that plagued state regulators for several years. These conditions especially affected new participants in the market, as the only dispensaries that had been permitted to open for retail sales on January 1, 2020, were the existing medical providers.[46] The medical market had been dominated by well-financed vertically integrated suppliers that had been selected by former governor Rauner's administration, leading to the perception that the medical market was controlled by forces hostile to changing market structures. As Juan Aguirre, an activist for social equity in Illinois, explained, "It's a very strategic play that the multi state operators own these licenses . . . they [the MSOs] have taken to lobbying heavily their state legislatures to convince them that this still is a dangerous drug that needs to be regulated and tightly controlled."[47] Expanding the initial network of retailers was delayed for over a year until the state legislature fixed some inconsistencies in the previously passed legislation, which finally allowed the first licenses to be awarded.[48]

The details of what happened in Illinois are important, as many other states have encountered challenges when setting up licensing systems, especially those with more complex preferences written into the fine print. While Illinois's CTRA had envisioned eventually awarding at least 500 licenses across all categories, interest in the first round far surpassed expectations; the state eventually received more than 4,000 applications.[49] This demonstrates a strong interest in acquiring these opportunities, though the state's process for assigning licenses would soon lead state regulators astray.

State law mandated that the licenses be awarded to the highest-scoring applications in each category and region. In a push to make sure that these licenses went to social equity applicants, 20 percent of the final score was supposed to be awarded to those that fit special requirements, including any business that was 51 percent owned either by residents of disproportionately impacted areas or people who had personal or family experience with a cannabis arrest or conviction or whose employee base fit these criteria.[50] Another part of the CTRA gave additional credit to businesses that encouraged veteran participation, however, awarding an additional five "bonus points" for these applicants. This meant that applicants were capable of achieving more than perfect scores if they were able to find the "social equity veteran unicorn" to join their ownership team. At least twenty-one of the groups in the initial applicant pool were able to get this bonus, collectively representing 232 applicants with a more than perfect score.[51] This confusing result led to lawsuits and negative press, and after an allegation of self-dealing from one of the applicants who also worked at scoring entity KPMG,[52] state regulators decided to suspend the awarding of licenses.

These hiccups collectively meant that the state only issued its first licenses to social equity applicants in November 2022, nearly three years after the legal cannabis market in Illinois had gotten underway. While state legislators envisioned that cannabis legalization would give an economic boost to communities of color as well as the state, many applicants spent these two-plus years in regulatory limbo, forced to maintain a physical location and operating expenses despite not having the legal capacity to commence operations.[53] Additionally, a program established by state legislators to provide financing to social equity applicants also encountered delays, depriving the emerging industry of critical capital during a vulnerable period.[54] As the first licenses and loan awards were made in late 2022, some from among the original group of applicants had been forced to leave the industry, providing an opportunity for more established operators—including MSOs—to enter the legal cannabis market.[55] Ricky Hendon, a former state senator and winning applicant, discussed his own frustration with this situation in late 2021: "It's been a two-year delay. People have rent and mortgages to pay and you still have to raise capital to get [a dispensary] off the ground. This isn't about people being hell-bent on making money."[56]

In the first two years of legal cannabis, the state collected well over $1 billion in tax revenue, with fiscal year 2022 revenues totaling $445 million.[57] The revenue-sharing component that directs 25 percent of state tax proceeds into the Restore, Reinvest, and Renew (R3) grant program to directly benefit communities impacted by cannabis criminalization and other symptoms of poverty has so far led to over $100 million in announced grants to nonprofit organizations. These organizations work in areas that were selected according to criteria such as the highest rates of gun injury, unemployment, and child poverty, as well as those with a designation as a Disproportionately Impacted Area according to the Illinois Department of Community and Economic Development.[58] The R3 grants have gone out in at least three regular funding rounds, as well as a special round announced in summer 2021 focused on combating increasing youth violence.[59]

With the R3 program still in its early days, there remains skepticism that state and local governments in Illinois have the technical capacity to deliver widespread social change with cannabis money, given the state's reputation for public corruption. Unlike most states with legal cannabis that place responsibility for cannabis regulation in one distinct agency, Illinois's comparatively opaque regulatory structure divides responsibility among a patchwork of different agencies.[60] Additionally, the board responsible for directing the R3 funding was filled with many political appointees and did not have as much representation from impacted communities as Massachusetts would include in its similar funding initiative beginning in 2022.[61] That said, this funding has so far proved accessible to community organizations, and the state officials administering the fund have conducted follow-up research to ensure that they are reaching the best applicants and supporting their efforts to finish grant applications. While defining the geographic and programmatic scope of the funding proved confusing for some grant recipients, it is also clear that this money is serving a population that has not traditionally been targeted with this kind of intentional funding.[62]

Many of the organizations receiving these funds have also spoken of the way they make possible important on-the-ground work in their communities. A 2021 report by Afterschool for Children and Teens identified the partnerships that resulted from the R3 funds, including after-school math tutoring in Rockford, after-school clubs and activities in East St. Louis, workforce readiness training in Springfield, and social and emotional learning services for disconnected youth in the suburbs of Chicago.[63] Another organization that received $230,044 in funding from R3 grants—Land of Lincoln Legal Aid—provides community education and outreach services to help address client needs related to housing, debt, and the expungement of criminal records. On receiving this grant, the organization's executive director identified the link between the money and the work that they would do with it: "We are thrilled to receive this groundbreaking funding [since] we know a lot of community members are mistrustful of the legal system because of experiences they have had with the criminal justice system. As a result, they may avoid legal assistance altogether, even when an attorney could have a helped with a significant problem."[64]

Illinois's centralized legislative method of legalization was most effective in one regard. The expungement section of the CTRA mandated that the Illinois State Police would have six years to expunge any convictions for people with low-level offenses. However, the governor announced in late 2020 that the state police had already been successful in purging nearly half a million convictions, and Pritzker further pardoned another 9,219 individuals.[65] In Cook County, the state attorney's office took a bit longer but ultimately announced in 2022 that it had expunged over 15,191 convictions, with many of the convictions waiting to be addressed dating to before 1965, due to the higher burden for researching and documenting those cases.[66] Other counties in the state have until 2024 to conduct the remaining expungement work, though many have already completed it earlier than required. It is important that Illinois lawmakers opted to give the state authority in this realm, as opposed to simply directing counties or other local jurisdictions to act, since the state government has easier access to official records and a higher capacity to handle the overwhelming legal task of processing the volume of expungements that are required under these kinds of efforts.

Despite this progress, it is clear that much more work is needed—especially in the licensing and business support aspects of the program—if cannabis legalization is to serve its full purpose in helping to restore the trust of communities of color in local and state governments. State representative LaShawn Ford from Chicago stated this plainly, noting that "the people that we intended to be emerging in this market have not yet emerged because they are still tied up in court. And those are the Black people and Brown people that really actually have been a target of the war on drugs. So right now the law, for the intent, has failed."[67] Echoing this sentiment, cannabis entrepreneur and license applicant Frank Cowan described his own experience: "We're still spending money on attorneys, we're still spending money on zoning experts, I mean we're spending money and we don't have an end in sight. There will be some of us [social equity license holders] . . . that won't be financially situated to open because it's taken so long. People have lost employees because of this. People have lost financial backing because of this. If I were open I would probably add about 200 jobs."[68] Right now, many social equity license applicants see the main beneficiaries of recreational legalization as the medical providers who were able to start in that market from the very beginning of its existence.

In other words, much like developments in Massachusetts, the record for social equity in Illinois is so far mixed. The infusion of funding and institutional buy-in has clearly allowed for more progress toward racial justice than has been possible in Massachusetts and other states. Yet even today there is still clearly a gap in trust and access between the communities of color that were targeted as part of cannabis criminalization and the communities that are benefiting from legalization. There is certainly an easily perceptible gap between how state officials in the Pritzker administration describe the progress made toward social equity and how those in communities of color, particularly elected officials in the legislature, have perceived the impact of legalization. Any effort to further engage with this policy problem will require understanding the true purpose of social equity, which is to ensure that communities impacted by criminalization actually see tangible benefits from legalization.

THE PROMISE OF LOCAL APPROACHES TO SOCIAL EQUITY

These drives for social equity are far from new, and a previous political and legal campaign is instructive. The effort to legalize gambling in Illinois decades earlier had encountered similar discussions, though the ultimate result was political capitulation to a state-run monopoly that would redistribute its profits to general state funding needs such as education or capital projects.[69] Then-state representative Lewis Caldwell, a social worker who had studied gambling enforcement himself, had instead proposed local legalization of gambling in Illinois because "the Black community needs the jobs."[70] Speculation that gamblers would be spending social service payments helped weaken support for this proposal, though Lewis loudly protested the lack of any evidence of this. It is clear that these themes of disparate enforcement and economic justice are long-standing in cities such as Chicago, where decades of police enforcement operations—whether targeted at narcotics or gambling—have left a legacy of exclusion and trauma that has been disproportionately borne by people of color.

To that end, an alternative path forward for social equity has been charted by a city in the Chicagoland suburbs. Like much of the northeast corner of Illinois, Evanston has a reputation as a liberal haven much like Cambridge, Massachusetts, earning the city a reputation as the "People's Republic of Evanston."[71] Fittingly, then, Evanston has made national headlines in recent years for a proposal to pay Black residents reparations. The local campaign for this program began in 2019 when the city council passed a resolution acknowledging the city's painful history of racial discrimination and segregation.[72] This past includes the legacy of the Potawatomi Tribes, who once lived on the land which Evanston now occupies but were forcefully relocated by the federal government,[73] as well as the town's namesake, John Evans, who participated in a massacre of 150 Native Americans.[74] The first Evanston resident of African descent was a slave purchased by a local family.[75] The resolution also referred to the city's participation in decades of discrimination in housing and government services, which led to economic stagnation for the city's Black residents, many of whom are finding it increasingly difficult to afford to remain in the city as the cost of living goes up and up.[76] This situation for Black residents has become even starker in recent years as the percentage of the city's population which is Black has continued to decline.[77]

After the Evanston City Council made this first step, the council's Equity and Empowerment Commission spent the following months hearing community feedback and working on solutions, including considering where the money could be found to fund any program and what the most effective form of reparations might be. While there was broad skepticism of the city's capacity to actualize this plan, the commission moved forward to recommend in September 2019 that the city council adopt a program of racial reparations that included housing assistance, economic development for businesses, and education assistance for the African American residents of Evanston. The council's November 2019 resolution adopting this plan called for these programs to be financed from disbursements derived from taxes on the cannabis businesses that would open in the city as a result of the legalization that had recently passed the legislature.[78]

One of the loudest voices on the council in favor of these measures was Robin Rue Simmons, a councilor first elected in 2017. Simmons had grown up in the segregated part of Evanston's 5th Ward, and after beginning her career in real estate and the local business community she became convinced of the need for further government measures to desegregate homeownership and provide racial minorities greater access to safe housing more broadly. During her term on the council, Simmons served as both the local champion and national face of the reparations campaign. She methodically worked with her community to bolster the case for Evanston to address harms that could be confronted at the local level, focusing on what could be achieved in practical terms even if it fell short of full justice in an abstract sense.[79] This included highlighting the recent history of cannabis enforcement by the Evanston Police Department—a report by city officials showed that from 2017–2019, Black individuals made up 71 percent and 57 percent of cannabis-related arrests and citations, respectively, despite making up around only 15 percent of the population in the most recent census.[80] After leaving the council in

2021, Simmons has continued her advocacy campaign in favor of national reparations.[81]

In large part due to Simmons's influence, the Evanston City Council adopted the first formal resolution authorizing its reparations program in 2021. The plan envisioned that the initial $10 million of the revenue that the city expects to receive from cannabis establishment taxes, as well as donations to be received from other sources, would be dedicated to financing its activities. It proposed spending up to $400,000 to help sixteen local Black residents obtain or sustain a home in the city of Evanston. Potential applicants could qualify for funding as a direct descendent of a Black resident of the city who lived there after 1919 in an effort to target those who had directly experienced segregation in Evanston.[82]

After receiving hundreds of applications for this funding pool, Evanston hosted the first raffle drawing in early 2022 to select the initial sixteen recipients of reparations benefits. Each beneficiary was eligible to receive up to $25,000. One of them was Stephen Frazier, an eighty-five-year-old Black resident of Evanston who grew up in and worked for the city for decades, including as an assistant city manager in the 1970s. Frazier was quoted in local media as saying that "it means enduring something that I had the fortitude to do. . . . [I]t's a way of acknowledging it was wrong."[83] Another recipient, Louis Weathers, recounted the history of segregation he personally experienced and reported planning to lend the funds he was to receive to help his son reduce his mortgage. Weathers and others also relayed frustration about the limited uses the funds were eligible for, though they acknowledged the importance of this measure and those similar to it nationally.[84] After the initial batch of reparations payments went out, the city had not made any additional awards to the potential recipients who qualified for the program as of March 2023. Most of those who qualified had lived and worked in Evanston's segregated 5th Ward for decades, and in the time since the drawing, at least six of them died without receiving any benefits from the program.[85]

Evanston has proposed to continue the disbursements to the remaining recipients qualified by city staff under the program. Funding the remaining applicants was projected to cost approximately $3.5 million, which the city was struggling to raise given that state licensing delays had only resulted in one of the projected three cannabis businesses opening in Evanston.[86] More recently, the city approved the idea of using real estate transfer tax revenues and one-time pandemic relief funds to fulfill its obligations under the reparations program, making it clear that local leaders remain committed to this work despite Rue Simmons herself leaving the council.[87] Meanwhile, her replacement representing the 5th Ward, Alderman Bobby Burns, has taken matters to diversify the ownership of Illinois cannabis ownership into his own hands by proposing to open a craft grower in Chicago's historically

Black Pullman neighborhood. Burns connected his efforts in this realm to his own experience as a student in Evanston's high school who occasionally used cannabis, and called for the state to make sure cannabis businesses were successful precisely because "we've tied the success of cannabis to this important social initiative."[88]

Despite success at winning over the local government, the discussion in Evanston is impacted by similar narratives about deservedness that have haunted other proposals for reparations. As Simmons noted, she has received many critical responses to her work: "You already have reparations, it's called Section eight and link card, you're lazy, just go get a job. They call it the ghetto lottery. They said it was reverse racism. They called me stupid. I mean, just the list went on. . . . I didn't respond to it initially, I would just delete them right away because it was so nasty. And I just I like to reject things that don't strengthen or build."[89] Still, it is notable that the first official reparations to be paid to Black Americans from government coffers were funded by legal cannabis sales, and it demonstrates, at least on a small scale, the creative potential for linking legalization to social equity. As Rue Simmons explained, "We just decided to take this first step, not perfect, not complete, certainly a first step in its infancy stages. But we said yes to reparations, we said yes to repair in a tangible, measurable way with funding we put our, our dollars, where are our values are stated."[90] In this sense, Evanston's importance is perhaps similar to Colorado's role in pioneering cannabis legalization: it has shown that it is possible to win political support for some form of reparations, even if this first step has been in practical terms somewhat limited.

That said, Evanston's example also demonstrates the potential challenges of tying the fight for reparations or any other kind of social equity program directly to the development of the legal cannabis market, which is subject to a number of pressures that conspire to make it difficult for entrepreneurs of color to begin and sustain businesses. Although local government in and of itself is limited in its capacity to enact change, however, much of the practical gains for social equity must be built and sustained on the local level—and the perfect cannot be the enemy of the good. Perhaps the most important lesson here is similar to the one shown in chapter 6 by the movement to ensure social equity businesses in the city of Cambridge, Massachusetts: the development of new policy models in this space is dependent on the tenacity and ingenuity of local activists willing to speak up and, when necessary, run for office themselves to effectuate change, regardless of what's happening in other jurisdictions or at the state or national level.

HAS ILLINOIS DONE BETTER?

When Governor Pritzker and Illinois legislators sketched out an ambitious plan for a socially equitable legalization of cannabis in 2019, none of them could imagine that less than a year later a global epidemic would seriously impair government operations and completely derail the prospects for building an inclusive industry. Partly as a result of COVID-19, Illinois has run into some of the same challenges that previous states encountered in setting up licit markets, such as ensuring an adequate supply of products. At the same time, the gathering strength of the dominant MSOs in the cannabis industry continues to hinder the prospects for creating equitable space for those with experience in the legacy market for cannabis. However, policymakers in Illinois should be commended for their commitment to getting many of the details right and, when circumstances changed, revisiting their initial assumptions and enacting amendments to the legislation.

While Illinois has not avoided many of the same problems that Massachusetts encountered when attempting to encourage equity in the legalized recreational market for cannabis, there have been important developments that still pushed the movement for equitable cannabis legalization forward. For example, Illinois legislators were successful in ensuring that expungement for previous offenses would be as far reaching and automated as possible, providing what is so far the greatest possible reach for this policy. Likewise, local policies in cities like Evanston can serve as guiding inspiration for efforts to further develop sustainable policies to direct the resources made available by legalization to the communities impacted by criminalization and the broader array of discriminatory policies associated with it.

Illinois's chief regulatory official, Danielle Perry, frames these developments as a precedent for future legalization measures, noting that "I don't like to have a conversation with a state that's thinking about legalizing, if they don't have [social equity] in there. . . . I think it's important for us to figure out ways to continue to diversify this industry, but to do it in a way where the application process itself is not burdensome on people." Importantly, however, Perry also recognizes that this is a work in progress: "Nationally, we have conversations all the time about the right way to do that. I don't know that anybody has found the perfect way."[91]

The fight for cannabis legalization began as a populist campaign guided by a small group of activists and endorsed by voters in a select group of states with the courage to see an off-ramp from the prohibitionist approach embraced by previous generations. However, as this book and others argue, the societal challenges that came with criminalization and the lived consequences of it borne by communities of color demand a more comprehensive response than can be delivered at the ballot box. What Illinois's experience—along with New York's, discussed in the next chapter—shows is that fully addressing these harms often requires participation of elected officials, at both the state and local levels. Legislators in particular are often able to better understand the communities they represent and demand comprehensive solutions for their constituents; they are also often more interested in ensuring the political and institutional success of the programs they create as opposed to those that might be initiated by activist groups and ratified by voters. Using this form of representation, legislators in states across the Northeast and Midwest have begun to envision a different form of cannabis legalization that incorporates the voices of communities of color, particularly those where legacies of segregation and criminalization have made wealth generation difficult. It is still early days for these efforts, but their prospects for success are intriguing.

NOTES

1. CBS News, "Chad Roberston Case: Amtrak Officer Charged with Murder in Unarmed Man's Shooting," *CBS News*, February 17, 2017, https://www.cbsnews.com/news/chad-robertson-case-amtrak-officer-charged-with-murder-in-unarmed-mans-shooting/.

2. Declan Desmond, "2 Years Later, Amtrak Officer Who Fatally Shot Minneapolis Man Acquitted," *Bring Me the News*, March 1, 2020, https://bringmethenews.com/minnesota-news/2-years-later-amtrak-officer-who-fatally-shot-minneapolis-man-acquitted.

3. Edward L. Lascher Jr., Michael G. Hagen, and Steven A. Rochlin, "Gun Behind the Door? Ballot Initiatives, State Policies and Public Opinion," *Journal of Politics* 58, no. 3 (1996): 760–75, https://www.jstor.org/stable/2960443.

4. See *KHQA*, "Gov. Rauner Signs IL Marijuana Decriminalization Bill Into Law," July 29, 2016, https://khqa.com/news/state/gov-rauner-signs-il-marijuana-decriminalization-bill-into-law; and Jaclyn Driscoll, "Illinois Governor Approves Medical Cannabis As Alternative for Opioids," *NPR Illinois*, August 28, 2018, https://www.nprillinois.org/health-harvest/2018-08-28/illinois-governor-approves-medical-cannabis-as-alternative-for-opioids.

5. Tina Sfondeles, "Gov. Rauner Not High on Legalizing Marijuana: 'That's a Mistake,'" *Chicago Sun-Times*, December 2, 2017, https://chicago.suntimes.com/2017/12/2/18317912/gov-rauner-not-high-on-legalizing-marijuana-that-s-a-mistake.

6. Shelby Bremer, "Pritzker Says He Wants to Legalize Marijuana in Illinois," *NBC5 Chicago*, updated November 9, 2018, https://www.nbcchicago.com/news/politics/pritzker-legalize-marijuana-in-illinois/169294/.

7. *Chillinois Podcast*, "#196—Danielle Perry," podcast, 1:59:37, April 22, 2022, https://soundcloud.com/chillinoispodcast/196-danielle-perry.

8. Richard J. Bonnie and Charles H. Whitebread, *The Marihuana Conviction: A History of Marihuana Prohibition in the United States* (Charlottesville: University of Virginia Press, 1974), 3.

9. George N. Leighton and Charles S. Bargiel, "A History of Illinois Drug Control Laws from 1818 to 1975," *UIC Law Review* 9, no. 1 (1975): 149.

10. Leighton and Bargiel, "Illinois Drug Control," 150–52.

11. Leighton and Bargiel, "History of Illinois Drug Control," 153–55.

12. Bonnie and Whitebread, *Marihuana Conviction*, 47.

13. Paul S. Taylor, "Crime and the Foreign Born: The Problem of the Mexican," in Edith Abbott, *Report on Crime and Criminal Justice in Relation to the Foreign Born for National Commission on Law Observance and Enforcement*, 200–25 (Washington, DC: Government Printing Office, 1931), https://www.ojp.gov/pdffiles1/Digitization/44548NCJRS.pdf.

14. Leighton and Bargiel, "Illinois Drug Control," 153.

15. Leighton and Bargiel, "Illinois Drug Control," 156.

16. Bonnie and Whitebread, *Marihuana Conviction*, 104.

17. Leighton and Bargiel, "Illinois Drug Control," 155–56.

18. Pamela Platt, "Legislative Note—Legal Analysis of Marijuana Legislation in Illinois," *DePaul Law Review* 22, no. 1 (1972): 281–83, https://via.library.depaul.edu/cgi/viewcontent.cgi?article=2856&context=law-review.

19. Leighton and Bargiel, "Illinois Drug Control," 157–59

20. *People v. McCabe*, 49 Ill. 2d 338 (1971), https://law.justia.com/cases/illinois/supreme-court/1971/42674-6.html.

21. Platt, "Legislative Note," 294.

22. Platt, "Legislative Note," 298.

23. Matthew Vaz, *Running the Numbers: Race, Police, and the History of Urban Gambling* (Chicago: University of Chicago Press, 2020), 25–29.

24. Vaz, *Running the Numbers*, 39–41.

25. US Senate, *Final Report of the Special Committee to Investigate Organized Crime in Interstate Commerce* (Washington, DC: Government Printing Office, 1951), archived at http://stoppredatorygambling.org/wp-content/uploads/2012/12/Kefauver-Committee-Final-report.pdf.

26. Vaz, *Running the Numbers*, 51.

27. Vaz, *Running the Numbers*, 48.

28. Vaz, *Running the Numbers*, 55–56.

29. Vaz, *Running the Numbers*, 145–48.

30. Richard Nixon et al., "Oval Office Conversation 498-5," May 13, 1971, from Common Sense for Drug Policy's archive of Nixon White House tape recordings, https://www.csdp.org/research/nixonpot.txt.

31. David Jackson, "The Law and Richard M. Daley," *Chicago*, May 13, 2011, https://www.chicagomag.com/chicago-magazine/september-1988/the-law-and-richard-m-daley/.

32. NORML, "Chicago Considers Marijuana Decriminalization Plan," blog post, September 23, 2004, https://norml.org/news/2004/09/23/chicago-considers-marijuana-decriminalization-plan/.

33. Civilian Office of Police Accountability (Chicago), "Summary Report of Investigation," Log no. 1087742, March 10, 2021, 1–5, https://loevy-content-uploads.s3.amazonaws.com/uploads/2022/08/COPA-Report-1087742.SRI_.pdf.

34. Jamie Kalven, "Operation Smoke and Mirrors," *The Intercept*, October 6, 2016, https://theintercept.com/2016/10/06/in-the-chicago-police-department-if-the-bosses-say-it-didnt-happen-it-didnt-happen/.

35. Ben Joravsky, "Joshua Tepfer—Ronald Watts," podcast, 57:00, in *The Ben Joravsky Show*, produced by Chicago *Reader*, January 11, 2022, https://chicagoreader.com/columns-opinion/podcasts/ben-joravsky-show-podcast-episodes/.

36. See Ballotpedia, "Colorado Constitution," Article V, Section 1.5.5, https://ballotpedia.org/Colorado_Constitution.

37. See Ballotpedia, "Massachusetts Constitution," Article XLVIII, Section II.2, available at https://ballotpedia.org/Massachusetts_Constitution.

38. Associated Press, "Illinois Considers Legalizing Marijuana for a Fiscal Boost," *Fox 2 Now*, March 26, 2017, https://fox2now.com/news/illinois-considers-legalizing-marijuana-for-a-fiscal-boost/.

39. Dean Olsen, "Illinois Legislators Lay Out Plans for Recreational Marijuana Proposal," *Herald & Review* (Decatur, IL), January 29, 2019, https://herald-review.com/news/state-and-regional/govt-and-politics/illinois-legislators-lay-out-plans-for-recreational-marijuana-proposal/article_36da662d-3db1-5224-8745-cf75df1b5276.html.

40. Kyle Jaeger, "Illinois Senate Approves Marijuana Legalization Bill," *Marijuana Moment*, May 29, 2019, https://www.marijuanamoment.net/illinois-senate-approves-marijuana-legalization-bill/.

41. Liz Nagy, "Illinois Senate Passes Marijuana Legalization Bill, Sends It Back to Illinois House," *ABC 7 Chicago*, May 30, 2019, https://abc7chicago.com/illinois-marijuana-cannabis-legalization-bill/5322315/.

42. Craig Wall and Sarah Schulte, "Illinois Marijuana Law Signed by Governor JB Pritzker Tuesday, Takes Effect January 1, 2020," *ABC 7 Chicago*, June 25, 2019, https://abc7chicago.com/illinois-marijuana-law-in-jb-pritzker-recreation-weed-2020/5362982/.

43. Tom Schuba, "State Sen. Toi Hutchinson Appointed as Illinois' Pot Czar," *Chicago Sun-Times*, September 26, 2019, https://chicago.suntimes.com/cannabis/2019/9/26/20886313/state-senator-toi-hutchinson-appointed-illinois-pot-czar.

44. Cate Cauguiran and Craig Wall, "Illinois House Passes Marijuana Legalization Bill, Approves Balanced Budget," *ABC 7 Chicago*, June 1, 2019, https://abc7chicago.com/illinois-passes-recreational-marijuana-senate-house-weed-il/5324375/.

45. Tom Schuba, "Recreational Weed Sales Drop to $35 Million in February as Shortages Continue," *Chicago Sun-Times*, March 4, 2020, https://chicago.suntimes.com/cannabis/2020/3/4/21165299/recreational-weed-sales-drop-to-35-million-in-february-as-shortages-continue.

46. Ally Marotti, "Illinois Delays Awarding 75 Licenses for New Marijuana Dispensaries Amid Coronavirus Outbreak," *Chicago Tribune*, April 29, 2020, https://www.chicagotribune.com/coronavirus/ct-coronavirus-illinois-marijuana-dispensary-delays-20200429-ao2nooa5hzgnnbmfulw4w5sdma-story.html.

47. Matthew Rees, "Social Equity and Cannabis Legalisation in Illinois: Creating Equitable Societies?" Master's thesis, University of Sheffield, UK, 2021–2022, 35.

48. Shia Kapos, "Lawyers, Race and Money: Illinois' Messy Weed Experiment," *Politico*, September 18, 2021, https://www.politico.com/news/2021/09/18/illinois-weed-experiment-512626.

49. Mike Fourcher, "KPMG Contract Allowed Recent College Graduates to Score Illinois Dispensary Applications," *Grown In*, September 29, 2020, https://grownin.com/2020/09/29/kpmg-contract-allowed-recent-college-graduates-to-score-illinois-dispensary-applications/.

50. Illinois Department of Commerce and Economic Opportunity, "Social Equity Cannabis Loans," fact sheet, https://idfpr.illinois.gov/Forms/AUC/SocialEquityCannabisLoans%20One-Pager.pdf.

51. Sanford Stein, "What Happened in Illinois Part I," *Cannabis Law*, March 15, 2022, https://cannabislaw.com/what-happened-in-illinois-part-i/.

52. Tom Schuba, "Finalist for Marijuana Dispensary Licenses Also Works for Firm That Graded Applications," *Chicago Sun-Times*, September 8, 2020, https://chicago.suntimes.com/cannabis/2020/9/8/21427810/kpmg-illinois-new-marijuana-pot-licenses-hamd-kamal.

53. Amanda Vinicky, "The Illinois Marijuana Industry Was Supposed to Bring Equity: Advocates Say Those Promises Are Falling Short," *WTTW*, September 28, 2022, https://news.wttw.com/2022/09/28/illinois-marijuana-industry-was-supposed-bring-equity-advocates-say-those-promises-are.

54. Illinois Department of Commerce and Economic Opportunity, *2022 Annual Cannabis Report* (Springfield: Illinois Department of Commerce and Economic Opportunity, 2022), 2, https://dceo.illinois.gov/content/dam/soi/en/web/dceo/aboutdceo/reportsrequiredbystatute/2023-loans-and-grants-to-social-equity-applicant-report.pdf?wcmmode=disabled.

55. Vinicky, "Illinois Marijuana Industry."

56. Kapos, "Lawyers, Race and Money."

57. Illinois (State of), "Gov. Pritzker Announces Record-Breaking $445 Million in FY 2022 for Total Tax Reported for Adult-Use Cannabis," news release, July 25, 2022, https://www.illinois.gov/news/press-release.25213.html.

58. Illinois Justice Project, "Restore, Reinvest, and Renew (R3 Program)," https://www.iljp.org/r3program; and Illinois R3 (Restore, Reinvest, and Renew) Program, "Eligibility," State of Illinois, last updated December 15, 2021, https://r3.illinois.gov/eligibility/.

59. Illinois R3 (Restore, Reinvest, and Renew) Program, "Pritzker Administration Awards $3.5 Million in Restore, Reinvest, and Renew Program Grants in Response to Summer Violence," news release, July 15, 2021, https://r3.illinois.gov/news/2021-07-15-r3-update.

60. Illinois Office of the Lieutenant Governor, "Restore, Reinvest, and Renew Program Board (R3PB)," November 15, 2021, https://r3.illinois.gov/downloads/R3ProgramBoardMembers.pdf.

61. Illinois Office of the Lieutenant Governor, "Restore, Reinvest, and Renew Program Board (R3PB)."

62. Lauren Weisner, “The Illinois Restore, Reinvest, and Renew (R3) Grant Program: Examining Grant Applicant Feedback,” Illinois Criminal Justice Information Authority, October 22, 2021, https://icjia.illinois.gov/researchhub/articles/the-illinois-restore-reinvest-and-renew-r3-grant-program-examining-grant-applicant-feedback/.

63. ActNow! “Afterschool as a Substance Misuse and Violence Prevention Tool: Funding Youth Development Programs Through Adult-Use Cannabis Tax Revenue in Illinois,” brochure, 2021, https://actnowillinois.org/wp-content/uploads/2021/03/AA-IL-ACT-Now-R3-030921-FINAL.pdf.

64. Amanda Vinicky, “More Than 2 Years After Illinois Legalized Recreational Marijuana, Some Say Law Falls Short of Promise,” *WTTW*, April 21, 2022, https://news.wttw.com/2022/04/21/more-2-years-after-illinois-legalized-recreational-marijuana-some-say-law-falls-short; and Illinois Criminal Justice Information Authority, “SFY23 R3 Grant Awards,” June 22, 2022, https://agency.icjia-api.cloud/uploads/SFY_23_R3_Grants_List_4a515603da.pdf.

65. Illinois (State of), “Pritzker Administration Announces Nearly 500,000 Cannabis Arrest Records Expunged Four Years Ahead of Schedule,” news release, December 31, 2020, https://www.illinois.gov/news/press-release.22566.html.

66. Ivan Pereira, “Chicago Prosecutors Expunge 15,000 Cannabis Convictions,” *ABC News*, April 20, 2022, https://abcnews.go.com/US/chicago-prosecutors-expunge-15000-cannabis-convictions/story?id=84197307.

67. Vinicky, “2 Years After Illinois Legalized.”

68. Vinicky, “2 Years After Illinois Legalized.”

69. Illinois Lottery, “Where the Money Goes,” https://www.illinoislottery.com/giving-back/where-the-money-goes.

70. Vaz, *Running the Numbers*, 146.

71. Jeff P. Smith (@jeffpsmith), “CSNA Mayoral Forum Qs. #9, #10: Gentrification; People’s Republic of Evanston,” blog post, Central Street Neighbors Association, March 23, 2009, archived at https://archive.vn/20120707064753/http://centralstreetneighbors.com/?q=node/530.

72. For example, see Rachel Treisman, “In Likely First, Chicago Suburb of Evanston Approves Reparations for Black Residents,” *NPR*, March 23, 2021, https://www.npr.org/2021/03/23/980277688/in-likely-first-chicago-suburb-of-evanston-approves-reparations-for-black-reside.

73. Unitarian Church of Evanston, “Unitarian Church of Evanston Land Acknowledgement,” https://ucevanston.org/land-acknowledgment/; and Evanston (IL) Public Library, “Land Acknowledgment,” https://www.epl.org/land-acknowledgment/.

74. *Northwestern Magazine*, “John Evans and the Sand Creek Massacre,” Fall 2014, https://www.northwestern.edu/magazine/fall2014/campuslife/john-evans-and-the-sand-creek-massacre.html.

75. Larry Gavin, “Exhibit Shows History of Segregation and Redlining in Evanston,” *Evanston Round Table*, September 4, 2019, https://evanstonroundtable.com/2019/09/04/exhibit-shows-history-of-segregation-and-redlining-in-evanston/.

76. Evanston (IL) City Council, *Resolution: Commitment to End Structural Racism and Achieve Racial Equality*, Resolution 58-R-19, June 5, 2019, https://www.cityofevanston.org/home/showpublisheddocument/62674/637511531477970000

77. Bill Smith, "Evanston's Population Has Dropped: How to Respond?" *Evanston Now*, January 3, 2020, https://evanstonnow.com/evanstons-population-has-dropped-how-to-respond/.

78. Evanston (IL) City Council, *Resolution: Establishing a City of Evanston Funding Source Devoted to Local Reparations*, Resolution 126-R-19, November 14, 2019, https://www.cityofevanston.org/home/showpublisheddocument/62672/637511530122430000.

79. Devon Reid to Robin Rue Simmons, memo, April 18, 2019, https://www.cityofevanston.org/home/showpublisheddocument/71150/637854525387270000.

80. Shenicka Hohenkirk to Honorable Mayor and Members of the City Council, "Cannabis Arrests and Compliance Tickets," memo, November 20, 2019, https://www.cityofevanston.org/home/showpublisheddocument/55309/637190175978830000.

81. FirstRepair, "Our Founder: About Robin Rue Simmons," 2023, https://firstrepair.org/robin-rue/.

82. Kimberly Richardson to Honorable Mayor and Members of the City Council, "Adoption of Resolution 37-R-27, Authorizing the Implementation of the Evanston Local Reparations Restorative Housing Program and Program Budget," memo, March 22, 2021, 1–4, https://cityofevanston.civicweb.net/document/50624/Adoption%20of%20Resolution%2037-R-27,%20Authorizing%20the.pdf?handle=E11C7B73E1B6470DA42362AB80A50C46; and Morris (Dino) Robinson Jr. and Jenny Thompson, "Evanston Policies and Practices Directly Affecting the African American Community, 1900–1960 (and Present)," draft report, Evanston, IL, August 2020, https://www.cityofevanston.org/home/showpublisheddocument?id=59759.

83. *NBC 5 Chicago*, "Man Receives Evanston Reparations Program Award," video, May 13, 2022, https://www.nbcchicago.com/local/man-receives-evanston-reparations-program-award/2832568/.

84. Debbie-Marie Brown, "'I Didn't Think I Had a Chance': Meet One of Evanston's First 16 Reparations Recipients," *Evanston Round Table*, August 4, 2022, https://evanstonroundtable.com/2022/08/04/louis-weathers-reparations-grant-recipients/.

85. Adrienne Broaddus, "Evanston City Council Votes in Favor of Expanding Its Reparations Program to Repair Housing Discrimination," CNN.com, March 28, 2023, https://www.cnn.com/2023/03/27/us/evanston-illinois-reparations-housing-discrimination-expand/index.html.

86. Debbie-Marie Brown, "City OKs Paying Out $3.45 Million in Reparations," *Evanston Round Table*, August 9, 2022, https://evanstonroundtable.com/2022/08/09/city-approves-dispersal-of-3-45m-in-reparations/.

87. Bob Seidenberg, "A Reparations Program in Search of a Funding Source," *Evanston Round Table*, November 15, 2022, https://evanstonroundtable.com/2022/11/15/a-reparations-program-in-search-of-a-funding-source/.

88. Saul Pink, "Ald. Bobby Burns Cultivates New Approach to the Business and Politics of Marijuana," *Daily Northwestern* (Evanston, IL), October 28, 2022, https://dailynorthwestern.com/2022/10/28/city/ald-bobby-burns-cultivates-new-approach-to-the-business-and-politics/.

89. *Chicago Sun-Times*, "Evanston Ald. on First-in-the-Nation Reparations Bill," YouTube video, April 2, 2021, https://www.youtube.com/watch?v=6rZITSDO-UQ&ab_channel=ChicagoSun-Times.

90. *Chicago Sun-Times*, "First-in-the-Nation Reparations Bill."

91. *Chillinois Podcast*, "#196—Danielle Perry," podcast, 1:59:37, April 22, 2022, https://soundcloud.com/chillinoispodcast/196-danielle-perry.

Chapter 8

New York

Resources for Social Equity

In 2014, a Black New Yorker named Eric Garner was stopped by NYPD officer Daniel Pantaleo on the streets of Staten Island on suspicion of selling "loose" cigarettes, which are often smuggled and sold by and to poor individuals seeking to evade increasingly high taxes.[1] During the stop, which was captured on cell phone video, Pantaleo determined that Garner was uncooperative and put him into a chokehold, resulting in Garner's eventual death. Along with the police killing of Michael Brown later the same year, Garner's death is often seen as the beginning of the "Black Lives Matter" movement.

Garner's death is a tragic example of how local officials' efforts to enforce even mundane laws promoting the state's interest in maximizing revenue from tobacco taxes can be deadly to those in minority neighborhoods. When the state seeks to exert a great degree of control over individual autonomy on drug use, the consequences can be just as deadly. Although Garner's death made news across the country and led to a political row between New York's mayor and the NYPD, there was comparatively little uproar only several years earlier when eighteen-year-old Ramarley Graham was shot to death in front of his grandmother in the Bronx, while trying to flush cannabis down his bathroom toilet, by a police officer who had earlier stopped him and returned with a warrant. Although the officer was later forced to leave the police force and Graham's family was successful in obtaining a legal settlement in their favor, it spurred no mass movement to highlight the injustice of War on Drugs policies.[2]

While media attention on both Garner and Graham rightfully spoke to the arbitrary use of police violence in their cases, there was little discussion of the nature of legal regimes, the license they have given to law enforcement to conduct surveillance and exert social control in communities of color, and the incentives that policymakers and the state more generally have to maintain these systems. One of the few national politicians that made this connection in Garner's case was Kentucky senator and noted libertarian Rand Paul, who in 2014 pointed out that the New York legislature had as recently as 2010 increased the tax on cigarettes sold in New York City. Paul thought that "it's also important to know that some politician put a tax of $5.85 on a pack of cigarettes, so they've driven cigarettes underground so as not to make them so expensive."[3]

Underground markets have put much of the economic life of communities of color on the wrong side of the law, exposing participants in these economies to police misconduct. When violence does occur, it often puts victims on the defensive in media reporting that too frequently suggests that people of color should "know better" than to engage in these illicit activities given the risks. As the Drug Policy Alliance's executive director Kassandra Frederique put it: "People don't think Black people have the right to use drugs in the first place . . . [because] if you are Black there are certain rules" that are socially enforced. "You can't play guns in the street, you can't walk in the street with a hoodie up, you can't go into a Walmart and look at things . . . and the fact that you know the things that you are unable to do [and would still] have the audacity to think you could take a psychoactive substance is ridiculous." Because "you are breaking the rules," the thinking goes, "whatever happens to you, you deserve."[4]

There are far too many Garners and Grahams who fell victim to this kind of arbitrary racist zone of social disapproval that provided the legal and moral pretext for their murder at the hands of law enforcement. Black New Yorkers, like Black residents across the country, know that they have been targeted by law enforcement for pretextual reasons at disproportionate rates. Addressing the harm of criminalization more firmly requires addressing this collective trauma as much as any package of economic and criminal justice reforms could do. In recent years, the disparate realities that Black people face in these areas compared to white people have at least started to spur legislators to consider revamping drug laws—a development that is a particularly salient issue for New York's future because of the state's unique past.

As this chapter will demonstrate, New York is where much of the criminalized drug policy that has come to define the War on Drugs was itself born, and where it continued to find life for decades after that. Beyond the television screens where New York's "finest" were depicted arresting countless unnamed young men of color for various crimes of social disorder, the actual epidemic of criminal enforcement in both New York City and across the state represented one of the most strict and extensive systems of state sanctions for drug possession and sales across the country. Well into the twentieth century, New York's drug enforcement numbers—as evidenced by arrests and the criminal sentences that resulted—reflected an audacious commitment on the part of the state to regulate the economic and social fabric of communities of color. Set apart from a neoliberal tendency to shrink or limit the size of the state that has come to define politics in recent decades in an otherwise liberal hub, the expansion of police power to arrest, discipline, and imprison individuals attributable to the War on Drugs is the mark of a dystopian yet highly activist philosophy of intervention.

As one of the nation's political and cultural centers, New York has for many years been an example to the rest of the country of what a "tough on crime" approach to drug policy should look like. The so-called "Rockefeller Drug Laws" that New York first developed in the 1960s became a model of strict criminalization that many other states adopted, while mention of the "broken windows" and "stop-and-frisk" policing techniques that dominated the 1990s and 2000s immediately evoke New York City. Yet this situation is in many ways reversed when it comes to decriminalization: New York is a relatively recent entrant into the community of states that have legal cannabis, only joining its peers in 2021.

Similar to Illinois, voters in New York have no right to initiate a ballot petition to enact legislation, and the political culture of the state reflects population dynamics that often leave more conservative upstate legislators of both parties setting the priorities for the more liberal downstate population center. The victory for legalization was only born in the years after progressive Democrats broke a coalition of Republicans and conservative Democrats that had dominated the state senate and blocked policy reforms dear to activists on a number of social and criminal justice issues. This coalition had often been useful to then-governor Andrew Cuomo, who used the division to control the policy agenda in the state. After progressive Democrats took full control of the legislature, however, it set up a number of policy fights with a newly defensive Cuomo, including a challenge on how exactly to legalize cannabis in New York.[5]

While it took a few years—cannabis legalization was first considered and defeated in 2019—the state ultimately adopted a legalization measure in 2021. One effect of this state legislative history is that it delayed any serious legalization efforts in New York long enough that when its proponents finally succeeded they had more than two decades of cannabis policies from other states to examine as models of both what to do and what not to do. For example, legalization in New York has come with some of the major tools that Illinois adopted just the year before and which are being called for in other states to address the harms of criminalization.

So far, there are three distinct elements to New York's approach. First, a robust and state-directed expungement program that is intended to ensure that all of those who were arrested and convicted of cannabis offenses during the period of criminalization would have their records cleared. Second, it recognizes that those who had previous experience in the legacy market for cannabis need to have relatively low barriers to access ownership and management opportunities in the new regulated market. Lastly, it conceives that tax revenues derived from cannabis legalization should be distributed and invested in a way that gives tangible paths for those communities of color most impacted by criminalization to benefit from legalization, particularly by providing economic opportunities for residents beyond the regulated cannabis industry. Ensuring any one of these aspects of equitable legalization has proved challenging thus far, though New York legislators are seeking to build on the progress of other social equity programs from around the country. For example, New York has created a licensing preference system with more specific criteria than those of previous states. The success of this policy remains to be seen. As of this writing, it is still being implemented, with the funding stream for much of the social equity policy still to be determined.

The stakes of legalization in New York can't be higher. The inherently reactionary nature of state politics has threatened the political coalition for leniency and reduced state disciplining of communities of color. For example, a criminal justice reform bill passed in 2019 that made significant revisions to the bail system for those arrested and awaiting trial has been revised and faces greater skepticism from moderate Democrats, including the current New York City mayor, Eric Adams.[6] If the benefits of legalization do not reach communities of color, or conservatives are able to frame the legalization of cannabis as a larger contributor to crime and disorder, New York may yet come to symbolize a failure in legalization's thus far relentless spread rather than an important milestone in the use of social equity policies to redress past harms stemming from the War on Drugs.

CANNABIS CRIMINALIZATION

New York's history with cannabis criminalization is perhaps one of the most extensive in the nation. As quoted by a market participant: "New York can lay the claim . . . of being the marijuana arrests capital, and, you know, for many years having the experience where there were more people arrested than could even fit inside of Yankee Stadium, just for low level marijuana possession every single year."[7]

Similar to Illinois, New York has a particularly long history of establishing various forms of regulation that seek to minimize, if not prohibit, the use of drugs deemed harmful by society. In 1886, the state legislature required that all opium and morphine be properly labeled as such, which was then followed by further regulations in 1897 and 1900 that imposed restrictions on carrying narcotic substances while also creating new recordkeeping requirements for those who sought to distribute such substances.[8]

By 1907, the legislature became increasingly willing to impose harsh penalties on the use and trafficking of cocaine, which was an ingredient in a variety of patent medicines as well as soft drinks and other consumer products sold widely across the state and country.[9] With this new wave of legislation, possession without a valid prescription became a criminal offense, bringing a whole new group of individuals and behaviors under state control and criminal sanction. The Towns-Boylan Act in 1914 imposed many similar restrictions on opium, and further legislation over the ensuing years sought to harmonize these regulations with the prohibitions and legal structures of the federal Harrison Act.[10] This legislative movement culminated in 1918 with New York's Narcotic Drug Control Act, which imposed criminal penalties on the illegal transfer of drugs but allowed medically supervised consumption to take place.[11] However, federal efforts to control medical access for addicts resulted in a strict legal regime that most, if not all, prescribers were unable or unwilling to comply with. This in turn led the state legislature to repeal this version of drug control only three years later, in 1921, leaving New York without a statewide drug control law for several years.[12]

Later efforts to establish drug control in New York state beginning in 1927 were focused on using the criminal code to limit the use of various substances, including heroin, cocaine, and opiates. Penalties for violations were revived or even enhanced, and medical access was largely prohibited.[13] While cannabis was initially not included in these efforts, 1937's federal Marihuana Tax Act gave state legislators the push to align New York's drug law with the new policy. The state added cannabis to its control regime beginning in 1939; it added even greater legal penalties four years later.[14] Increasing focus on the problems of drug abuse prompted the state legislature to continue revising drug laws until 1967, when New York consolidated nearly all of its measures into a single location in the statute book that created a unified scheduling system for substances and uniform penalties for different classes of offenses. This system was subsequently brought into compliance with the federal Controlled Substances Act in 1973.[15]

As in many other places throughout the United States, New York's increasingly expansive and punitive drug control policies during the mid-twentieth century reflected its general push to regulate activities that policymakers deemed to be socially harmful. Similar to what occurred in Chicago, for example, enforcement of anti-gambling laws in New York City had hit a fever pitch by the mid-1950s, with arrests rising quickly and nearly hitting 45,000 after having declined somewhat from a previous peak in the mid-1940s.[16] Aggressive enforcement of gambling prohibition turned from a perhaps once-idealistic belief in the power of the state to reify and rectify problem behaviors into barely disguised economic warfare against communities of color. It also brought a predictable surge in law enforcement corruption as the often poorly paid agents of the state buckled and broke under the conflicting demands of tough street-level enforcement and the inherent challenges in following through with legal cases against those arrested, who were often released almost immediately. Even still, the brunt of the effort was visited on communities of color, where the gambling games employed thousands of hardworking residents who were implicated in the dragnet. Many workers were being added to police files as being associated with the gambling industry, which limited their employability outside the gambling trade and locked them into criminal activity.[17]

Before New Yorkers began to be arrested in the thousands during the last decades of the twentieth century in the name of drug control, then, racial disparities in anti-gambling arrests exemplified street-level police surveillance and intervention into communities of color across the state. This economic front in the war against poor Black communities shattered with court decisions in the 1960s that made gambling prosecutions much more difficult. New York eventually declared defeat in its pursuit of criminal prosecutions of gamblers and instead chose to legalize and regulate gambling through the New York State Lottery, a business that by the 2022 fiscal year had raised $3.6 billion in tax revenue. Though only amounting to a small portion of the $220 billion state budget, this figure takes on a different import when considered as representing the loss to communities of color that occurred when, in the early troubled years of its existence, the state lottery replicated the games common in illicit gambling rings that provided thousands of New Yorkers with a steady economic existence, leading to the slow erosion of these legacy operations.[18]

The relationship between the decline of gambling control and the rise of drug control is hinted at by a simple comparison of trends in arrests related to the two activities. After hitting a peak in 1956, gambling arrests sharply declined and less than ten years later were below a quarter of their previous level. Conversely, narcotics arrests in the city during the 1960s were on the rise. The two hit an inflection point around 1965, after which much of the public narrative about public disorder centered on drug use. Law enforcement had previously pushed the envelope of legality regarding enforcement of gambling laws, including warrantless searches of those suspected of being involved in gambling, as well as harassment arrests designed to disrupt or intimidate gambling operations.[19] Police enforcement of drug laws would pick up this tradition while becoming a legal beachhead for new forms of surveillance and harassment of communities of color.

THE ROCKEFELLER DRUG LAWS

During the 1970s, visitors to New York City often commented on its failing infrastructure, high crime, and public manifestations of poverty—including public drug use and other criminalized behavior. The smell of cannabis in the air in the middle of places like Times Square was a frequent reminder of this "bad" New York. It was partially a response to this context that in 1973—shortly after the federal government passed the Controlled Substances Act that scheduled all drugs—New York state adopted what became known as the "Rockefeller Drug Laws." Named for the moderate Republican governor in office at the time, Nelson Rockefeller, these laws provided strict criminal penalties for anyone arrested with small amounts of criminalized substances.[20]

Rockefeller's career spanned decades in public service, including as governor of New York for twelve years (1959–1971) and three unsuccessful campaigns for the presidency. Due to his personal position in the national spotlight, as well as the state's cultural influence on the rest of America, Rockefeller's political positions on drugs evolved in close relation to national trends. In particular, he had previously been known as a moderate on the question of drug enforcement; during the first part of his governorship, he favored rehabilitation and treatment for addicted people. Reflecting a broader national change toward punitive solutions for public perceptions of drug abuse and addiction, however, Rockefeller announced in his final term that leniency had failed, and he instead demanded the imposition of harsh criminal penalties for those convicted of selling drugs as both punishment and a deterrent. State policymakers have been dealing with the consequences of this shift ever sense, with legislators revising this regime several times.[21]

Strong historical evidence suggests that while Rockefeller had long been struggling with the issue of drug addiction and the public safety issues perceived to be connected with this issue, the origins of his punitive push lay in his admiration of how other countries confronted drug addiction and, in particular, trafficking. Rockefeller communicated with one confidant regarding policies in Japan, for example, where drug sellers were often punished with life sentences. The reform of drug laws that passed the New York state legislature in 1973 reflected this philosophy, with convictions for sale of relatively small amounts of any prohibited substance getting at least fifteen years in state prison. The law also removed much of the discretion given to judges and prosecutors to plead individuals down to lesser charges. Rockefeller himself ignored a number of warnings that the new laws would create intense pressure on state institutions, rejecting the treatment-oriented approach that had defined addiction policy in the 1960s and calling for "common sense" in dealing with the drug problem. He also latched on to public concern about drugs as reflected by leaders in the Black community as well as in letters he personally received, which often called for stark action to address the drug epidemic and less concern for individual rights than for community needs.[22] Although cannabis possession was removed from the highest enforcement tier in the regime under the administration of Rockefeller's successor, Hugh Carey, it nevertheless remained strictly prohibited.[23] Although that action reduced possession of small amounts of cannabis in general to a violation, possession of cannabis in "public view" remained a misdemeanor—a distinction which would allow law enforcement in New York City significant discretion to harass and arrest Black residents.[24]

This shift toward harsher New York drug laws by itself did not immediately lead to the sort of mass loss of opportunity for communities of color that the War on Drugs later entailed. For one thing, there was no rush to prosecute new classes of offenders. By the late 1970s, a state legislative commission called the new strict laws "disappointing," given the stable rates of convictions seen for drug crimes.[25] This ultimately reflected a delay, however, rather than any real continuity in enforcement strategies by legal authorities that simply had not yet received the resources that would allow them to scale up operations to the degree Rockefeller envisioned. This mismatch in priorities is reflected by New York City mayor John Lindsay's 1973 opposition to the laws. Although his warnings that the state prison population would increase by as much as 50 percent failed to emerge during his tenure in office, over the next two decades they would prove to be a profound understatement of the actual impact.[26]

Consider the following statistics. In 1978, the number of felony drug arrests in New York was a modest 7,972, a figure relatively unchanged from before the passage of the Rockefeller Drug Laws. Within five years, these arrests would double; five years after that, they would triple again. In other words, less than two decades after Rockefeller's reforms, the number of felony drug arrests increased by a factor of six. This crackdown may have begun with statewide drug policy reform, but the substantial increases in arrests and convictions developed for many years after that initial decision.[27]

The growth in enforcement actions reflects a profound change in politics and policy on the national, state, and city levels that had set in by the early 1980s. It was part and parcel of the same trend that the Kelling and Wilson "Broken Windows" article, published in 1982, represented. New York City mayor Ed Koch, elected in 1978 with a tough on crime agenda and in power throughout the 1980s, embraced this philosophy to great effect. While previous city officials had largely abandoned street-level enforcement, believing it to entail high costs yet ultimately having little effect on drug markets themselves, Koch and his leadership at the NYPD reversed this trend and created enforcement units in response to evolving public concern about open-air drug markets. Increasing budgets for the NYPD meant it could hire thousands of additional officers in the first half of the 1980s to confront this perceived crisis. The arrests for felony drug arrests in Manhattan and the Bronx reflect this, increasing at scale through the 1980s. This trend was most pronounced in Manhattan, where felony drug arrests nearly quadrupled during the 1980s.[28]

The perceptions of social disorder and consequent public demands for increased punitive control continued well into the 1990s, eventually resulting in the election of Mayor Rudy Giuliani in 1993 and the imposition of greater punitive police surveillance measures. This led to the so-called New York "Renaissance," which crested by the later half of the decade and the new millennium, although crime rates had already started to decrease enough in the years before Giuliani's election that Kevin McAllister, the main character of 1992's *Home Alone 2: Lost in New York*, could plausibly remain safe enough in the city to meet then–real estate developer Donald Trump in the lobby of his newly purchased hotel. Rather than challenging the racialized poverty of the later half of the twentieth century with its heavily policed population, the vision of social disorder seen in the finale of the movie is instead personified by the "Pigeon Lady" and her uplifting message that the viewer should "trust again."[29]

THE POLITICAL LEGACY OF NEW YORK CITY CRIME CONTROL

The version of social order now present in much of the tourist-friendly parts of Manhattan masks a larger city where the NYPD has often used the War on Drugs as a tool of societal and individual discipline. For example, under the "stop-and-frisk" policy which would come to be identified as a core initiative of former mayor Michael Bloomberg, NYPD officers could search individuals under a lower degree of suspicion if they believed that the individual in question might have a firearm or other dangerous weapon. Bloomberg later explained the thinking behind this policy:

> Ninety-five percent of murders—murderers and murder victims—fit one M.O. You can just take the description, Xerox it, and pass it out to all the cops. They are male, minorities, sixteen to twenty-five. . . . And that's where the real crime is. You've got to get the guns out of the hands of people that are getting killed. So you want to spend the money on a lot of cops in the streets. Put those cops where the crime is, which means in minority neighborhoods. So one of the unintended consequences is people say, "Oh my God, you are arresting kids for marijuana that are all minorities." Yes, that's true. Why? Because we put all

> the cops in minority neighborhoods. Yes, that's true. Why do we do it? Because that's where all the crime is. And the way you get the guns out of the kids' hands is to throw them up against the wall and frisk them. . . . And then they start . . . [thinking], "Oh I don't want to get caught." So they don't bring the gun. They still have a gun, but they leave it at home.[30]

NYPD officers were already stationed in and prioritizing criminal enforcement in minority neighborhoods as part of 1990s "tough on crime" efforts, and the enforcement actions under the stop-and-frisk policies furthered this ugly racial narrative. A later study found that over 90 percent of the people stopped under this program were young Black males, few of whom actually had a firearm or other dangerous weapon.[31] Very few of these stops—18 percent of 97,296 in the first year of the Bloomberg administration and 12 percent of 685,724 stops by its last year in 2011—resulted in a "hit," meaning officers issued some sort of citation or arrest.[32] Stop-and-frisk, while often justified as an officer-safety and crime-control measure, frequently served as social discipline for residents in these poorer neighborhoods, reinforcing an adversarial relationship with law enforcement for youth of color and decreasing social cohesion.

The scale of this enforcement mechanism would remain a persistent aspect of drug criminalization in New York. While felony drug arrests during the 1990s remained at the high plateau they had reached in the late 1980s, they then dissipated. This was partly because much drug enforcement would move to misdemeanor arrests by the early 2000s, when stop-and-frisk became the paradigmatic approach of the NYPD. Misdemeanor arrests in Manhattan peaked at nearly 30,000 per year in the late 1990s, well over the peak of felony drug arrests in that same borough. Similar arrest trends can be seen in Brooklyn and the Bronx.[33]

This system was uniquely expensive—according to an ACLU report on cannabis law enforcement across the country, New York stood far apart from other states in terms of the amount of money it spent supporting enforcement activities. This report estimated that New York spent nearly $677 million on cannabis enforcement in 2010—between police, courts, and correctional systems—which represents nearly three-fifths of all drug enforcement spending in the state that year. The ACLU's arrest statistics for that year found that Black New Yorkers were over four times as likely to be arrested for cannabis statewide, a statistic that itself was dwarfed by the numbers coming from New York City, where Black residents were over nine times as likely to be arrested as white residents.[34]

By 2018, the statewide racial disparity had decreased so that Black residents were "only" 2.6 times more likely to be arrested for cannabis than white residents, even as fewer residents overall and fewer African Americans specifically were arrested for possession.[35] But even in areas with much smaller numbers of possession arrests, there was still often a wide racial disparity in arrests. In upstate rural Steuben County, which according to the 2020 census was over 96 percent white and had little over a thousand Black residents, law enforcement managed to arrest Black residents at nearly twenty times the rate of white residents for cannabis possession.[36]

This overview of cannabis enforcement in New York demonstrates how prohibition was racially targeted and fundamentally unequal, whether this design was explicitly intended or not. As referenced in earlier chapters, New Yorkers (and all Americans) use cannabis at roughly equal rates across racial lines. White Americans who wished to indulge in cannabis use previous to legalization often had access to a private home to safely consume it in, something that many Black Americans, particularly those living in a densely crowded urban area such as New York City, simply did not have. While a relatively small proportion of Black residents of New York City live in public housing, they are significantly more likely to do so than members of other racial or ethnic groups—a situation which subjects much of their day-to-day life to possible state surveillance and interference.[37] The leases signed by residents of public housing projects strictly prohibit consumption or possession of any controlled substance, cannabis included (even after legalization). This created and perpetuates a degree of economic insecurity attached to potential drug use among many Black families, where any family member who might have a small stash of personal drugs would threaten housing for the entire family. Those individuals who do use drugs have few, if any, options for where to safely consume and likewise have little education on what safe use looks like.[38]

Even the election of progressive reformer Bill de Blasio as New York City's mayor in 2013 was not enough to stem the tide of arrests for simple possession of cannabis, as found by a Drug Policy Alliance (DPA) report from 2017.[39] As late as 2016, the NYPD made over 18,000 such arrests, with more than four-fifths of those being of Black people and Latinos.[40] The arrests were also distributed unevenly in geographic terms. Precinct 30, covering parts of West Harlem and Hamilton Heights and with a population that is approximately 84 percent Black and Hispanic, saw 677 marijuana possession arrests, of which 94 percent were of Black or Hispanic people. Conversely, in Precinct 19, covering the wealthier areas of the Upper East Side between 59th and 96th Streets—where the population is 10 percent Black and Hispanic—police officers only arrested 14 people for simple possession, though half of them were Black and Hispanic. In each of the fifteen precincts identified by DPA with the highest absolute numbers of cannabis arrests, at least 82 percent of these arrests were of Black and Hispanic people. In the fifteen precincts with the lowest proportions of Black and Hispanic residents (anywhere from

10–48 percent), the number of Black and Hispanic people arrested combined was more than half the total in every case.[41] In almost thirty years of data collected in the DPA report, NYPD had arrested 738,227 individuals for simple marijuana possession.[42]

As statistics such as these suggest, personal cannabis use and drug use more generally has historically been a privilege for mostly white Americans with the wealth to access a private home away from urban police surveillance. At the same time, Black drug use is culturally pathologized and often subject to media, and thus public, attention. Being involved in the drug trade has been a moneymaking activity for some white residents, but for many Black New Yorkers, it might often have been one of the few economic and material options available to achieve any form of stability or success. No surge in funding to law enforcement or revision of criminal penalties changed this basic economic necessity—to the contrary, time and again it only served to capture these individuals in the maw of a cruel and unforgiving criminal justice system. It remains to be seen whether that basic dynamic will change with the advent of cannabis legalization.

That said, social equity licensing and related programs might mean that the exact same individuals who have historically been persecuted for their involvement with cannabis can use what they're already doing to build wealth and economic opportunity. As one Black market participant in New York explained, "This is where we're right off the street. You're an expert. If you've been consuming for twenty years, fifteen years . . . you know what you're talking about. Now, you need to turn that street science into real science, right? Get some real knowledge behind" your intuitive experience. For this observer, this transition is both key to developing a trade and, crucially, dependent on the kind of outside help that a holistic social equity program might entail: "You like, oh, man, this weed always makes me tired. This weed always puts me up. You really 'splaining sativa indica or the terpenes that are affecting you; . . . you just don't know the terms yet. So matching that experience with professional terms, you know, really is going to turn us into businessmen."[43]

THE CAMPAIGN FOR LEGALIZATION

As in Illinois, New Yorkers advocating for an approach to cannabis use other than criminalization were unable to take advantage of ballot initiative access. Though there had been an effort in the first decades of the twentieth century to bring the initiative process to the Empire State, the resiliency of those in power in the political system proved this effort to be short-lived.[44] State legislators have allowed local initiatives to be proposed, but statewide binding laws and constitutional amendments may only be referred through the legislature.[45] Partially as a result, New York's political institutions have been remarkably resistant to reform until only recently.

The character and previous experience of New York's most recent governors also speaks to this resistance. Republican George Pataki, first elected in 1994 after defeating Mario Cuomo—in part by highlighting Cuomo's pardons as well as his opposition to the death penalty—served three terms and rebuffed any mention of reform during his time in office. The two popularly elected governors who came after Pataki had both previously served as attorney general and, perhaps in part because of that experience as the top law enforcement official in the state, were hardly enthused by proposals to scale down the War on Drugs. Eliot Spitzer was quickly ensnared in a prostitution scandal and stepped aside only a year after he took office, while Andrew Cuomo, first elected in 2010, had a familial legacy to redeem. Less than two weeks before his election, Cuomo declared an opposition to legalizing even the medical use of cannabis, leading one newspaper to declare that he would not let the state "go to pot."[46] Cuomo only budged on this issue nearly four years later, when he finally issued an executive order that allowed for the limited use of cannabis in therapeutic settings.[47]

By the next time Cuomo was up for reelection in 2018, the national context had changed drastically in favor of reform on cannabis. Several states, including regional neighbors Massachusetts and Maine, had voted in 2016 to legalize cannabis, bringing the substance to the state's eastern border. More importantly for Cuomo, progressive activists were seeing increasing success in breaking the centrist stranglehold on state politics, forcing Cuomo to seek to protect his left flank in advance of an expected primary challenge in 2018. Though this eventual challenge—led by actor and activist Cynthia Nixon—would fall far short of success, it provided Cuomo an opportunity to pivot on the cannabis issue in a way that would bring him closer to the ideological center of Democratic primary voters.[48]

Nixon herself campaigned fiercely in favor of cannabis legalization and pointed especially to the burden of criminalization that had fallen on the state's communities of color.[49] By the end of the 2018 campaign, Cuomo came out firmly in favor of legalization, and New York Democratic voters helped seal the deal by refusing to renominate a slate of legislators who had worked with Republicans to block Democratic priorities.[50] Perhaps most importantly for Cuomo, however, was the election of J. B. Pritzker in Illinois, who campaigned with the bold promise of legalizing cannabis. Although the famously circumspect Cuomo had officially disclaimed any interest in running for president, this new potential competitor was surely on his radar.[51]

The stage was set for what many believed would be a quick endorsement of legal cannabis from one of the largest states in the country. In 2018, Cuomo had given himself political and rhetorical cover for legalizing cannabis by asking the state Department of Health to assess the positive and negative effects of legalization.[52] This report was issued in July of that year and allowed the governor to begin his third term in office with a budget address where his administration could make a comprehensive argument in favor of legalization. The elements of the program were clearly drawn from other states, including a push for easy expungements and a recognition of the harm that criminalization had inflicted on communities of color.[53]

As soon as Cuomo became a champion of legalization, however, political rivalries and the politics of the moment conspired to delay legalization. Progressive Democrats in the legislature were inherently distrustful of the Cuomo administration's plan. After the 2018 election, this group was a far more powerful force within the state legislature than it had been before. During the legislature's 2019 session, the Cuomo administration and these progressive legislators diverged on how the tax revenues from legal cannabis would be distributed, with progressives pushing for more explicit guarantees about who would control the funds and how they would be allocated to affected communities.[54] Legislators advocating for social equity were willing to hold up legalization until they received structural reforms that would address the harms of criminalization, which extended the timeline in the 2019 session until it ended.[55] Then beginning in March 2020, the COVID-19 pandemic froze any discussions of cannabis legalization and social equity for months.

Still, advocates for legalization remained adamant about the need for further action. As one law enforcement supporter of legalization pointed out, "Decriminalization is a step in the right direction," but its influence is limited. "Look at cannabis [which] was decriminalized for the majority of my career yet people got arrested over and over again, they just got fined." While this was in many cases a better outcome than being imprisoned, this improvement was also frequently illusory because although "most of them . . . didn't go to jail, but they just [were charged a] ton of fines, which . . . when folks couldn't afford to pay those fines, they did go to jail, because they then got warrants for failure to pay a fine, they got put [in] the cell or sent to the county [jail], because they couldn't deal with that warrant."[56]

Finally, in March 2021, the New York legislature passed—and Andrew Cuomo signed—what came to be known as the Marihuana Regulation and Taxation Act (MRTA).[57] The MRTA provided for the full recreational legalization and regulation of this market by creating the Office of Cannabis Management (OCM), to be led by a five-member Cannabis Control Board (CCB). Unlike in neighboring Massachusetts, where legislation entrusted the implementation of equity guidelines to one commissioner, the MRTA provides that appointments "should, to the extent possible, be geographically and demographically representative of the state and communities historically affected by the war on drugs."[58] Most notably, the governor appoints three members of this board, with legislators appointing the two additional members.

While legislators may have expected that Cuomo would be the individual to appoint the original commissioners, he was forced to resign in August 2021 due to personal scandals weighing down his administration. This allowed his successor, Kathy Hochul, to make her mark on cannabis regulation from the start of her administration. Hochul's appointment to chair the CCB went to Tremaine Wright, a former state legislator from Brooklyn, and her choice to serve as executive director was Christopher Alexander, a lead advocate in the state for legalization through his previous work with the Drug Policy Alliance and his support for criminal justice reform more broadly.[59]

Alexander later spoke of the principles that informed the 2021 legalization push, outlining three key elements that he believed needed to be addressed in implementing the new policy. Even "before moving forward with legalization," according to Alexander, it was essential "to make sure we're dealing with the consequences of the harm that's been caused. In our story, that meant clearing quite a bit of arrests and convictions that were made in communities of color across the state." Second was a belief that the new industry "would be diverse and inclusive," which required writing provisions that could be "woven into the market architecture to ensure that there was a space for people to come in and meaningfully participate." Lastly, supporters wanted "to guarantee that whatever resources were created from legalization were reinvested back into communities that have been most impacted."[60]

To these ends, the MRTA followed up on the 2019 law that had automatically expunged previous cannabis convictions, which was estimated to impact the records of at least 202,000 people. Many of these records had been slated to be destroyed after the passage of decriminalization, though the COVID-19 pandemic delayed this in some cases. The MRTA called for the automatic expungement of a further 107,000 cases that involved any conduct that had later been made legal due to the law, including possession of under three ounces of cannabis and the right to grow up to six mature plants per household.[61] These expungements would allow affected individuals to avoid disclosing convictions for these activities on job license applications where they may have previously been a barrier to employment. For those whose records were not eligible for automatic expungement, individuals could petition for re-adjudication by a court.[62] This automatic process, like that seen in Illinois, is expected to reach many more impacted residents than the petition-based process set up in Massachusetts and other similar programs.

The implementation of the economic justice mission clearly draws on the experience of previous states that have adopted social equity programs, though there are also some noteworthy changes. For example, the MRTA requires awarding at least half of all recreational licenses to qualified social and economic equity applicants. Eligible applicants are defined as being from a "disproportionately impacted community," having an income lower than 80 percent of the median income in the community where the applicant lives, or having personal experience with cannabis criminalization involving themselves or close family. New York's approach was informed by previous states with high capital requirements that blocked otherwise eligible participants from joining the market, however, so the OCM was charged with prioritizing certain types of licenses—such as for businesses that focus on social consumption, are organized as cooperatives, or that provide a delivery service—to qualified applicants. All cannabis businesses were mandated to submit a "social responsibility framework" as part of their license application with a promise that adherence to this framework would be examined when making relicensing decisions.[63]

These programs are ambitious and in many ways still unfulfilled, so it is beyond the scope of this book to be able to critically evaluate their performance. They look likely to provide a useful test case for determining the ultimate power of a single state government agency to achieve social equity in a narrow market environment. A delivery market company official summarized OCM's regulatory balancing challenge: "I think New York took a really progressive approach and a holistic approach. And I'm really excited to see how they implement it. How [is] the regulator going to define success in this space? I don't view the industry as a zero sum game [and] . . . there are ways to make room for independent players and MSOs. And lots of different license types. And then, you know, let the market work itself out."[64]

Another key area of New York's vision of social equity, built upon other state frameworks, is the promise to reinvest the proceeds of cannabis tax revenues in communities impacted by criminalization. As in many other states, the legislature directed that cannabis tax revenue be deposited into a separate fund which would first pay for the expenses of the regulating agency. Forty percent of the remaining revenue goes to the State Lottery Fund to pay for educational expenses. Another 40 percent is allocated to the Community Grants Reinvestment Fund, which the OCM administers in conjunction with a Cannabis Advisory Board. Some of the services that residents in eligible communities can access these funds for include job placement and training, education, mental health treatment, housing, and re-entry services that help individuals adjust to life after incarceration. The remaining 20 percent of tax revenue is set to be distributed to the Drug Treatment and Public Education Fund, which is charged with reducing youth use of cannabis and developing materials for a public health campaign on the safe use of legal cannabis.[65]

It didn't take long for challenges with meeting the state's ambitious vision for social equity to occur, however. In April 2022, the Dormitory Authority of the State of New York (DASNY) announced a request for proposals for a social equity investment fund in which the state would put in an initial investment of $50 million, with private matching potentially totaling an additional $150 million.[66] In June of that year, DASNY, a quasi-state agency often criticized as a tool of insider pork barrel spending,[67] selected a duo comprising NBA Hall of Famer Chris Webber and sneaker entrepreneur Lavetta Wills as fund managers.[68] Several months later, media and public inquiries about the progress toward meeting the targets for attracting private financing, as well as questions about Walls's and Webber's past work, have continued to emerge, as DASNY refuses to answer many questions about the fund.[69] As state officials were forced to explore other avenues to put adequate resources into the fund,[70] prospective equity licensees have also expressed concern regarding the structure of facility acquisition services offered to them out of DASNY, including possible locations with high upfront costs that would require them to charge prohibitive prices and make their operations unsustainable.[71] This has led to a rocky rollout of legal cannabis across New York, with fewer than a dozen recreational dispensaries open across the state by mid-2023.[72]

Another key aspect of the licensing piece of New York's initiative is a restriction on social equity license holders that limits their capacity to sell or transfer their license in the first three years of operation. The intention was to encourage social equity participants to remain in the market and to encourage investment in those participants' businesses while preventing the purchase of those same licenses by out-of-state MSOs, a development that has occurred in many other places. In November 2022, the first licenses were awarded to twenty-eight individuals or entities intended to benefit those who had either personally been convicted of cannabis offenses or had a close family member who had. Because none of these establishments have opened yet and several years still need to pass before the three-year limitation period ends, it is too early to see what effects this restriction will have.[73]

HAS NEW YORK DONE BETTER?

It is fitting that legalization advocates in New York would have the mandate to think broadly about how cannabis legalization can advance racial justice, as for decades state and local law enforcement spent hundreds of millions of dollars ensuring that New York would be the center of criminalization. Those advocates who fought the long and difficult battle for years under indifferent or hostile political leadership should be commended for their work to ensure that the state's political institutions are held to account for decades of damage done to communities of color. However, it is much too early to determine whether the kind of social equity outcomes that the MRTA has laid out are effective in practice. Given the volatile nature of legalized cannabis markets, it is difficult to know whether the protections built in for social equity licensees are sufficient to make their participation in the legalized market durable against the guaranteed presence of well-financed and experienced MSOs.

New York state government must use its regulatory power and market position with care. Otherwise, the legalization of cannabis threatens to turn an economic activity that provides opportunities and avenues for success into a state-regulated oligopoly available to those few with access to capital and connections. This kind of distorted use of market power has already been seen in New York in the taxi and rideshare industry, where for decades a corrupt and racist monopoly disfavored both ownership and customer service opportunities for people of color, leading to the development of an underground "jitney" economy in unlicensed cabs in communities of color. Meanwhile, the legal monopoly on taxi medallions led to a separate legacy of economic exploitation for immigrants, in particular, who were often forced to take a ruining amount of debt in order to obtain one of these licenses.[74]

While the rise of Uber and similar rideshare services has often been compared to jitney cabs,[75] the reality is that these larger corporations rarely serve to expand economic opportunities for people of color who move into their legal businesses.[76] Rather than following in these tracks and closing off an economic opportunity for Black New Yorkers by making entry for legacy market participants difficult or impossible, cannabis legalization must instead serve as a bridge toward building a legal market that can advance the same kinds of economic opportunities that legacy suppliers were sometimes able to access, but without the risk, stigma, and other barriers associated with operating an illegal business.

It is also imperative that New York and states like it remain vigilant against political pressures to reassert the police as a vehicle for social and economic control of communities of color. The 2022 governor's election in New York featured a strong element of fear and concern about crime and social disorder.[77] Although incumbent Hochul ultimately won reelection over challenger Lee Zeldin, she did so by the narrowest margin in decades.[78] One telling sign from this race that the broader national conversation about cannabis may have really changed from only a few decades ago is that cannabis legalization itself did not emerge as a major issue. Only during one debate did Zeldin briefly point out his concern about youth exposure in public environments, while Hochul pivoted toward an argument for regulation and increased economic opportunities for communities of color.[79] Zeldin's larger message in this campaign was a critique of other criminal justice policies that Hochul and the Democratic-controlled legislature had enacted, such as bail reform. Nevertheless, the danger here is clear, as public paranoia about crime and public safety has previously led to the kinds of policies that count arrests and bodies in prison as the policy outcomes, rather than working to deliver real public safety.

That such an outcome would undermine any successes in social equity specific to cannabis even if the target of aggressive law enforcement lay elsewhere was outlined by a cannabis industry expert who suggested that "I think people are starting to realize how much cannabis legalization and cannabis criminalization [are] ingrained in police reform." He went on to explain that social equity in cannabis without broader criminal justice reform would likely fail to help the people it was intended to help because cannabis has often been the excuse for negative action rather than the root cause. This is clear from the fact that "people like myself, you know, a middle-class white dude, I've never felt the effects of criminalization of cannabis, . . . I've never once worried in my entire life about getting arrested or going to jail for cannabis. I'm aware of the privilege." Conversely, "when you start looking at these other communities, you walk outside you have a possession of a joint or something ludicrous, or something, you know, minimal, your whole life could be uprooted." While cannabis legalization should solve that immediate problem, he concluded, it "isn't going to solve the, you know, institutional racism and everything that comes with it."[80]

The same expert worried that there was a real danger that apathy surrounding the need for any future change would set in during the post-legalization phase. Without a sense of urgency to keep working on broader reform, it seems all too likely that legalization could be viewed as an end in itself rather than the first step in reforming a whole suite of policies that criminalization of cannabis worked in concert with to oppress communities of color. This would be similar to what happened with gambling in New York (and Chicago, among other places) in the middle of the twentieth century when local law enforcement shifted their focus from anti-gambling to anti-drug initiatives. Without any attempt to overhaul policing tactics or to reform broader racist ideas about the importance of controlling the social lives of people of color, law enforcement personnel could simply use the surveillance and enforcement tactics that they were already familiar with to target drugs instead. In the current context, this mistake would be akin to legalizing cannabis but maintaining stop-and-frisk policing techniques, mandatory minimum sentencing guidelines, extended pretrial detentions, and all of the other elements of the imprisonment machine that defined the War on Drugs era. Dismantling these and similar policies will be a key benchmark in ensuring that the full potential of legalization is achieved.

The quotation from Kassandra Frederique of the Drug Policy Alliance that appeared in the introduction to this chapter, about the cultural perception of Black people "getting what they deserve" if they are punished for using illegal drugs, continues with the following admonition: "When we talk about

Black Lives Matter, are we talking about Black drug users? Are we talking about Black people who decided to sell drugs? Are we talking about some people who attended a music festival and took some drugs to enhance their experience? It is disgusting to people to think that we want to be in another state recreationally, because we are not allowed recreation. And we are also not allowed compassion."[81] With the goal of redressing this kind of discriminatory mindset—and the restrictions it promotes and justifies—it is imperative that social equity policies allow Black New Yorkers and others across the country to realize a fully liberated experience. It is also imperative that these be viewed as an initial step toward the kind of broader criminal justice reform and cultural readjustment that will be required for truly lasting change.

NOTES

1. Frances A. Stillman et al., "Out of View but in Plain Sight: The Illegal Sale of Single Cigarettes," *Journal of Urban Health* 91, no. 2 (2014): 355–65, https://doi.org/10.1007%2Fs11524-013-9854-3.
2. Matt Flegenheimer and Al Baker, "Officer Fatally Shoots Teenager in Bronx," *New York Times*, February 2, 2012.
3. Sara Fischer, "Rand Paul Blames Eric Garner's Death on High NYC Cigarette Tax," *CNN*, December 4, 2014, https://www.cnn.com/2014/12/03/politics/rand-paul-eric-garner-taxes/index.html.
4. Drug Policy Alliance, "Liberation for Black Drug Users | Reform 2015," YouTube video, August 20, 2020, https://www.youtube.com/watch?v=ue9t6eF_N5M&ab_channel=DrugPolicyAlliance.
5. Blake Zeff, "Another Cuomo Noninterference Story Falls Apart," *Politico*, September 2, 2014, https://www.politico.com/states/new-york/albany/story/2016/05/another-cuomo-noninterference-story-falls-apart-049022.
6. *Weekend Edition Sunday*, "New York Is Debating Bringing Back Cash Bail," *NPR*, April 3, 2002, https://www.npr.org/2022/04/03/1090498735/new-york-is-debating-bringing-back-cash-bail.
7. Quoted in Kaelan Castetter, "Putting Equity First with Melissa Moore NYS Director for the Drug Policy Alliance," podcast, 18:48, February 26, 2021, in *Empire State of Cannabis*, produced by CannaBuff, https://anchor.fm/empire-state-of-cannabis/episodes/Putting-Equity-First-with-Melissa-Moore-NYS-Director-for-the-Drug-Policy-Alliance-er4q4e/a-a4osgio. For reference, Yankee Stadium's capacity for baseball games is 46,537 people, so this benchmark was hit in 2000 and from 2009 to 2011. See Bryan Hoch, "Yankee Stadium to Open at 20% Capacity," MLB.com, March 20, 2021, https://www.mlb.com/news/yankee-stadium-to-open-2021-with-limited-seating; and Harry G. Levine and Loren Siegel, *Unjust and Unconstitutional: 60,000 Jim Crow Marijuana Arrests in Mayor de Blasio's New York* (New York: Marijuana Arrest Research Project and the Drug Policy Alliance,

2017), 6–7, https://drugpolicy.org/sites/default/files/Marijuana-Arrests-NYC--Unjust-Unconstitutional--July2017_2.pdf.

8. Thomas M. Quinn and Gerald T. McLaughlin, "The Evolution and Present Status of New York Drug Control Legislation," *Buffalo Law Review* 22, no. 3 (1973): 707–8.

9. Quinn and McLaughlin, "New York Drug Control," 709–11.

10. Quinn and McLaughlin, "New York Drug Control," 713.

11. Quinn and McLaughlin, "New York Drug Control," 715–18.

12. Quinn and McLaughlin, "New York Drug Control," 718–19.

13. Quinn and McLaughlin, "New York Drug Control," 721–22; and Richard J. Bonnie and Charles H. Whitebread, *The Marihuana Conviction: A History of Marihuana Prohibition in the United States* (Charlottesville: University of Virginia Press, 1974), 50.

14. Quinn and McLaughlin, "New York Drug Control," 722–23.

15. Quinn and McLaughlin, "New York Drug Control," 722, 732.

16. Matthew Vaz, *Running the Numbers: Race, Police, and the History of Urban Gambling* (Chicago: University of Chicago Press, 2020), 85.

17. Vaz, *Running the Numbers*, 89–92.

18. Vaz, *Running the Numbers*, 147–50.

19. Vaz, *Running the Numbers*, 93–95. The US Supreme Court's *Mapp v. Ohio* (1961) decision establishing the requirement that law enforcement searches require warrants originated from a gambling enforcement operation.

20. Julilly Kohler-Hausmann, "'The Attila the Hun Law': New York's Rockefeller Drug Laws and the Making of a Punitive State," *Journal of Social History* 44, no. 1 (2010): 72–75, http://www.jstor.org/stable/40802109.

21. Mason B. Williams, "How the Rockefeller Laws Hit the Streets: Drug Policing and the Politics of State Competence in New York City, 1973–1989," *Modern American History* 4, no. 1 (2021): 72–82, https://doi.org/10.1017/mah.2020.23.

22. Kohler-Hausmann, "'Attila the Hun Law,'" 72.

23. Kohler-Hausmann, "'Attila the Hun Law,'" 88.

24. Erica Bond et al., "Marijuana Enforcement in New York State, 1990–2017," Research Brief, Data Collaborative for Justice, John Jay College of Criminal Justice, February 2019, 3–4, https://datacollaborativeforjustice.org/wp-content/uploads/2020/04/Marijuana-Brief.pdf.

25. Joint Committee on New York Drug Law Evaluation, Association of the Bar of the City of New York Drug Abuse Council, Inc., *The Nation's Toughest Drug Law: Evaluating the New York Experience* (Washington, DC: National Institute of Law Enforcement and Criminal Justice, 1978), 13, https://www.ojp.gov/pdffiles1/Digitization/43315NCJRS.pdf.

26. Williams, "Rockefeller Laws," 67.

27. Williams, "Rockefeller Laws," 87–89.

28. Williams, "Rockefeller Laws," 80.

29. Chris Columbus, dir., *Home Alone 2: Lost in New York* (Los Angeles, CA: Twentieth Century Fox, 1992).

30. Audio of Bloomberg's remarks available at Benjamin Dixon (@BenjaminPDixon), "Audio of @MikeBloomberg's 2015 @AspenInstitute speech where

he explains that 'you can just Xerox (copy)' the description of male, minorities 16–25 and hand to copes," Twitter, February 10, 2020, 3:58 p.m., https://twitter.com/BenjaminPDixon/status/1226973723720396808.

31. Williams, "Rockefeller Laws," 90.

32. National Association for the Advancement of Colored People, *Born Suspect: Stop-and-Frisk Abuses and the Continued Fight to End Racial Profiling in America* (Baltimore, MD: NAACP, 2014), 11, https://www.prisonpolicy.org/scans/naacp/Born_Suspect_Report_final_web.pdf.

33. Williams, "Rockefeller Laws," 87–89.

34. Ezekiel Edwards, Will Bunting, and Lynda Garcia, *The War on Marijuana in Black and White: Billions of Dollars Wasted on Racially Biased Arrests* (New York: ACLU, 2013), 167, https://www.aclu.org/report/report-war-marijuana-black-and-white.

35. Ezekiel Edwards et al., *A Tale of Two Countries: Racially Targeted Arrests in the Era of Marijuana Reform* (New York: ACLU, 2020), 79, https://www.aclu.org/report/tale-two-countries-racially-targeted-arrests-era-marijuana-reform.

36. Edwards et al., *Tale of Two Countries*, 79.

37. Howard Husock, "How New York Can End the Public Housing Trap," in "New York City Reborn: 2021," special issue, *City Journal*, https://www.city-journal.org/new-york-public-housing-trap.

38. Benjamin T. Metcalf, US Department of Housing and Urban Development, to All Multifamily Regional Directors et al., "Subject: Use of Marijuana in Multifamily Assisted Properties," memo, December 29, 2014, https://www.hud.gov/sites/documents/USEOFMARIJINMFASSISTPROPTY.PDF; and Patrick Sisson, "Public Housing Tenants Still Face Stiff Penalties for Pot, Even in States Where It's Legal," *Curbed*, November 13, 2019, https://archive.curbed.com/2019/11/13/20962970/marijuana-section-8-medical-pot-public-housing.

39. Levine and Siegel, *Unjust and Unconstitutional*, 3–5.

40. Levine and Siegel, *Unjust and Unconstitutional*, 20.

41. Levine and Siegel, *Unjust and Unconstitutional*, 24–25.

42. Levine and Siegel, *Unjust and Unconstitutional*, 22.

43. Quoted in Kaelan Castetter, "From Legacy to Legal with Reggie Keith CEO of Canna-House," podcast, 33:44, June 28, 2021, in *Empire State of Cannabis*, produced by CannaBuff, https://anchor.fm/empire-state-of-cannabis/episodes/From-Legacy-to-Legal-with-Reggie-Keith-CEO-of-Canna-House-e13j89a.

44. Initiative and Referendum Institute, University of Southern California, "New York," accessed December 30, 2022, http://www.iandrinstitute.org/states/state.cfm?id=41.

45. Initiative and Referendum Institute, "New York."

46. Lore Croghan and Glenn Blain, "I Won't Let New York Go to Pot: Governor Hopeful Andrew Cuomo Says He Is Against Medical Marijuana," *Daily News* (New York), October 25, 2010, https://www.nydailynews.com/new-york/won-new-york-pot-governor-hopeful-andrew-cuomo-medical-marijuana-article-1.188416.

47. Reuters, "New York Gov. Cuomo to Allow Limited Use of Medical Marijuana," January 14, 2014, https://www.reuters.com/article/usa-marijuana

-newyork/new-york-gov-cuomo-to-allow-limited-use-of-medical-marijuana-paper-idUSL6N0KF00620140105.

48. J. David Goodman, "Cuomo Moves Closer to Marijuana Legalization in New York," *New York Times*, July 13, 2018, https://www.nytimes.com/2018/07/13/nyregion/marijuana-new-york-cuomo-legalization.html.

49. Vivian Wang, "Cynthia Nixon Puts Legalizing Marijuana Front and Center of Campaign," *New York Times*, April 11, 2018, https://www.nytimes.com/2018/04/11/nyregion/cynthia-nixon-marijuana-legalization.html.

50. Vivian Wang, "Democratic Insurgents Topple 6 New York Senate Incumbents," *New York Times*, September 13, 2018, https://www.nytimes.com/2018/09/13/nyregion/state-senate-election-results-idc-klein.html.

51. Alisa Wiersema, Kendall Karson, and Josh Margolin, "'Draft Cuomo 2020' Groundswell Emerges Amid the New York Governor's Coronavirus Response," *ABC News*, March 31, 2020, https://abcnews.go.com/Politics/draft-cuomo-2020-groundswell-emerges-amid-york-governors/story?id=69879290.

52. Tom Angell, "Cuomo Administration Report Backs Marijuana Legalization in New York," *Forbes*, July 13, 2018, https://www.forbes.com/sites/tomangell/2018/07/13/gov-cuomo-releases-report-backing-marijuana-legalization-in-new-york/?sh=42fd42b04c06.

53. Andrew M. Cuomo, *State of the State 2021: Reimagine, Rebuild, Renew* (Albany: New York State, 2021), 83–86, https://www.governor.ny.gov/sites/default/files/atoms/files/SOTS2021Book_Final.pdf.

54. Vivian Wang and Jesse McKinley, "Marijuana Legalization Isn't Dead Yet in New York," *New York Times*, June 17, 2019, https://www.nytimes.com/2019/06/17/nyregion/ny-marijuana-legalization.html.

55. Joseph Spector and Jon Campbell, "Why Legalizing Marijuana in New York Failed, but Decriminalizing It Passed," *Democrat & Chronicle* (Albany, NY), June 21, 2019, https://www.democratandchronicle.com/story/news/politics/albany/2019/06/21/why-legalizing-pot-new-york-failed-but-decriminalizing-passed/1521505001/.

56. Quoted in Kaelan Castetter, "The War on Drugs with Chief Brendan Cox," podcast, 34:09, March 15, 2022, in *Empire State of Cannabis*, produced by CannaBuff, https://anchor.fm/empire-state-of-cannabis/episodes/The-War-on-Drugs-with-Chief-Brendan-Cox-e1fosi7.

57. Ivan Pereira, "New York Legalizes Recreational Marijuana, Expunges Former Pot Convictions," *ABC News*, March 31, 2021, https://abcnews.go.com/US/york-legalizes-recreational-marijuana-expunges-pot-convictions/story?id=76775175.

58. *Marihuana Regulation and Taxation Act of 2021*, NY S. 854-A, 2021–2022 regular session (2021), 8, https://legislation.nysenate.gov/pdf/bills/2021/S854A.

59. New York Governor's Press Office "Governor Hochul Announces Confirmations of Tremaine Wright and Christopher Alexander to Lead Implementation of the Marijuana Regulation and Taxation Act," news release, September 1, 2021, https://www.governor.ny.gov/news/governor-hochul-announces-confirmations-tremaine-wright-and-christopher-alexander-lead.

60. Transform Drug Policy Foundation, "Legalising Cannabis for Good | Chris Alexander," YouTube video, December 7, 2022, https://youtu.be/mrqI3SiPgAE.

61. New York State Association of Counties, *The Marijuana Regulation and Taxation Act: A Summary* (Albany: New York State Association of Counties, 2021), 7, https://www.nysac.org/files/MRTA_Summary.pdf.

62. Brendan Kennedy, "Up in Smoke: How Expungement of Cannabis Crimes Will Work Under the MRTA," New York State Bar Association, April 22, 2021, https://nysba.org/up-in-smoke-how-expungement-of-cannabis-crimes-will-work-under-the-mrta/.

63. Office of Cannabis Management, New York, "What Is In the Law: Social and Economic Equity," fact sheet, 2022, https://cannabis.ny.gov/system/files/documents/2022/02/cannabis-management-fact-sheet-social-equity_0_0.pdf.

64. Quoted in Kaelan Castetter, "NY's Cannabis Marketplace with Lobbyist Katie Neer," podcast, 35:11, June 2, 2021, in *Empire State of Cannabis*, produced by CannaBuff, https://anchor.fm/empire-state-of-cannabis/episodes/NYs-Cannabis-Marketplace-with-Lobbyist-Katie-Neer-e1229hj.

65. New York State Office of Cannabis Management, "What Is In the Law: Taxation and Revenue," fact sheet, 2022, https://cannabis.ny.gov/system/files/documents/2022/04/cannabis-management-fact-sheet-taxation-03.pdf.

66. Dormitory Authority of the State of New York, "New York Social Equity Cannabis Investment Fund," solicitation no. 7585, issue date May 12, 2022, https://www.dasny.org/opportunities/rfps-bids/2022/new-york-social-equity-cannabis-investment-fund.

67. Chris Bragg, "Dorm Authority: NY's Deepest Pork Barrel," *Times-Union* (Albany, NY), updated December 19, 2016, https://www.timesunion.com/tuplus-local/article/1-9B-pork-barrel-titan-10803778.php.

68. New York Governor's Press Office, "Governor Hochul Announces Major Progress Toward Advancing Equity in Cannabis," news release, June 22, 2022, https://www.governor.ny.gov/news/governor-hochul-announces-major-progress-toward-advancing-equity-cannabis.

69. Brad Racino and Sean Teehan, "Smoke and Mirrors: Inside the Murky $200M Effort to Kickstart NY's Marijuana Industry," Syracuse.com, December 1, 2022, https://www.syracuse.com/marijuana/2022/12/smoke-and-mirrors-inside-the-murky-200m-effort-to-kickstart-nys-marijuana-industry.html.

70. Brad Racino, "New York State's $200 Million Social Equity Fund (Appears?) Close to Being Funded," Cannabis Insider, NYup.com, May 26, 2023, https://www.newyorkupstate.com/cannabis-insider/2023/05/new-york-states-200-million-cannabis-social-equity-fund-appears-close-to-being-funded.html.

71. Concerned CAURD Licensees to Reuben R. McDaniel III, Chris Alexander, and Tremaine Wright, May 9, 2023, available at https://www.documentcloud.org/documents/23809208-caurd-licensee-grievances.

72. New York State Office of Cannabis Management, "Dispensary Location Verification," accessed June 18, 2023, https://cannabis.ny.gov/dispensary-location-verification.

73. New York State Cannabis Control Board, "Cannabis Control Board Approves First Conditional Adult Use Retail Dispensary Licenses," news release, November 2022, https://cannabis.ny.gov/system/files/documents/2022/11/ccb-approves-first-caurd-licenses.pdf.

74. Brian M. Rosenthal, "'They Were Conned': How Reckless Loans Devastated a Generation of Taxi Drivers," *New York Times*, May 19, 2019, https://www.nytimes.com/2019/05/19/nyregion/nyc-taxis-medallions-suicides.html.

75. Kaitlyn A. Laurie, "Capping Uber in New York City: Ramifications for Ride-shares, the Road, and Outer-Borough Residents," *Fordham Urban Law Journal* 46, no. 4 (2019): 966, https://ir.lawnet.fordham.edu/ulj/vol46/iss4/5/.

76. Edward Ongweso Jr., "Civil Rights Groups Say Uber Actively Hurts Black People," *Vice*, September 23, 2020, https://www.vice.com/en/article/7kpn9z/civil-rights-groups-say-uber-actively-hurts-black-people.

77. Erin Durkin, "How Blood-and-Guts Headlines Propelled Republicans in New York," *Politico*, November 12, 2022, https://www.politico.com/news/2022/11/12/zeldin-hochul-crime-midterms-new-york-00066287.

78. Rebecca C. Lewis and Shantel Destra, "Kathy Hochul Ekes Out a Victory in the Closest Governor's Race in Decades," *City & State New York*, November 9, 2022, https://www.cityandstateny.com/politics/2022/11/kathy-hochul-ekes-out-victory-closest-governors-race-decades/379511/.

79. *Eyewitness News ABC7NY*, "Hochul, Zeldin Spar Over Crime, Trump in Debate for New York Governor," YouTube video, October 26, 2022, https://www.youtube.com/watch?v=EI0_5v6Ljdk&ab_channel=EyewitnessNewsABC7NY.

80. Quoted in Kaelan Castetter, "How Suburbs Delay Legalization with Policy Analyst Sarah McGovern," podcast, 24:14, August 14, 2020, in *Empire State of Cannabis*, produced by CannaBuff, https://anchor.fm/empire-state-of-cannabis/episodes/How-Suburbs-Delay-Legalization-with-Policy-Analyst-Sarah-McGovern-ei0973.

81. Drug Policy Alliance, "Liberation for Black Drug Users."

Chapter 9

The War on Drugs and the Fight for Racial Justice in Federal Legalization

The prospect of the federal government recognizing the increasing retreat from War on Drugs policies occurring in the states has been a hazy prospect from the moment Colorado and Washington began this trend. Yet public polling demonstrates a clear tipping point in approximately 2012 or 2013 when the average voter seems to have decided that current policies on criminalization were ineffective—at least regarding cannabis. Since then, greater numbers of Americans have supported the legality of recreational sales and possession of cannabis. By late 2021, Gallup put the rate of Americans who support legal cannabis at 68 percent, a number many weed enthusiasts would not have dared to dream of as recently as a decade ago.[1]

This polling is not reflected in the official policy of the federal government, however, which still lists cannabis as a Schedule 1 controlled substance, nor does it seem to square with the views of those concentrated in federal law enforcement supervisory positions. Each of the two most recent presidents, Donald Trump and Joe Biden (notably representing both major parties), have continued to oppose federal legalization.[2] This is despite many of the tantalizing political benefits that could accrue to them—after all, the 2020 presidential election was one where the two-thirds of Americans who supported recreational use did not have a major party candidate who shared their beliefs. Trump's first attorney general, Jeff Sessions, publicly voiced his perspective that stoners were worse than members of the Ku Klux Klan.[3] Trump's second attorney general, William Barr, was also opposed to legalization, although he did acknowledge that Congress had a role to play in setting policy, reminding senators during his confirmation hearing that they had the option of changing the law.[4] However, support among congresspeople in the decade since the first state adopted legalization has been slow and often relegated to the margins of each political party, with individual federally elected officials deferring to the voters in their own states.

The most consistent supporters of liberalization in Congress over the last decade hail from states with legal markets. One notable example is former senator Cory Gardner of Colorado, a Republican first elected in 2014 during a wave year for his party. Gardner opposed the legalization amendment, but after his election he became a champion of the industry in his own state.[5] In 2019, *Playboy* magazine called Gardner a "power broker" for cannabis policy in the US Senate.[6] Gardner's politically expedient conversion on the cannabis issue, as well as his reluctance to embrace Trump, did not give him enough political cover to survive as a moderate Republican in an increasingly liberal state, and he was defeated for reelection in 2020. However, Gardner's opponent in that election and successor in the Senate was none other than former Colorado governor John Hickenlooper, the once fervent opponent of cannabis legalization who has turned into an evangelist for his state's version of regulated legalization. As Hickenlooper noted about his transformation: "I feel pretty darn sure now that [cannabis legalization] is such a better—in terms of almost every measure—such a better societal decision than what I grew up in. I've personally gone and talked to either the General Assembly or the governors in a half-dozen states . . . [a]nd literally, there is no attack, no anxiety, that we don't have a pretty good answer for."[7]

Despite his optimism, Hickenlooper's description of his experience notably focuses on the policymakers in statehouses instead of the US Congress. However, many equity *activists*—along with other people from across the country and political spectrum who have moved beyond the "should it be legal" discussion on federal legalization—are now focused on helping to shape what the legal market for cannabis will look like in the days and years after the federal government bends to majority opinion, as well as on the reality of what is already happening in many states. Shaping this reality by advocating to build on much of the progress made on social equity at the state and local levels will be a difficult task. Among the important hurdles to pursuing equity in a national market are the established MSOs inside the legal industry—as well as larger companies that remain outside of the industry for now—that might capture the market with a flood of capital and a wealth of experience complying with (and at times evading) strict regulations, pursuing profit rather than policy outcomes. These companies include large tobacco companies that have long been eyeing the cannabis industry as a natural complement to their existing businesses, especially once federal officials remove the barriers that currently make interstate commerce in cannabis impossible.

To understand why an interstate trade of cannabis products without provisions to actively support entrants with limited access to capital or who have been otherwise harmed by decades of criminalization would instantly flatten the market, consider the larger producers that dominate the consumer market for alcohol. While the success of the craft beer industry (among other "craft" products) has demonstrated the existence of a consumer appetite for niche markets, the scale of these producers relative to the overall market size is modest. Craft beer producers supply roughly 27 percent of the domestic beer market, as measured by sales.[8] In cannabis, by contrast, the market in many places has been able to mature and diversify, in no small part due to the artificially inflated prices that many legal suppliers are able to charge. Many of these suppliers are not able to sustain price decreases below a certain threshold, however, as the costs for many of their factors of production are related to their participation in a quasi-legal trade. As outlined in chapter 3, not being able to deduct business expenses from your federal tax return or running an all-cash business because you can't contract with a credit card provider entails costs that most other businesses do not have to bear. Likewise, legal restrictions tied to their licenses often prohibit or limit licensed operators from increasing their production to make up for lower prices that the market may demand. Even without federal action, several states have seen supply gluts that have served to push prices down and imperil small cannabis operators.[9] The entry of large, well-capitalized firms that can benefit from economies of scale and cost efficiencies derived from having complex national or international logistics operations already in place would almost inevitably run these and many other small operators out of business.

In a sign of what is likely to come if and when cannabis is legalized at the federal level, British American Tobacco partnered in 2022 with a private capital company associated with rapper Snoop Dogg to invest in a German cannabis startup in that country's emerging legal market.[10] Likewise, large conglomerates such as Philip Morris[11] and Anheuser-Busch[12] in the tobacco and alcohol industries are eyeing additional investments across the spectrum of cannabis products that have emerged in recreational markets, including vaping devices, beverages, and ice cream. Meanwhile, celebrities such as Whoopi Goldberg are increasingly investing in cannabis.[13] In early 2021, Aaron Goines, a Black man who owns a small Wareham, Massachusetts, cannabis business, shared his fears of what a legalized national market for cannabis would look like for him: "If the capital markets opened up to cannabis tomorrow, having that liquidity would be like throwing gasoline on a fire. Massive players from alcohol and tobacco and big ag[riculture] and big pharma will come in and go crazy in this space. . . . If farms in the Midwest start growing thousands of acres, it's game over for most of us."[14]

In short, even if there have been both profound political and cultural changes around cannabis in the last decade, the stubborn reality of the entrenched degree of criminalization that federal policy has created continues to harm both individual consumers as well as the market as a whole. While the status quo has allowed some states to experiment with creating preferences for social equity, the legally contradictory nature of recreational cannabis without federal reform precludes interstate commerce and may ultimately limit the ability of states to intervene in market behavior. Various reforms under consideration in Congress today have begun to consider what an equitable federal solution for legal cannabis might look like, attracting a flood of legislative proposals but no consensus. Important gaps here still exist, particularly around how the federal government can address the individual and collective impacts of criminalization across the country.

CANNABIS CONTROL AT THE NATIONAL LEVEL

Easily lost in this overall discussion of whether the federal government will ever implement full legalization on a national level is that the federal government has itself been supporting the production and distribution of cannabis for the entirety of the War on Drugs era. In the college town of Oxford, home to "Ole Miss," or the main campus of the University of Mississippi, and located in the northwestern part of the state, the nation's only federally legal cannabis farm is quietly operated through a partnership between the university's School of Pharmacy and the National Institute of Mental Health. In 1968, NIMH contracted with then-chair of the pharmacy department Norman Doorenbos to provide the federal government with a supply of cannabis for research and medical purposes. A year later, the first seeds from as far away as Afghanistan and Korea were planted, beginning a quiet but lucrative contract for the school that has lasted until the current day.

This program survived the passage of the Controlled Substances Act (CSA), though the arrangement significantly changed as a result—federal approval for cannabis research and medical use soon became regulated through the National Institute for Drug Abuse (NIDA) that was established a few years later. Since then, the farm has supplied hundreds of medical patients who are registered with the federal government with boxes of rolled joints, as well as cannabis for the small number of research projects that NIDA approves. During the enhancement of the drug war in the 1980s, the Reagan administration chose Dr. Carlton Turner, who had headed the program at the Mississippi farm for over ten years, to became Reagan's chief drug advisor in 1981.[15] Turner's appointment demonstrated the importance that federal authorities placed on cannabis, though he attracted negative attention during his tenure in the White House for linking cannabis use and homosexuality.[16] By the mid-2000s, the Mississippi farm was regularly growing over a thousand kilograms of cannabis yearly and engaging in efforts to develop different delivery mechanisms for THC, including arm patches and extracts.[17]

Only three years before the federally sponsored cannabis farm started operating, infamous drug researcher Timothy Leary was arrested at the US–Mexico border when he took responsibility for a small amount of cannabis found in his romantic partner's underclothes. Leary was subsequently arrested by federal officials for violating the Marihuana Tax Act, eventually being convicted and sentenced to three decades in prison. The paradox of cannabis enforcement at the time was that compliance with this federal law—payment of a tax stamp for possessing cannabis—would have exposed Leary to criminal penalties in the state of Texas, where cannabis was illegal. Leary's ensuing appeals of his conviction eventually led the US Supreme Court to determine in *Leary v. United States* (1969) that this requirement amounted to an unconstitutional violation of the Fifth Amendment right against self-incrimination, declaring the Marihuana Tax Act void and providing the nation an opportunity to revisit cannabis criminalization.[18]

Leary, whom Richard Nixon once called "the most dangerous man in America,"[19] was hardly a sympathetic hero, however. He was fired by Harvard University in 1963 for his research into psychedelics and represented much of what law-and-order Americans believed to be fueling disorder in society in the 1960s. What Leary undid in 1969, Nixon redid two years later with the passage of the CSA, solidifying the status of cannabis within the federal drug control regime for another five decades.

Established in 1974 as a follow-up to the CSA, NIDA oversees a wide array of federal programs supposedly aimed at fighting drug abuse. Yet the cannabis farm in Mississippi represents an effective legal monopoly for the domestic production of cannabis products, and the institute has notably rebuffed potential competitors from entering this narrow market. One of these efforts came from the University of Massachusetts Amherst, where the late Lyle Cracker fought beginning in 2001 to develop another location to grow and harvest cannabis for the federal government. Cracker's application was shuffled between federal agencies in an elongated process that lasted at least a decade. Even the transition between the George W. Bush and Barack Obama administrations and a letter from Massachusetts's two senators was not enough to convince NIDA to fold. In denying Cracker's application, motivated in part by claims of low potency and quality in the cannabis produced at the Mississippi farm, NIDA asserted that approving an additional site would undermine the American government's obligations under international treaties to control the production and sale of cannabis. This position would later be refuted by the State Department itself, demonstrating that NIDA had little concern for either the law or the cannabis it produced.[20]

The Failure of Federal Anti-Drug Messaging

Overall, the President's National Drug Control Budget requested $42.5 billion in federal spending for fiscal year 2022—this includes nearly $20 billion for treatment, over $10 billion to support domestic law enforcement, $5.8 billion for interdiction, and $2.9 billion for prevention.[21] Using this budget number as a proxy for yearly spending, this would indicate that the federal government has likely spent well in excess of a trillion dollars—at least in inflation-adjusted terms—fighting the War on Drugs, rivaling either of the wars in Afghanistan and Iraq in financial scale and likely far exceeding the human toll in lives taken or otherwise ruined.[22]

For all of this spending, very few people are arrested and convicted by federal authorities for cannabis possession and sales. When President Biden announced an executive order in late 2022 to pardon all individuals convicted of simple cannabis possession, this clemency only affected approximately 6,500 people, a tiny percentage of the millions that have been arrested at the state and local levels over recent decades.[23] The federal money spent on drug enforcement is only a small fraction of the total amount of spending across all levels of government on drug enforcement, but federal spending and mandates nevertheless enable a great deal of the enforcement actions taken by states and have shaped the institutional character of the War on Drugs.[24] President Biden indirectly acknowledged that states might finally be pushing back against federal influence, however, when he framed his executive order as a response to the fact that "sending people to prison for possessing marijuana has upended too many lives and incarcerated people for conduct that many states no longer prohibit."[25]

Beyond financial incentives and enforcement mandates to bring states into the War on Drugs, decades of federal messaging since the Nixon administration has also been aimed at both youth and adults to try to convince Americans to abstain from a variety of drugs, including cannabis. Millions of Americans have grown up on a steady diet of these entreaties—perhaps best exemplified by the "Just Say No" campaign that Nancy Reagan adopted from Black activists in Oakland (as discussed in chapter 2)—with billions of dollars spent to create and distribute them. These efforts' overall message and focus has sometimes shifted, but the discouragement of cannabis use has always been a significant element of them.

Another major piece of the anti-drug campaign has been educational programs like Drug Abuse Resistance Education, more commonly known as DARE, first developed in the early 1980s as a partnership between law enforcement and school officials in Los Angeles. This program and its related messaging spread to schools across the country as it achieved federal funding, with President Reagan first declaring National DARE Day in 1988.[26] DARE.

educational programs vary depending on the community, though many schools actively partner with law enforcement and facilitate police officers coming to schools in order to deliver anti-drug and anti-gang messaging. These police officers at times have encouraged students to report any use of drugs that they were aware of, potentially implicating fellow students or their parents. For example, a North Carolina eleven-year-old brought cannabis he found at home to his school's DARE officer in 2010, leading to the arrest of his parents.[27]

For many Americans who went through middle and high school beginning in the 1980s and 1990s, DARE was a significant and even ubiquitous aspect of their educational experiences. In schools with active DARE programs, students were given a wide array of "swag," including T-shirts, sweatshirts, and other clothing, leading many school campuses to have a subtle yet constant broadcast of the messaging that the program sought to spread.[28] This trend occurred at much the same time that American schools also instituted a wave of zero-tolerance campaigns related to violence between students and weapons on campus in response to school safety fears, particularly after the Columbine shooting in 1998.[29] During this period, schools also increasingly became centers of surveillance that served to exclude students of color, who faced disciplinary suspensions and expulsions for behavior at overwhelmingly disproportionate rates compared to white students—mimicking the broader trends of mass incarceration and the War on Drugs.[30] This confluence of harsh and disproportionate treatment has come to be recognized in scholarly and activist circles as the "school-to-prison pipeline" and has led to the exclusion for decades of students of color from the educational system, with many of them being pushed into the criminal justice system instead.[31] Yet even today, numerous American students across the country continue to participate in the DARE program.[32]

But was this anti-drug messaging effective in reducing drug use? Decades of significant scholarly research, as well as anecdotal wisdom, have rarely found anything other than an extremely short-term effect from the approach that DARE represents.[33] One of the reasons why is illustrated by a famous television ad produced during the 1980s that has come to be known by its very simple narrative: "your brain on drugs." In the ad, an unnamed man, played by television actor John Roselius, asks whether anyone has any questions about the impact of drugs, before cracking an egg into a frying pan and telling the audience that "this is your brain on drugs."[34] This brute-force approach would characterize many government-sponsored efforts to convince Americans to abstain from drugs, but the lack of nuance convinced few teens that what they were seeing reflected their actual lives and social environments—which were, seemingly inevitably, much more complex and filled with a wide variety of personal experiences and perspectives on drug use.

In fact, DARE has often been criticized by scholars and government officials for introducing youth to information about drugs in the first place, creating a sense of negative association and curiosity that might cause some individuals to try those substances for themselves.[35] Some scholars even discuss a "boomerang" effect, with cohorts of students who were presented with DARE messaging later using drugs at higher rates than those who were not exposed.[36] By 2001, the US surgeon general placed DARE on a list of ineffective prevention programs.[37] Two years later, officials from the federal Government Accountability Office were unable to find any evidence that these programs were effective.[38]

However, NIDA did not need outside scholarly research to question the effectiveness of the anti-drug messaging that the federal government was sponsoring. In addition to the institute's cannabis farm and participation in federal anti-drug policy in partnership with the Office of National Drug Control Policy (ONDCP), NIDA also sponsored a research effort through the University of Michigan that has come to be known as Monitoring the Future (MTF). This survey has been given to approximately 50,000 eighth-, tenth-, and twelfth-grade students across the country since 1975, asking a variety of questions about their lives. Topics include religion, the influence of parents, societal factors, and perceptions about—as well as use of—drugs.[39] Many social science and public health scholars owe a heavy debt to the MTF survey for providing results that have led to their publications, though few know its funding source and larger purpose. Most importantly for drug policy researchers, the questions focus on a variety of both legal and illegal drugs, including alcohol, tobacco, cannabis, and other substances, evaluated on a lifetime, past-year, and past-month basis, allowing scholars representing many different perspectives on the War on Drugs to make their cases. More recently, the MTF data has been featured in both sides of an emerging debate about whether cannabis legalization in different states has led to a corresponding increase in youth use.

Using NIDA's own MTF survey, it is clear that decades of anti-drug messaging and federal enforcement have been a failure. Lifetime drug use—measuring anyone who claimed at least one-time use of any of the tracked substances, including both legal and illegal ones—among twelfth-grade students reached an all-time high of around 65 percent in the late 1970s and early 1980s, with a sharp fall to about 40 percent by the early 1990s. Use again peaked at higher than 50 percent by the beginning of the twenty-first century and has slowly leveled off in the years since then, with a sharp drop in the last four years to just over 40 percent. Monthly rates have followed a consistent trend over the same time period, though at a lower rate—starting in the late 1970s, nearly 40 percent of students reported having used drugs in the last thirty days and by 2022, approximately 25 percent of twelfth-grade students nationwide were reporting having used any drug over the last thirty days. The last decade of increasingly liberal access to recreational cannabis, specifically the years from 2013 to 2019 (the last year before COVID-19), does not seem to have increased the nationwide rate of usage.[40] This has been consistently reflected in state-by-state analyses which usually show little change in youth use as recreational markets are established.[41]

More recently, youth drug use significantly dropped in the two years of data ending in 2022. It is difficult to pin down exactly what has occurred here, though some impacts of the COVID-19 pandemic and the resulting changes in schooling and social interactions among youth seem clearly influential. While there was the possibility that the decreases might reflect a measurement challenge—such as that the increased proportion of students who took the MTF survey at home impacted their willingness to be candid—federal officials worked to ensure that this was not a factor by conducting additional analyses to validate the drop.[42] It seems clearer that the disruption and isolation of the pandemic has decreased access to these substances for youth, leading to lower rates of usage during the time period of severe school closures in 2020 and 2021. Usage rates in 2022 began to recover to pre-pandemic rates for some substances, including twelfth-graders' use of alcohol, but other usage rates, including those for cannabis and vaping tobacco, remained steady.[43]

It has long been apparent to many that the federal government's efforts to control the use and distribution of cannabis—to say nothing of other drugs—over the last half century have represented an embarrassing failure, even if the enormous criminal justice cost of the War on Drugs is not factored in. A global pandemic has proved more successful in reducing youth use of cannabis than the billions of dollars spent on federal, state, and local efforts that are intentionally dedicated to the purpose. The most prominent persuasion campaigns have been utterly unpersuasive yet are often allowed to persist despite the fact that research sponsored—and even sometimes executed—by the federal government itself determined its inefficacy. And while the federal government directly financed much of the work of criminal enforcement, its indirect coordination of these pursuits has allowed local police officers across the country to create a dragnet for Black and brown Americans in places like New York, where NYPD officers have cited tens of thousands of individuals for cannabis possession, primarily young men of color.

THE COLE MEMO AND FEDERAL-STATE INTERACTIONS

The disconnects between a stated federal policy on the continued illegality of cannabis, the practice of limited federal enforcement, and public support for legal cannabis might seem incongruous with principles of democratic accountability as well as effective administration of government. On the one hand, laws that are on the books should be enforced; on the other, laws that are unpopular should also be reformed or repealed. However, this status quo is instead a logical product of our federal system, particularly its reliance on the federal government to gather and maintain social consensus on issues that have a national character. While popular attitudes about cannabis (among other drugs) have long been more complicated than its legal status might suggest, a culture of prohibition persisted in law enforcement and among elected officials who effectively precluded discussion of liberalization until activists simply went around them to adopt legalization via ballot measures.

Perhaps because of this, lawmakers in many states have been reluctant to address the numerous issues that have developed in legalized markets. At the same time, the states that have adopted measures to restrict or withdraw from criminal enforcement of cannabis prohibition have hobbled federal efforts to use the CSA to disrupt cannabis markets not only in their states but more generally. There were initial attempts by the federal government to crack down on state-sanctioned medical legalization in the 1990s and early 2000s, most prominently in California. These efforts were nearly all complete failures, however, as federal officials ended up mired in an expensive and lengthy court fight with state-licensed dispensaries that had earned some public sympathy and even support from local officials.[44]

After the Obama administration intervened during the 2010 ballot initiative campaign in California to recommend that voters not approve Proposition 19,[45] the Justice Department began to back off direct messaging to voters during political campaigns starting in 2012. This was both a political as well as an institutional move—Obama needed many of the younger voters that would otherwise have shown up to support cannabis in Colorado, and there was no longer enough support for prohibition amongst core Democratic voters.[46] Likewise, these early ballot initiatives' focus on instituting a highly regulated approach to legalization in both medical and recreational states gave federal officials cover to soften their stance.

Even as the Food and Drug Administration has maintained its classification of cannabis as a Schedule 1 drug, a concrete shift in federal law enforcement toward cannabis in the year after Colorado and Washington legalized recreational use came in the form of the so-called Cole Memo. Issued by the Justice Department in 2013, it directed US attorneys across the nation to defer to local laws and regulation for both adult use and medical cannabis.[47] This policy was similar in spirit to a long-proposed federal budget rider often called the "Rohrabacher-Farr Amendment"—named for two members of Congress from California and Colorado, respectively—that was originally introduced in 2001 and finally adopted for the first time in 2014. This budget rider forbade the Justice Department from using federal funds to intervene in states where medical cannabis was legal.[48]

Though rescinded in 2018, the Cole Memo for a time gave states the clearest guidelines for how federal officials would regard legal cannabis regimes going forward and helped inform the decisions of state officials responsible for cannabis regulation. In particular, the memo had eight policy aims for regulated cannabis markets that would preclude further federal enforcement if enacted. States had to prevent the following: distribution to minors; the collection of revenues for organized crime; interstate diversion; the use of cannabis as a cover for other forms of crime such as trafficking other drugs; the use of weapons or violence; drugged driving; the cultivation of cannabis on public lands; and usage on federal property. The memo also emphasized that cannabis regulation must be effective in practice, not just in design, and that federal officials reserved the right to intervene if state regulation failed to prevent any of the above activities.[49]

Even if the Cole Memo represented a softening of the federal government's position on regulated markets, the two-faced nature of federal policy became clear as individuals across the country continue to face legal consequences for interacting with cannabis. Such outcomes include failed federal background checks for medically registered cannabis patients,[50] denied naturalization during the immigration process due to admission of use of cannabis in a recreationally legal state,[51] and denied clearances for federal employees who admit to using cannabis during their security reviews.[52] Likewise, cannabis businesses operating in regulated markets still are not permitted to deduct normal business expenses on their federal tax returns, a legacy of the extra scrutiny that drugs were given in federal law during the War on Drugs.[53] Many Americans seem to think that state legalization of cannabis represents the end of the War on Drugs in their individual lives, yet the collateral consequences continue to fall on those around them.

The Cole Memo's provision that state officials should work to ensure that cannabis sold in one state is not diverted into other jurisdictions touches on a particularly challenging area. Today, each state with legal cannabis nominally operates as its own hermetically sealed market, with the existing federal laws on the books making any interstate trade in state-legal cannabis a practical no-go. There is some evidence of diversion from legal markets, even as many states with those legal markets seek to create so-called "seed-to-sale" tracking systems for legally produced cannabis in order to discourage this practice. Even so, diversion would be rather simple, and it likely does occur even if we assume that most producers in the legal market comply with seed-to-sale tracking and do not sell cannabis marked for destruction out of the back door. While there is common speculation that this occurs at times when the cannabis market is oversaturated—Washington state went through such a period of oversupply in the years after legalization first passed—it is not clear that diversion is in fact widespread or the source of much legacy market supply.[54] Either way, the Cole Memo's bar on interstate trade in cannabis helped to set up each individual state's cannabis market on a direct collision course with a potential consolidation that only direct action by Congress is likely able to address.

After Jeff Sessions became attorney general in 2017, he undertook a review of the Obama administration's federal policy on cannabis, eventually resulting in the Justice Department withdrawing the Cole Memo in early 2018.[55] The public conversion of Cory Gardner to legalization advocate became especially important in the wake of this decision, as Gardner placed holds on some of Donald Trump's Justice Department nominees and only relented after Trump himself promised to maintain the status quo on federal policy.[56] This unhealthy but consistent status quo has continued to the present—after President Biden took office in 2021, his attorney general signaled that he would readopt a policy much like that in the original Cole Memo, though Biden's Justice Department had not yet issued a formal policy on the matter as of this book's writing.[57]

This federal inaction has left little room for further progress. Despite New York's legalization of cannabis in 2021 turning Senate Majority Leader Chuck Schumer into a champion of federal legalization,[58] the Biden administration's lack of any concrete commitment on this issue short of congressional legislation has perpetuated the policy stagnation seen across the country. Even where there is bipartisan agreement on problems in the current market—such as the vaping-related vitamin E acetate epidemic in 2019 and a more recent rash of robberies and crime impacting legal dispensaries due to their continued need to receive large amounts of cash[59]—Congress has proved incapable of arriving at any consensus on even limited solutions.

POLICY PATHWAYS: RESCHEDULING OR DE-SCHEDULING

One of the major controversies on the federal level even today is the debate over whether cannabis should be rescheduled or de-scheduled. This somewhat arcane federal regulatory distinction has a great deal of real-world consequences for those who would like to participate in legal cannabis markets. Cannabis's current designation as a Schedule I substance indicates that the federal government believes it has no accepted medical use while having a high potential for abuse. While there is a great deal of contention regarding the latter characterization, the collective judgments of nearly every state in the country with some legalized access to medical cannabis should call into question the accuracy of the former.[60] If cannabis were to be rescheduled, this would put it into one of the four other categories outlined by the CSA. Access to substances on any one of the schedules, even the least controlled Schedule V—which consists of substances such as cough suppressant steroids that have a "lower" potential for abuse—is tightly controlled.

There are two options for changing the schedule of a drug: administrative and legislative. The CSA does lay out a process where the US secretary of health and human services (HHS) or another "interested party" can file a petition with the attorney general to reschedule cannabis. The attorney general can then direct the secretary of HHS to examine the scientific evidence regarding knowledge and use of the drug as well as the public health effects of abuse and dependence on the drug. HHS can then recommend that the drug not be controlled at all, recommend control outside of the drug scheduling regime, or provide any other potential regulatory response, though the final decision is ultimately up to the attorney general.[61] This complex scheme demonstrates the criminal justice orientation of the War on Drugs, with scientific evidence being ultimately judged by the same criminal justice system that is responsible for the prosecution and incarceration of millions of people of color.

To demonstrate the difficulty of this pathway, a recent example may be worth considering. In 2018, the federal government received a petition from a company called Advanced Imaging Projects to de-schedule a chemical known as [18F]FP-CIT.[62] This substance is derived from cocaine but has shown a great deal of promise in research for treatments of Parkinson's disease. Advanced Imaging Projects is a company that has in the past worked on so-called "orphan drugs," often expensive treatments targeted toward rare diseases. With this petition, it seemed that the pharmaceutical player was working to bring a new substance to market based on [18F]FP-CIT to be called Fluoroseek, primarily to aid in the evaluation of Parkinson's patients in highly controlled radiological lab environments. By November 2021, the Drug Enforcement Administration announced that HHS had determined that [18]FFP-CIT did not conform to the conditions for Schedule II, or any other schedule, and thus was not subject to regulation under the CSA. This action received six comments on Regulations.gov, the federal website for public comments on administrative decisions, with all but one supporting the FDA's decision and noting the potential benefits of the action. The exception was this likely sarcastic and hastily written comment which dissented from the other positive views: "Reschedule cocaine, or any cocaine derivative is insane! Are the whacked at the DEA on drug? This sends the wrong signal, that somehow cocaine is less malignant than cannabis is very irresponsible. This is a bad idea."[63] In any case, federal regulators moved forward with de-scheduling the substance in November 2022, though it is not clear whether Advanced Imaging Projects will move forward with marketing this treatment.

The prospect of de-scheduling cannabis without additional federal legislation or action to address the harms of the War on Drugs has been noted by social equity activists as an incomplete solution. De-scheduling—or even rescheduling to a less stringent level such as Schedule II or even Schedule V—would leave large corporations in the driver's seat for commercialization of cannabis across state borders. At the same time, the perceived removal of federal regulatory guardrails preventing youth access and diversion would also likely unleash a costly political backlash from the exact kinds of voters that ballot initiative organizers in states like Colorado and Massachusetts once sought to convince about the efficacy of regulation. Therefore, despite ample evidence that the majority of Americans now support revisiting the legal status of cannabis, regulators are unlikely on their own to respond to public pressure to use the tools at their disposal to change how the federal government views cannabis.

The legislative approach, by contrast, would potentially provide for more explicit deliberation about what a national framework for a legal cannabis market could look like while plausibly allowing for more clarity about the relationship between the federal and state governments than the current situation entails. Trump's second attorney general, Bill Barr, expressed approval for national legislation during his confirmation hearing in 2019. Although he made clear that he was personally opposed to legalization, he opined that "the current situation is untenable, it's almost like a backdoor nullification of a federal law. To me, it's a binary choice. Either have a federal law prohibiting marijuana everywhere, . . . [or] if we want a federal approach with states having their own laws, let's get there the right way" through explicit congressional action authorizing it.[64]

Barr's successor, Merrick Garland, spoke to the problematic ambiguity of the current state of affairs during his own confirmation hearing two years later, albeit in somewhat different terms. Garland asserted the necessity of a continued role for the Justice Department "to be sure there are no end-runs around the state laws that criminal enterprises are doing. So that kind of enforcement should be continued." At the same time, the overall approach according to Garland should be one of deference to state laws because "I don't think it's a good use of our resources, where states have already authorized. That only confuses people, obviously, within the state."[65] Notably, Garland also signaled a realization of the equity issue with cannabis, at least the way that aggressively pursuing nonviolent possession charges can deeply impact individual lives—especially for people of color—while bringing little social benefit. In light of this, he advocated a need to focus "our charging and arresting on violent crimes and others that deeply affect our society, and not have such an overemphasis on marijuana possession, for example, which has disproportionately affected communities of color and damaged them after the original arrest because of the inability to get jobs."[66]

The legislative path is also seemingly simpler than the regulatory one and should theoretically prove appealing to members of Congress given the persistent and even loud signs that voters on both sides of the aisle support the relaxation of federal rules on cannabis access. One powerful sign of potential conservative support for legalization, for example, came in 2016, when Florida voters considered Amendment 2 to expand the use of medical cannabis in that state. While Donald Trump was winning Florida in his first presidential campaign, Amendment 2 earned the support of over 70 percent of the voting population, easily clearing the state constitution's threshold of 60 percent support needed to approve popularly initiated amendments. Individual members of Congress have also come out in support of some type of reform, including otherwise highly conservative officials such as Republican Matt Gaetz, who helped write Florida's first medical cannabis law while serving in the state legislature in 2014.[67]

Despite the potential for political benefit and legislative success that recent history such as this implies, Congress has yet to act. Still, it can at any time pass a law that changes a drug's schedule listing or even removes it from the CSA schema. As discussed in the next section, there is proposed legislation before Congress right now that would in fact do exactly this. Whether it will move forward in the face of legislative gridlock and politicians' evergreen fears about being seen as "soft on crime" or other pejoratives remains to be seen.

President Biden's announcement in October 2022 that he would pardon simple cannabis possession offenses was received with great fanfare and, in some small way, marked an official recognition that the federal criminalization of cannabis would soon come to an end. Biden also encouraged governors to issue similar orders to help the many more Americans who had been impacted under state laws. At least one governor has done so—Oregon's Kate Brown announced a month later that she would pardon over 45,000 residents who had been convicted of simple possession of cannabis.[68] Biden's executive order also included an additional request to the attorney general and the HHS secretary to "expeditiously" initiate a review of cannabis's designation as a Schedule I substance. It is unclear what sort of timetable for federal action this executive order sets up, with many veteran activists remaining skeptical that the executive branch agencies that have supported prohibition for decades would quickly change paths.[69]

The clearest implications of removing cannabis from the purview of the CSA would be the likelihood of creating interstate commerce in cannabis while in turn threatening much of the regulatory apparatuses that states have created to protect consumers and ensure that social equity remains a priority in the recreational market. The challenge here lies in a constitutional concept known as the "dormant commerce clause," which holds that Congress has the exclusive authority to regulate economic activity across state lines, preventing states themselves from creating rules that might otherwise limit business activity in some protected markets. Courts have generally held that Congress must explicitly invoke the Constitution's commerce clause to delegate additional authority to states to impose their own market restrictions, and absent this authority, laws that might impose "economic protectionism" are subject to higher levels of legal scrutiny.[70] This constitutional principle was used in a 2019 Supreme Court case challenging a Tennessee residency requirement for alcohol licensees in which the court held that Tennessee's rule violated the commerce cause even though a provision in the Twenty-First Amendment expressed that states would continue to have authority to regulate alcohol after the end of Prohibition.[71] Given these sorts of barriers to state-level regulation, any chance of preserving social equity outcomes under national legalization will require a comprehensive federal legislative solution to challenge the paradigm of what it takes to regulate a substance whose use comes with consequences for public health and safety but for which a prohibition model has completely failed.

Shaleen Title, the longtime cannabis equity activist and former member of the Massachusetts Cannabis Control Commission whose work was discussed in chapter 6, is one of many who have recognized the need to prioritize social equity for cannabis at the outset of legalization while giving future regulators on the federal and state levels space to develop and learn in forming better rules that address concerns around public health and market consolidation. Title spoke to this in a 2022 policy paper on preventing monopolies in the cannabis industry, noting that "the biggest lesson from Big Tobacco and Big Tech is that free and open competition is not an issue we can safely figure out after the fact." For Title, this means that "sensible regulation [of cannabis] to prevent excessive corporate power, protect public health, and serve the public good must not become a sidenote" because a failure to avoid this would lead to a failure to "reap the benefits of competition and enjoy an innovative market."[72] While many cannabis activists and scholars have in the past pointed to alcohol as a model for cannabis regulation, Title's larger point is that policy leaders can't simply copy and paste the regulatory model from another sector and expect that we will automatically develop markets and regulations that serve the public good. Cannabis should instead be an opportunity to develop a new framework that moves away from stigma as the basis for regulation by using experience and science to guide regulatory decisions.

CURRENT LEGISLATION

The most recent congressional efforts to address cannabis's legal status include the proposed Marijuana Opportunity Reinvestment and Expungement (MORE) Act, sponsored by representative Jerry Nadler of New York. This law has passed the House in the last two sessions of Congress but has yet to be considered by the Senate. The MORE Act would completely de-schedule cannabis; remove cannabis-related convictions as a disqualifying offense for federal benefits, including welfare, food stamps, and education assistance; and impose a 5 percent federal excise tax on cannabis. Part of this revenue would be used to serve communities impacted by the War on Drugs, both through reinvestment in the communities themselves and also by providing technical assistance and grants for states which choose to create equity licensing systems. When the Congressional Budget Office scored the proposed legislation, staffers found that the taxes to be collected and the savings to federal enforcement efforts would add billions to federal coffers over the next decade.[73] This bill has received limited bipartisan support from Republicans in the two votes it has received in the House, including from Matt Gaetz and his fellow Floridian Brian Mast.

The MORE Act represents some progress in the discussion around federal legalization. But it is unlikely to fully address the consolidation that will likely ensue once large corporations begin entering the recreational market, as it only provides a limited range of financial assistance for those impacted by the War on Drugs to start their own businesses and does not pose any substantial challenge to interstate cannabis companies. Other legislation has been proposed to address different understandings of the federal cannabis policy paradox, particularly in areas that impact large corporations and classes of professional workers.

After widespread reporting of the compliance challenges that banking institutions faced in order to serve the cannabis market, for example, representative Ed Perlmutter introduced the Safe and Fair Enforcement (SAFE) Act in 2019, which would allow financial institutions to serve the industry without threat of legal penalty from the federal government. As noted in chapter 3, many cannabis businesses today operate on a primarily cash basis, which increases their cost of doing business and makes them more susceptible to violent crime. By 2022, dozens of robberies across several states with legal cannabis led to a renewed push for the SAFE Act's passage.[74] Particularly influential was the death of twenty-nine-year old Jordan Brown of Washington state, a cannabis dispensary employee who was murdered by a pair of underage boys.[75] A similar bill known as the Claiming Law Around Insurance of Marijuana Act (CLAIM) has been proposed to allow cannabis enterprises to more easily acquire different types of standard business insurance.[76] Other legislation was proposed in 2022 to allow additional avenues to research the medical use of cannabis and allow physicians to discuss cannabis with patients.[77]

While many of the proposed bills are aimed at helping or clarifying laws around operating a cannabis business, members of Congress have also recently demonstrated clear interest in addressing some of the ways that federal law impacts individual Americans who use cannabis. In 2021, for example, the late Don Young introduced the Gun Rights and Marijuana Act, which would allow cannabis users to honestly complete the required forms for a federal background check needed to purchase a firearm.[78] Brendan Boyle similarly introduced the Destigmatizing in Immigration Act that would remove cannabis use as a disqualifying factor in immigration cases, clearing the way for new Americans to no longer fear that their legal cannabis use would become an issue during stressful immigration cases.[79] And for those medical patients who would seek to legally consume cannabis in federally subsidized housing, Eleanor Holmes Norton introduced the Marijuana in Federal Assisted Housing Parity Act, which would prevent evictions and loss of benefits for these residents.[80]

Still, the stigma of cannabis use has not entirely evaporated from the halls of Congress—Representative Tom Rice recently reintroduced a bill known as the Welfare for Needs Not Weeds Act, a measure that has been consistently proposed since 2014 which would prevent federal benefit cards, such as SNAP food aid, from being used to purchase cannabis.[81] The connection between drug use and welfare has a consistent legacy of late twentieth-century stereotypes—many of them racist—about those who receive public benefits. That this proposed bill is largely if not entirely a political stunt is evident in the fact that there are already provisions that make it difficult for those who possess federal EBT cards to use those funds directly on legal cannabis purchases.[82]

Even with all of this legislative activity, the 117th Congress (2021–2022) ended up being a bust for any movement on federal liberalization. Senator Schumer and other congressional advocates of legislation like the SAFE and MORE Acts worked to combine many of the provisions into a larger package called the Cannabis Administration and Opportunity Act and to attach this larger bill onto a variety of must-pass legislation that the narrow Democratic majorities in Congress could get to the floor. This approach seemed to bring imminent congressional passage of some modest amount of federal reform at several points during the second half of 2022, but Republican opponents of legalization such as senator Mitch McConnell were successful in mobilizing allies to threaten to block any legislation that would include these measures.[83] During his tenure as senate majority leader until 2021, McConnell had already successfully helped pass two Farm Bills that clarified the legal status of hemp, an important crop in his state of Kentucky. These bills also liberalized access to non-THC products that have CBD, a chemical that helps to relax some individuals and has some clinical applications.[84] As minority leader, however, McConnell has shown little interest in helping to advance the cause of legal cannabis despite the clear public support for congressional action.

REPARATIONS FOR FEDERAL WRONGS: THE CAUTIONARY TALE OF THE *PIGFORD* CASE

An important and shameful legacy of federal policy that should be considered when determining how to move forward on legalization is the plight of Black farmers who sought recompense from the 1999 settlement of the *Pigford v. Glickman* class action lawsuit. Indirectly, their claims went all the way back to the failure of Reconstruction-era economic reforms, particularly the choice to avoid land reform in favor of the millions of formerly enslaved Black individuals across the South. The business of farming—particularly small farming—heavily favored the white planter class that had dominated the region since before the Civil War. While the federal government began to provide more extensive economic support to farmers in the twentieth century, the decline of smaller-scale farming in the face of factory farming and more mechanized methods of agriculture disproportionately impacted Black farmers. This was in part because the US Department of Agriculture (USDA) systematically discriminated against them for loans and other forms of aid. Much of this aid was distributed locally using a selection system that often completely excluded Black farmers, and the USDA's civil rights office was effectively defunct, leaving these farmers with no recourse. Even when farmers were not denied aid outright, they were often subjected to additional scrutiny and delays that caused them financial harm.[85]

In 1997, a group of 400 farmers led by plaintiff Timothy Pigford filed suit against the USDA on behalf of what was thought to be at least 2,000 farmers impacted by this discriminatory behavior. The plaintiffs were granted class action status and the case was eventually settled. Under the terms of legislation later passed by Congress, over $2 billion was supposed to be paid to tens of thousands of African American farmers who were denied benefits by the USDA. One of the largest claims went to the former owners of the New Communities, a collective land trust in Georgia that a small group of Black farmers had owned and been forced to sell after the USDA denied them emergency loans in the mid-1980s that it routinely gave to white farmers with little delay. The USDA under the Reagan administration had closed its regional civil rights office and discarded complaints that were received about the delays.[86] The New Communities group, including a woman named Shirley Sherrod, received $13 million from the settlement in 2009 to compensate them for these harms.[87]

Despite the enabling congressional legislation, the *Pigford* claims process spanned the following two decades and included allegations of fraud against settlement recipients, though few claimants ended up having these allegations sustained.[88] The institutional legacy of this case came to a head in 2010, when Sherrod—who was by that point the leader of the USDA Office of Rural Development in Georgia—was quoted in a story featured in conservative media stating that she would not help white farmers, sparking a bipartisan furor that led to a dramatic roadside call where Sherrod was summarily fired. When the full video was released, however, Sherrod's words came in the context of recounting the difficult legacy of her own family's legacy with racism, but she also made clear that she was able to help the white farmers who came to her and ultimately befriend them. While Sherrod was ultimately offered her job back, she declined, and her experience became a harbinger of the larger discourse on the legacy of racist policies and the presumed responsibility of Black Americans to engage in responsibility politics to even receive recognition of past wrongs.[89]

The *Pigford* case—and its later role in helping to undermine the career of a Black public servant—shows the complicated political and institutional dynamics of reparations politics on the federal level. As seen here, in the previously unsuccessful efforts to establish a national reparations commission described in chapter 3, and in the local effort to create reparations in Evanston, Illinois, detailed in chapter 7, it remains difficult to even publicly broach many of the hard discussions regarding the impacts of slavery, segregation, and continuing discrimination on Americans of color. It often proves difficult to agree on basic facts, such as the existence of previous harms, without even getting to the point of determining the financial impact or the policy design of the relief. Any effort to account for the impact of the federal government in cannabis prohibition—particularly the racially oriented impacts of state-level enforcement that federal policy abetted—will have to grapple with these sorts of difficult conversations to determine levels of causality regarding who bears the responsibility for the impacts of criminalization. And that's even before crafting the legislation to respond in an appropriate way.

CONCLUSION: FINDING SOCIAL EQUITY IN FEDERAL LAW

During the COVID-19 pandemic, states across the country decreed that cannabis businesses were "essential operations," allowing them to remain open to customers during the widespread business closures that came during lockdowns. The political and moral implications of this decision seemed ironic to prisoners such as Craig Cesal, who had been convicted on federal charges in 2002 because his automotive body shop occasionally worked on refrigerated trucks that participated in the interstate smuggling of cannabis. He wrote in 2020:

> While the marijuana purveyors carry on in their marijuana stores, the local county jails are busy identifying prisoners they can release if they determine they are not a danger to the community. Local jails are working to reduce jail populations to staunch the spread of coronavirus. All but violent offenders, including marijuana slingers, are being released, since they are not a threat to anyone. If marijuana proprietors are not a threat to the community, a community made up of the People of the US, why are taxpayers spending over $50,000 per year to keep me in this box?[90]

Cesal had been sentenced to life in prison for drug smuggling despite never having actually touched or transported cannabis himself.[91]

Freed in 2020 as part of the widespread release of nonviolent prisoners from federal prisons, Cesal was eventually pardoned by former President Trump on his way out of office in January 2021.[92] Cesal has since become an activist for prison reform and has participated in advocacy efforts for decriminalization, including pointing out potential flaws that would have limited relief provided by the proposed MORE Act.[93] In the editorial that he wrote from prison in 2020, Cesal estimates that thousands of federal prisoners were still serving sentences for crimes where cannabis distribution was a factor, suggesting the immense reach that a social equity approach to cannabis legalization at the federal level will have in redressing the harms of criminalization.

As Cesal's experience makes plain and as this chapter has demonstrated, the path for cannabis legalization at the federal level remains hazy despite the apparent shift in public opinion about both the merits and costs of criminalization. Yet even where progress has been made—either in redressing past convictions or crafting proposed legislation—the prospects of having an integrated and diverse ownership structure in a future legal market are unlikely without a further shift in political support that actively positions that as a goal of the movement. As a result, many advocates of social equity policy are apathetic about federal legalization, viewing it as a threat to the fragile progress made in a handful of states. The inspiration to "regulate cannabis like alcohol" instead points to a highly centralized industry that has a limited, if still developing, capacity for niche and craft producers to establish themselves.

Despite this pessimism, however, it is likely that social equity supporters represent an important, if not critical, group that would need to sign off on federal legalization. Advocates have learned from previous experiences where licensing schemes were established on the front end to benefit established providers in exchange for legalization support, but at a long-term cost. For example, the campaign for legislative adoption in New York demonstrated this kind of savvy on the part of many cannabis advocates who were able to examine the experience of legalization in other states and point to those examples as they worked to prevent equity from taking a back seat to other interests.

It is clear from the support of figures ranging from Chuck Schumer to Matt Gaetz that advocates of social equity policies have significantly impacted the federal debate over legalization, making it difficult if not impossible to imagine that Congress would be able to ignore these demands in creating a comprehensive policy. Much like the legislative solutions to criminalization that were adopted in Illinois and New York, political demands to address the legacy of criminalization have become a part of the narrative regarding cannabis legalization itself. The key question is how long it will take to get the momentum to build a true coalition for legalization. While the current status quo may allow the space for social equity policies to develop and sustain themselves in artificially limited circumstances, full legalization of any type will represent a threat to these markets. Still, although the narrow Republican House majority brought in by the 2022 midterm elections will likely pose a stumbling block for any congressional progress on cannabis policy for much, if not all, of the 118th Congress, it is far easier in 2023 to imagine the end of federal prohibition than it was in 2013 or 2003.

NOTES

1. Every year since 1969, Gallup has asked Americans, "Do you think the use of marijuana should be legal or not?" 2013 was the first year that more than half answered, "Yes," and support has never been below that figure again. See Jeffrey M. Jones, "Marijuana Views Linked to Ideology, Religiosity, Age," Gallup, November 15, 2022, https://news.gallup.com/poll/405086/marijuana-views-linked-ideology-religiosity-age.aspx.

2. NORML, "Petition to Biden and Trump: End Marijuana Prohibition," circa 2020, https://norml.org/petition-to-biden-and-trump-end-marijuana-prohibition/.

3. Michael Roberts, "AG Nom Jeff Sessions Thought KKK Was Okay Until He Learned They Smoked Pot?" *Westword*, November 18, 2016, https://www.westword.com/news/ag-nom-jeff-sessions-thought-kkk-was-okay-until-he-learned-they-smoked-pot-8515997.

4. Sarah N. Lynch, "US Attorney General Nominee Will Not Target Law Abiding Marijuana Businesses," Reuters, January 15, 2019, https://www.reuters.com

/article/us-usa-trump-barr-marijuana/u-s-attorney-general-nominee-will-not-target-law-abiding-marijuana-businesses-idUSKCN1P92JO.

5. Michael Roberts, "Marijuana: Cory Gardner to Be Targeted for Vote Against Defunding Federal MMJ Raids," *Westword*, June 3, 2014, https://www.westword.com/news/marijuana-cory-gardner-to-be-targeted-for-vote-against-defunding-federal-mmj-raids-5882999.

6. Matt Laslo, "How a Republican Senator Became the Biggest Cannabis Power Broker in Congress," *Playboy*, November 1, 2019, https://www.playboy.com/read/cory-gardner-cannabis.

7. John Ingold, "Marijuana Legalization in Colorado Is 10 Years Old: Here's the Story of How It Happened," *Colorado Sun*, November 7, 2022, https://coloradosun.com/2022/11/07/colorado-marijuana-legalization-history-amendment-64/.

8. Statista, "Craft Beer Share of Retail Beer Market in the United States from 2012 to 2021," 2022, https://www.statista.com/statistics/1093653/craft-beer-dollar-share-of-us-beer-market/.

9. Paul Demko, "A National Weed Glut Is Causing Prices to Plummet and Imperiling Businesses," *Politico*, December 25, 2022, https://www.politico.com/news/2022/12/25/weed-prices-business-michigan-00075485.

10. Mumbi Gitau, "Big Tobacco Jumps into Germany's Pot Industry Alongside Snoop Dogg," *Bloomberg*, September 26, 2022, https://www.bloomberg.com/news/newsletters/2022-09-26/bat-tobacco-company-joins-snoop-dogg-in-german-marijuana-industry.

11. *MJBizDaily*, "Tobacco Giant Philip Morris Eyes Marijuana Market Opportunities," updated December 17, 2021, https://mjbizdaily.com/tobacco-giant-philip-morris-eyes-marijuana-market-opportunities/.

12. Stefan Sykes, "Cannabis Drinks Pop Up As Companies Bet on the Growing Market for Legal Marijuana," *CNBC*, updated August 31, 2022, https://www.cnbc.com/2022/08/30/cannabis-drinks-companies-hope-to-capitalize-on-growing-market.html.

13. Hazey Taughtme and K. Michael Williams, "Driven by Necessity," *Black Cannabis*, April 2021, https://blackcannabismagazine.com/april2021/.

14. Dan Adams, "Federal Marijuana Reform Looms After Senate Flip—and Massachusetts Could End Up a Loser," *Boston Globe*, January 22, 2021, https://www.bostonglobe.com/2021/01/22/marijuana/federal-marijuana-reform-looms-after-senate-flip-massachusetts-could-end-up-loser/.

15. Emily Dufton, *Grass Roots: The Rise and Fall and Rise of Marijuana in America* (New York: Basic Books, 2017), 147–49.

16. Elizabeth Kastor, "The Great Drug Debate," *Washington Post*, October 22, 1986, https://www.washingtonpost.com/archive/lifestyle/1986/10/22/the-great-drug-debate/df37470c-2763-444c-be93-3a1ae842b022/.

17. University of Mississippi School of Pharmacy, "Marijuana Research: History," https://pharmacy.olemiss.edu/marijuana/history/.

18. *Leary v. United States*, 395 U.S. 6 (1969), https://caselaw.findlaw.com/us-supreme-court/395/6.html.

19. Laura Mansnerus, "Timothy Leary, Pied Piper of Psychedelic 60's, Dies at 75," *New York Times*, June 1, 1996, https://www.nytimes.com/1996/06/01/us/timothy-leary-pied-piper-of-psychedelic-60-s-dies-at-75.html?sec=&spon=&pagewanted=all.

20. Tom Angell, "State Department Says DEA Is Wrong on Marijuana Monopoly," Marijuana.com, May 6, 2016, archived at https://web.archive.org/web/20181011133436/https://www.marijuana.com/news/2016/05/state-department-says-dea-is-wrong-on-marijuana-monopoly/.

21. White House Office of National Drug Control Policy, "National Drug Control Budget: FY 2023 Funding Highlights," March 2022, https://www.whitehouse.gov/wp-content/uploads/2022/03/FY-2023-Budget-Highlights.pdf.

22. Brown University, "Costs of the 20-Year War on Terror: $8 Trillion and 900,000 Deaths," news release, September 1, 2021, https://www.brown.edu/news/2021-09-01/costsofwar.

23. John Hudak, "Biden's Cannabis Pardons: A Long Overdue Reassessment of the War on Drugs," *How We Rise* (blog), Brookings Institution, October 7, 2022, https://www.brookings.edu/blog/how-we-rise/2022/10/07/bidens-cannabis-pardons-a-long-overdue-reassessment-of-the-war-on-drugs/.

24. Hudak, "Biden's Cannabis Pardons."

25. Office of the White House, "Statement from President Biden on Marijuana Reform," October 6, 2022, https://www.whitehouse.gov/briefing-room/statements-releases/2022/10/06/statement-from-president-biden-on-marijuana-reform/.

26. Rosie Cima, "DARE: The Anti-Drug Program That Never Actually Worked," *Priceonomics*, December 19, 2016, https://priceonomics.com/dare-the-anti-drug-program-that-never-actually/.

27. Jeff Rivenbark and Tom Roussey, "Elementary Student Brings Pot to School to Turn in His Parents," *WBTV*, updated November 14, 2010, https://www.wbtv.com/story/13330034/couple-facing-drug-charges-after-child-tips-off-cop-at-school/.

28. Cima, "DARE."

29. NPR, "15 Years After Columbine, Are Schools Safer?" *Tell Me More* radio broadcast, 11:36, April 18, 2014, recording and transcript available at https://www.npr.org/2014/04/18/304526475/15-years-after-columbine-are-schools-any-safer.

30. Mikki L. Smith, "A Generation at Risk: The Ties Between Zero Tolerance Policies and the School-to-Prison Pipeline," *McNair Scholars Research Journal* 8 (2015): 125–41, https://commons.emich.edu/cgi/viewcontent.cgi?article=1094&context=mcnair.

31. Nancy A. Heitzeg, "'Education or Incarceration': Zero Tolerance Policies and the School to Prison Pipeline," *Forum on Public Policy* no. 2 (2009), 8–13, https://files.eric.ed.gov/fulltext/EJ870076.pdf.

32. This observation has been confirmed by my yearly informal survey of students in both undergraduate and graduate classes taught in the Boston area. See also D.A.R.E. (Drug Abuse Resistance Education), "D.A.R.E. Hometowns—U.S.A. and International,," https://dare.org/where-is-d-a-r-e/.

33. For example, see Richard R. Clayton, Anne M. Cattarello, and Bryan M. Johnstone, "The Effectiveness of Drug Abuse Resistance Education (Project

DARE): 5-Year Follow-Up Results," *Preventive Medicine* 25, no. 3 (1996): 307–18, https://doi.org/10.1006/pmed.1996.0061; and Steven L. West and Keri K. O'Neal, "Project D.A.R.E. Outcome Effectiveness Revisited," *American Journal of Public* Health 94, no. 6 (2004): 1027–29, https://doi.org/10.2105%2Fajph.94.6.1027.

34. Roselius himself later voted in favor of California's cannabis legalization initiative in 2016. German Lopez, "In the 1980s, He Warned That 'This Is Your Brain on Drugs.' In 2016, He Voted to Legalize Marijuana," *Vox*, October 26, 2016, https://www.vox.com/policy-and-politics/2016/10/26/13417270/marijuana-legalization-brain-on-drugs.

35. German Lopez, "Why Anti-Drug Campaigns Like DARE Fail," *Vox*, September 1, 2014, https://www.vox.com/2014/9/1/5998571/why-anti-drug-campaigns-like-dare-fail.

36. Cima, "DARE."

37. Reuters, "Youth Violence Epidemic Not Over, Surgeon General Warns," *New York Times*, January 18, 2001, https://www.nytimes.com/2001/01/18/health/youth-violence-epidemic-not-over-surgeon-general-warns.html.

38. US Government Accountability Office, *Youth Illicit Drug Use Prevention: DARE Long-Term Evaluations and Federal Efforts to Identify Effective Programs*, GAO-03–172R, January 15, 2003, 5–7, https://www.gao.gov/assets/gao-03-172r.pdf.

39. Monitoring the Future, University of Michigan, "About MTF," https://monitoringthefuture.org/about/.

40. Richard A. Miech et al., *Monitoring the Future National Survey Results on Drug Use, 1975–2022: Secondary School Students* (Ann Arbor: Institute for Social Research, University of Michigan, 2023), 117–23, https://monitoringthefuture.org/wp-content/uploads/2022/12/mtf2022.pdf.

41. Christopher P. Salas-Wright et al., "Trends in Perceived Access to Marijuana Among Adolescents in the United States: 2002–2015," *Journal of Studies on Alcohol and Drugs* 78, no. 5 (2017): 778–79, https://doi.org/10.15288/jsad.2017.78.771; and D. Mark Anderson et al., "Association of Marijuana Laws with Teen Marijuana Use: New Estimates from the Youth Risk Behavior Survey," *JAMA Pediatrics* 173, no. 9 (2019): 879–81, https://doi.org/10.1001/jamapediatrics.2019.1720.

42. National Institute on Drug Abuse, "Percentage of Adolescents Reporting Drug Use Decreased Significantly in 2021 as the COVID-19 Pandemic Endured," news release, December 15, 2021, https://nida.nih.gov/news-events/news-releases/2021/12/percentage-of-adolescents-reporting-drug-use-decreased-significantly-in-2021-as-the-covid-19-pandemic-endured.

43. National Institute on Drug Abuse, "Most Reported Substance Use Among Adolescents Held Steady in 2022," news release, December 15, 2022, https://nida.nih.gov/news-events/news-releases/2022/12/most-reported-substance-use-among-adolescents-held-steady-in-2022.

44. Martin A. Lee, *Smoke Signals: A Social History of Marijuana—Medical, Recreational, and Scientific* (New York: Scribner, 2012), 258–59.

45. Peter Hecht, *Weed Land: Inside America's Marijuana Epicenter and How Pot Went Legit* (Berkeley: University of California Press, 2014), 190–91.

46. Emily Crick, Mark Cooke, and Dave Bewley-Taylor, "Selling Cannabis Regulation: Learning from Ballot Initiatives in the United States in 2012," Policy Brief 6, Global Drug Policy Observatory, November 2014, 11, https://www.swansea.ac.uk/media/Selling-Cannabis-Regulation.pdf.

47. James M. Cole, "Memorandum to All United States Attorneys," August 29, 2013, https://www.justice.gov/iso/opa/resources/3052013829132756857467.pdf.

48. US House of Representatives, H.Amdt.332 to H.R.2578, 114th Cong. (2015–2016), https://www.congress.gov/amendment/114th-congress/house-amendment/332.

49. Cole, "Memorandum."

50. National Instant Criminal Background Check Business Unit, "Information and Examples of the Application of Title 18, United States Code (U.S.C.), Section 922, Subsection (g)(3): Persons Who Are Unlawful Users Of or Addicted to Any Controlled Substance," National Instant Criminal Background Check System (NICS) Section, Federal Bureau of Investigation, May 2, 2019, 6, https://www.justice.gov/file/1385186/download.

51. Michael Karlik, "Feds Properly Denied Colorado Woman's Citizenship Request for Marijuana Use, Judge Says," *Colorado Politics*, updated December 9, 2022, https://www.coloradopolitics.com/news/feds-properly-denied-colorado-womans-citizenship-request-for-marijuana-use-judge-says/article_9e83588a-5570-11ed-b5c2-cb07f84192ae.html.

52. Aaron Herreras Szot, "Marijuana Use Can Still Be a Problem for Security Clearance Applicants," *Government Executive*, January 20, 2022, https://www.govexec.com/defense/2022/01/marijuana-use-can-still-be-problem-security-clearance-applicants/360933/.

53. Will Yakowicz, "The Sexiest Story of Taxes and Marijuana: The History of Tax Code 280e," *Inc.*, June 29, 2016, https://www.inc.com/will-yakowicz/how-cpas-tax-lawyers-fighting-irs-for-marijuana.html.

54. Cultiva Law, "Overproduction, Diversion, and the 'New' Marijuana Black Market," blog post, May 22, 2018, https://cultivalaw.com/overproduction-diversion-and-the-new-marijuana-black-market/.

55. US Department of Justice, "Justice Department Issues Memo on Marijuana Enforcement," news release, January 4, 2018, https://www.justice.gov/opa/pr/justice-department-issues-memo-marijuana-enforcement.

56. Burgess Everett, "Colo. Senator: Trump Easing Up on Pot Crackdown," *Politico*, April 13, 2018, https://www.politico.com/story/2018/04/13/cory-gardner-marijuana-522862.

57. Kyle Jaeger, "Biden AG Pick Restates Pledge to Respect State Marijuana Laws, in Writing," *Marijuana Moment*, March 1, 2021, https://www.marijuanamoment.net/biden-ag-picks-restates-pledge-to-respect-state-marijuana-laws-in-writing/.

58. Natalie Fertig, "Schumer Launches Long-Shot Bid for Legal Weed," *Politico*, July 14, 2021, https://www.politico.com/news/2021/07/14/schumer-launches-long-shot-bid-for-legal-weed-499584.

59. Natalie Fertig, "Cannabis Crime Wave Boosts Banking Prospects on Capitol Hill," *Politico*, May 10, 2022, https://www.politico.com/news/2022/05/10/cannabis-crime-wave-banking-capitol-hill-00030330.

60. For an overview of medical cannabis legalization, see National Conference of State Legislatures, "State Medical Cannabis Laws," updated September 12, 2022, https://www.ncsl.org/health/state-medical-cannabis-laws.

61. John Hudak and Grace Wallack, "How to Reschedule Marijuana, and Why It's Unlikely Anytime Soon," *FixGov* (blog), Brookings Institution, February 13, 2015, https://www.brookings.edu/blog/fixgov/2015/02/13/how-to-reschedule-marijuana-and-why-its-unlikely-anytime-soon/.

62. Drug Enforcement Administration, "Schedules of Controlled Substances: Removal of (18F)FP-CIT from Control," *Federal Register* 86, no. 211 (November 4, 2021): 60785–90, https://www.govinfo.gov/content/pkg/FR-2021-11-04/pdf/2021-23852.pdf.

63. Regulations.gov, "Comment on FR Doc # 2021–23852," Comment ID DEA-2021-0025-008, https://www.regulations.gov/comment/DEA-2021-0025-0008.

64. Davis Richardson, "Trump's Attorney General Pick Bill Barr Breaks with Jeff Sessions over Weed Policy," *Observer*, January 15, 2019, https://observer.com/2019/01/attorney-general-pick-bill-barr-breaks-with-jeff-sessions-weed-policy/.

65. *MJBizDaily*, "Attorney General Nominee Garland Signals Friendlier Marijuana Stance," updated December 17, 2021, https://mjbizdaily.com/attorney-general-nominee-merrick-garland-signals-friendlier-marijuana-stance/.

66. *MJBizDaily*, "Attorney General Nominee Garland."

67. Tribune News Service, "Matt Gaetz Helped Set Off Florida's Marijuana 'Green Rush': Some of His Friends, Allies Scored Big," *Tampa Bay* (FL) *Times*, May 9, 2021, https://www.tampabay.com/news/florida-politics/2021/05/09/matt-gaetz-helped-set-off-floridas-marijuana-green-rush-some-of-his-friends-allies-scored-big/.

68. Andrew Selsky, "Oregon's Governor Pardons Thousands for Pot Convictions," Associated Press, November 21, 2022, https://apnews.com/article/biden-oregon-crime-district-of-columbia-kate-brown-4e15853ff264fba36ca978b33f20c94f.

69. Bruce Barcott, "President Biden's Marijuana 'Review' Could Be a Deadly Trap," *Leafly*, October 13, 2022, https://www.leafly.com/news/politics/president-bidens-marijuana-review-could-be-a-deadly-trap.

70. Geoffrey Lawrence, "First Circuit Makes Clear Cannabis Is Subject to Interstate Commerce Clause," *Reason*, September 13, 2022, https://reason.org/commentary/first-circuit-makes-clear-cannabis-is-subject-to-interstate-commerce-clause/.

71. Amy Howe, "Opinion Analysis: A Total Victory for Total Wine in 21st Amendment Dispute," *SCOTUSblog*, June 16, 2019, https://www.scotusblog.com/2019/06/opinion-analysis-a-total-victory-for-total-wine-in-21st-amendment-dispute/.

72. Shaleen Title, "Bigger Is Not Better: Preventing Monopolies in the National Cannabis Market," Ohio State Legal Studies Research Paper no. 678, Drug Enforcement and Policy Center (2022), 10–11, https://dx.doi.org/10.2139/ssrn.4018493.

73. Congressional Budget Office, *H. R. 3884, MORE Act of 2020* (December 4, 2020), https://www.cbo.gov/publication/56882.

74. Associated Press, "Pot Shop Robberies Are Fueling Calls for a US Banking Bill," *NPR*, April 20, 2022, https://www.npr.org/2022/04/20/1093841615/pot-shop-robberies-are-fueling-calls-for-a-u-s-banking-bill.

75. Sara Jean Green, "Seattle Police Arrest 15-Year-Old Wanted in Deadly Tacoma Pot Shop Robbery; 2 Remain At Large," *Seattle Times*, updated April 12, 2022, https://www.seattletimes.com/seattle-news/law-justice/seattle-police-arrest-15-year-old-wanted-in-deadly-tacoma-pot-shop-robbery-2-remain-at-large/.

76. Jay Virdi, "Understanding the Federal SAFE and CLAIM Acts," *mg Magazine*, June 23, 2021, https://mgmagazine.com/business/understanding-the-federal-safe-and-claim-acts/.

77. Kristine Blackwood et al., "President Biden Signs Bill Clearing the Way for Medical Cannabis Research," legal advisory, Arnold & Porter, December 7, 2022, https://www.arnoldporter.com/en/perspectives/advisories/2022/12/medical-cannabis-research.

78. *GovTrack Insider*, "GRAM Act Would Allow State-Legal Marijuana Use As Acceptable Answer on Federal Firearm Background Check," July 15, 2021, https://govtrackinsider.com/gram-act-would-allow-state-legal-marijuana-use-as-acceptable-answer-on-federal-firearm-background-6b4aef161c55.

79. 117th Congress, *H. R. 1614 (IH)—Destigmatizing in Immigration Act*, 2021, https://www.govinfo.gov/app/details/BILLS-117hr1614ih.

80. Kyle Jaeger, "Congressional Bill Filed to Protect Marijuana Consumers from Losing Public Housing," *Marijuana Moment*, May 14, 2021, https://www.marijuanamoment.net/congressional-bill-filed-to-protect-marijuana-consumers-from-losing-public-housing/.

81. Melissa Kuipers Blake and Osiris Morel, "Cannabis Legislation Wrap Up for 2021," client alert, Brownstein Hyatt Farber Schreck, January 12, 2022, https://www.bhfs.com/insights/alerts-articles/2022/cannabis-legislation-wrap-up-for-2021.

82. David Mikkelson, "Can You Use Food Stamps to Purchase Marijuana?" *Snopes*, September 12, 2014, https://www.snopes.com/2014/09/13/welfare-for-weed/.

83. Natalie Fertig, "Schumer Makes Last-Ditch Push for Cannabis Banking Bill," *Politico*, December 16, 2022, https://www.politico.com/news/2022/12/16/schumer-cannabis-banking-bill-00074258.

84. John Hudak, "The Farm Bill, Hemp Legalization and the Status of CBD: An Explainer," *FixGov* (blog), Brookings Institution, December 14, 2018, https://www.brookings.edu/blog/fixgov/2018/12/14/the-farm-bill-hemp-and-cbd-explainer/.

85. Congressional Research Service, *The* Pigford *Cases: USDA Settlement of Discrimination Suits by Black Farmers*, May 29, 2013, archived at https://www.everycrsreport.com/reports/RS20430.html.

86. Kate Pickert, "When Shirley Sherrod Was First Wronged by the USDA," *Time*, July 23, 2010, archived at https://web.archive.org/web/20100829162023/http://www.time.com/time/nation/article/0,8599,2006058,00.html?xid=rss-fullnation-yahoo.

87. Debbie Elliott, "5 Decades Later, New Communities Land Trust Still Helps Black Farmers," *NPR*, October 3, 2019, https://www.npr.org/2019/10/03/766706906/5-decades-later-communities-land-trust-still-helps-black-farmers.

88. Susan A. Schneider, "Discrimination at USDA: Response to USDA," *Agricultural Law* (blog), May 1, 2013, http://aglaw.blogspot.com/2013/05/discrimination-at-usda-response-to-new.html.

89. Pickert, "Shirley Sherrod."

90. Craig Cesal, "Reflections of an 'Essential' Businessman Doing Life Without Parole," Foundation for Economic Education, June 8, 2020, https://fee.org/articles/reflections-of-an-essential-businessman-doing-life-without-parole/.

91. Andrew Ward, "Most Affected: Craig Cesal Remained Positive and Defiant Despite Life Behind Bars," *High Times*, March 11, 2021, https://hightimes.com/activism/most-affected-craig-cesal-remained-positive-defiant-despite-life-behind-bars/.

92. Office of the White House, "Statement from the Press Secretary Regarding Executive Grants of Clemency," news release, January 20, 2021, https://trumpwhitehouse.archives.gov/briefings-statements/statement-press-secretary-regarding-executive-grants-clemency-012021/.

93. *NBC*, "Chicago Man Serving Life for Marijuana Granted Clemency After 19 Years in Prison," video, July 7, 2022, archived at https://news.yahoo.com/chicago-man-serving-life-marijuana-025002678.html.

Conclusion

FROM "HALLOWEEN SADISM" TO HARM REDUCTION: MOVING TOWARD EQUITY

Every Halloween, millions of young Americans dress up in festive costumes across the country and participate in the annual ritual of knocking on their neighbors' doors to ask for candy and other treats. With few exceptions, this ritual passes with little acclaim. If all you had to go on was the local evening news, however, this might not be your impression. Year after year in many communities, public figures and the news media participate in a complementary ritual with a less savory past. Take for instance a 2021 television segment on *WXYZ-TV* in Detroit, Michigan—a state with legal cannabis—that aired just before the holiday.[1] Viewers of this segment were advised about the colorful and attractive cannabis-infused candies that were offered in stores across the state, including unlicensed products. Some parents, when asked about this, expressed a clear alarm about the possibility of their children getting cannabis candies and a desire to check the candy this year to avoid such an event. The only countering voice was that of a local police chief, who underscored that although this added "a whole new element" to the danger, the candies were rather expensive and consequently not that likely to show up in an unsuspecting tyke's bag.

This second ritual is of course an exercise in cultural paranoia. Legalization has led to an increase in accidental youth ingestion, though this is most often attributable to adults keeping their personal supply of cannabis in places their children could reach.[2] While it is understandable that some parents may want to take every precaution to ensure their child's safety, this fear has long been derided given the complete lack of evidence that cannabis-infused candies have ever actually been given to children on Halloween, as well as the lack of understanding about drug use embedded in the notion that they might. Namely, few of those who choose to use drugs recreationally have any interest in sharing them with the children of strangers, for both moral and economic reasons. Joel Best, a sociologist from the University of Delaware, calls this trope "Halloween sadism" and has consistently looked for even one confirmed report of this occurring. As of 2021, his search was still unfruitful.[3]

While it is darkly comical to repeatedly see these news reports every Halloween, such stories create active harm. Costumed children roaming streets in search of candy in the late fall are at far more risk of being hit by a car in the middle of the street than at the hands of any pretend predator who somehow manages to master the art of cleanly placing razor blades in apples.[4] Much as continuing to emphasize the latter may help us soothe our concern for the safety of children, it is wildly irresponsible to pretend as though this is a helpful exercise in minimizing the harms that could befall them. It leads to the same misplaced impulses that arise when one ignores or is never taught the fact that the average child is far more at risk of being subjected to sexual abuse at the hands of a family member or other trusted figure than those of a stranger.[5] The common misperception that child abductions by strangers are common often does a disservice to parents' efforts to protect their children from adults they might otherwise trust.

THE SPECIAL CONCERNS OF YOUTH

I began this book's conclusion with the panic surrounding cannabis and Halloween rather than considerations of social equity because it illustrates one of the primary motivations that lead many to call for criminal prohibition of cannabis and other drugs: the specter of youth drug use. This concern frames most discussions of drug policy today in the United States and was an important part of the debate over legalization in each state which I have discussed in this book, and it will surely continue to generate heated discussion in both liberal and conservative areas of the country as the wave of cannabis liberalization continues to spread across the country. It would be irresponsible to ignore this concern in any serious consideration of drug policy, and so I will deal frankly with it here for the sake of my readers and with respect for the complex questions that it engenders.

That youth will be a target for bad actors is of course a deeply rooted fear. We most often seek to shield children—those dear to us and the larger population as a whole—from most worldly threats and harm, in a way that prioritizes this outcome over nearly any other pursuit, no matter how noble. This desire has often arisen to complicate racial activism, for example, most prominently in recent decades during the effort by federal courts to desegregate schools. In the Civil Rights Movement and its immediate aftermath, white parents often recoiled at the idea that their children would go to school alongside Black children and resented the idea that their children's education might be sacrificed in support of a social ideal of integration, forming a constituency that sought to defy court orders and the demands of civil rights leaders to fulfill the spirit of *Brown v. Board of Education*.[6] Even today, the challenge of fighting against the de facto school segregation that continues to persist in many areas of the United States often rests on the willingness of parents to cooperate with the idea of uncertainty in their children's education—or else to send them to private school or move into suburbia. One such parent quoted in a 2016 *New York Times* story on this subject summed up why this fear is so hard to overcome when they protested that "my kid's not an experiment."[7]

Even today, this fear of exceptional risks to youth rings true. Conservative political leaders throughout the country warn of ever new menaces in their efforts to reassert control over a changing world and build their own political careers. States where these sentiments are most powerful even seek to limit discussion of sexuality, gender, and racial disparities themselves, as seen most prominently in Florida's recent adoption of the Stop Woke Act.[8] At least fifteen states have considered—and Tennessee has actually passed—legislation to classify "drag" shows as adult oriented and to limit establishments hosting them to areas away from schools and other places associated with children.[9] States and school boards have removed from curricula the writings of scholars who have been critical of racially discriminatory policies in recent decades, such as Michelle Alexander, in response to their efforts,[10] limiting the opportunity for students of all backgrounds to understand the different perspectives that have helped shape policy and practice for the last two decades.

STIGMA, FEAR, AND PUBLIC POLICY

Drugs, and our use of them, mediate much of human society and the experiences and relationships which both bind humans together and, sometimes, push them apart from one another. Every adult in the United States has been forced to consider questions about their own potential use and misuse of substances at some point in their lives, whether for religious, moral, health, emotional, relational, professional, or other reasons. The substances in question can be anything from caffeine—which some faiths consider to be a drug worthy of prohibition, many adults seek to carefully regulate their own usage of, and parents restrict their children from accessing—to alcohol, cannabis, heroin, cocaine, Adderall, and any number of others, whether licit or not.

The reasons why we make these considerations are informed both by our larger knowledge of the world as well as our own practical experiences with those same substances, though at times these two sources of knowledge can in fact be locked in diametric tension. For example, our fears about the potential for safety, dependence, or exposure to societal consequences can be in direct conflict with a desire for the satisfaction and perceived rejuvenation that may occur when using those substances. The former—which in many cases may be characterized as "stigma"—may help us make good decisions in some cases, but it may also cloud the decision-making process with a sense of fear and apprehension that leads not just to self-judgment but also judgment of others. Stigma often serves to amplify the harms and the fear of drug use, resulting in a narrative about the same that does not reflect the reality that many people, youth among them, recognize and which alienates any value that stigma might otherwise hold.

This stigmatized knowledge and the judgment of others that nearly always follows from it often leads to poorly conceived public policy. The key variable here is risk, and stigma unfortunately clouds any attempt at a candid and careful consideration of various elements of risk and the policies that might seek to minimize (though not eliminate) them. In place of this kind of careful consideration, stigma can be found across the spectrum of drug policy in the United States today, from the inconsistently enforced prohibition on alcohol use by people under the age of twenty-one on college campuses, to the scourge of addiction and death that followed the opioid crisis that was felt in rural communities across America but not in the boardrooms of the drug companies that drove the crisis.

This call for consideration is not an invitation for licentiousness, especially for vulnerable populations such as children. It is instead a simple observation that those youth are paying careful attention to the messages that they are receiving—at home, in school, and in the political and social discourse of the current moment—and up to this point, attempts by elders to infuse this message with a healthy dose of prohibitionist sloganizing have simply been failures. Alongside this messaging, youth are exposed to a powerful array of experiential learning from peers, family, and society about the use and abuse of drugs, and any incongruence between what they might receive in school regarding their own relationship with drugs and what they see going on around them will eventually make ineffective or even harmful any dosage of "this is your brain on drugs" sloganizing. By continuing to engage in this effort, both elders and the youth they seek to aid are hurt.

Along with the clear data that demonstrates the futility of most anti-drug messaging,[11] considering drug use in these terms should liberate discourse on drug policy from the moralist pursuit of purification which the ample evidence of the twentieth century lays bare as a failure. In its place, we can build a twenty-first-century approach founded on the principles of harm reduction and authentically caring for others. This policy should consider the harms that both drugs themselves and their use place upon individuals, families, and societies, but it should also take into account the harms that result from control policies and enforcement actions that are intended to prevent individuals from seeking to access those drugs. Where those policies and actions subject individuals, families, and the communities in which they reside to enough harm as to defeat their nominal purpose of promoting public and individual safety, we should dismantle them and consider whether a different set of controls, or none at all, is in fact better in a holistic sense.

In thinking about who is best suited to take the lead in crafting these new approaches, two phrases come to mind. "Nothing about us without us" is an older phrase made new again in recent decades by the disability rights movement, though the sentiment is easily recognized in political organizing across time and space.[12] "The people closest to the pain should be closest to the power" is a similar phrase that is nevertheless distinct enough to warrant inclusion here because it is common in organizing spaces today and amplified by activists and politicians such as Boston congresswoman Ayanna Pressley (who has made it a cornerstone of her public profile).[13] Taken together, those phrases tell us both where we have come from as well as where we should go when dealing with the many thorny issues of regulating the use and productive trade in various substances that may have a negative impact on individual users and the common good. As they relate to who should properly make decisions about the application of state authority, particularly coercive power, these phrases strongly center on the need for intentional inclusivity and democratic provision of both the burdens and benefits of access and use of drugs.

For decades, those in power have sought to limit or prohibit "problematic" drug use, often resorting to the blunt tools of the criminal justice system, reasoning that the incredible consequences that legal codes can impose would surely scare those using substances away from this behavior. For many, even most, this may have actually worked, but for many others this simply represented an alienation and an exclusion from society. We simply cannot afford—on either an individual or a collective level—to continue this approach. It's a bad use of scarce public resources, and in many cases an individual's exposure to the criminal justice system actually makes their addiction worse or even exposes them to other harmful use patterns of a substance that they had not previously encountered. Regardless, imposing pain under the color of state authority to punish an individual's use, possession, or purchase of substances is a poor substitute for actually developing supportive services that empower individuals to regulate their own consumption. It is bad policy in part because it so often fails to temper or even exacerbates the problem it is deployed to fix, and in part because the actual expense of incarceration for hundreds of thousands of Americans convicted of drug crimes is vastly greater than what it could cost to provide even a modest safety net for those experiencing drug addiction issues.[14]

It is also bad policy for the United States in particular because it is fundamentally undemocratic. While those in power are often subjected to many of the same desires to use substances, whether illegal or not, they often manage to adapt the law to give themselves the license to continue their use, and other times they openly flout their codes while relying on the inability or unwillingness of law enforcement to equally apply the law. It is an unfortunate side effect that in those few cases when a member of the "elite" actually does use substances in an illegal way and faces consequences for that action, such as Patrick Kennedy's 2013 incident described earlier in this book, the individual most often credits the legal consequences of their behavior as the impetus for them seeking help with their own problematic use. This reinforces the primacy of the legal in determining how we can help individuals, as well as society, set positive patterns in their substance use—despite the fact that an outcome such as Kennedy's is far more likely precisely because he was already advantaged to begin with.

The idea that a criminal approach is bad policy is not the same thing as saying that people perpetuating harms should be allowed to continue without accountability. To the contrary, the idea of accountability is a key value in the recovery community that has been developed to help support people who do want to change problematic behaviors—as it should be. But rather than being accountable to the state, this context stresses the idea of being accountable on the personal, family, social, and professional levels, and the recovery community—along with the industry of coaches, centers, and other business models—has developed a web of support that seeks to aid those navigating difficult personal challenges and individual trauma in order to establish healthy relationships with substances, whether that means moderation or total elimination of use. Substituting legal consequences as a shortcut for controlling perceived substance abuse, especially without establishing and providing access to such supportive services, simply serves to criminalize trauma and poverty, as those who have wealth or power can afford these services and are often able to use them to weave around the legal consequences during troubling periods, while those who are disadvantaged in some way are simply locked up.

While replacing users' criminal accountability to the state with a more holistic approach is one crucial way forward to a more just drug policy, the state also has an important role to play in demonstrating its accountability to its own citizens for the decades of harm that criminalization has wrought. In this effort, the goals of both social equity and social justice broadly defined should become more fully aligned, at least in terms of drug policy. This alignment can be an important building block in the quest to restore trust among communities of color in the fairness of political and social institutions and would serve to bring many individual members of these communities out of the exclusion to which society has condemned them. It would also help ensure that future efforts to control harms from substance use do not fall on these or other structurally disempowered communities.

Fear and stigma don't just drive debates around drug use, of course—they unhelpfully shape countless narratives that inform and drive public policy today. Whether that is fear of a foreign nation, public health crisis, economic calamity, natural disaster, or social condition, the most impactful narratives are often those that we are able to see or imagine occurring to ourselves or those immediately around us. Drug addiction is one of the social conditions in recent decades which has hit communities across America and has not perfectly discriminated across color lines or between the rich and the poor, even if the way that drug addiction is recognized and addressed is still very different depending on which side of these persistent social divides you find yourself.

The face of drug addiction is often stigmatized—frequently in racialized terms—leading to a cultural idea that there is a metaphorical "other" group seeking to spread misery and exploit drugs' power. This can appear as a more trivial display of paranoia—see the Halloween media ritual described at the beginning of this chapter—but it is also a major component of what public leaders will point to when discussing the threat of drug use. One recurrent theme in this book is how debate over youth use of cannabis has frequently been central to larger political considerations of cannabis legalization—and has often played important roles in both legalization campaigns and in informing the specific regulatory policies that ballot initiatives and legislators have put into place. But this was in many ways simply the logical outgrowth of the fact that concern about youth use first motivated—or at least justified—many of the drug criminalization efforts that federal and state governments implemented over the course of the last century and more.

Even today, some public leaders, particularly those on the right, still actively and knowingly exploit similar fears of drug use and addiction to pursue public policies designed not to control or limit any specific epidemic but instead to build their own political power and recognition by playing on public anxieties about youth exposure to drugs. Even if many of these public leaders today might ignore cannabis does not mean that this trend will continue. The embryonic legal cannabis market waited in fear during the years of the Trump administration when many activists worried that federal prohibition—far from being nearly dead—would come roaring back to life at the hands of Attorney General Jeff Sessions. These fears may not have come to pass, but a future conservative administration could certainly choose to follow the clear letter of federal law still currently on the books and expose a variety of legal operators, state officials, and intermediary businesses to criminal charges for participating in a highly regulated industry. Should this happen, it seems likely that hope for any sort of industry or legal protection will wither, and many state legislators might no longer view legalization as a safe investment of time or political capital.

Even more regressive outcomes are of course possible, up to and including retrenchment into an enhanced War on Drugs—particularly if Donald Trump or anyone inspired by him takes the presidency back. That this is a plausible outcome rather than simply a different form of fear mongering is suggested by the Philippines, whose president, Rodrigo Duterte, oversaw a wave of state-sponsored violence beginning shortly after his election in 2016. Duterte openly bragged about previously murdering drug users, and during his first speech as president he called for citizens to commit vigilante justice against those selling drugs. As a result, over a thousand "drug traffickers" died within a week of his inauguration, and over the six years of his presidency at least 30,000 Filipinos died as a result of this targeting, with little attention to due process. As with previous attempts at prohibition in other contexts, such as the United States, Duterte's campaign was exemplified by accusations of corruption and a focus on low-level offenders, while many larger participants escaped scrutiny or accountability. By the end of his term in office, drug availability in the Philippines had remained consistent despite the loss of numerous lives and social cohesion.[15] Yet during his own time in office, Trump expressed sympathy for Duterte's campaign.[16]

While not eliminating the possibility of a Philippines-style turn in the United States, legal protections for cannabis specifically and a more holistic revision of federal drug policy more generally would at least raise the barrier for such an outcome when the policy preferences or political instincts of those in national office inevitably change. At the end of the day, even if some supporters of cannabis legalization refuse to acknowledge it as a matter of racial justice, the opponents of legalization certainly see it this way. For those that would seek to remove discussion of racial justice from the American discourse, cannabis legalization is a direct threat. Even if much of the focus of these political actors is currently on book bans and other cultural battles,[17] it would take little effort for political opportunism to stoke fear and anxiety regarding legal cannabis as well. Consider that reports of schools stockpiling litterboxes in classrooms sparked a right-wing furor over supposed "gender indoctrination" creating a wave of bathroom-challenged youth, as well as a large degree of venom directed at school officials across the country. Never mind that the litterboxes themselves—which only existed in some limited cases—actually reflected an attempt by school officials to provide supplies for classrooms in the case of an extended lockdown or school shooting.[18]

If the Philippines represents a cautionary tale of the possibilities that might follow from a perpetuation of the status quo, the vision for a drug policy informed by harm reduction rather than a punishment philosophy can look at a limited number of countries worldwide that have taken steps in this direction. The most notable example is Portugal, which radically changed its drug policy in the early twenty-first century. Historically, the dictatorship that persisted in the country prior to 1974 had strongly controlled drug use, often using these measures to marginalize and silence opposition. When Portugal began seeing a large uptick in intravenous needle sharing and HIV/AIDs cases that came from this practice, however, policymakers decided to confront this challenge by overhauling its drug control regime rather than redoubling previous efforts.[19]

Although some media has portrayed Portugal's new policy as legalization or even full decriminalization, this is largely a misconception. Instead, the new strategy changed the control structure to focus on how the individual who was caught possessing drugs may be a harm to themselves or society. Trafficking cases are still prosecuted using the criminal code, but those caught with a personal supply (defined as ten days' worth of use) are diverted out of the justice system to a series of panels that have the power to impose an array of restrictions up to and including fines. The membership of these panels is important, as they tend to include people who are focused on social service provision—including treatment—rather than punitive solutions. Many sanctions that the committee might impose are stayed pending the individual going to therapy of their own volition. Importantly, Portugal has also invested a great deal of resources into building a treatment pipeline, ensuring that organizations that offer substitution therapy as well as a variety of treatment intensities, both inpatient and outpatient, are easy to access. Notably, one of the main goals of the Portuguese control strategy is to focus on behaviors that cause stigmatization of drug users, such as public use and open-air drug markets—the idea is to identify these behaviors as reflective of a need for public services and not punitive control.[20]

Portugal's policy has often been cited by reformers across the world, though few countries or jurisdictions have copied the structure wholesale. Cannabis decriminalization in the United States certainly has at times been a notable example of the philosophy's promise, though a coalition of both law enforcement and public health voices has emerged in nearly every state to criticize these moves, along with further liberalization measures, as removing one of the few ways that problematic drug use could be regulated and individuals could be at least introduced into treatment. The limitations of a full decriminalization approach emerge more concretely when looking at the state of Oregon, where voters in 2020 passed Measure 110, which decriminalized possession of small amounts of all drugs. Those who are caught with such substances would instead be given a citation, which would be dismissed if they called a drug treatment hotline. This support is far less than what is provided in Portugal, however, and treatment rates have been far less than supporters suggested would develop, while problematic use has continued for some.[21] One of the lessons would seem to be that just as criminalization imposed blunt and simplistic mechanisms for addressing the harms that can come from substance use, simplistic approaches to decriminalization may similarly be limited in the good that they can achieve beyond the obvious—though substantial in its own right—diversion of people away from the criminal justice system. Along with such benefits, a social equity approach can add a redress of past harms and a chance at more holistic progress in the future.

WHERE DO WE GO FROM HERE?

Scarcely ten years after legal recreational sales of cannabis began in Colorado, the federal prospect for reform of cannabis policy—or drug policy more generally—seems ever hazier. While there is plenty of political support for some sort of change, few can agree on the full picture of this reform, and little can be accomplished without reaching consensus that the status quo is unacceptable. The fact is, the current situation does benefit many cannabis market incumbents, particularly the MSOs that have established themselves in medical and recreational operations across the country. These MSOs are often less than transparent with and accountable to consumers, citizens, or regulators, creating barriers to developing the kind of market suppliers that would be willing to address larger public fears of increased youth use, as well as ensuring that products are tested and safe for consumption. Increasingly, both the quality of these companies' cannabis as well as the funding behind their operations have come into question, putting pressure on state regulators to enhance their scrutiny of legal cannabis market players.

An example of this is Curaleaf, one of the cannabis companies mentioned in chapter 3. Beginning in 2022, Curaleaf has faced growing scrutiny about much of the earlier financing that helped the company grow into additional markets over the early years of legalization, particularly a series of loans from now-sanctioned Russian oligarch Roman Abramovich.[22] Cannabis market suppliers in these formative years required large infusions of capital to get established, comply with extensive state regulations, and pay a large tax burden due to the shunned status of the substance.[23] Despite the best intentions of federal officials who had drafted the Cole Memo to encourage legal cannabis markets to avoid money from illicit sources, as well as state officials who often sought to understand the benefactors of the web of capital that came into play, many cannabis companies such as Curaleaf have financing connections that undermine public trust in the industry.

Full federal legalization of cannabis might result in a wave of consolidation that would make companies like Curaleaf obsolete, but it would also incentivize the entry of big brands into the market that would do little to address these larger questions of public trust. Public health scholars have long been critical of the marketing practices of large companies in both the tobacco and the alcohol industries,[24] and it is doubtful that these larger brands would be successful in respecting concerns about the ever-expanding amount of colorful cannabis products potentially promoting youth use, which generations of business-savvy cannabis entrepreneurs have variously sought to and been successful at addressing.

The halting solutions to the problems of criminalization proposed in the drug policy debate demonstrate the inadequacy of any one approach to reform. The drug policy reform movement, having helped to usher in regulated markets for cannabis, has often turned its attention to new fronts in recent years, succeeding in efforts to decriminalize all drug possession in Oregon in 2020 and to regulate psilocybin in Colorado in 2022. While laudable for their immediate goals of reducing harm, these efforts contribute to a patchwork of regulation across the country and do little to move toward a larger national reform of drug laws and enforcement-first approaches that will be truly transformative in how American society addresses drug use and abuse. Reaching these ends is of course made more difficult by those who still oppose legalizing cannabis or taking a different approach to the War on Drugs than that pioneered by Harry Anslinger, Richard Nixon, and Ronald Reagan and their belief in the power of ever-increasing penalties to deter both users and sellers. This legacy clearly persists in the thinking of people like former president Donald Trump, now running for another term in office, who has called for those convicted of drug crimes to receive the death penalty and has even expressed a desire to make these executions more gruesome in an effort to shock and awe those watching into presumed sobriety.[25]

While youth use is therefore far from the only drug policy issue that needs to be addressed in any holistic reform effort, the fact that it can be so easily weaponized toward supporting punitive approaches to control makes it an especially important area to focus on in terms of both creating new cultural narratives and innovating new policies. Instead of using the protection of youth as a cudgel for social punishment or a pretext for economic protectionism, we must embrace a better approach that first recognizes the role of youth in setting their own path toward adulthood. This has already been crucial to the early movement for cannabis legalization, as the increasingly large number of youth arrested for cannabis offenses just before legalization campaigns were successfully undertaken touched people from across race and class lines. What is notable about these millions of arrests is that their legacy today is less directly about the pervasive criminal justice system interactions that they spawned than that this widespread exposure to the War of Drugs helped to turn a large portion of the voting age population against such policies.

Much like alcohol prohibition in the early twentieth century, many aspects of the campaign to criminalize cannabis have finally led to greater public awareness about the impacts of criminalization and the demands to scale back the powers of law enforcement to conduct these widespread dragnets.

One of the major critiques that Black Americans have had about the War on Drugs—whether focused on cannabis or more broadly—is the pretext that this effort has given law enforcement to conduct surveillance and violence against communities of color and limit their opportunities for growth in either personal or economic terms. Many critics of cannabis legalization more generally and social equity policies more specifically rightly point out that legalizing cannabis by itself will not eliminate such pretexts because there are still any number of dangerously ambiguous laws, as well as law enforcement personnel willing to use the discretion for which they are trusted on a daily basis to harass and control citizens of color. This should not discourage those who argue for liberalization of policies regarding cannabis and other substances, however, but instead point to an opportunity to broaden the scope of reform and the coalition to achieve this more comprehensive policy change.

Perhaps the most important decision that cannabis regulators must make when working to transition both consumers and suppliers away from the legacy market is a commitment to not use the tools of the previous regime as a shortcut for achieving a shortsighted policy goal of either revenue maximization or public safety more generally. This means that regulators should not partner with law enforcement to raid or otherwise obstruct unregulated cannabis suppliers, unless as an absolute last result. The strength of the legacy market can be explained in many ways, but the harsh truth is that many of those suppliers who still participate in this unregulated market are following a completely rational path, especially in the context of high regulations and taxes that deter those who would happily go "legal" from even getting their foot in the door.

There is a new generation of Americans of color who are leading the way for these suppliers, and by extending a helping hand to them rather than using the heavy hand of the police state, public officials can help build wealth in communities of color in a small yet still extremely significant way. The pace of change on cannabis legalization has been so swift that many Americans who have grown up with the criminalization of cannabis simply being an unquestioned fact are still getting used to the idea that at least on a consumer level, cannabis possession and use are increasingly now a given. It is important to ensure that cannabis consumers are legally protected and safe in this new world, which features threats ranging from large criminal organizations such as Mexican gangs that might use the profits from cannabis sales to fund violence or the trafficking of other substances, to dangerous chemicals and pesticides used in the illegal production of cannabis over decades of stigmatization. But legalization efforts must also pay close attention to full legal protection for the entire cannabis industry, such as suppliers, distributors, and ancillary businesses, as well as ensuring employment and ownership opportunities in these sectors for at least some of those who have been left to the mercy of the criminal justice system due to criminalization.

One element in this fight over legal protections is a key battle between cannabis oligopolists and the broader legalization movement over home growing of cannabis. While most states that have legalized cannabis have provided some allowance for individuals to grow their own plants, some companies and regulators have viewed the effort to dismantle the legacy market as an opportunity to limit consumers' rights to secure their own supply. This right was protected in many of the early ballot initiatives that passed across the country, but state legislators proved more skeptical—Illinois still explicitly prohibits home grow,[26] while New Jersey regulators declined to extend home grow protections to consumers (although this has increased pressure on the state legislature there to address this issue).[27] Policymakers should take a skeptical eye toward arguments to limit home grow across both the medical and recreational markets for cannabis, however, especially when these efforts are being directed by an industry that may hope to capture the market entirely and limit consumer freedom.

Another especially important path to ensuring broad opportunities in the world of legal cannabis is making sure that there is representation within the ranks of regulators for Americans of color, particularly those with direct experience of criminalization. Many of these potential regulators—such as Shaleen Title and the new generation of activists who have taken up the tools of policy that she exemplifies—are not simply "waiting their turn" and are instead demanding the space they need to occupy. For those regulators who may not be aware of the racialized history of legalization, it is crucial that they arrive in their roles willing to listen and consider the viewpoints of both new entrepreneurs and the voices of those who have been selling and buying cannabis for decades, often at the mercy of agents of the state. I have tried to highlight these narratives throughout this book so that they might be considered by regulators who would in turn come away with at least a willingness to continue listening.

Once we are willing to listen to the voices of those impacted by the criminalization of cannabis, it is my hope that comprehensive federal legalization will be the next step. Whatever federal revenues are derived from legalization should first be directed toward addressing the harms of criminalization. This could be done in any number of ways, but one compelling and obvious solution is to use existing resources of the federal government, such as Small Business Administration grant and loan programs, to help build a new diverse generation of cannabis entrepreneurs and provide them the opportunity to build capital for themselves, their families, and their communities. More generally, federal funding can also be directed at high-impact interventions that build wealth and support opportunities for communities of color in areas from which they have been historically denied, such as education and housing.

It is also my hope that by acknowledging some of the past harms of racism and white supremacy—not just those related directly to drug policy, but in terms of structural racism more generally—we can build a bridge to a larger conversation about the generational wealth and opportunity gaps that exist in America today. Some leaders, like Robin Rue Simmons, have already used the advent of cannabis legalization as a starting point for discussing and implementing reparations for slavery and racial discrimination. Where this groundwork has begun to be laid can in turn become a way into discussing a larger agenda of economic and social justice for communities of color.

Martin Luther King Jr. stated in 1963 that the debt of justice owed to Black Americans was being rejected, and in the six decades since then most attempts to even discuss this debt have continually been rejected as well. King refused to believe that the Bank of Justice was insolvent, however, and cannabis legalization has provided one modest opportunity to demonstrate that Americans are willing to pay the debts for which we are responsible. This long-fought and rare opportunity is why it is so important that issues of racial justice be addressed at the outset of discussions regarding legalization. Without underscoring the racial disparity that has been embedded in cannabis criminalization for nearly a century, few can fully appreciate the need for concentrated action ensuring that social equity policies are part of any legalization program that hopes to truly undo and redress the harms of that legacy. Staying "woke" will ensure that cannabis legalization is truly just on its own terms so that it can become an important cornerstone in the larger campaign for racial justice that we will continue to fight for in the coming years.

NOTES

1. *WXYZ-TV Detroit*, "Police Warn of Marijuana Edibles That Look Like Candy Ahead of Halloween," YouTube video, October 21, 2021, https://www.youtube.com/watch?v=7G07RJAZLFo&ab_channel=WXYZ-TVDetroit%7CChannel7.

2. US Food and Drug Administration, "FDA Warns Consumers About the Accidental Ingestion by Children of Food Products Containing THC," news release, June 16, 2022, https://www.fda.gov/food/alerts-advisories-safety-information/fda-warns-consumers-about-accidental-ingestion-children-food-products-containing-thc; and Winter Roth et al., "Changes in California Cannabis Exposures Following Recreational Legalization and the COVID-19 Pandemic," *Clinical Toxicology* 60, no.

5 (2022): 632–38, https://www.tandfonline.com/doi/full/10.1080/15563650.2021.2006212.

3. Joel Best, "Halloween Sadism," blog post, JoelBest.net, https://www.joelbest.net/halloween-sadism.

4. State Farm, "Halloween Is 'Deadliest Day' of the Year for Child Pedestrian Fatalities," news release, October 23, 2012, https://www.prnewswire.com/news-releases/halloween-is-deadliest-day-of-the-year-for-child-pedestrian-fatalities-175397121.html.

5. Rape, Abuse and Incest National Network, "Children and Teens: Statistics," https://www.rainn.org/statistics/children-and-teens.

6. Matthew Delmont, "The Lasting Legacy of the Busing Crisis," *Atlantic*, March 29, 2016, https://www.theatlantic.com/politics/archive/2016/03/the-boston-busing-crisis-was-never-intended-to-work/474264/.

7. Nikole Hannah-Jones, "Choosing a School for My Daughter in a Segregated City," *New York Times Magazine*, June 9, 2016, https://www.nytimes.com/2016/06/12/magazine/choosing-a-school-for-my-daughter-in-a-segregated-city.html?_r=1.

8. Katie Reilly, "Florida's Governor Just Signed the 'Stop Woke Act': Here's What It Means for Schools and Businesses," *Time*, April 22, 2022, https://time.com/6168753/florida-stop-woke-law/.

9. Reuters, "Tennessee Takes Lead in Republican Efforts to Restrict Drag Shows," *NBC News*, February 23, 2023, https://www.nbcnews.com/nbc-out/out-politics-and-policy/tennessee-takes-lead-republican-effort-restrict-drag-shows-rcna72080.

10. Dana Goldstein, "Inside the College Board's Revised African American Studies Curriculum," *New York Times*, February 1, 2023, https://www.nytimes.com/2023/02/01/us/ap-african-american-studies-course.html.

11. See chapter 9 for a discussion of the ineffectiveness of DARE and similar prohibitionist-oriented youth programming.

12. Eli A. Wolff and Mary Hums, "'Nothing About Us Without Us'—Mantra for a Movement," *HuffPost*, updated September 6, 2017, https://www.huffpost.com/entry/nothing-about-us-without-us-mantra-for-a-movement_b_59aea450e4b0c50640cd61cf.

13. Pressley includes the phrase in the first paragraph of the "about" page on her official website. See "Meet Ayanna," AyannaPressley.com, accessed July 5, 2023, https://ayannapressley.com/about/.

14. Gary A. Zarkin et al., "Benefits and Costs of Substance Abuse Treatment Programs for State Prison Inmates: Results from a Lifetime Simulation Model," *Health Economics* 21, no. 6 (2011): 633–52, https://doi.org/10.1002/hec.1735.

15. Tom Allard and Karen Lema, "Exclusive: 'Shock and Awe' Has Failed in Philippines Drug War, Enforcement Chief Says," Reuters, February 7, 2020, https://www.reuters.com/article/us-philippines-drugs-performance-exclusi/exclusive-shock-and-awe-has-failed-in-philippines-drug-war-enforcement-chief-says-idUSKBN2010IL.

16. Joshua Berlinger and Elise Labott, "Trump Praises Duterte's Deadly Drug War in Leaked Transcript," CNN.com, May 24, 2017, https://www.cnn.com/2017/05/24/politics/donald-trump-rodrigo-duterte-phone-call-transcript/index.html.

17. Andrew Jack, "Growing List of Books Targeted in America's School Culture Wars," *Financial Times*, November 20, 2022, https://www.ft.com/content/5d9ce954-ed2e-4c15-81d8-91a5b2a88905.

18. Tyler Kingkade et al., "How an Urban Myth About Litter Boxes in Schools Became a GOP Talking Point," *NBC News*, October 14, 2022, https://www.nbcnews.com/tech/misinformation/urban-myth-litter-boxes-schools-became-gop-talking-point-rcna51439.

19. Ximene Rêgo et al., "20 Years of Portuguese Drug Policy—Developments, Challengers and the Quest for Human Rights," *Substance Abuse Treatment, Policy, and Policy* 16 (2021), https://doi.org/10.1186/s13011-021-00394-7.

20. Lauren Frayer, "In Portugal, Drug Use Is Treated as a Medical Issue, Not a Crime," *NPR*, April 18, 2017, https://www.npr.org/sections/parallels/2017/04/18/524380027/in-portugal-drug-use-is-treated-as-a-medical-issue-not-a-crime.

21. Dirk VanderHart, "Addiction Experts Tell Oregon Lawmakers the State Has Been Too Lax on Drug Use," OPB.org, September 21, 2022, https://www.opb.org/article/2022/09/21/oregon-decriminalize-drugs-measure-110-addiction-treatment/.

22. Bill Alpert, "How a Prominent Russian Oligarch Helped Start America's Cannabis Industry," *Barron's*, January 4, 2023, https://www.barrons.com/articles/russian-oligarch-roman-abramovich-curaleaf-cannabis-industry-51674507683.

23. Mike Baker and William K. Rashbaum, "As Russian Money Poured into Cannabis, Giuliani Allies Scrambled to Partake," *New York Times*, updated October 24, 2019, https://www.nytimes.com/2019/10/23/us/kukushkin-giuliani-russia-cannabis-marijuana.html.

24. Jennfier L. Brown et al., "Spinning a Global Web: Tactics Used by Big Tobacco to Attract Children at Tobacco Points-of-Sale," *Tobacco Control* (2022), http://dx.doi.org/10.1136/tobaccocontrol-2021-057095; and Douglas A. Gentile et al., "Beer Advertisements and Adolescent Drinking Knowledge, Expectancies, and Behavior," *Addictive Behaviors Reports* 10 (2019), https://doi.org/10.1016/j.abrep.2019.100226.

25. Cheryl Teh, "Trump Has Been Asking His Advisers Questions Like 'What Do You Think of Firing Squads' When Planning His Campaign Messaging: *Rolling Stone*," *Business Insider*, February 14, 2023, https://www.businessinsider.com/donald-trump-firing-squad-guillotine-ask-advisers-report-2023-2.

26. Austin Berg, "What You Need to Know About Marijuana Legalization in Illinois," blog post, Illinois Policy Institute, January 1, 2020, https://www.illinoispolicy.org/what-you-need-to-know-about-marijuana-legalization-in-illinois/.

27. Kyle Jaeger, "New Jersey Governor Says State Should 'Revisit' Marijuana Home Grow Ban After Market Matures," *Marijuana Moment*, November 2, 2022, https://www.marijuanamoment.net/new-jersey-governor-says-state-should-revisit-marijuana-home-grow-ban-after-market-matures/.

Bibliography

117th Congress. *H. R. 1614 (IH)—Destigmatizing in Immigration Act.* 2021. https://www.govinfo.gov/app/details/BILLS-117hr1614ih.

ABC News. "Tapes Reveal Nixon's Prejudices Again." March 22, 2002. https://abcnews.go.com/GMA/story?id=126236&page=1.

Abbott, David. "Trulieve Amazing: Trulieve Deal to Acquire Harvest Finalized, Creating Nationwide Cannabis Empire." *Tucson Weekly*, October 23, 2021. https://www.tucsonweekly.com/tucson/trulieve-amazing-trulieve-deal-to-acquire-harvest-finalized-creating-nationwide-cannabis-empire/Content?oid=31459407.

Abdelfatah, Rund, and Ramtin Arablouei. "Strange Fruit." Podcast, 31:00. In *Throughline*, produced by Rund Abdelfatah et al., August 22, 2019. https://www.npr.org/transcripts/752909807.

ACLU of Ohio. *Overcharging, Overspending, Overlooking: Cuyahoga County's Costly War on Drugs*. Cleveland: ACLU of Ohio, 2011.

ActNow! "Afterschool as a Substance Misuse and Violence Prevention Tool: Funding Youth Development Programs Through Adult-Use Cannabis Tax Revenue in Illinois." Brochure, 2021. https://actnowillinois.org/wp-content/uploads/2021/03/AA-IL-ACT-Now-R3-030921-FINAL.pdf.

Adams, Dan. "Federal Marijuana Reform Looms After Senate Flip—and Massachusetts Could End Up a Loser." *Boston Globe*, January 22, 2021. https://www.bostonglobe.com/2021/01/22/marijuana/federal-marijuana-reform-looms-after-senate-flip-massachusetts-could-end-up-loser/.

———. "Follow the Money in Fight Over Cambridge Pot Policy." *Boston Globe*, July 1, 2019. https://www.bostonglobe.com/news/marijuana/2019/07/01/follow-money-fight-over-cambridge-pot-policy/GORrl0PgO5J9jRSt1yYsYO/story.html.

———. "Marijuana Trade Group Drops Lawsuit Against State After Backlash." *Boston Globe*, January 25, 2021. https://www.bostonglobe.com/2021/01/25/marijuana/dispensary-trade-group-drops-lawsuit-against-state-after-backlash/.

———. "Q&A with Outgoing Cannabis Commissioner Shaleen Title." *Boston Globe*, December 29, 2020. https://www.bostonglobe.com/2020/12/29/marijuana/qa-with-outgoing-cannabis-commissioner-shaleen-title/.

———. "SJC Says Boston Judge Erred in Denying Marijuana Expungement." *Boston Globe*, September 8, 2022. https://www.bostonglobe.com/2022/09/08/marijuana/sjc-says-boston-judge-erred-denying-marijuana-expungement/.

———. "Sweeping Cannabis Bill Becomes Law, After Yearslong Effort on Reforms." *Boston Globe*, August 11, 2022. https://www.bostonglobe.com/2022/08/11/marijuana/sweeping-cannabis-bill-becomes-law-after-yearslong-effort-reforms/.

———. "'An Utter Failure': Law Meant to Clear Old Convictions, Including for Marijuana Possession, Helps Few." *Boston Globe*, November 28, 2021. https://www.bostonglobe.com/2021/11/28/marijuana/an-utter-failure-law-meant-clear-old-convictions-including-marijuana-possession-helps-few/.

akchuk. "Ronald Reagan: 'Marijuana . . . Is Probably the Most Dangerous Drug.'" YouTube video, September 4, 2014. https://www.youtube.com/watch?v=VxHBx6H-xFo&ab_channel=akchuk.

Aldridge, Derrick P. "Atlanta Compromise Speech." In *New Georgia Encyclopedia*. Last edited October 1, 2020. https://www.georgiaencyclopedia.org/articles/history-archaeology/atlanta-compromise-speech/.

Alexander, Erika, and Whitney Dow, dirs. *The Big Payback: Fear and Reparations in the American Suburb*. Color Farm Media, 2023.

Alexander, Michelle. *The New Jim Crow: Mass Incarceration in the Age of Colorblindness*. New York: New Press, 2010.

Allard, Tom, and Karen Lema. "Exclusive: 'Shock and Awe' Has Failed in Philippines Drug War, Enforcement Chief Says." Reuters, February 7, 2020. https://www.reuters.com/article/us-philippines-drugs-performance-exclusi/exclusive-shock-and-awe-has-failed-in-philippines-drug-war-enforcement-chief-says-idUSKBN2010IL.

Alpert, Bill. "How a Prominent Russian Oligarch Helped Start America's Cannabis Industry." *Barron's*, January 4, 2023. https://www.barrons.com/articles/russian-oligarch-roman-abramovich-curaleaf-cannabis-industry-51674507683.

Altman, David G., Douglas W. Levine, George Howard, and Hal Hamilton. "Tobacco Farmers and Diversification: Opportunities and Barriers." *Tobacco Control* 5, no. 3 (1996): 192–98. https://www.jstor.org/stable/20207199.

Amendment 64 Implementation Task Force. *Task Force Report on the Implementation of Amendment 64: Regulation of Marijuana in Colorado*. Denver, CO, March 13, 2013. https://fliphtml5.com/gnse/nzgj.

American Bar Association. *Collateral Consequences of Criminal Convictions: Judicial Bench Book*. Chicago, IL: American Bar Association, March 2018. https://www.ojp.gov/pdffiles1/nij/grants/251583.pdf.

American Beverage Licensees. "America's Beer, Wine and Spirits Retailers Create 2.03 Million Jobs and $122.63 Billion in Direct Economic Impact." News release, October 23, 2018. https://ablusa.org/americas-beer-wine-spirits-retailers-create-2-03-million-jobs-122-63-billion-in-direct-economic-impact/.

Anderson, D. Mark, Benjamin Hansen, Daniel I. Rees, and Joseph J. Sabia. "Association of Marijuana Laws with Teen Marijuana Use: New Estimates from the Youth Risk Behavior Surveys." *JAMA Pediatrics* 173, no. 9 (2019): 879–81. https://doi.org/10.1001/jamapediatrics.2019.1720.

Andreas, Peter. "Drugs and War: What Is the Relationship?" *Annual Review of Political Science* 22, no. 1 (2019): 57–73. https://doi.org/10.1146/annurev-polisci-051017-103748.

Angell, Tom. "Cuomo Administration Report Backs Marijuana Legalization in New York." *Forbes*, July 13, 2018. https://www.forbes.com/sites/tomangell/2018/07/13/gov-cuomo-releases-report-backing-marijuana-legalization-in-new-york/?sh=42fd42b04c06.

———. "State Department Says DEA Is Wrong on Marijuana Monopoly." Marijuana.com, May 6, 2016. Archived at https://web.archive.org/web/20181011133436/https://www.marijuana.com/news/2016/05/state-department-says-dea-is-wrong-on-marijuana-monopoly/.

Anslinger, H. F. "Marijuana—Assassin of Youth." With Courtney Ryley Cooper. *Reader's Digest*, February 1938. Reprint available at https://www.druglibrary.org/schaffer/history/e1930/mjassassinrd.htm.

APB Speakers. "Pot, Power and Politics—Wanda James." YouTube video, January 3, 2022. https://www.youtube.com/watch?v=ZqU0JCNXFq8&ab_channel=APBSpeakers.

Arthur L. Carter Journalism Institute, New York University. "Ta-Nehisi Coates' 'The Case for Reparations' Named Top Work of Journalism of the Last Decade." News release, October 14, 2020. https://www.nyu.edu/about/news-publications/news/2020/october/ta-nehisi-coates---the-case-for-reparations--named-top-work-of-j.html.

Asch, Beth J., Michael L. Hansen, Rosanna Smart, David Knapp, and Daniel Schwam. *An Empirical Assessment of the US Army's Enlistment Waiver Policies: An Examination in Light of Emerging Societal Trends in Behavioral Health and the Legalization of Marijuana*. Santa Monica, CA: RAND Corporation, 2021. https://www.rand.org/pubs/research_reports/RR4431.html.

Associated Press. "Illinois Considers Legalizing Marijuana for a Fiscal Boost." *Fox 2 Now*, March 26, 2017. https://fox2now.com/news/illinois-considers-legalizing-marijuana-for-a-fiscal-boost/.

———. "Kent State Massacre: 50 Years Since Four Students Were Killed by the National Guard." *MarketWatch*, May 4, 2020. https://www.marketwatch.com/story/kent-state-massacre-50-years-since-four-student-were-killed-by-the-national-guard-2020-05-04.

———. "Pot Shop Robberies Are Fueling Calls for a US Banking Bill." *NPR*, April 20, 2022. https://www.npr.org/2022/04/20/1093841615/pot-shop-robberies-are-fueling-calls-for-a-u-s-banking-bill.

———. "Want to Grow Arkansas Medical Marijuana? Here's How Much You'll Need to Pay Annually." *The Cannabist*, January 5, 2017. https://www.thecannabist.co/2017/01/05/arkansas-medical-marijuana-grow-fee-2/70668/.

Auxier, Richard, and Nikhita Airi. *The Pros and Cons of Cannabis Taxes*. Washington, DC: Tax Policy Center, September 28, 2022. https://www.taxpolicycenter.org/publications/pros-and-cons-cannabis-taxes/full.

Baker, Mike, and William K. Rashbaum. "As Russian Money Poured into Cannabis, Giuliani Allies Scrambled to Partake." *New York Times*, updated October 24,

2019. https://www.nytimes.com/2019/10/23/us/kukushkin-giuliani-russia-cannabis-marijuana.html.

Ballotpedia. "Colorado Constitution," Article V, Section 1.5.5. https://ballotpedia.org/Colorado_Constitution.

———. "Colorado Marijuana Legalization Initiative, Amendment 64 (2012)." https://ballotpedia.org/Colorado_Marijuana_Legalization_Initiative,_Amendment_64_(2012).

———. "Colorado Marijuana Possession, Initiative 44 (2006)." https://ballotpedia.org/Colorado_Marijuana_Possession,_Initiative_44_(2006).

———. "Colorado Proposition 122, Decriminalization and Regulated Access Program for Certain Psychedelic Plants and Fungi Initiative (2022)." https://ballotpedia.org/Colorado_Proposition_122,_Decriminalization_and_Regulated_Access_Program_for_Certain_Psychedelic_Plants_and_Fungi_Initiative_(2022).

———. "Colorado Proposition AA, Taxes on the Sale of Marijuana (2013)." https://ballotpedia.org/Colorado_Proposition_AA,_Taxes_on_the_Sale_of_Marijuana_(2013).

———. "Colorado Springs, Colorado, Ballot Question 300, Allow for Retail Marijuana Establishments Initiative (November 2022)." https://ballotpedia.org/Colorado_Springs,_Colorado,_Ballot_Question_300,_Allow_for_Retail_Marijuana_Establishments_Initiative_(November_2022).

———. "Massachusetts Constitution." Article XLVIII, Section II.2. https://ballotpedia.org/Massachusetts_Constitution.

———. "Massachusetts Marijuana Legalization, Question 4 (2016)." https://ballotpedia.org/Massachusetts_Marijuana_Legalization,_Question_4_(2016).

———. "Massachusetts Medical Marijuana Initiative, Question 3 (2012)." https://ballotpedia.org/Massachusetts_Medical_Marijuana_Initiative,_Question_3_(2012).

———. "Massachusetts Question 2, Change Marijuana Possession from Criminal to Civil Penalties Initiative (2008)." https://ballotpedia.org/Massachusetts_Question_2,_Change_Marijuana_Possession_from_Criminal_to_Civil_Penalties_Initiative_(2008).

———. "Ohio Casino Approval and Tax Distribution, Amendment 3 (2009)." https://ballotpedia.org/Ohio_Casino_Approval_and_Tax_Distribution,_Amendment_3_(2009).

———. "Ohio Initiated Monopolies Amendment, Issue 2 (2015)." Note 15. https://ballotpedia.org/Ohio_Initiated_Monopolies_Amendment,_Issue_2_(2015)#cite_note-green-15.

———. "Ohio Marijuana Legalization Initiative, Issue 3 (2015)." https://ballotpedia.org/Ohio_Marijuana_Legalization_Initiative,_Issue_3_(2015).

———. "Presidential Election in Massachusetts, 2016." https://ballotpedia.org/Presidential_election_in_Massachusetts,_2016.

———. "Presidential Election in South Dakota, 2020." https://ballotpedia.org/Presidential_election_in_South_Dakota,_2020.

———. "South Dakota Constitutional Amendment A, Marijuana Legalization Initiative (2020)." https://ballotpedia.org/South_Dakota_Constitutional_Amendment_A,_Marijuana_Legalization_Initiative_(2020).

Balmert, Jessie. "Marijuana Policy Project Drops Ohio Medical Marijuana Initiative." *Cincinnati* (OH) *Enquirer*, May 28, 2016. https://www.cincinnati.com/story/news/politics/2016/05/28/marijuana-policy-project-drops-ohio-medical-marijuana-initiative/85083418/.

Balta, Hugo. "Racial Bias in Home Appraisals." *Chicago Reporter*, March 25, 2022. https://www.chicagoreporter.com/racial-bias-in-home-appraisals/.

Bane, Jason. "Smoking Weed 'Makes Denver SAFER!'" *5280*, October 13, 2005. https://www.5280.com/smoking-weed-makes-denver-safer/.

Baradaran, Mehrsa. *The Color of Money: Black Banks and the Racial Wealth Gap*. Cambridge, MA: Harvard University Press, 2017.

———. "The Real Roots of 'Black Capitalism.'" *New York Times*, March 31, 2019. https://www.nytimes.com/2019/03/31/opinion/nixon-capitalism-blacks.html.

Barcott, Bruce. "President Biden's Marijuana 'Review' Could Be a Deadly Trap." *Leafly*, October 13, 2022. https://www.leafly.com/news/politics/president-bidens-marijuana-review-could-be-a-deadly-trap.

Barcott, Bruce, and Beau Whitney. *Jobs Report 2022*. With Max Savage Levenson and Chris Kudialis. Seattle, WA: Leafly, 2002. https://leafly-cms-production.imgix.net/wp-content/uploads/2022/02/22132544/LeaflyJobsReport2022.pdf.

Bartlett, Jessica. "Revolutionary Clinics Drops Lawsuit Over Cannabis License Restrictions in Cambridge." *Boston Business Journal*, January 28, 2021. https://www.bizjournals.com/boston/news/2021/01/28/revolutionary-clinics-drops-lawsuit-over-cannabis.html.

Baum, Dan. "How to Win the War on Drugs." *Harper's Magazine*, April 2016.

BDSA. "Cannabis by the Numbers." Slide deck, Beer Marketer's Insights conference, May 12, 2022. https://bdsa.com/wp-content/uploads/2022/05/BDSA_Cannabis-by-the-Numbers_Beer-Marketers-Insights-Presentation_May-2022-1.pdf.

Becker, Deborah, and Hafsa Quraishi. "Thousands to Split $14M in Mass. Drug Lab Scandal." *WBUR*, August 26, 2022. https://www.wbur.org/news/2022/08/26/massachusetts-drug-convictions-tampering-settlement-disbursement.

Becker, Gary S., and Kevin M. Murphy. "A Theory of Rational Addiction." *Journal of Political Economy* 96, no. 4 (1988): 675–700. https://www.jstor.org/stable/1830469.

Berg, Austin. "What You Need to Know About Marijuana Legalization in Illinois." Blog post. Illinois Policy Institute, January 1, 2020. https://www.illinoispolicy.org/what-you-need-to-know-about-marijuana-legalization-in-illinois/.

Berlinger, Joshua, and Elise Labott. "Trump Praises Duterte's Deadly Drug War in Leaked Transcript." CNN.com, May 24, 2017. https://www.cnn.com/2017/05/24/politics/donald-trump-rodrigo-duterte-phone-call-transcript/index.html.

Best, Joel. "Halloween Sadism." Blog post. JoelBest.net. https://www.joelbest.net/halloween-sadism.

Bickers, John M. "The Power to Do What Manifestly Must Be Done: Congress, the Freedmen's Bureau, and Constitutional Imagination." *Roger Williams University Law Review* 12, no. 1 (2006): 86–89.

Big Hope Project. "Our Mission." https://www.bighopeproject.org/our-mission/.

———. "Programs." https://www.bighopeproject.org/programs/.

———. "Team." https://www.bighopeproject.org/team/harry-jean-jacques/.

Bird, Malcolm G. "Legalized Cannabis in Canada: Federalism, Policy, and Politics." In *High Time: The Legalization and Regulation of Cannabis in Canada*, edited by Andrew Potter and Daniel Weinstock, 22–35. Montreal: McGill-Queen's University Press, 2019.

Birkeland, Bente. "With Proposition BB, Colorado Votes on Marijuana Tax Money—Again." *KUNC*, October 20, 2015. https://www.kunc.org/politics/2015-10-20/with-proposition-bb-colorado-votes-on-marijuana-tax-money-again#stream/0.

Blackwood, Kristine, et al. "President Biden Signs Bill Clearing the Way for Medical Cannabis Research." Legal advisory. Arnold & Porter, December 7, 2022. https://www.arnoldporter.com/en/perspectives/advisories/2022/12/medical-cannabis-research.

Blake, Melissa Kuipers, and Osiris Morel. "Cannabis Legislation Wrap Up for 2021." Client alert. Brownstein Hyatt Farber Schreck, January 12, 2022. https://www.bhfs.com/insights/alerts-articles/2022/cannabis-legislation-wrap-up-for-2021.

Blum, Deborah. "The Chemist's War." *Slate*, February 19, 2010. https://slate.com/technology/2010/02/the-little-told-story-of-how-the-us-government-poisoned-alcohol-during-prohibition.html.

Bond, Erica, Cecilia Low-Weiner, Meredith Patten, et al. "Marijuana Enforcement in New York State, 1990–2017." Research Brief. Data Collaborative for Justice, John Jay College of Criminal Justice, February 2019. https://datacollaborativeforjustice.org/wp-content/uploads/2020/04/Marijuana-Brief.pdf.

Bonni, Joe. "You Down with MPP?" *Boston Weekly Dig*, February 11, 2003. Reprint available at http://www.mapinc.org/drugnews/v03/n237/a06.html?127.

Bonnie, Richard J., and Charles H. Whitebread. *The Marihuana Conviction: A History of Marihuana Prohibition in the United States*. Charlottesville: University of Virginia Press, 1974.

Borchardt, Jackie. "Libertarians, Green Party Oppose ResponsibleOhio's Marijuana Legalization Plan." Cleveland.com, May 29, 2015. https://www.cleveland.com/open/2015/05/libertarians_green_party_oppos.html.

———. "Ohio Medical Marijuana: 'Racial Quota' for Grow Licenses Ruled Unconstitutional." *Cincinnati* (OH) *Enquirer*, November 16, 2018. https://www.cincinnati.com/story/news/2018/11/16/ohio-medical-marijuana-court-finds-racial-quota-unconstitutional/2023545002/.

Boston (City of). "Boston Equity Program for Cannabis Businesses." Boston.gov, last updated February 17, 2023. https://www.boston.gov/departments/economic-development/cannabis-equity-program.

———. *City of Boston: State Election—November 8, 2016, Question 4: Marijuana*. Boston.gov. https://www.boston.gov/sites/default/files/embed/0/036_-_2016_-_11-08-16_-_question_4_-_marijuana.pdf.

Boston Business Journal. "Cannabis Commission Backs Giving Minority Groups Exclusive Access to Delivery Licenses in Massachusetts." *MassLive*, April 29, 2019. https://www.masslive.com/marijuana/2019/04/cannabis-commission-backs-giving-minority-groups-exclusive-access-to-delivery-licenses-in-massachusetts.html.

Boston Globe. "Ted Kennedy and the Chappaquiddick Incident | Boston Globe." YouTube video, August 26, 2009. https://www.youtube.com/watch?v=ZNHbDikvXlU&ab_channel=TheBostonGlobe.

Bowen, Max. "Is Pot Pie Shrinking? Advocates, Store Owners Assess Whether Cannabis Market Oversaturated." *Daily Hampshire* (MA) *Gazette*, December 30, 2022. https://www.gazettenet.com/The-shrinking-pot-pie-49299488.

Bragg, Chris. "Dorm Authority: NY's Deepest Pork Barrel." *Times-Union* (Albany, NY), updated December 19, 2016. https://www.timesunion.com/tuplus-local/article/1-9B-pork-barrel-titan-10803778.php.

Breathes, William. "Colorado Cannabis Time Capsule, 1923: 'Mexican Dope Ring Operating in Denver,'" *Westword*, June 20, 2014. https://www.westword.com/news/cannabis-time-capsule-1923-mexican-dope-ring-operating-in-denver-5902872.

———. "Colorado Cannabis Time Capsule, 1929: Legislators Make Sale and Cultivation a Felony." *Westword*, December 21, 2012. https://www.westword.com/news/colorado-cannabis-time-capsule-1929-legislators-make-sale-and-cultivation-a-felony-5856142.

Bremer, Shelby. "Pritzker Says He Wants to Legalize Marijuana in Illinois." *NBC5 Chicago*, updated November 9, 2018. https://www.nbcchicago.com/news/politics/pritzker-legalize-marijuana-in-illinois/169294/.

Brennan, Noel. "A Look at Diversity in the Cannabis Industry on 420." *9News*, April 20, 2022. https://www.9news.com/article/news/local/diversity-in-cannabis-industry-420/73-b5116cbe-7797-4553-8f59-64a031eacca4.

Broaddus, Adrienne. "Evanston City Council Votes in Favor of Expanding Its Reparations Program to Repair Housing Discrimination." CNN.com, March 28, 2023. https://www.cnn.com/2023/03/27/us/evanston-illinois-reparations-housing-discrimination-expand/index.html.

Brown, Debbie-Marie. "City OKs Paying Out $3.45 Million in Reparations." *Evanston Round Table*, August 9, 2022. https://evanstonroundtable.com/2022/08/09/city-approves-dispersal-of-3-45m-in-reparations/.

———. "'I Didn't Think I Had a Chance': Meet One of Evanston's First 16 Reparations Recipients." *Evanston Round Table*, August 4, 2022. https://evanstonroundtable.com/2022/08/04/louis-weathers-reparations-grant-recipients/.

Brown, Jennfier L., Debra Rosen, Maria G. Carmona, Natalia Parra, Mark Hurley, and Joanna E. Cohen. "Spinning a Global Web: Tactics Used by Big Tobacco to Attract Children at Tobacco Points-of-Sale." *Tobacco Control* (2022). http://dx.doi.org/10.1136/tobaccocontrol-2021-057095.

Brown University. "Costs of the 20-Year War on Terror: $8 Trillion and 900,000 Deaths." News release, September 1, 2021. https://www.brown.edu/news/2021-09-01/costsofwar.

Brownsberger, Will. "Criminal Justice Reform at a Glance." Blog post. WillBrownsberger.com, May 6, 2018. https://willbrownsberger.com/criminal-justice-package-at-a-glance/.

———. "The Marijuana Compromise." Blog post. WillBrownsberger.com, July 16, 2017. https://willbrownsberger.com/the-marijuana-compromise/.

Bunch, Joey. "Polis Signs Social Equity Bill for Colorado Marijuana Industry." *Colorado Politics*, updated November 8, 2021. https://www.coloradopolitics.com/legislature/polis-signs-social-equity-bill-for-colorado-marijuana-industry/article_a93b9574-ba5b-11ea-bb74-8b1553a52c63.html.

Burd-Sharps, Sarah, and Rebecca Rasch. *Impact of the US Housing Crisis on the Racial Wealth Gap Across Generations*. New York: Social Science Research Council, 2015.

Burkland, Eric, David Cobb, Bill Denihan, Jack Fisher, Gordon Gough, and Élise Spriggs. "Official Argument Against Issue 3." Ohio Secretary of State. August 17, 2015. https://www.sos.state.oh.us/globalassets/ballotboard/2015/3-against.pdf.

Butler, Gavin. "Companies Are Getting Rid of Drug Tests Because They Can't Find Enough Workers." *Vice*, September 17, 2021. https://www.vice.com/en/article/y3d7kx/companies-employers-drug-tests-labour-shortage.

California NORML. "Jury Acquits Eugene Davidovich/DA Re-Targets Lambert." Blog post, March 28, 2010. https://www.canorml.org/jury-acquits-eugene-davidovichda-re-targets-lambert/.

Calvey, Mark. "Angel Investors Are High on Legal Marijuana's Opportunities." *San Francisco Business Times*, August 15, 2014. https://www.bizjournals.com/sanfrancisco/blog/2014/08/marijuana-cannabis-pot-angel-investing-startups.html.

Campaign for a Safe and Healthy MA. "Neighborhoods." YouTube video, October 18, 2016. https://www.youtube.com/watch?v=bjtmo2M3Exw&ab_channel=PBSNewsHour.

Campos, Isaac. *Home Grown: Marijuana and the Origins of Mexico's War on Drugs*. Chapel Hill: University of North Carolina Press, 2012.

Cannabis Regulatory Agency, State of Michigan. "What Are the Capitalization Requirements for Each Type of License?" https://www.michigan.gov/cra/faq/licensing-list/apps-new/what-are-the-capitalization-requirements-for-each-type-of-license.

———. "Why Is Marijuana Sometimes Spelled with an 'H' and Other Times Spelled with a 'J'?" https://www.michigan.gov/cra/faq/licensing-list/additional-new/why-is-marijuana-sometimes-spelled-with-an-h-and-other-times-spelled-with-a-j.

Cantor, Donald J. "The Criminal Law and the Narcotics Problem." *Journal of Criminal Law and Criminology* 51, no. 5 (1961): 512–27. https://scholarlycommons.law.northwestern.edu/cgi/viewcontent.cgi?article=4977&context=jclc.

Carr, Erin Lee, dir. *How to Fix a Drug Scandal*. TV series. Jigsaw Productions, 2020.

Castetter, Kaelan. "From Legacy to Legal with Reggie Keith CEO of Canna-House." Podcast. 33:44. In *Empire State of Cannabis*, produced by Cannabuff, June 28, 2021. https://anchor.fm/empire-state-of-cannabis/episodes/From-Legacy-to-Legal-with-Reggie-Keith-CEO-of-Canna-House-e13j89a.

———. "How Suburbs Delay Legalization with Policy Analyst Sarah McGovern." Podcast, 24:14. In *Empire State of Cannabis*, produced by Cannabuff, August 14, 2020. https://anchor.fm/empire-state-of-cannabis/episodes/How-Suburbs-Delay-Legalization-with-Policy-Analyst-Sarah-McGovern-ei0973.

———. "NY's Cannabis Marketplace with Lobbyist Katie Neer." Podcast, 35:11. In *Empire State of Cannabis*, produced by Cannabuff, June 2, 2021. https://anchor.fm/empire-state-of-cannabis/episodes/NYs-Cannabis-Marketplace-with-Lobbyist-Katie-Neer-e1229hj.

———. "Putting Equity First with Melissa Moore NYS Director for the Drug Policy Alliance." Podcast, 18:48. In *Empire State of Cannabis*, produced by Cannabuff, February 26, 2021. https://anchor.fm/empire-state-of-cannabis/episodes/Putting-Equity-First-with-Melissa-Moore-NYS-Director-for-the-Drug-Policy-Alliance-er4q4e/a-a4osgio.

———. "The War on Drugs with Chief Brendan Cox." Podcast, 34:09. In *Empire State of Cannabis*, produced by Cannabuff, March 15, 2022. https://anchor.fm/empire-state-of-cannabis/episodes/The-War-on-Drugs-with-Chief-Brendan-Cox-e1fosi7.

Cauguiran, Cate, and Craig Wall. "Illinois House Passes Marijuana Legalization Bill, Approves Balanced Budget." *ABC 7 Chicago*, June 1, 2019. https://abc7chicago.com/illinois-passes-recreational-marijuana-senate-house-weed-il/5324375/.

Caulkins, Jonathan P. "Are Mandatory Minimum Drug Sentences Cost-Effective?" Research Brief RB-6003. RAND Corporation, 1997. https://www.rand.org/pubs/research_briefs/RB6003.html.

Caulkins, Jonathan P., and Peter Reuter. "How Drug Enforcement Affects Drug Prices." *Crime and Justice* 39, no. 1 (2010): 213–71. https://www.jstor.org/stable/10.1086/652386.

CBS News. "Chad Robertson Case: Amtrak Officer Charged with Murder in Unarmed Man's Shooting." February 17, 2017. https://www.cbsnews.com/news/chad-robertson-case-amtrak-officer-charged-with-murder-in-unarmed-mans-shooting/.

Cebul, Brent. "Tearing Down Black America." *Boston Review*, July 22, 2020. https://www.bostonreview.net/articles/brent-cebul-tearing-down-black-america/.

Cesal, Craig. "Reflections of an 'Essential' Businessman Doing Life Without Parole." Foundation for Economic Education, June 8, 2020. https://fee.org/articles/reflections-of-an-essential-businessman-doing-life-without-parole/.

Chappell, Bill. "Amazon Will Stop Testing Job Seekers for Marijuana and Now Backs Legalizing Weed." *NPR*, June 2, 2021. https://www.npr.org/2021/06/02/1002409858/amazon-wont-test-jobseekers-for-marijuana.

Chernenko, Sergey, and David S. Scharfstein. "Racial Disparities in the Paycheck Protection Program." NBER Working Paper 29748. National Bureau of Economic Research, February 2022. https://doi.org/10.3386/w29748.

Chicago Sun-Times. "Evanston Ald. on First-in-the-Nation Reparations Bill." YouTube video, April 2, 2021. https://www.youtube.com/watch?v=6rZITSDO-UQ&ab_channel=ChicagoSun-Times.

Childs, Jason, and George Hartner. "Displacing the Illicit Cannabis Market: Challenges and Trade-Offs." In *The High North: Cannabis in Canada*, edited by Andrew

D. Hathaway and Clayton James Smith McCann, 73–96. Vancouver, BC: UBC Press, 2022.

Chillinois Podcast. "#196—Danielle Perry." Podcast, 1:59:37. April 22, 2022. https://soundcloud.com/chillinoispodcast/196-danielle-perry.

Christian Science Monitor. "Tobacco, Government, and the Reagan Team." January 2, 1981. https://www.csmonitor.com/1981/0102/010218.html.

Cima, Rosie. "DARE: The Anti-Drug Program That Never Actually Worked." *Priceonomics*, December 19, 2016. https://priceonomics.com/dare-the-anti-drug-program-that-never-actually/.

City of Aurora (CO). *Financial Performance Report: Fourth Quarter, 2020*. https://cdn5-hosted.civiclive.com/UserFiles/Servers/Server_1881137/File/Business%20Services/Marijuana%20Regulations/2020%20Q4%20MJ.pdf.

———. "Retail Marijuana Delivery and Social Equity." https://www.auroragov.org/business_services/marijuana_and_hemp_licensing/retail_marijuana_delivery_and_social_equity.

City of Denver (CO). *The Denver Collaborative Approach: Leading the Way in Municipal Marijuana Management*. Denver: City of Denver, 2022. https://www.denvergov.org/files/assets/public/business-licensing/documents/marijuana-annual-report-2022.pdf.

Civilian Office of Police Accountability (Chicago, IL). "Summary Report of Investigation." Log no. 1087742. March 10, 2021. https://loevy-content-uploads.s3.amazonaws.com/uploads/2022/08/COPA-Report-1087742.SRI_.pdf.

Clayton, Richard R., Anne M. Cattarello, and Bryan M Johnstone. "The Effectiveness of Drug Abuse Resistance Education (Project DARE): 5-Year Follow-Up Results." *Preventive Medicine* 25, no. 3 (1996): 307–18. https://doi.org/10.1006/pmed.1996.0061.

CNBC. "For Wanda James Being in the Cannabis Industry Isn't About Making Money; It's About Social Justice." Video, January 22, 2021. https://www.cnbc.com/video/2021/01/22/for-wanda-james-being-in-the-cannabis-industry-is-about-social-justice.html.

Coates, Ta-Nehisi. "The Case for Reparations." *The Atlantic*, June 2014. https://www.theatlantic.com/magazine/archive/2014/06/the-case-for-reparations/361631/.

Cole, James M. "Memorandum to All United States Attorneys." August 29, 2013. https://www.justice.gov/iso/opa/resources/3052013829132756857467.pdf.

Coley, Rebekah Levine, Claudia Kruzik, Marco Ghiani, Naoka Carey, Summer Sherburne Hawkins, and Christopher F. Baum. "Recreational Marijuana Legalization and Adolescent Use of Marijuana, Tobacco, and Alcohol." *Journal of Adolescent Health* 69, no. 1 (2021): 41–49. https://doi.org/10.1016/j.jadohealth.2020.10.019.

Colorado Bureau of Investigation, Department of Public Safety. "Marijuana Pardons." https://cbi.colorado.gov/sections/biometric-identification-and-records-unit/marijuana-pardons.

Colorado Department of Education. "BEST Grant Program." https://www.cde.state.co.us/capitalconstruction/best.

———. "Marijuana Tax Revenue and Education." Updated November 2, 2022. https://www.cde.state.co.us/communications/2021marijuanarevenue.

Colorado Department of Local Affairs. "Regional Data Lookup." https://coloradodemography.github.io/population/data/regional-data-lookup/.

Colorado Department of Revenue. "Marijuana Tax Reports." https://cdor.colorado.gov/data-and-reports/marijuana-data/marijuana-tax-reports.

Colorado Department of Revenue, Specialized Business Group. "MED Licensee Demographic Information." https://sbg.colorado.gov/med/MED-licensee-demographic-information.

———. "Social Equity: Equity, Diversity and Inclusion Is a Priority for the State of Colorado." https://sbg.colorado.gov/med/social-equity.

Colorado General Assembly. "An Act Concerning Certain Criminal Marijuana Offenses." HB 21-1090. https://cbi.colorado.gov/sites/cbi/files/documents/HB%2021-1090%2C%20concerning%20certain%20MJ%20offenses_final%20act.pdf.

———. "Explore the Colorado State Budget." https://leg.colorado.gov/explorebudget/.

———. "HB20-1424: Social Equity Licenses in Regulated Marijuana." Bill Summary. https://leg.colorado.gov/bills/HB20-1424.

Colorado Legislative Council. *Dangerous Drugs and Drug Abuse Control*. Research Publication No. 127, December 1967, 8–23. http://hermes.cde.state.co.us/drupal/islandora/object/co:2584/datastream/OBJ/view.

———. "Proposition AA: Retail Marijuana Taxes." Fiscal Impact Statement, September 24, 2013. https://www.leg.state.co.us/LCS/Initiative%20Referendum/1314initrefr.nsf/b74b3fc5d676cdc987257ad8005bce6a/e3e37fa33a36873887257b6c0077ac93/$FILE/Retail%20Marijuana%20Taxes_FN.pdf.

Colorado Marijuana Initiative 2012. "What If? Latino Voices for Amendment 64." YouTube video, October 31, 2012. https://www.youtube.com/watch?v=8KycY5QuI0Y&ab_channel=ColoradoMarijuanaInitiative2012.

Colorado Office of the Secretary of State. *Official Publication of the Abstract of Votes Cast for the 2005 Coordinated, 2006 Primary, 2006 General*. https://www.sos.state.co.us/pubs/elections/Results/Abstract/pdf/2000-2099/2006AbsractBook.pdf.

Columbus, Chris, dir. *Home Alone 2: Lost in New York*. Los Angeles, CA: Twentieth Century Fox, 1992.

Commonwealth Museum, Boston, Massachusetts. "The Stamp Tax Crisis of 1765." Traveling Exhibit: Road to Revolution. https://www.sec.state.ma.us/mus/pdfs/Stamp-Tax-Crisis.pdf.

Commonwealth v. Leis, 355 Mass. 189 (1969). https://casetext.com/case/commonwealth-v-leis.

CompaniesMarketCap.com. "Curaleaf." Revenue History for Curaleaf. https://companiesmarketcap.com/curaleaf/revenue/.

Concepcion v. United States, 597 U.S. ___ (2022). https://www.supremecourt.gov/opinions/21pdf/20-1650_new_4gci.pdf.

Concerned CAURD Licensees to Reuben R. McDaniel III, Chris Alexander, and Tremaine Wright. May 9, 2023. Available at https://www.documentcloud.org/documents/23809208-caurd-licensee-grievances.

Congressional Budget Office. *H. R. 3884, MORE Act of 2020*. December 4, 2020. https://www.cbo.gov/publication/56882.

Congressional Research Service. "The Application of Internal Revenue Code Section 280E to Marijuana Businesses: Selected Legal Issues." Report no. R46709, March 10, 2021. https://crsreports.congress.gov/product/pdf/R/R46709.

———. *The* Pigford *Cases: USDA Settlement of Discrimination Suits by Black Farmers*. May 29, 2013. Archived at https://www.everycrsreport.com/reports/RS20430.html.

Cooper, Renée. "Thousands Still Eligible for Record Expungement Two Years After Illinois Legalizes Recreational Marijuana." WCIA.com, September 16, 2021. https://www.wcia.com/news/target3/thousands-still-eligible-for-record-expungement-two-years-after-illinois-legalizes-recreational-marijuana/.

Cox, Kiana, and Khadijah Edwards. "3. Reparations for Slavery." Pew Research Center, August 30, 2022. https://www.pewresearch.org/race-ethnicity/2022/08/30/black-americans-views-on-reparations-for-slavery/.

Creason, Joe. "Economic Empowerment and Cannabis in Somerville." *Somerville* (MA) *Times*, September 1, 2021. https://www.thesomervilletimes.com/archives/110833.

Crick, Emily, Mark Cooke, and Dave Bewley-Taylor. "Selling Cannabis Regulation: Learning from Ballot Initiatives in the United States in 2012." Policy Brief 6, Global Drug Policy Observatory, November 2014. https://www.swansea.ac.uk/media/Selling-Cannabis-Regulation.pdf.

Crocker, Phyllis L. "Appointed But (Nearly) Prevented from Serving: My Experiences as a Grand Jury Foreperson." *Ohio State Journal of Criminal Law* 2 (2004): 291–98. https://kb.osu.edu/bitstream/handle/1811/72870/OSJCL_V2N1_289.pdf.

Croghan, Lore, and Glenn Blain. "I Won't Let New York Go to Pot: Governor Hopeful Andrew Cuomo Says He Is Against Medical Marijuana." *Daily News* (New York), October 25, 2010. https://www.nydailynews.com/new-york/won-new-york-pot-governor-hopeful-andrew-cuomo-medical-marijuana-article-1.188416.

Cultiva Law. "Overproduction, Diversion, and the 'New' Marijuana Black Market." Blog post, May 22, 2018. https://cultivalaw.com/overproduction-diversion-and-the-new-marijuana-black-market/.

Cuomo, Andrew M. *State of the State 2021: Reimagine, Rebuild, Renew*. Albany: New York State, 2021. https://www.governor.ny.gov/sites/default/files/atoms/files/SOTS2021Book_Final.pdf.

Daley, Mariah. "Maurice Shumate Released from 15-Year-Sentence." Blog post. Last Prisoner Project, February 23, 2022. https://www.lastprisonerproject.org/maurice-shumate-released-from-15-year-sentence.

Daniel, Seth. "How Buffer Zone Rules Are Impacting Cannabis Dispensaries in Some Boston Neighborhoods." *WBUR*, October 4, 2021. https://www.wbur.org/news/2021/10/04/blue-hill-avenue-marijuana-shops-buffer.

DARE (Drug Abuse Resistance Education). "D.A.R.E. Hometowns—U.S.A. and International." https://dare.org/where-is-d-a-r-e/.

Darity, William A., Jr., and A. Kirsten Mullen. *From Here to Equality: Reparations for Black Americans in the Twenty-First Century*. Chapel Hill: University of North Carolina Press, 2020.

Davenport, Steven, Jonathan P. Caulkins, and Mark A.R. Kleiman. "Controlling Underage Access to Legal Cannabis." *Case Western Reserve Law Review* 65, no. 3 (2015): 541–66. https://scholarlycommons.law.case.edu/cgi/viewcontent.cgi?article=1041&context=caselrev.

Davis, Jonathan M., Bruce Mendelson, Jay J. Berkes, Katie Suleta, Karen F. Corsi, and Robert E. Booth. "Public Health Effects of Medical Marijuana Legalization in Colorado." *American Journal of Preventive Medicine* 50, no. 3 (2016): 373–79. https://doi.org/10.1016/j.amepre.2015.06.034.

DeCosta-Klipa, Nik. "How a Debate in Cambridge Over Recreational Marijuana Turned Ugly." Boston.com, September 26, 2019. https://www.boston.com/news/local-news/2019/09/26/cambridge-marijuana-debate/.

"Defendant Harvest Grows, LLC's Brief in Opposition." In *Pharmacann Ohio, LLC v. Jacqueline T. Williams, et al.*, 17 CV 10962, Franklin County (OH) Court of Common Pleas, September 14, 2018, 3–6. https://fcdcfcjs.co.franklin.oh.us/CaseInformationOnline/imageLinkProcessor.pdf?coords=iwFK2JLKokC9bTKnDIhvqy%2FdIhlAJt0e52Z9FEjXDo%2B12Z1myqYs9btFX%2BnYnXsia8lqfJySIi6L%2FwAXZQaqT1gsg%2FvlfxQ%2B8Ny7jSgUoHX5avdupg4rp9LsX8eoz7T0YkcCPGVSRI2gQSKL8yloZZTk6BsAxRJ6k0YipD4M0Kw%3D.

DeForge, Jeanette. "State Cannabis Law Offers Licenses for Marginalized Populations But Few Apply, Experts Said in Holyoke Panel Discussion." *MassLive*, updated June 24, 2019. https://www.masslive.com/news/2019/06/state-cannabis-law-offers-licenses-for-marginalized-populations-but-few-apply-experts-said-in-holyoke-panel-discussion.html.

Delamont, Kieran. "Legacy to Legal Brands Are Taking Over the Cannabis Industry." Blog post. Leafly.ca, last updated February 10, 2022. https://www.leafly.ca/news/canada/once-illegal-brands-are-taking-over-the-legal-cannabis-market.

Delmont, Matthew. "The Lasting Legacy of the Busing Crisis." *The Atlantic*, March 29, 2016. https://www.theatlantic.com/politics/archive/2016/03/the-boston-busing-crisis-was-never-intended-to-work/474264/.

Demko, Paul. "A National Weed Glut Is Causing Prices to Plummet and Imperiling Businesses." *Politico*, December 25, 2022. https://www.politico.com/news/2022/12/25/weed-prices-business-michigan-00075485.

Denver Post. "Amendment 64 Is the Wrong Way to Legalize Marijuana." Editorial. October 12, 2012. https://www.denverpost.com/2012/10/12/editorial-amendment-64-is-the-wrong-way-to-legalize-marijuana/.

Derenoncourt, Ellora, Chi Hyun Kim, Moritz Kuhn, and Moritz Schularick. "The Wealth of Two Nations: The US Racial Wealth Gap, 1860–2020." NBER Working Paper 30101. National Bureau of Economic Research, June 2022. https://doi.org/10.3386/w30101.

Desmond, Declan. "2 Years Later, Amtrak Officer Who Fatally Shot Minneapolis Man Acquitted." *Bring Me the News*, March 1, 2020. https://bringmethenews.com/minnesota-news/2-years-later-amtrak-officer-who-fatally-shot-minneapolis-man-acquitted.

Dinan, John, and Jac C. Heckelman. "Support for Repealing Prohibition: An Analysis of State-Wide Referenda on Ratifying the 21st Amendment." *Social Science Quarterly* 95, no. 3 (2014): 636–51. https://doi.org/10.1111/ssqu.12077.

Dixon, Benjamin (@BenjaminPDixon). "Audio of @MikeBloomberg's 2015 @AspenInstitute speech where he explains that 'you can just Xerox (copy)' the description of male, minorities 16–25 and hand to copes." Twitter, February 10, 2020, 3:58 p.m. https://twitter.com/BenjaminPDixon/status/1226973723720396808.

D'Mello, Colin. "Cannabis Customers Have Been Complaining Ontario's Pot Is 'Too Dry.'" *CTV News*, December 7, 2020. https://toronto.ctvnews.ca/cannabis-customers-have-been-complaining-ontario-s-pot-is-too-dry-1.5220170.

Doonan, Samantha M., and Julie K. Johnson. *A Baseline Review and Assessment of Cannabis Use and Public Safety: Part 2; 94C Violations and Social Equity; Literature Review and Preliminary Data in Massachusetts.* Boston, MA: Massachusetts Cannabis Control Commission, April 2019. https://mass-cannabis-control.com/wp-content/uploads/2019/04/1.-RR2-94C-Violations-FINAL.pdf.

Dormitory Authority of the State of New York. "New York Social Equity Cannabis Investment Fund." Solicitation no. 7585. Issue date May 12, 2022. https://www.dasny.org/opportunities/rfps-bids/2022/new-york-social-equity-cannabis-investment-fund.

Douglass, Frederick. "Frederick Douglass on Prohibition." *San Marcos* (TX) *Free Press*. May 19, 1887. Available at https://texashistory.unt.edu/ark:/67531/metapth295657/m1/1/?q=frederick%20douglass.

Driscoll, Jaclyn. "Illinois Governor Approves Medical Cannabis As Alternative for Opioids." *NPR Illinois*, August 28, 2018. https://www.nprillinois.org/health-harvest/2018-08-28/illinois-governor-approves-medical-cannabis-as-alternative-for-opioids.

Drug Policy Alliance. *Federal Byrne Grants: Drug War Funds Available for Drug Treatment*. New York: Drug Policy Alliance, September 2010. https://drugpolicy.org/sites/default/files/FactSheet_ByrneJAG_Sept.%202010.pdf.

———. "Federal Student Aid Access." https://drugpolicy.org/issues/federal-student-aid-access.

———. "Liberation for Black Drug Users | Reform 2015." YouTube video, August 20, 2020. https://www.youtube.com/watch?v=ue9t6eF_N5M&ab_channel=DrugPolicyAlliance.

Dufton, Emily. *Grass Roots: The Rise and Fall and Rise of Marijuana in America*. New York: Basic Books, 2017.

Durkin, Erin. "How Blood-and-Guts Headlines Propelled Republicans in New York." *Politico*, November 12, 2022. https://www.politico.com/news/2022/11/12/zeldin-hochul-crime-midterms-new-york-00066287.

Edge, Megan, and Laurel Andrews. "Timeline: Notable Moments in 40 Years of Alaska's History with Marijuana." *Anchorage Daily News*. April 14, 2014. https://www.adn.com/cannabis-north/article/alaska-weed-history/2014/04/14/.

Edwards, Ezekiel, Will Bunting, and Lynda Garcia. *The War on Marijuana in Black and White: Billions of Dollars Wasted on Racially Biased Arrests*. New York: ACLU, 2013. https://www.aclu.org/report/report-war-marijuana-black-and-white.

Edwards, Ezekial, Emily Greytak, Brooke Madubuonwu, et al. *A Tale of Two Countries: Racially Targeted Arrests in the Era of Marijuana Reform*. New York: ACLU, 2020. https://www.aclu.org/report/tale-two-countries-racially-targeted-arrests-era-marijuana-reform.

Elliott, Debbie. "5 Decades Later, New Communities Land Trust Still Helps Black Farmers." *NPR*, October 3, 2019. https://www.npr.org/2019/10/03/766706906/5-decades-later-communities-land-trust-still-helps-black-farmers.

Ellis, Grant Smith. "About Grant Smith Ellis." Patreon. https://www.patreon.com/GrantSmithEllis.

———. "Episode 1: Shaleen Title and Joe Gilmore." In *Cannabis Policy Watch*, produced by Cannabis Policy Watch, January 12, 2022. https://anchor.fm/grant-smith-ellis/episodes/Episode-1-Shaleen-Title-and-Joe-Gilmore-e1crrqe.

Elton, Catherine. "How Has Boston Gotten Away with Being Segregated for So Long?" *Boston*, December 8, 2020. https://www.bostonmagazine.com/news/2020/12/08/boston-segregation/.

Esposito, Michael H., Hedwig Lee, Margret T. Hicken, Lauren C. Porter, and Jerald R. Herting. "The Consequences of Contact with the Criminal Justice System for Health in the Transition to Adulthood." *Longitudinal and Life Course Studies* 8, no. 1 (2017): 57–74. https://doi.org/10.14301%2Fllcs.v8i1.405.

Evans, Mark David. *The Consequences of Conviction: Sanctions Beyond the Sentence Under Colorado Law*. Denver: Office of the Colorado State Public Defender, 2019. https://www.coloradodefenders.us/wp-content/uploads/2019/12/Consequences-of-Conviction-2019-Edition-1.pdf.

Evanston (IL) City Council. *Resolution: Commitment to End Structural Racism and Achieve Racial Equality*. Resolution 58-R-19, June 5, 2019. https://www.cityofevanston.org/home/showpublisheddocument/62674/637511531477970000.

———. *Resolution: Establishing a City of Evanston Funding Source Devoted to Local Reparations*. Resolution 126-R-19, November 14, 2019. https://www.cityofevanston.org/home/showpublisheddocument/62672/637511530122430000.

Evanston (IL) Public Library. "Land Acknowledgment," https://www.epl.org/land-acknowledgment/.

Everett, Burgess. "Colo. Senator: Trump Easing Up on Pot Crackdown." *Politico*, April 13, 2018. https://www.politico.com/story/2018/04/13/cory-gardner-marijuana-522862.

Eyewitness News ABC7NY. "Hochul, Zeldin Spar Over Crime, Trump in Debate for New York Governor." YouTube video, October 26, 2022. https://www.youtube.com/watch?v=EI0_5v6Ljdk&ab_channel=EyewitnessNewsABC7NY.

Faber, Keith, Ryan Smith, Mike Curtin, and David Leland. "Vote YES on Issue 2: Protect Our Constitution from Monopoly Interests." Ohio Secretary of State, 2015. https://www.sos.state.oh.us/globalassets/ballotboard/2015/2-for.pdf.

Fang, Lee. "Pharma Company Funding Anti-Pot Fight Worried About Losing Business, Filings Show." *The Intercept*, September 12, 2016. https://theintercept.com/2016/09/12/pharma-opioid-marijuana/.

Feldscher, Jacqueline. "NASA Paid SpaceX for Safety Review After Musk Smoked Pot." *Politico*, October 16, 2019. https://www.politico.com/news/2019/10/16/nasa-musk-weed-048099.

Fernandez, Cynthia. "Top Ranked Ohio Dispensary Applicants Largely Out-of-State MSOs." *Grown In*, February 9, 2022. https://grownin.com/2022/02/09/top-ranked-ohio-dispensary-applicants-largely-out-of-state-msos/.

Fertig, Natalie. "Cannabis Crime Wave Boosts Banking Prospects on Capitol Hill." *Politico*, May 10, 2022. https://www.politico.com/news/2022/05/10/cannabis-crime-wave-banking-capitol-hill-00030330.

———. "Schumer Launches Long-Shot Bid for Legal Weed." *Politico*, July 14, 2021. https://www.politico.com/news/2021/07/14/schumer-launches-long-shot-bid-for-legal-weed-499584.

———. "Schumer Makes Last-Ditch Push for Cannabis Banking Bill." *Politico*, December 16, 2022. https://www.politico.com/news/2022/12/16/schumer-cannabis-banking-bill-00074258.

FirstRepair. "Our Founder: About Robin Rue Simmons." 2023. https://firstrepair.org/robin-rue/.

Firth, Caislin L., Julie E. Maher, Julia A. Dilley, Adam Darnell, and Nicholas P. Lovrich. "Did Marijuana Legalization in Washington State Reduce Racial Disparities in Adult Marijuana Arrests?" *Substance Use & Misuse* 54, no. 9 (2019): 1582–87. https://doi.org/10.1080/10826084.2019.1593007.

Fischer, Sara. "Rand Paul Blames Eric Garner's Death on High NYC Cigarette Tax." *CNN*, December 4, 2014. https://www.cnn.com/2014/12/03/politics/rand-paul-eric-garner-taxes/index.html.

Flegenheimer, Matt, and Al Baker. "Officer Fatally Shoots Teenager in Bronx." *New York Times*, February 2, 2012.

Fourcher, Mike. "KPMG Contract Allowed Recent College Graduates to Score Illinois Dispensary Applications." *Grown In*, September 29, 2020. https://grownin.com/2020/09/29/kpmg-contract-allowed-recent-college-graduates-to-score-illinois-dispensary-applications/.

Frank, John. "Colorado Governor Is Considering the Release of Nearly 40 Inmates with Marijuana Convictions." *Denver Post*, February 6, 2018. https://www.denverpost.com/2018/02/06/colorado-governor-marijuana-commutation/.

———. "It Wasn't Just Cash: How Texting Cannabis Voters and Tech Outreach Strategies Lifted Jared Polis to Victory." *Colorado Sun*, November 8, 2018. https://coloradosun.com/2018/11/08/how-jared-polis-won/.

———. "Meet America's First Pot Governor, Colorado's Jared Polis." *Colorado Sun*, January 7, 2019. https://coloradosun.com/2019/01/07/americas-first-marijuana-governor-colorado-jared-polis/.

Franklin County (OH) Clerk of Court. Records for Case No. 17 CV 010962 [*Pharmacann*]. https://fcdcfcjs.co.franklin.oh.us/CaseInformationOnline/caseSearch?7oZ5BTzAMXQc39QqOAVT.

Frayer, Lauren. "In Portugal, Drug Use Is Treated as a Medical Issue, Not a Crime." *NPR*, April 18, 2017. https://www.npr.org/sections/parallels/2017/04/18/524380027/in-portugal-drug-use-is-treated-as-a-medical-issue-not-a-crime.

Freddie Mac. "Racial and Ethnic Valuation Gaps in Home Purchase Appraisals." Research note, September 20, 2021. https://www.freddiemac.com/research/insight/20210920-home-appraisals.

French, Lynette. "We Support Patients' Rights to Grow Their Own Medicine." Blog post. Surterra.com, December 13, 2022. https://www.surterra.com/blog/florida-homegrow.

Frist, Bill. "How Former US Representative Patrick Kennedy's Own Experience with Addiction Led Him to Become One of Our Nation's Most Ardent Mental Healthcare Champions." *Forbes*, June 21, 2021. https://www.forbes.com/sites/billfrist/2021/06/21/how-former-us-representative-patrick-kennedys-own-experience-with-addiction-led-him-to-become-one-of-our-nations-most-ardent-mental-healthcare-champions/?sh=6380bf59232e.

Gaetz, Matt. "Proud to Support the MORE Act." Video. Gaetz.House.Gov, September 30, 2021. https://gaetz.house.gov/media/videos/matt-gaetz-proud-support-more-act.

Gallup. "Tobacco and Smoking." In Depth: Topics A to Z. Accessed February 24, 2023. https://news.gallup.com/poll/1717/tobacco-smoking.aspx.

Garmon, Margaret Ann, ed. "Legal Chronology May 5, 1970–January 4, 1979." Special Collections and Archives, Kent State University Libraries. https://www.library.kent.edu/special-collections-and-archives/legal-chronology-may-5-1970-january-4-1979.

Garcia, Nic. "Hickenlooper Pardons 26 Coloradans for Theft, Drug and Other Convictions." *Denver Post*, updated January 25, 2019. https://www.denverpost.com/2018/08/23/hickenlooper-pardons-26-coloradans/.

Gately, Iain. *Tobacco: A Cultural History of How an Exotic Plant Seduced Civilization*. New York: Grove Press, 2001.

Gathright, Alan. "Pot Vote Prompts Worldwide Attention." *Rocky Mountain News* (Denver, CO), November 4, 2005. Reprinted in "US CO: Pot Vots Prompts Worldwide Attention," Media Awareness Project. http://www.mapinc.org/drugnews/v05/n1726/a03.html?1332.

Gavin, Larry. "Exhibit Shows History of Segregation and Redlining in Evanston." *Evanston Round Table*, September 4, 2019. https://evanstonroundtable.com/2019/09/04/exhibit-shows-history-of-segregation-and-redlining-in-evanston/.

Gelb, Adam, Phillip Stevenson, Adam Fifield, et al. "More Imprisonment Does Not Reduce State Drug Problems." Issue brief. Pew Charitable Trusts, March 8, 2018. https://www.pewtrusts.org/en/research-and-analysis/issue-briefs/2018/03/more-imprisonment-does-not-reduce-state-drug-problems.

Gellerman, Bruce. "Busing Left Deep Scars on Boston, Its Students." *WBUR*, September 5, 2014. https://www.wbur.org/news/2014/09/05/boston-busing-effects.

———. "'It Was Like a War Zone': Busing in Boston." *WBUR*, September 5, 2014. https://www.wbur.org/news/2014/09/05/boston-busing-anniversary.

Gentile, Douglas A., Brooke J. Arterberry, Patrick K. Bender, and Kristi A. Costabile. "Beer Advertisements and Adolescent Drinking Knowledge, Expectancies, and Behavior." *Addictive Behaviors Reports* 10 (2019). https://doi.org/10.1016/j.abrep.2019.100226.

Gerald R. Ford Presidential Library and Museum. "President Gerald R. Ford's Proclamation 4417." https://www.fordlibrarymuseum.gov/library/speeches/760111p.htm.

Gettman, Jon. *Marijuana in Ohio: Arrests, Usage, and Related Data*. Bulletin of Cannabis Reform, October 19 2009. Available as Exhibit 0E321-F20 in *Pharmacann Ohio, LLC v. Jacqueline T. Williams, et al.*, 17 CV 10962, Franklin County (OH) Court of Common Pleas, https://fcdcfcjs.co.franklin.oh.us/CaseInformationOnline/imageLinkProcessor.pdf?coords=RWTMrj%2FpXxxnvWeMIaP4Fc2M8tS8n7OK18L2LAK%2BiysF86xAMuDIBcjYaYUvJUapNloEODZbWuwCd5MOuQuE702oCENELdfn7Rv1AWy5piytM5NaDeKtThbRI6M%2BHShT9fNy%2FUzzRDbzCxI7IFkWTXgkHDwDVXVM%2F7FSqxLQtqU%3D.

Gettman, Jon B. *The Impact of Drug and Marijuana Arrests on Local Communities in Massachusetts*. Boston: Massachusetts Cannabis Control Commission, December 8, 2017. https://masscannabiscontrol.com/wp-content/uploads/2017/12/Impact-of-Drug-and-Marijuana-Arrests-on-Local-Communities-in-Massachusetts.pdf.

Gettman, Jon B., Emily Whitfield, and Matthew Allen. *The War on Marijuana in Black and White: A Massachusetts Update*. Boston: ACLU Foundation of Massachusetts, 2016. https://www.aclum.org/sites/default/files/tr-report-10-2016-final-with-cover.pdf.

Gitau, Mumbi. "Big Tobacco Jumps into Germany's Pot Industry Alongside Snoop Dogg." *Bloomberg*, September 26, 2022. https://www.bloomberg.com/news/newsletters/2022-09-26/bat-tobacco-company-joins-snoop-dogg-in-german-marijuana-industry.

Gitlin, Todd. *The Sixties: Years of Hope, Days of Rage*. Rev. ed. New York: Bantam, 1993.

Glick, Daniel. "Marijuana Prohibition Began with These Arrests in 1937." Leafly.com, last updated July 28, 2020. https://www.leafly.com/news/politics/drug-war-prisoners-1-2-true-story-moses-sam-two-denver-drifters-became-cannabis-pioneers.

Global Commission on Drug Policy. *Enforcement of Drug Laws: Refocusing on Organized Crime Elites*. Geneva, Switzerland: Global Commission on Drug Policy, 2020. https://www.globalcommissionondrugs.org/wp-content/uploads/2020/06/2020report_EN_web_100620.pdf.

Goldstein, Dana. "Inside the College Board's Revised African American Studies Curriculum." *New York Times*, February 1, 2023. https://www.nytimes.com/2023/02/01/us/ap-african-american-studies-course.html.

Gonzalez v. Raich, 545 U.S. 1 (2005).

Goode, Jo C., et al. "'Jaisel Was Dirty': Marijuana Vendors Detail Bribes Demanded by Former Mayor Correia." *Herald News* (Fall River, MA), May 5, 2021. https://www

.heraldnews.com/story/news/courts/2021/05/05/live-updates-corruption-fraud-trial-former-fall-river-mayor-jasiel-correia-marijuana-extortion-bribe/4952528001/.

Goodman, J. David. "Cuomo Moves Closer to Marijuana Legalization in New York." *New York Times*, July 13, 2018. https://www.nytimes.com/2018/07/13/nyregion/marijuana-new-york-cuomo-legalization.html.

Goodwin, Doris Kearns. *The Fitzgeralds and the Kennedys*. New York: Simon and Schuster, 1987.

Gould, Barbara, Taylor Deutschle, Robert J. Letourneau, Rosemary Robinson, and Patrick T. McHenry. "Vote Yes on Issue 3." Ohio Secretary of State, 2015. https://www.sos.state.oh.us/globalassets/ballotboard/2015/3-for.pdf.

GovTrack Insider. "GRAM Act Would Allow State-Legal Marijuana Use As Acceptable Answer on Federal Firearm Background Check." July 15, 2021. https://govtrackinsider.com/gram-act-would-allow-state-legal-marijuana-use-as-acceptable-answer-on-federal-firearm-background-6b4aef161c55.

Grand View Research. "Report Summary: Legal Marijuana Market Size, Share and Trends Analysis Report by Product Type (Flower, Oil and Tinctures), by Application (Medical, Adult Use), by Region (North America, Europe, APAC, LATAM, Africa), and Segment Forecasts, 2023–2030." https://www.grandviewresearch.com/industry-analysis/legal-marijuana-market.

Green, Emma. "Why the Catholic Church Is Leading the Fight Against Legal Pot in Massachusetts." *The Atlantic*, November 1, 2016. https://www.theatlantic.com/politics/archive/2016/11/boston-archdiocese-marijuana-legalization/505997/.

Green Market Report. "Black History Month Spotlight: Akele Parnell." February 10, 2022. https://www.greenmarketreport.com/black-history-month-spotlight-akele-parnell/.

Green, Sara Jean. "Seattle Police Arrest 15-Year-Old Wanted in Deadly Tacoma Pot Shop Robbery; 2 Remain At Large." *Seattle Times*, updated April 12, 2022. https://www.seattletimes.com/seattle-news/law-justice/seattle-police-arrest-15-year-old-wanted-in-deadly-tacoma-pot-shop-robbery-2-remain-at-large/.

Grove, Jelena. "What Is the 280e Tax Code and How Is It a Liability for Social Equity Licensees in 2020?" *This Is Our Dream* (blog). Accessed December 15, 2022. https://thisisourdream.com/what-is-the-280e-tax-code-and-how-is-it-a-liability-for-social-equity-licensees-in-2020/.

Hamilton, Jessica R., Samantha M. Doonan, and Julie K. Johnson. *Special Report: A Baseline Review and Assessment of the Massachusetts Cannabis Industry's Required Positive Impact Plans*. Boston: Massachusetts Cannabis Control Commission, October 2019. https://masscannabiscontrol.com/wp-content/uploads/2019/10/Special_Report_A_Baseline_Review_and_Assessment_of_the_Massachusetts_Cannabis-Industry%E2%80%99s_Required_Positive_Impact_Plans-Oct-2019.pdf.

Hancock, Michael B. "Mayor Hancock Reflects on 10 Years of Legalized Recreational Marijuana in the Mile High City." YouTube video, April 20, 2022. https://www.youtube.com/watch?v=JXUsjraDyow&ab_channel=MichaelB.Hancock.

Hannah-Jones, Nikole. "Choosing a School for My Daughter in a Segregated City." *New York Times Magazine*, June 9, 2016. https://www.nytimes.com/2016/06/12/magazine/choosing-a-school-for-my-daughter-in-a-segregated-city.html?_r=1.

Hannan, Caleb. "The Don Draper of Pot." *Politico*, December 3, 2013. https://www.politico.com/magazine/story/2013/12/the-don-draper-of-pot-mason-tvert-100609/.

Hansen, Jolene. "The Making of an MSO." *Cannabis Business Times*, July 2022. https://www.cannabisbusinesstimes.com/article/standard-wellness-ohio-multistate-operator-cannabis-jared-maloof/.

Harris, Katharine Neill, and William Martin. "Persistent Inequities in Cannabis Policy." *Judges' Journal* 60, no. 1 (2021): 9–13.

Harvard Chan-NIEHS Center for Environmental Health. "Racial Residential Segregation in Greater Boston." July 18, 2022. https://storymaps.arcgis.com/stories/bd15a5eb9eae49cda09bfa7368272f89.

Hathaway, Andrew D., Amir Mostaghim, Patricia G. Erickson, Kat Kolar, and Geraint Osborne. "'It's Really No Big Deal': The Role of Social Supply Networks in Normalizing Use of Cannabis by Students at Canadian Universities." *Deviant Behavior* 39, no. 12 (2018): 1672–80. https://doi.org/10.1080/01639625.2017.1411047.

Hawkins, Matt. "Marijuana Investing: The Pros and Cons of MSOs." *Kiplinger*, last updated September 22, 2021. https://www.kiplinger.com/investing/stocks/marijuana-stocks/603477/marijuana-investing-the-pros-and-cons-of-msos.

Haynes, George H. "How Massachusetts Adopted the Initiative and Referendum." *Political Science Quarterly* 34, no. 3 (1919): 454–75.

Healy, Beth. "OneUnited Moves to Foreclose on Historic Church." *Boston Globe*, February 29, 2012. https://www.bostonglobe.com/business/2012/02/29/oneunited-bank-taking-steps-foreclose-charles-street-african-methodist-episcopal-church/TXwcVjuDZlCv4m1MA8B6NM/story.html.

Hecht, Peter. *Weed Land: Inside America's Marijuana Epicenter and How Pot Went Legit*. Berkeley: University of California Press, 2014.

Heitzeg, Nancy A. "Education or Incarceration: Zero Tolerance Policies and the School to Prison Pipeline." *Forum on Public Policy* no. 2 (2009): 8–13. https://files.eric.ed.gov/fulltext/EJ870076.pdf.

Herd, Denise A. "Prohibition, Racism and Class Politics in the Post-Reconstruction South." *Journal of Drug Issues* 13, no. 1 (1983): 77–94. https://doi.org/10.1177/002204268301300105.

Herreras Szot, Aaron. "Marijuana Use Can Still Be a Problem for Security Clearance Applicants." *Government Executive*, January 20, 2022. https://www.govexec.com/defense/2022/01/marijuana-use-can-still-be-problem-security-clearance-applicants/360933/.

Herrington, A. J. "California Bill Filed to Accelerate Cannabis Conviction Expungements." *High Times*, January 27, 2022. https://hightimes.com/news/california-bill-filed-to-accelerate-cannabis-conviction-expungements/.

Hersh, Ed. "Smoke Shops, Convenience Stores, and an Open Secret." *West Side Rag*, June 6, 2022. https://www.westsiderag.com/2022/06/06/smoke-shops-convenience-stores-and-an-open-secret.

Herzberg, David. *White Market Drugs: Big Pharma and the Hidden History of Addiction in America*. Chicago: University of Chicago Press, 2020.

History Colorado. "Growing Reason." Vimeo video, April 1, 2019. https://vimeo.com/317484359.

Hoch, Bryan. "Yankee Stadium to Open at 20% Capacity." MLB.com, March 20, 2021. https://www.mlb.com/news/yankee-stadium-to-open-2021-with-limited-seating.

Hodson, Tom. "Ian James: Personal Passion for Marriage Equality." *WOUB*, June 18, 2013. https://woub.org/2013/06/18/ian-james-personal-passion-marriage-equality/.

Hohenkirk, Shenicka, to Honorable Mayor and Members of the City Council. "Cannabis Arrests and Compliance Tickets." Memo, November 20, 2019. https://www.cityofevanston.org/home/showpublisheddocument/55309/637190175978830000.

Horn, James. "Transformations of Virginia: Tobacco, Slavery, and Empire." Forum introduction. *William and Mary Quarterly* 68, no. 3 (2011): 327–31.

Howe, Amy. "Opinion Analysis: A Total Victory for Total Wine in 21st Amendment Dispute." *SCOTUSblog*, June 16, 2019. https://www.scotusblog.com/2019/06/opinion-analysis-a-total-victory-for-total-wine-in-21st-amendment-dispute/.

Hudak, John. "Biden's Cannabis Pardons: A Long Overdue Reassessment of the War on Drugs." *How We Rise* (blog). Brookings Institution, October 7, 2022. https://www.brookings.edu/blog/how-we-rise/2022/10/07/bidens-cannabis-pardons-a-long-overdue-reassessment-of-the-war-on-drugs/.

———. "The Farm Bill, Hemp Legalization and the Status of CBD: An Explainer." *FixGov* (blog). Brookings Institution, December 14, 2018. https://www.brookings.edu/blog/fixgov/2018/12/14/the-farm-bill-hemp-and-cbd-explainer/.

Hudak, John, and Grace Wallack. "How to Reschedule Marijuana, and Why It's Unlikely Anytime Soon." *FixGov* (blog). Brookings Institution, February 13, 2015. https://www.brookings.edu/blog/fixgov/2015/02/13/how-to-reschedule-marijuana-and-why-its-unlikely-anytime-soon/.

Humphreys, Brad R. "Legalized Sports Betting, VLT Gambling, and State Gambling Revenues: Evidence from West Virginia." *Eastern Economic Journal* 47 (2021): 9–28. https://doi.org/10.1057/s41302-020-00178-0.

Husock, Howard. "How New York Can End the Public Housing Trap." In "New York City Reborn: 2021." Special issue, *City Journal*. https://www.city-journal.org/new-york-public-housing-trap.

Illinois Criminal Justice Information Authority. "SFY23 R3 Grant Awards." June 22, 2022. https://agency.icjia-api.cloud/uploads/SFY_23_R3_Grants_List_4a515603da.pdf.

Illinois Department of Commerce and Economic Opportunity. *2022 Annual Cannabis Report*. Springfield: Illinois Department of Commerce and Economic Opportunity, 2022. https://dceo.illinois.gov/content/dam/soi/en/web/dceo/aboutdceo/reportsrequiredbystatute/2023-loans-and-grants-to-social-equity-applicant-report.pdf?wcmmode=disabled.

———. "Social Equity Cannabis Loans." Fact sheet. https://idfpr.illinois.gov/Forms/AUC/SocialEquityCannabisLoans%20One-Pager.pdf.

Illinois Justice Project. "Restore, Reinvest, and Renew (R3 Program)." https://www.iljp.org/r3program.

Illinois Lottery. "Where the Money Goes." https://www.illinoislottery.com/giving-back/where-the-money-goes.

Illinois Office of the Lieutenant Governor. "Restore, Reinvest, Renew Program Board (R3PB)." November 15, 2021. https://r3.illinois.gov/downloads/R3ProgramBoardMembers.pdf.

Illinois R3 (Restore, Reinvest, Renew) Program. "Eligibility." State of Illinois. Last updated December 15, 2021. https://r3.illinois.gov/eligibility/.

———. "Pritzker Administration Awards $3.5 Million in Restore, Reinvest, and Renew Program Grants in Response to Summer Violence." News release, July 15, 2021. https://r3.illinois.gov/news/2021-07-15-r3-update.

Illinois (State of). "Gov. Pritzker Announces Record-Breaking $445 Million in FY 2022 for Total Tax Reported for Adult-Use Cannabis." News release, July 25, 2022. https://www.illinois.gov/news/press-release.25213.html.

———. "Pritzker Administration Announces Nearly 500,000 Cannabis Arrest Records Expunged Four Years Ahead of Schedule." News release, December 31, 2020. https://www.illinois.gov/news/press-release.22566.html.

Ingles, Jo. "Longtime Lawmaker Who Sponsored Med Pot Bills Reacts to House Passed Plan." Statehouse News Bureau, May 11, 2016. https://www.statenews.org/government-politics/2016-05-11/longtime-lawmaker-who-sponsored-med-pot-bills-reacts-to-house-passed-plan.

Ingold, John. "Marijuana Legalization in Colorado Is 10 Years Old: Here's the Story of How It Happened." *Colorado Sun*, November 7, 2022. https://coloradosun.com/2022/11/07/colorado-marijuana-legalization-history-amendment-64/.

Initiative and Referendum Institute, University of Southern California. "New York." Accessed December 30, 2022. http://www.iandrinstitute.org/states/state.cfm?id=41.

InsaneNutter. "Chris Rock—How Not to Get Your Ass Kicked by the Police!" YouTube video, February 2, 2007. https://www.youtube.com/watch?v=uj0mtxXEGE8&ab_channel=InsaneNutter.

iNSIGHTS Lab. *2019 High Costs Campaign Evaluation: Denver Teens Survey, November–December 2019*. iNSIGHTS Lab, 2020. https://www.thehighcosts.com/wp-content/uploads/2020/02/HighCosts_2019Post-CampaignSurvey_Results.pdf.

Irons, Meghan E., and Zoe Greenberg. "'It's a Shame': Some Black Residents See Lost Opportunity as Janey, Campbell Concede in Boston Mayoral Race." *Boston Globe*, updated September 14, 2021. https://www.bostonglobe.com/2021/09/14/metro/march-history-this-boston-mayoral-race-black-residents-pause-reflect/.

Jack, Andrew. "Growing List of Books Targeted in America's School Culture Wars." *Financial Times*, November 20, 2022. https://www.ft.com/content/5d9ce954-ed2e-4c15-81d8-91a5b2a88905.

Jackson, David. "The Law and Richard M. Daley." *Chicago*, May 13, 2011. https://www.chicagomag.com/chicago-magazine/september-1988/the-law-and-richard-m-daley/.

Jaeger, Kyle. "Biden AG Pick Restates Pledge to Respect State Marijuana Laws, in Writing." *Marijuana Moment*, March 1, 2021. https://www.marijuanamoment.net/biden-ag-picks-restates-pledge-to-respect-state-marijuana-laws-in-writing/.

———. "Congressional Bill Filed to Protect Marijuana Consumers from Losing Public Housing." *Marijuana Moment*, May 14, 2021. https://www.marijuanamoment.net/congressional-bill-filed-to-protect-marijuana-consumers-from-losing-public-housing/.

———. "Illinois Senate Approves Marijuana Legalization Bill." *Marijuana Moment*, May 29, 2019. https://www.marijuanamoment.net/illinois-senate-approves-marijuana-legalization-bill/.

———. "New Jersey Governor Says State Should 'Revisit' Marijuana Home Grow Ban After Market Matures." *Marijuana Moment*, November 2, 2022. https://www.marijuanamoment.net/new-jersey-governor-says-state-should-revisit-marijuana-home-grow-ban-after-market-matures/.

John F. Kennedy Presidential Library and Museum. "John F. Kennedy and Ireland." https://www.jfklibrary.org/learn/about-jfk/jfk-in-history/john-f-kennedy-and-ireland.

Johnson, Akilah. "Boston. Racism. Image. Reality." Spotlight. *Boston Globe*, December 10, 2017. https://apps.bostonglobe.com/spotlight/boston-racism-image-reality/series/image/.

Johnson, Alan. "Group Aims for 2015 Ballot Issue to Legalize Marijuana." *Columbus* (OH) *Dispatch*, December 19, 2014. Archived at https://perma.cc/M69K-5RGF?type=image.

Johnson, Nick. *Grass Roots: A History of Cannabis in the American West*. Corvallis: Oregon State University Press, 2017.

Joint Committee on New York Drug Law Evaluation, Association of the Bar of the City of New York Drug Abuse Council, Inc. *The Nation's Toughest Drug Law: Evaluating the New York Experience*. Washington, DC: National Institute of Law Enforcement and Criminal Justice, 1978. https://www.ojp.gov/pdffiles1/Digitization/43315NCJRS.pdf.

Jones, Jeffrey M. "Marijuana Views Linked to Ideology, Religiosity, Age." Gallup, November 15, 2022. https://news.gallup.com/poll/405086/marijuana-views-linked-ideology-religiosity-age.aspx.

Joravsky, Ben. "Joshua Tepfer—Ronald Watts." Podcast, 57:00. In *The Ben Joravsky Show*, produced by Chicago *Reader*, January 11, 2022. https://chicagoreader.com/columns-opinion/podcasts/ben-joravsky-show-podcast-episodes/.

Joshi, Apoorva. "Explainer: Three Strikes Laws and Their Effects." Blog post. Interrogating Justice, July 23, 2021. https://interrogatingjustice.org/mandatory-minimums/three-strikes-laws-and-effects/.

Journal Entry of Dismissal in *Pharmacann Ohio, LLC v. Ohio Department of Commerce*, 18AP-954 Ohio 10th App. (2021). https://fcdcfcjs.co.franklin.oh.us/CaseInformationOnline/imageLinkProcessor.pdf?coords=jBX5qMK4lyzo

%2BekULz0dG%2FPnKFt5rM1jzkpv9Cg1HwK5UNdcMYcw3LOixQ1V%2B%2FxBsMQA8qS7T3IcqJhLxpFWcoLzP42a2e1sxt5SK%2FVPOe6kR77%2F0%2FXR%2FGv6vMBqbqzLY%2FdRgx2LUw%2BlBLFbEqBp2VJfrirf60f2woi7R8A5Ig0%3D.

Justia.com. "Financing a Cannabis Business." Last reviewed September 2022. https://www.justia.com/cannabis-law/financing-a-cannabis-business/.

Kalven, Jamie. "Operation Smoke and Mirrors." *The Intercept*, October 6, 2016. https://theintercept.com/2016/10/06/in-the-chicago-police-department-if-the-bosses-say-it-didnt-happen-it-didnt-happen/.

Kapos, Shia. "Lawyers, Race and Money: Illinois' Messy Weed Experiment." *Politico*, September 18, 2021. https://www.politico.com/news/2021/09/18/illinois-weed-experiment-512626.

Karlik, Michael. "Feds Properly Denied Colorado Woman's Citizenship Request for Marijuana Use, Judge Says." *Colorado Politics*, updated December 9, 2022. https://www.coloradopolitics.com/news/feds-properly-denied-colorado-womans-citizenship-request-for-marijuana-use-judge-says/article_9e83588a-5570-11ed-b5c2-cb07f84192ae.html.

Kastor, Elizabeth. "The Great Drug Debate." *Washington Post*, October 22, 1986. https://www.washingtonpost.com/archive/lifestyle/1986/10/22/the-great-drug-debate/df37470c-2763-444c-be93-3a1ae842b022/.

Kealy, Sean J. "Marijuana Legalization and the Role of the Massachusetts Legislature." *Boston University Law Review* 101 (2021): 1173–1202. https://www.bu.edu/bulawreview/files/2021/07/KEALY.pdf.

Kennedy, Brendan. "Up in Smoke: How Expungement of Cannabis Crimes Will Work Under the MRTA." New York State Bar Association, April 22, 2021. https://nysba.org/up-in-smoke-how-expungement-of-cannabis-crimes-will-work-under-the-mrta/.

Keyes, Katherine M., Noah T. Kreski, Hadley Ankrum, et al. "Frequency of Adolescent Cannabis Smoking and Vaping in the United States: Trends, Disparities and Concurrent Substance Use, 2017–19." *Addiction* 117, no. 8 (2022): 2316–24. https://doi.org/10.1111/add.15912.

Keyes, Katherine M., Melanie Wall, Tianshu Feng, Magdalena Cerdá, and Deborah S Hasin. "Race/Ethnicity and Marijuana Use in the United States: Diminishing Differences in the Prevalence of Use, 2006–2015." *Drug and Alcohol Dependence* 179, no. 1 (2017): 379–86. https://doi.org/10.1016/j.drugalcdep.2017.07.027.

Khan, Shariq. "US Pot Sellers Stash Cash as Banks Leave Them High and Dry." Reuters, May 24, 2021. https://www.reuters.com/world/us/us-pot-sellers-stash-cash-banks-leave-them-high-dry-2021-05-24/.

KHQA. "Gov. Rauner Signs IL Marijuana Decriminalization Bill Into Law." July 29, 2016. https://khqa.com/news/state/gov-rauner-signs-il-marijuana-decriminalization-bill-into-law.

Kilroy, Ashley. *Turn Over a New Leaf: Report*. Denver, CO: [Denver Department of Excise and Licenses], September 4, 2019. https://www.denvergov.org/files/assets/public/marijuana-info/documents/tonl_report.pdf.

King, Ryan S., and Marc Mauer. "The War on Marijuana: The Transformation of the War on Drugs in the 1990s." *Harm Reduction Journal* 3 (2006): 1–17. https://doi.org/10.1186/1477-7517-3-6.

Kingkade, Tyler, Ben Goggin, Ben Collins, and Brandy Zadrozny. "How an Urban Myth About Litter Boxes in Schools Became a GOP Talking Point." *NBC News*, October 14, 2022. https://www.nbcnews.com/tech/misinformation/urban-myth-litter-boxes-schools-became-gop-talking-point-rcna51439.

Klammer, Sean. "Responsible Ohio: Successes, Failures, and the Future of Adult Marijuana Use in Ohio." *Ohio State Law Journal Furthermore* 79 (2018).

Knieriem, Declan J. "Cambridge City Council Weighs Recreational Marijuana Legislation." *Harvard Crimson* (Cambridge, MA), June 30, 2019. https://www.thecrimson.com/article/2019/6/30/city-council-recreational-marijuana/.

Kohler-Hausmann, Julilly. "'The Attila the Hun Law': New York's Rockefeller Drug Laws and the Making of a Punitive State," *Journal of Social History* 44, no. 1 (2010): 71–95. http://www.jstor.org/stable/40802109.

Konsko, Lindsay. "Why You Can't Always Buy Marijuana with a Credit Card." Blog post. NerdWallet.com, January 18, 2014. https://www.nerdwallet.com/article/credit-cards/buy-marijuana-credit-card.

Krane, Kris. "Company-Led Ballot Initiatives May Be Good for the Cannabis Industry, But Are They Good Policy?" *Forbes*, September 19, 2019. https://www.forbes.com/sites/kriskrane/2019/09/19/company-led-ballot-initiatives-may-be-good-for-the-cannabis-industry-but-are-they-good-policy/?sh=4a57b8549195.

Kuhn, Anthony. "3 Consequences of Using Marijuana After Your State 'Legalizes.'" *Military Times*, April 14, 2021. https://www.militarytimes.com/opinion/commentary/2021/04/14/3-consequences-of-using-marijuana-after-your-state-legalizes/.

Kuhn, Clifford, and Gregory Mixon. "Atlanta Race Massacre of 1906." In *New Georgia Encyclopedia*. Last edited November 14, 2002. https://www.georgiaencyclopedia.org/articles/history-archaeology/atlanta-race-massacre-of-1906/.

Kuziemko, Ilyana, and Steven D. Levitt. "An Empirical Analysis of Imprisoning Drug Offenders." NBER Working Paper 8489. National Bureau of Economic Research, September 2001. https://www.nber.org/papers/w8489.

Kyvig, David E. *Repealing National Prohibition*. 2nd ed. Kent, OH: Kent State University Press, 2000.

Lamonica, Aukje K, Miriam Boeri, and Timothy Anderson. "Gaps in Medical Marijuana Policy Implementation: Real-Time Perspectives from Marijuana Dispensary Entrepreneurs, Health Care Professionals and Medical Marijuana Patients." *Drugs: Education, Prevention and Policy* 23, no. 5 (2016): 422–34. https://doi.org/10.3109/09687637.2016.1150963.

Lampe, Joanna R. "The Controlled Substances Act (CSA): A Legal Overview for the 117th Congress." Report No. R45948, Congressional Research Service, updated February 5, 2021. https://sgp.fas.org/crs/misc/R45948.pdf.

Lane, Tyler J., and Wayne Hall. "Traffic Fatalities within US States that Have Legalized Recreational Cannabis Sales and Their Neighbours." *Addiction* 114, no. 5 (2019): 847–56. https://doi.org/10.1111/add.14536.

Lascher, Edward L., Jr., Michael G. Hagen, and Steven A. Rochlin. "Gun Behind the Door? Ballot Initiatives, State Policies and Public Opinion." *Journal of Politics* 58, no. 3 (1996): 760–75. https://www.jstor.org/stable/2960443.

Laslo, Matt. "How a Republican Senator Became the Biggest Cannabis Power Broker in Congress." *Playboy*, November 1, 2019. https://www.playboy.com/read/cory-gardner-cannabis.

Lassiter, Matthew D. "Impossible Criminals: The Suburban Imperatives of America's War on Drugs." *Journal of American History* 102, no. 1 (2015): 126–40.

Last Prisoner Project. *2021 Annual Report*. Denver, CO: Last Prisoner Project, 2021. https://irp.cdn-website.com/08efa45c/files/uploaded/Annual%20Report%202021%20%282%29.pdf.

———. "Exactly How Many People Are Locked Up for Weed?" Accessed December 16, 2022. https://www.lastprisonerproject.org/cannabis-prisoner-scale.

Laurie, Kaitlyn A. "Capping Uber in New York City: Ramifications for Rideshares, the Road, and Outer-Borough Residents." *Fordham Urban Law Journal* 46, no. 4 (2019): 942–1003. https://ir.lawnet.fordham.edu/ulj/vol46/iss4/5/.

Lawrence, Geoffrey. "First Circuit Makes Clear Cannabis Is Subject to Interstate Commerce Clause." *Reason*, September 13, 2022. https://reason.org/commentary/first-circuit-makes-clear-cannabis-is-subject-to-interstate-commerce-clause/.

Leary v. United States, 395 U.S. 6 (1969). https://caselaw.findlaw.com/us-supreme-court/395/6.html.

Lee, Martin A. *Smoke Signals: A Social History of Marijuana—Medical, Recreational, and Scientific*. New York: Scribner, 2012.

Legislative Council of the Colorado General Assembly. *Analysis of the 2006 Ballot Proposals*. Research Publication No. 554, September 14, 2006. https://myctbl.cde.state.co.us/sites/default/files/pdf/blue-book/BlueBook2006.pdf.

Leighton, George N., and Charles S Bargiel. "A History of Illinois Drug Control Laws from 1818 to 1975." *UIC Law Review* 9, no. 1 (1975).

Lekhtman, Alexander. "Frustrations Boil Over Massachusetts Cannabis Equity Delays." *Filter*, January 17, 2020. https://filtermag.org/massachusetts-cannabis-equity-protests/.

Levine, Harry G., Jon B. Gettman, and Loren Siegel. *210,000 Marijuana Possession Arrests in Colorado, 1986–2010*. New York: Marijuana Arrest Research Project, 2012. http://marijuana-arrests.com/docs/210,000-Marijuana-Arrests-In-Colorado.pdf.

Levine, Harry G., and Craig Reinarman. 1991. "From Prohibition to Regulation: Lessons from Alcohol Policy for Drug Policy." *Milbank Quarterly* 69, no. 3 (1991): 461–94. https://doi.org/10.2307/3350105.

Levine, Harry G., and Loren Siegel. *Unjust and Unconstitutional: 60,000 Jim Crow Marijuana Arrests in Mayor de Blasio's New York*. New York: Marijuana Arrest Research Project and the Drug Policy Alliance, 2017. https://drugpolicy.org/sites/default/files/Marijuana-Arrests-NYC--Unjust-Unconstitutional--July2017_2.pdf.

Levy, Marc. "Judge Has a New Rejection for Dispensary Lawsuit to Break Two-Year Head Start on Recreational Pot." CambridgeDay.com, October 10, 2020. https:

//www.cambridgeday.com/2020/10/10/judge-has-a-new-rejection-for-dispensary-lawsuit-to-break-two-year-head-start-on-recreational-pot/.

Lewis, Rebecca C., and Shantel Destra. "Kathy Hochul Ekes Out a Victory in the Closest Governor's Race in Decades." *City & State New York*, November 9, 2022. https://www.cityandstateny.com/politics/2022/11/kathy-hochul-ekes-out-victory-closest-governors-race-decades/379511/.

Leydon, Stephanie. "How a Long-Ago Map Created Racial Boundaries That Still Define Boston." *GBH*, November 12, 2019. https://www.wgbh.org/news/local-news/2019/11/12/how-a-long-ago-map-created-racial-boundaries-that-still-define-boston.

Linebaugh, Kate, and Ryan Knutson. "The Highs and Lows of Diversifying the Cannabis Industry." Podcast, 17:30. In *The Journal*, co-produced by the *Wall Street Journal* and Gimlet Media, December 20, 2022. https://www.wsj.com/podcasts/the-journal/the-highs-and-lows-of-diversifying-the-cannabis-industry/0dde3849-c4c3-44db-99a2-9f0225f8283f.

Lisi, Clemente. "Recreational Marijuana Legalization Becomes New Front in the Culture Wars Following Midterms." *Religion Unplugged*, November 11, 2022. https://religionunplugged.com/news/2022/11/10/2022-midterm-elections-catholic-bishops-increasingly-vocal-against-recreational-marijuana-use-fall-short-following-passage-in-missouri-and-maryland.

Lopez, German. "In the 1980s, He Warned That 'This Is Your Brain on Drugs.' In 2016, He Voted to Legalize Marijuana." *Vox*, October 26, 2016. https://www.vox.com/policy-and-politics/2016/10/26/13417270/marijuana-legalization-brain-on-drugs.

———. "Why Anti-Drug Campaigns Like DARE Fail." *Vox*, September 1, 2014. https://www.vox.com/2014/9/1/5998571/why-anti-drug-campaigns-like-dare-fail.

Lynch, Mona. *Selective Enforcement of Drug Laws in Cuyahoga County, Ohio: A Report on the Racial Effects of Geographic Disparities in Arrest Patterns.* Report. Citizens for a Safe and Fair Cleveland, 2008. http://realneo.us/system/files/DrugArrestsCuyahoga.pdf.

Lynch, Sarah N. "US Attorney General Nominee Will Not Target Law Abiding Marijuana Businesses." Reuters, January 15, 2019. https://www.reuters.com/article/us-usa-trump-barr-marijuana/u-s-attorney-general-nominee-will-not-target-law-abiding-marijuana-businesses-idUSKCN1P92JO.

MacLaury, Judson. "The Federal Government and Negro Workers Under President Woodrow Wilson." Paper presented at annual meeting of the Society for History in the Federal Government, Washington, DC, March 16, 2000. https://www.dol.gov/general/aboutdol/history/shfgpr00.

Mahamad, Syed, and David Hammond. "Retail Price and Availability of Illicit Cannabis in Canada." *Addictive Behaviors* 90 (2019): 402–8. https://doi.org/10.1016/j.addbeh.2018.12.001.

Malcolm X. "Speech at Ford Auditorium (1965)." BlackPast.org, July 26, 2010. https://www.blackpast.org/african-american-history/speeches-african-american-history/1965-malcolm-x-speech-ford-auditorium/.

Mansnerus, Laura. "Timothy Leary, Pied Piper of Psychedelic 60's, Dies at 75." *New York Times*, June 1, 1996. https://www.nytimes.com/1996/06/01/us/timothy-leary-pied-piper-of-psychedelic-60-s-dies-at-75.html?sec=&spon=&pagewanted=all.

Manta, Ashley. "Remembering the San Francisco Cannabis Buyers Club, the Nation's First Dispensary." Leafly.com, last updated July 28, 2020. https://www.leafly.com/news/lifestyle/san-francisco-cannabis-buyers-club-nations-first-american-dispensary.

Marihuana Regulation and Taxation Act of 2021. NY S. 854-A. 2021–2022 regular session (2021). https://legislation.nysenate.gov/pdf/bills/2021/S854A.

Marijuana Policies of Ohio Taskforce. *Marijuana and Ohio: Past, Present, Potential*. June 2015.

Marijuana Policy Project. "Cannabis Tax Revenue in States that Regulate Cannabis for Adult Use." Last updated April 5, 2022. https://www.mpp.org/issues/legalization/cannabis-tax-revenue-states-regulate-cannabis-adult-use/.

———. "Colorado Passes Proposition AA Tax Measure." Blog post, November 8, 2013. https://blog.mpp.org/tax-and-regulate/colorado-passes-proposition-aa-tax-measure/.

———. "Our History." https://www.mpp.org/about/history/.

Marotti, Ally. "Illinois Delays Awarding 75 Licenses for New Marijuana Dispensaries Amid Coronavirus Outbreak." *Chicago Tribune*, April 29, 2020. https://www.chicagotribune.com/coronavirus/ct-coronavirus-illinois-marijuana-dispensary-delays-20200429-ao2nooa5hzgnnbmfulw4w5sdma-story.html.

Martin Luther King, Jr. Research and Education Institute, Stanford University. "Freedom's Ring." Accessed December 13, 2022. https://freedomsring.stanford.edu/?view=Speech.

———. "Poor People's Campaign." In *Martin Luther King, Jr. Encyclopedia*. https://kinginstitute.stanford.edu/encyclopedia/poor-peoples-campaign.

Massachusetts Cannabis Control Commission. *Cannabis Use Trends in Massachusetts, Findings from the International Cannabis Policy Study, 2019 and 2020*. Boston: Massachusetts Cannabis Control Commission, 2022), 67. https://masscannabiscontrol.com/wp-content/uploads/2022/09/International-Cannabis-Policy-Study-2019-2020.pdf.

———. *Guidance for Identifying Areas of Disproportionate Impact*. Boston: Massachusetts Cannabis Control Commission, April 2018. https://mass-cannabis-control.com/wp-content/uploads/2018/04/Guidance-for-Identifying-Areas-of-Disproportionate-Impact.pdf.

———. *Guidance on Equity Programs*. Boston: Massachusetts Cannabis Control Commission, June 2020. https://masscannabiscontrol.com/wp-content/uploads/062020_Guidance_Equity.pdf.

Massachusetts General Court. *Acts and Resolves Passed by the General Court of Massachusetts in the Year 1911*. Boston: Wright & Potter, 1911. https://archive.org/details/actsresolvespass1911mass/.

———. *Acts and Resolves Passed by the General Court of Massachusetts in the Year 1914*. Boston: Wright & Potter, 1914. https://archive.org/details/actsresolvespass1914mass/.

———. *An Act to Ensure Safe Access to Marijuana*. Bill H. 3818 (2017). https://malegislature.gov/Laws/SessionLaws/Acts/2017/Chapter55.

Massachusetts General Laws. *Cannabis Control Commission*. Part I, Title II, Chapter 10, Section 76. https://malegislature.gov/Laws/GeneralLaws/PartI/TitleII/Chapter10/Section76.

Massachusetts Marijuana Initiative 2016. "Yes on 4—Families (:30)." YouTube video, October 25, 2016. https://www.youtube.com/watch?v=lCBqLr-2NTc&ab_channel=TheTelegraph.

———. "Yes on 4 Is a Vote for Social Justice." YouTube video, October 7, 2016. https://www.youtube.com/watch?v=HgVdADbtXhY&ab_channel=MassachusettsMarijuanaInitiative2016.

Massachusetts Office of the Inspector General. *Investigation of the Drug Laboratory at the William A. Hinton State Laboratory Institute, 2002–2012*. Boston, March 4, 2014. https://www.mass.gov/doc/investigation-of-the-drug-laboratory-at-the-william-a-hinton-state-laboratory-institute-2002-0/download.

Mass Moments. "August 8, 1954: Central Artery Project Announced." https://www.massmoments.org/moment-details/central-artery-project-announced.html.

Mathurin, Desiree. "Denver's Trying to Make Cannabis Delivery a More Attractive Business—and Exclusive to Social Equity Licensees." Denverite.com, September 19, 2022. https://denverite.com/2022/09/19/denvers-trying-to-make-cannabis-delivery-a-more-attractive-business-and-exclusive-to-social-equity-licensees/.

McDonald, Danny. "The Whiter the Boston Neighborhood, the Easier It Can Be to Find a Restaurant with a License to Serve Booze, Report Shows." *Boston Globe*, June 20, 2022.

McDonnell, Sean. "Cleveland School of Cannabis Starts Online Program for Home Growers of Marijuana." Cleveland.com, August 17, 2022. https://www.cleveland.com/business/2022/08/cleveland-school-of-cannabis-starts-online-program-for-home-growers-of-marijuana.html.

McGreevy, Patrick. "Kennedy Group Puts $2 Million into Fight Against Pot-Legalization Measures." *Los Angeles Times*, August 1, 2016. https://www.latimes.com/politics/la-pol-ca-patrick-kennedy-marijuana-legalization-opposition-20160801-snap-story.html.

McLaughlin, Tim. "Insys Founder Faces Stiff Prison Sentence, $100 Mln-Plus in Forfeiture." Reuters, January 23, 2020. https://www.reuters.com/article/insys-opioids/insys-founder-faces-stiff-prison-sentence-100-mln-plus-in-forfeiture-idUSL1N29R1A4.

Mehrtens, Savannah. "Colorado Officials, Cannabis Industry Leaders Celebrate 10th Anniversary of Amendment 64." *Denver Gazette*, updated December 29, 2022. https://denvergazette.com/news/marijuana/colorado-officials-cannabis-industry-leaders-celebrate-10th-anniversary-of-amendment-64/article_4a888cf0-4a71-11ed-84ad-57fdab26121d.html.

Melnick, Mark, and Nicoya Borella. *City of Boston: Race Distribution by Wards, 2010 Census Population*. Boston: Boston Redevelopment Authority, April 2011. https://www.bostonplans.org/getattachment/d1ba4403-b97e-4d6b-9561-9331fd0e4629.

Merritt, Jeralyn. "Shaky Path for Colorado's Marijuana Ballot Initiative." *5280*, January 20, 2005. https://www.5280.com/shaky-path-for-colorados-marijuana-ballot-initiative/.

Merzbach, Scott. "Raid! National Guard, State Police Descend on 81-Year-Old's Property to Seize Single Pot Plant." *Daily Hampshire* (MA) *Gazette*, September 30, 2016. https://www.gazettenet.com/MarijuanaRaid-HG-100116-5074664.

Metcalf, Benjamin T., US Department of Housing and Urban Development, to All Multifamily Regional Directors et al. "Subject: Use of Marijuana in Multifamily Assisted Properties." Memo, December 29, 2014. https://www.hud.gov/sites/documents/USEOFMARIJINMFASSISTPROPTY.PDF.

Mettler, Suzanne. *Soldiers to Citizens: The G.I. Bill and the Making of the Greatest Generation*. New York: Oxford University Press, 2005.

Michelson, Melissa R., and Joe Tafoya. "The Latino Politics of Proposition 19: Criminal Justice and Immigration." In *Something's in the Air: Race, Crime, and the Legalization of Marijuana*, edited by Katherine Tate, James Lance Taylor, and Mark Q. Sawyer, 115–25. New York: Routledge, 2013.

Miech, Richard A., Lloyd D. Johnston, Megan E. Patrick, Patrick M. O'Malley, Jerald G. Bachman, and John E. Schulenberg. *Monitoring the Future National Survey Results on Drug Use, 1975–2022: Secondary School Students*. Ann Arbor: Institute for Social Research, University of Michigan, 2023. https://monitoringthefuture.org/wp-content/uploads/2022/12/mtf2022.pdf.

Mikkelson, David. "Can You Use Food Stamps to Purchase Marijuana?" *Snopes*, September 12, 2014. https://www.snopes.com/2014/09/13/welfare-for-weed/.

Minneapolis Journal. "Finish War Ordered on Marihuana." October 17, 1937. Available at https://www.leafly.com/news/politics/drug-war-prisoners-1-2-true-story-moses-sam-two-denver-drifters-became-cannabis-pioneers.

Minority Cannabis Business Association. "Legal Status." Connecticut Equity Project State Briefing. https://minoritycannabis.org/equitymap/connecticut.

Miron, Jeffrey A., and Jeffrey Zwiebel. "Alcohol Consumption During Prohibition." *American Economic Review* 81, no. 2 (1992): 242–47. https://www.jstor.org/stable/2006862.

MJBizDaily. "Attorney General Nominee Garland Signals Friendlier Marijuana Stance." Updated December 17, 2021. https://mjbizdaily.com/attorney-general-nominee-merrick-garland-signals-friendlier-marijuana-stance/.

———. "Curaleaf Finalizes Grassroots Deal, Grows Marijuana Footprint to 23 States." March 18, 2022. https://mjbizdaily.com/curaleaf-finalizes-grassroots-acquisition-grows-marijuana-footprint-to-23-states/.

———. "Tobacco Giant Philip Morris Eyes Marijuana Market Opportunities." Updated December 17, 2021. https://mjbizdaily.com/tobacco-giant-philip-morris-eyes-marijuana-market-opportunities/.

Monitoring the Future, University of Michigan. "About MTF." https://monitoringthefuture.org/about/.

Morales, Karen. "Thousands of Drug Cases to Be Dismissed by State DAs." *Bay State Banner* (Dorchester, MA), December 8, 2017. https://www.baystatebanner.com/2017/12/08/thousands-of-drug-cases-to-be-dismissed-by-state-das/.

Moyer, Jeffrey. "Implementing Social Equity: Opportunities and Challenges from Marijuana Legalization in Massachusetts." In *Stoneover: The Observed Lessons and Unanswered Questions of Cannabis Legalization*. Edited by Nikolay Anguelov and Jeffrey Moyer, 83–108. Lanham, MD: Lexington Books, 2022.

———. "Innovation Through Popular Diffusion: Seeking Social Equity Through Cannabis Legalization in Massachusetts." Ph.D. diss., University of Massachusetts Boston, 2020. https://scholarworks.umb.edu/doctoral_dissertations/597/.

MRCC. "Weed Is Now Legal in MA | What Are The Rules? | Lawyers Tell Us How #WeedTalk Ep 1." YouTube video, March 9, 2017. https://www.youtube.com/watch?v=l65C3qPvr_U&t=39s&ab_channel=MRCC.

Mulvihill, Maggie. "Judge Declines Mass Dismissal of Cases from Tainted Drug Lab." *WBUR*, October 7, 2021. https://www.wbur.org/news/2021/10/07/dookhan-farak-drug-lab-tampering-dismissal-superior-court-ruling.

Mulvihill, Maggie, and Jon Schuppe. "Epic Massachusetts Crime Lab Scandal May Involve Even Broader Wrongdoing, Judge Says." *NBC News*, September 22, 2022. https://www.nbcnews.com/news/us-news/massachusetts-crime-lab-drug-testing-scandal-rcna48940.

Murray, Jon. "Cautious Approach on Marijuana Legalization Has Reaped Millions to Help Aurora's Homeless." *Denver Post*, updated December 30, 2018. https://www.denverpost.com/2018/12/28/aurora-marijuana-taxes-benefits-homeless/.

Nagy, Liz. "Illinois Senate Passes Marijuana Legalization Bill, Sends It Back to Illinois House." *ABC 7 Chicago*, May 30, 2019. https://abc7chicago.com/illinois-marijuana-cannabis-legalization-bill/5322315/.

Nasaw, David. *The Patriarch: The Remarkable Life and Turbulent Times of Joseph P. Kennedy*. New York: Penguin, 2013.

National Association for the Advancement of Colored People. *Born Suspect: Stop-and-Frisk Abuses and the Continued Fight to End Racial Profiling in America*. Baltimore, MD: NAACP, 2014. https://www.prisonpolicy.org/scans/naacp/Born_Suspect_Report_final_web.pdf.

National Association of Attorneys General. "The Master Settlement Agreement." https://www.naag.org/our-work/naag-center-for-tobacco-and-public-health/the-master-settlement-agreement/.

National Commission on Marihuana and Drug Abuse. *Marihuana: A Signal of Misunderstanding*. New York: Signet, 1972. https://babel.hathitrust.org/cgi/pt?id=mdp.39015015647558&view=1up&seq=6.

National Conference of State Legislatures. "Deep Dive: Marijuana." https://www.ncsl.org/bookstore/state-legislatures-magazine/marijuana-deep-dive.aspx.

———. "State Medical Cannabis Laws." Updated September 12, 2022. https://www.ncsl.org/health/state-medical-cannabis-laws.

National Drug Intelligence Center. "Marijuana." *Ohio Drug Threat Assessment*. April 2001. https://www.justice.gov/archive/ndic/pubs/659/marijuan.htm.

National Governors' Conference Center for Policy Research and Analysis. *Marijuana: A Study of State Policies and Penalties*. Washington, DC: National Institute of Law Enforcement and Criminal Justice, November 1977. https://www.ojp.gov/pdffiles1/Digitization/43880NCJRS.pdf.

National Instant Criminal Background Check Business Unit. "Information and Examples of the Application of Title 18, United States Code (U.S.C.), Section 922, Subsection (g)(3): Persons Who Are Unlawful Users Of or Addicted to Any Controlled Substance." National Instant Criminal Background Check System (NICS) Section, Federal Bureau of Investigation. May 2, 2019. https://www.justice.gov/file/1385186/download.

National Institute on Drug Abuse. "Drug Overdose Death Rates." https://nida.nih.gov/research-topics/trends-statistics/overdose-death-rates.

———. "Most Reported Substance Use Among Adolescents Held Steady in 2022." News release, December 15, 2022. https://nida.nih.gov/news-events/news-releases/2022/12/most-reported-substance-use-among-adolescents-held-steady-in-2022.

———. "Percentage of Adolescents Reporting Drug Use Decreased Significantly in 2021 as the COVID-19 Pandemic Endured." News release, December 15, 2021. https://nida.nih.gov/news-events/news-releases/2021/12/percentage-of-adolescents-reporting-drug-use-decreased-significantly-in-2021-as-the-covid-19-pandemic-endured.

National Museum of American History. "Redress Payments." https://americanhistory.si.edu/righting-wrong-japanese-americans-and-world-war-ii/redress-payments.

Naymik, Mark, and Brent Larkin. "Campaign to Legalize Marijuana Use in Ohio Quietly Underway and Borrows Page from Casino Campaign." Cleveland.com, December 18, 2014. Archived at https://perma.cc/5WL9-QCT5.

NBC. "Chicago Man Serving Life for Marijuana Granted Clemency After 19 Years in Prison." Video, July 7, 2022. Archived at https://news.yahoo.com/chicago-man-serving-life-marijuana-025002678.html.

NBC 5 Chicago. "Man Receives Evanston Reparations Program Award." Video, May 13, 2022. https://www.nbcchicago.com/local/man-receives-evanston-reparations-program-award/2832568/.

NBC News. "Treatment or Jail: Patrick Kennedy Wages Anti-Pot Crusade." February 17, 2014. https://www.nbcnews.com/storyline/legal-pot/treatment-or-jail-patrick-kennedy-wages-fierce-anti-pot-crusade-n22256.

Neighborhood View. "Neighborhood View: Shaleen Title on Regulating Cannabis, Racial Equity, Etc." YouTube video, February 6, 2018. https://www.youtube.com/watch?v=wi8iazOkarE&ab_channel=NeighborhoodView.

Nellis, Ashley. *The Color of Justice: Racial and Ethnic Disparity in State Prisons*. Washington, DC: Sentencing Project, 2021. https://www.sentencingproject.org/app/uploads/2022/08/The-Color-of-Justice-Racial-and-Ethnic-Disparity-in-State-Prisons.pdf.

New Frontier Data. "New Frontier Data Projects Annual US Cannabis Sales to More than Double to $72B by 2030." News release, March 23, 2022. https://www.globenewswire.com/en/news-release/2022/03/23/2408755/0/en/New-Frontier-Data-Projects-Annual-U-S-Cannabis-Sales-to-More-Than-Double-to-72B-by-2030.html.

New York Governor's Press Office. "Governor Hochul Announces Confirmations of Tremaine Wright and Christopher Alexander to Lead Implementation of the Marijuana Regulation and Taxation Act." News release, September 1, 2021. https:

//www.governor.ny.gov/news/governor-hochul-announces-confirmations-tremaine-wright-and-christopher-alexander-lead.

———. "Governor Hochul Announces Major Progress Toward Advancing Equity in Cannabis." News release, June 22, 2022. https://www.governor.ny.gov/news/governor-hochul-announces-major-progress-toward-advancing-equity-cannabis.

New York State Association of Counties. *The Marijuana Regulation and Taxation Act: A Summary*. Albany: New York State Association of Counties, 2021. https://www.nysac.org/files/MRTA_Summary.pdf.

New York State Cannabis Control Board. "Cannabis Control Board Approves First Conditional Adult Use Retail Dispensary Licenses." News release, November 2022. https://cannabis.ny.gov/system/files/documents/2022/11/ccb-approves-first-caurd-licenses.pdf.

New York State Office of Cannabis Management. "Dispensary Location Verification." Accessed June 18, 2023. https://cannabis.ny.gov/dispensary-location-verification.

———. "What Is in the Law: Social and Economic Equity." Fact sheet, 2022. https://cannabis.ny.gov/system/files/documents/2022/02/cannabis-management-fact-sheet-social-equity_0_0.pdf.

———. "What Is in the Law: Taxation and Revenue." Fact sheet, 2022. https://cannabis.ny.gov/system/files/documents/2022/04/cannabis-management-fact-sheet-taxation-03.pdf.

New York Times. "How the Skakel-Moxley Murder Case Unfolded Over Four Decades." November 2, 2020. https://www.nytimes.com/article/skakel-moxley-murder-case.html.

———. "Roosevelt Asks Narcotic War Aid." March 22, 1935. Reprinted at Schaffer Library of Drug Policy, https://www.druglibrary.net/schaffer/History/e1930/rooseveltasks.htm.

Nikki and Swami. "The Hardscrabble Origins of California's Fabled 'Emerald Triangle' (Part II)." *Merry Jane*, August 29, 2017. https://merryjane.com/culture/the-hardscrabble-origins-of-californias-fabled-emerald-triangle-part-ii.

Nixon, Richard, et al. "Oval Office Conversation 498-5." May 13, 1971. Available at Common Sense for Drug Policy's archive of Nixon White House tape recordings: https://www.csdp.org/research/nixonpot.txt.

NORML. "Chicago Considers Marijuana Decriminalization Plan." Blog post, September 23, 2004. https://norml.org/news/2004/09/23/chicago-considers-marijuana-decriminalization-plan/.

———. "Petition to Biden and Trump: End Marijuana Prohibition." Circa 2020. https://norml.org/petition-to-biden-and-trump-end-marijuana-prohibition/.

Northwestern Magazine. "John Evans and the Sand Creek Massacre." Fall 2014. https://www.northwestern.edu/magazine/fall2014/campuslife/john-evans-and-the-sand-creek-massacre.html.

NPR. "15 Years After Columbine, Are Schools Safer?" *Tell Me More* radio broadcast, 11:36, April 18, 2014. Recording and transcript available at https://www.npr.org/2014/04/18/304526475/15-years-after-columbine-are-schools-any-safer.

Oaksterdam University. "Trusted Leaders in Cannabis Education and Certification." https://oaksterdamuniversity.com/about/.

O'Donnell, Jayne, and David Robinson. "People Are Vaping a Deadly Substance Along with THC: Why Isn't Vitamin E Acetate Illegal?" *USA Today*, updated November 25, 2019. https://www.usatoday.com/story/news/health/2019/11/15/vitamin-e-acetate-deadly-thc-vape-additive-no-regulations-cdc/2569828001/.

O'Driscoll, Patrick. "Denver Votes to Legalize Marijuana Possession." *USA Today*, November 3, 2005. http://usatoday30.usatoday.com/news/nation/2005-11-03-pot_x.htm.

Office of the White House. "Statement from President Biden on Marijuana Reform." October 6, 2022. https://www.whitehouse.gov/briefing-room/statements-releases/2022/10/06/statement-from-president-biden-on-marijuana-reform/.

———. "Statement Ffrom the Press Secretary Regarding Executive Grants of Clemency." News release, January 20, 2021. https://trumpwhitehouse.archives.gov/briefings-statements/statement-press-secretary-regarding-executive-grants-clemency-012021/.

Ohio Criminal Sentencing Commission. "History of Marijuana Laws in Ohio." In Sara Andrews to Ohio Criminal Sentencing Commission Members and Advisory Committee. "Re: History of Marijuana Laws in Ohio and Supplemental Interesting Reports." Memo, October 19, 2015. https://www.supremecourt.ohio.gov/Boards/Sentencing/resources/general/historyMarijuana.pdf.

Ohio General Assembly. "An Act to Amend Sections 109.42 . . . 5149.311 of the Revised Code and to Amend Section 3 of Am. Sub. H.B. 130 of the 127th General Assembly." Am. Sub. H. B. No. 86, 129th General Assembly. http://archives.legislature.state.oh.us/BillText129/129_HB_86_EN_N.pdf.

———. "An Act to Amend Section 2925.11 of the Revised Code to Eliminate the 'Medical Purposes' Affirmative Defense to the Offense of Possession of Marihuana." S. B. 2, 122nd General Assembly. http://archives.legislature.state.oh.us/bills.cfm?ID=122_SB_2.

Ohio House of Representatives, Republican Newsroom. "Medical Marijuana Legislation Passes Ohio House." May 10, 2016. https://ohiohouse.gov/news/republican/medical-marijuana-legislation-passes-ohio-house-77939.

Ohio Legislative Service Commission. *Drug Abuse Control*. Staff Research Report No. 86. Columbus, Ohio, March 1967.

Ohio Secretary of State. "2015 Official Election Results." https://www.ohiosos.gov/elections/election-results-and-data/2015-official-elections-results/.

———. "Issue 3: Grants a Monopoly for the Commercial Production and Sale of Marijuana for Recreational and Medicinal Purposes." 2015. https://www.ohiosos.gov/globalassets/ballotboard/2015/3-language.pdf.

Ohio State University Moritz College of Law. "Cannabis on the Ballot: Lessons Learned from the Marijuana Reform Movement." YouTube video, October 27, 2022. https://www.youtube.com/watch?v=R8FQ8gHvoPM&ab_channel=TheOhioStateUniversityMoritzCollegeofLaw.

———. "Making the Case for Data-Driven Sentencing Reform in Ohio." YouTube video, May 25, 2022. https://youtu.be/cFcGRkUvrr8.

———. "Ohio Cannabis Reform in Focus: Medical Marijuana." YouTube video, April 14, 2022. https://www.youtube.com/watch?v=6nJ3YwddjyE&ab_channel=TheOhioStateUniversityMoritzCollegeofLaw.

———. "Social Equity 2.0: Expanding Horizons." YouTube video, December 13, 2021. https://www.youtube.com/watch?v=SHz_qQ-TcGQ&ab_channel=TheOhioStateUniversityMoritzCollegeofLaw.

———. "Social Equity 2.0: Lessons from Recent State Developments." YouTube video, December 13, 2021. https://www.youtube.com/watch?v=OAUYY6YpIZY.

———. "Where Do We Go from Here? Criminal Justice Reform in Ohio." YouTube video, January 6, 2022. https://youtu.be/2pzRVbzL1qs.

Oklahoma Commission to Study the Tulsa Race Riot of 1921. *Final Report*. February 28, 2001. https://www.okhistory.org/research/forms/freport.pdf.

Olsen, Dean. "Illinois Legislators Lay Out Plans for Recreational Marijuana Proposal." *Herald & Review* (Decatur, IL), January 29, 2019. https://herald-review.com/news/state-and-regional/govt-and-politics/illinois-legislators-lay-out-plans-for-recreational-marijuana-proposal/article_36da662d-3db1-5224-8745-cf75df1b5276.html.

Omi, Michael, and Howard Winant. *Racial Formation in the United States*. 3rd ed. New York: Routledge, 2015.

Ongweso, Edward, Jr. "Civil Rights Groups Say Uber Actively Hurts Black People." *Vice*, September 23, 2020. https://www.vice.com/en/article/7kpn9z/civil-rights-groups-say-uber-actively-hurts-black-people.

Pacula, Rosalie Liccardo, and Russell Lundberg. "Why Changes in Price Matter When Thinking About Marijuana Policy: A Review of the Literature on the Elasticity of Demand." *Public Health Reviews* 35 (2013). https://doi.org/10.1007/BF03391701.

Parents Involved in Community Schools v. Seattle School District No. 1, 551 U.S. 701 (2007).

Pattillo, Mary E. "Sweet Mothers and Gangbangers: Managing Crime in a Black Middle-Class Neighborhood." *Social Forces* 76, no. 3 (1998): 747–74. https://www.jstor.org/stable/3005693.

Pawel, Miriam. "California Ballot Initiatives Are Powerful: The Powerful Have Noticed." *New York Times*, November 5, 2018. https://www.nytimes.com/2018/11/05/opinion/california-ballot-initiatives-direct-democracy.html.

PBS. "A Social History of America's Most Popular Drugs." Frontline: Drug Wars, October 2000. https://www.pbs.org/wgbh/pages/frontline/shows/drugs/buyers/socialhistory.html.

———. "Unintended Consequences of Prohibition." *Prohibition: A Film by Ken Burns and Lynn Novick*. https://www.pbs.org/kenburns/prohibition/unintended-consequences.

Peck, Emily. "The Rise and Fall of a Black Banking Icon." Axios.com, February 28, 2022. https://www.axios.com/2022/02/28/the-rise-and-fall-of-a-black-banking-icon.

People v. McCabe, 49 Ill. 2d 338 (1971). https://law.justia.com/cases/illinois/supreme-court/1971/42674-6.html.

Pereira, Ivan. "Chicago Prosecutors Expunge 15,000 Cannabis Convictions." *ABC News*, April 20, 2022. https://abcnews.go.com/US/chicago-prosecutors-expunge-15000-cannabis-convictions/story?id=84197307.

———. "New York Legalizes Recreational Marijuana, Expunges Former Pot Convictions." *ABC News*, March 31, 2021. https://abcnews.go.com/US/york-legalizes-recreational-marijuana-expunges-pot-convictions/story?id=76775175.

Pfaff, John. *Locked In: The True Causes of Mass Incarceration and How to Achieve Real Reform*. New York: Basic Books, 2017.

Pharmacann Ohio, LLC v. Ohio Department of Commerce, 17 CV 10962, Franklin County (OH) Court of Common Pleas (2018). https://fcdcfcjs.co.franklin.oh.us/CaseInformationOnline/imageLinkProcessor.pdf?coords=FVu%2F%2FDLIvfuxMC7HxgEcx%2Bn4GY33YqowI40W0qo4RynoIV3M3h6Ho4Ri9cmOYUBjoNR7eZOWk0cZsBi4xl9oNa3Wi4Tos2XAGucl%2BrYogNKgr%2BjEKk4CQmCNk5IUpWyAEkVdSt146bbgwhB00S%2F4wUc%2B7zk4tUetgQFJ%2BcHqLzw%3D.

Pickert, Kate. "When Shirley Sherrod Was First Wronged by the USDA." *Time*, July 23, 2010. Archived at https://web.archive.org/web/20100829162023/http://www.time.com/time/nation/article/0,8599,2006058,00.html?xid=rss-fullnation-yahoo.

Pierson, Emma, Camelia Simoiu, Jan Overgoor, et al. "A Large-Scale Analysis of Racial Disparities in Police Stops Across the United States." *Nature Human Behaviour* 4, no. 7 (2020): 736–45. https://www.nature.com/articles/s41562-020-0858-1.

Pinho, Kirk. "Black Homeowners in Metro Detroit Face Greatest Home Value Disparity in Nation." *Crain's Detroit Business*, January 17, 2021. https://www.crainsdetroit.com/real-estate/black-homeowners-metro-detroit-face-greatest-home-value-disparity-nation.

Pink, Saul. "Ald. Bobby Burns Cultivates New Approach to the Business and Politics of Marijuana." *Daily Northwestern* (Evanston, IL), October 28, 2022. https://dailynorthwestern.com/2022/10/28/city/ald-bobby-burns-cultivates-new-approach-to-the-business-and-politics/.

Plaisance, Mike. "History Made with 1st Purchases of Recreational Marijuana in Northampton, Massachusetts." *MassLive*, November 20, 2018. https://www.masslive.com/news/2018/11/history_made_with_1st_purchase.html.

Platt, Pamela. "Legislative Note—Legal Analysis of Marijuana Legislation in Illinois." *DePaul Law Review.* 22, no. 1 (1972): 277–301. https://via.library.depaul.edu/cgi/viewcontent.cgi?article=2856&context=law-review.

Pollan, Michael. *How to Change Your Mind: What the New Science of Psychedelics Teaches Us About Consciousness, Dying, Addiction, Depression, and Transcendence*. New York: Penguin, 2018.

Poole, Mary. *The Segregated Origins of Social Security: African Americans and the Welfare State*. Chapel Hill: University of North Carolina Press, 2006.

Practical Law Commercial Transactions. "Massachusetts Reopens Recreational Marijuana Businesses Following COVID-19 Closure." May 20, 2020. https://content.next.westlaw.com/practical-law/document/I91d43d4599d911eabea3f0dc9fb69570/Legal-Update-Massachusetts-Reopens-Recreational-Marijuana-Businesses

-Following-COVID-19-Closure?viewType=FullText&originationContext=document&transitionType=DocumentItem&ppcid=612fed1d39ef49d38d501caed192046d&contextData=(sc.Default)

Pratt, Chastity, and Alexandra Schmidt. "Michigan Approves Recreational Marijuana: What You Need to Know." *Bridge Michigan*, November 6, 2018. https://www.bridgemi.com/michigan-government/michigan-approves-recreational-marijuana-what-you-need-know.

Pressley, Ayanna. "Meet Ayanna." AyannaPressley.com. Accessed July 5, 2023. https://ayannapressley.com/about/.

Price, Gregory N. "The Cost of Government Deposits for Black-Owned Commercial Banks." *Review of Black Political Economy* 23, no. 1 (1994): 9–24. https://doi.org/10.1007/BF02895738.

Prop AA. "Prop AA Update with Rick Ridder—Sept. 27, 2013." YouTube video, September 27, 2013. https://www.youtube.com/watch?v=nUc9lQzjpJ8&ab_channel=PropAA.

Provine, Doris Marie. *Unequal Under Law: Race in the War on Drugs.* Chicago: University of Chicago Press, 2007.

Quinn, Thomas M., and Gerald T. McLaughlin. "The Evolution and Present Status of New York Drug Control Legislation." *Buffalo Law Review* 22, no. 3 (1973): 705–36.

Quirion, Pauline. "Governor Bakers Signs Cannabis Social Equity Bill Making Expungement of Decriminalized Cases Easier." Blog post. MassLegalServices, August 12, 2022. https://www.masslegalservices.org/content/governor-baker-signs-cannabis-social-equity-bill-making-expungement-decriminalized-cases.

Racino, Brad. "New York State's $200 Million Social Equity Fund (Appears?) Close to Being Funded." Cannabis Insider, NYup.com, May 26, 2023. https://www.newyorkupstate.com/cannabis-insider/2023/05/new-york-states-200-million-cannabis-social-equity-fund-appears-close-to-being-funded.html.

Racino, Brad, and Sean Teehan. "Smoke and Mirrors: Inside the Murky $200M Effort to Kickstart NY's Marijuana Industry." Syracuse.com, December 1, 2022. https://www.syracuse.com/marijuana/2022/12/smoke-and-mirrors-inside-the-murky-200m-effort-to-kickstart-nys-marijuana-industry.html.

Rape, Abuse and Incest National Network. "Children and Teens: Statistics." https://www.rainn.org/statistics/children-and-teens.

Rashidian, Nushin. "Is Responsible Ohio's Mascot Buddie 'The Joe Camel of Marijuana'?" *The Guardian*, October 21, 2015. https://www.theguardian.com/us-news/2015/oct/21/buddie-responsible-ohio-mascot-joe-camel-big-business.

Reed, Jack K. *Impacts of Marijuana Legalization in Colorado*. Denver: Colorado Division of Criminal Justice, July 2021. https://cdpsdocs.state.co.us/ors/docs/reports/2021-SB13-283_Rpt.pdf.

Rees, Jonathan. *The Chemistry of Fear: Harvey Wiley's Fight for Pure Food.* Baltimore, MD: Johns Hopkins University Press, 2021.

Rees, Matthew. "Social Equity and Cannabis Legalisation in Illinois: Creating Equitable Societies?" Master's thesis, University of Sheffield, UK, 2021–2022.

Rêgo, Ximene, Maria João Oliveira, Catarina Lameira, and Olga S. Cruz. "20 Years of Portuguese Drug Policy—Developments, Challengers and the Quest for Human

Rights." *Substance Abuse Treatment, Policy, and Policy* 16 (2021). https://doi.org/10.1186/s13011-021-00394-7.

Regulate Marijuana Like Alcohol. "Initiative Text." 2021. https://justlikealcohol.com/initiative-text/.

Regulations.gov. "Comment on FR Doc # 2021-23852." Comment ID DEA-2021-0025-008. https://www.regulations.gov/comment/DEA-2021-0025-0008.

Reid, Devin, to Robin Rue Simmons. Memo, April 18, 2019. https://www.cityofevanston.org/home/showpublisheddocument/71150/637854525387270000.

Reilly, Katie. "Florida's Governor Just Signed the 'Stop Woke Act': Here's What It Means for Schools and Businesses." *Time*, April 22, 2022. https://time.com/6168753/florida-stop-woke-law/.

ResponsibleOhio. "Legalizing Ohio: An Introduction." YouTube video, August 6, 2015. https://www.youtube.com/watch?v=bCOwAIvQM9Y; screenshot archived at https://web.archive.org/web/20151203172122/https://www.youtube.com/watch?v=bCOwAIvQM9Y.

Restaurant Opportunities Centers United. *Ending Jim Crow in America's Restaurants: Racial and Gender Segregation in the Restaurant Industry*. New York: ROC United, 2015. https://laborcenter.berkeley.edu/pdf/2015/racial-gender-occupational-segregation.pdf.

Reuter, Peter, ed. *Understanding the Demand for Illegal Drugs*. Washington, DC: National Academies Press, 2010. https://doi.org/10.17226/12976.

Reuter, Peter, and Mark A. R. Kleiman. "Risks and Prices: An Economic Analysis of Drug Enforcement." *Crime and Justice* 7 (1986): 289–340. https://www.jstor.org/stable/1147520.

Reuters. "New York Gov. Cuomo to Allow Limited Use of Medical Marijuana." January 14, 2014. https://www.reuters.com/article/usa-marijuana-newyork/new-york-gov-cuomo-to-allow-limited-use-of-medical-marijuana-paper-idUSL6N0KF00620140105.

———. "Tennessee Takes Lead in Republican Efforts to Restrict Drag Shows." *NBC News*, February 23, 2023. https://www.nbcnews.com/nbc-out/out-politics-and-policy/tennessee-takes-lead-republican-effort-restrict-drag-shows-rcna72080.

———. "Youth Violence Epidemic Not Over, Surgeon General Warns." *New York Times*, January 18, 2001. https://www.nytimes.com/2001/01/18/health/youth-violence-epidemic-not-over-surgeon-general-warns.html.

Richardson, Davis. "Trump's Attorney General Pick Bill Barr Breaks with Jeff Sessions over Weed Policy." *Observer*, January 15, 2019. https://observer.com/2019/01/attorney-general-pick-bill-barr-breaks-with-jeff-sessions-weed-policy/.

Richardson, Kimberly, to Honorable Mayor and Members of the City Council. "Adoption of Resolution 37-R-27, Authorizing the Implementation of the Evanston Local Reparations Restorative Housing Program and Program Budget." Memo, March 22, 2021. https://cityofevanston.civicweb.net/document/50624/Adoption%20of%20Resolution%2037-R-27,%20Authorizing%20the.pdf?handle=E11C7B73E1B6470DA42362AB80A50C46.

Richtsmeier, Seth. "Equity, Not Equality: How Massachusetts Is Ensuring a Diverse Cannabis Industry." Blog post. Cannabis Creative. https://cannabiscreative

.com/blog/equity-not-equality-how-massachusetts-is-ensuring-a-diverse-cannabis-industry/.

Rivenbark, Jeff, and Tom Roussey. "Elementary Student Brings Pot to School to Turn In His Parents." *WBTV*, updated November 14, 2010. https://www.wbtv.com/story/13330034/couple-facing-drug-charges-after-child-tips-off-cop-at-school/.

Roberts, Chris. "Biden White House Admits Firing Staffers for Marijuana, But Still Employs Some Past Pot Users." *Forbes*, March 19, 2021. https://www.forbes.com/sites/chrisroberts/2021/03/19/biden-white-house-blasted-for-punishing-staffers-for-using-marijuana/?sh=6975ecd631a8.

Roberts, Michael. "AG Nom Jeff Sessions Thought KKK Was Okay Until He Learned They Smoked Pot?" *Westword*, November 18, 2016. https://www.westword.com/news/ag-nom-jeff-sessions-thought-kkk-was-okay-until-he-learned-they-smoked-pot-8515997.

———. "Marijuana: $1K Fine, Year in Jail for Possession Possible But Unlikely, Says Lakewood PD." *Westword*, September 7, 2012. https://www.westword.com/news/marijuana-1k-fine-year-in-jail-for-possession-possible-but-unlikely-says-lakewood-pd-5842109.

———. "Marijuana: Attorney Rob Corry on Today's Joint Rally in Boulder." *Westword*, September 23, 2013. https://www.westword.com/news/marijuana-attorney-rob-corry-on-todays-free-joint-rally-in-boulder-5821177?storyPage=2.

———. "Marijuana: Cory Gardner to Be Targeted for Vote Against Defunding Federal MMJ Raids." *Westword*, June 3, 2014. https://www.westword.com/news/marijuana-cory-gardner-to-be-targeted-for-vote-against-defunding-federal-mmj-raids-5882999.

———. "Marijuana: Wanda James on Closure of Edible Business, MMJ Banking, Obama and More." *Westword*, October 10, 2012. https://www.westword.com/news/marijuana-wanda-james-on-closure-of-edibles-business-mmj-banking-obama-and-more-5830735.

Robinson, Greg. "The Paradox of Reparations: Japanese Americans and African Americans at the Crossroads of Alliance and Conflict." In *Minority Relations: Intergroup Conflict and Cooperation*, edited by Greg Robinson and Robert S. Chang, 159–88. Oxford: University Press of Mississippi, 2016.

Robinson, Jeffrey. *Who's* Really *in Prison for Marijuana?* Washington, DC: Office of National Drug Control Policy, 2005. https://www.ojp.gov/sites/g/files/xyckuh241/files/media/document/whos_in_prison_for_marij.pdf.

Robinson, Morris (Dino), Jr., and Jenny Thompson. "Evanston Policies and Practices Directly Affecting the African American Community, 1900–1960 (and Present)." Draft report, Evanston, IL, August 2020. https://www.cityofevanston.org/home/showpublisheddocument?id=59759.

Rogeberg, Ole. "Taking Absurd Theories Seriously: Economics and the Case of Rational Addiction Theories." *Philosophy of Science* 71, no. 3 (2004): 263–85. https://doi.org/10.1086/421535.

Rogers, Dan. "Rogers Financial." https://dancannabis.com/.

Ronald Reagan Presidential Library and Museum. "Jelly Belly® Jelly Beans and Ronald Reagan." https://www.reaganlibrary.gov/reagans/ronald-reagan/jelly-bellyr-jelly-beans-and-ronald-reagan.

Rosario, Isabella. "The Unlikely Story Behind Japanese Americans' Campaign for Reparations." CodeSwitch, *NPR*, March 24, 2020. https://www.npr.org/sections/codeswitch/2020/03/24/820181127/the-unlikely-story-behind-japanese-americans-campaign-for-reparations.

Rosenthal, Brian M. "'They Were Conned': How Reckless Loans Devastated a Generation of Taxi Drivers." *New York Times*, May 19, 2019. https://www.nytimes.com/2019/05/19/nyregion/nyc-taxis-medallions-suicides.html.

Roth, Winter, Mitchell Tam, Carrie Bi, et al.. "Changes in California Cannabis Exposures Following Recreational Legalization and the COVID-19 Pandemic." *Clinical Toxicology* 60, no. 5 (2022): 632–38. https://www.tandfonline.com/doi/full/10.1080/15563650.2021.2006212.

Rothstein, Richard. *The Color of Law: A Forgotten History of How Our Government Segregated America*. New York: Liveright, 2017.

Rubino, Joe. "Denver Tweaks Marijuana Delivery Rules as Businesses Struggle to Get Off the Ground." *Denver Post*, September 19, 2022. https://www.denverpost.com/2022/09/19/denver-marijuana-delivery-licenses-regulations-cannabis-social-equity/.

Safer Colorado. "Press Room." November 10, 2006. Archived at http://web.archive.org/web/20061110033754/http://safercolorado.org/safer-doc.

Salas-Wright, Christopher P., Sehun Oh, Trenette Clark Goings, and Michael G. Vaughn. "Trends in Perceived Access to Marijuana Among Adolescents in the United States: 2002–2015." *Journal of Studies on Alcohol and Drugs* 78, no. 5 (2017): 771–80. https://doi.org/10.15288/jsad.2017.78.771.

Santaella-Tenorio, Julian, Katherine Wheeler-Martin, Charles J. DiMaggio, et al. "Association of Recreational Cannabis Laws in Colorado and Washington State with Changes in Traffic Fatalities, 2005–2017." *JAMA Internal Medicine* 180, no. 8 (2020): 1061–68. https://doi.org/10.1001/jamainternmed.2020.1757.

Sarkissian, Arek. "Trump Doesn't Inhale, But the Cannabis Industry Is Betting His Supporters Do." *Politico*, October 8, 2019. https://www.politico.com/states/florida/story/2019/10/08/trump-doesnt-inhale-but-cannabis-is-betting-his-supporters-do-1221139.

Schaneman, Bart. "Minority Cannabis Ownership Negligible in Colorado, But New Social Equity Law Aims to Spur Progress." *MJBizDaily*, updated December 17, 2021. https://mjbizdaily.com/minority-cannabis-ownership-negligible-in-colorado-but-new-law-aims-to-spur-progress/.

Scharfenberg, David. "Massachusetts' Public Schools Are Highly Segregated: It's Time We Treated That Like the Crisis It Is." *Boston Globe*, updated December 11, 2020. https://www.bostonglobe.com/2020/12/11/opinion/massachusetts-public-schools-are-highly-segregated-its-time-we-treated-that-like-crisis-it-is/.

Schneider, Susan A. "Discrimination at USDA: Response to USDA." *Agricultural Law* (blog), May 1, 2013. http://aglaw.blogspot.com/2013/05/discrimination-at-usda-response-to-new.html.

Schoenberg, Shira. "Marijuana Trade Association Drops Delivery Lawsuit Amid Public Pressure." *CommonWealth*, January 25, 2021. https://commonwealthmagazine.org/drug-addiction/drugs/marijuana-trade-association-drops-delivery-lawsuit-amid-public-pressure/.

Schrad, Mark Lawrence. "The Forgotten History of Black Prohibitionism." *Politico*, February 6, 2021. https://www.politico.com/news/magazine/2021/02/06/forgotten-black-history-prohibition-temperance-movement-461215.

———. "Let's Raise a Glass to What Prohibition Accomplished." *Politico*, December 4, 2022. https://www.politico.com/news/magazine/2022/12/04/liquor-capitalism-prohibition-repeal-day-00072067.

———. *Smashing the Liquor Machine: A Global History of Prohibition*. New York: Oxford University Press, 2021.

Schuba, Tom. "Finalist for Marijuana Dispensary Licenses Also Works for Firm That Graded Applications." *Chicago Sun-Times*, September 8, 2020. https://chicago.suntimes.com/cannabis/2020/9/8/21427810/kpmg-illinois-new-marijuana-pot-licenses-hamd-kamal.

———. "Recreational Weed Sales Drop to $35 Million in February as Shortages Continue." *Chicago Sun-Times*, March 4, 2020. https://chicago.suntimes.com/cannabis/2020/3/4/21165299/recreational-weed-sales-drop-to-35-million-in-february-as-shortages-continue.

———. "State Sen. Toi Hutchinson Appointed as Illinois' Pot Czar." *Chicago Sun-Times*, September 26, 2019. https://chicago.suntimes.com/cannabis/2019/9/26/20886313/state-senator-toi-hutchinson-appointed-illinois-pot-czar.

Seidenberg, Bob. "A Reparations Program in Search of a Funding Source." *Evanston Round Table*, November 15, 2022. https://evanstonroundtable.com/2022/11/15/a-reparations-program-in-search-of-a-funding-source/.

Selsky, Andrew. "Oregon's Governor Pardons Thousands for Pot Convictions." Associated Press, November 21, 2022. https://apnews.com/article/biden-oregon-crime-district-of-columbia-kate-brown-4e15853ff264fba36ca978b33f20c94f.

Selvarajah, Eswaran. *Gentrification of Codman Square Neighborhood: Fact or Fiction?* With contributions by Vidhee Garg. Boston: Codman Square Neighborhood Development Corporation, July 31, 2014. https://www.csndc.com/wp-content/uploads/2020/10/Gentrification-Internal-Analysis-Eswaran-Final-July-25-2014.pdf.

Sensible Colorado. "History of Colorado's Medical Marijuana Laws." 2013. http://sensiblecolorado.org/history-of-co-medical-marijuana-laws/.

Sentencing Project. "Growth in Mass Incarceration: Prison Population Over Time." Accessed December 14, 2022. https://www.sentencingproject.org/research/.

Sfondeles, Tina. "Gov. Rauner Not High on Legalizing Marijuana: 'That's a Mistake.'" *Chicago Sun-Times*, December 2, 2017. https://chicago.suntimes.com/2017/12/2/18317912/gov-rauner-not-high-on-legalizing-marijuana-that-s-a-mistake.

Sheehan, Brynn E., Richard A. Grucza, and Andrew D. Plunk. "Association of Racial Disparity of Cannabis Possession Arrests Among Adults and Youths with Statewide Cannabis Decriminalization and Legalization." *JAMA Health Forum* 2, no. 10 (2021). https://doi:org/10.1001/jamahealthforum.2021.3435.

Shi, Yuyan, and Di Liang. "The Association Between Recreational Cannabis Commercialization and Cannabis Exposures Reported to the US National Poison Data System." *Addiction* 115, no. 10 (2020): 1890–99. https://doi.org/10.1111/add.15019.

Shoag, Daniel, and Nicholas Carollo. "The Causal Effect of Place: Evidence from Japanese-American Internment." Working paper, January 2020. https://scholar.harvard.edu/shoag/publications/long-run-causal-impact-place-evidence-income-and-mobility-effects-japanese.

Simplifya.com. "A Simple Way to Estimate Cost of Compliance." Blog post, December 1, 2021. https://www.simplifya.com/simple-way-to-estimate-cost-of-compliance/.

Sinclair, J. Andrew, Jaclyn R. Kimble, and R. Michael Alvarez. "Why Did Proposition 19 Fail?" In *Something's in the Air: Race, Crime, and the Legalization of Marijuana*, edited by Katherine Tate, James Lance Taylor, and Mark Q. Sawyer, 54–64. New York: Routledge, 2014.

Sisson, Patrick. "Public Housing Tenants Still Face Stiff Penalties for Pot, Even in States Where It's Legal." *Curbed*, November 13, 2019. https://archive.curbed.com/2019/11/13/20962970/marijuana-section-8-medical-pot-public-housing.

Small, Melvin. "The Election of 1968." *Diplomatic History* 28, no. 4 (2004): 513–28. https://doi.org/10.1111/j.1467-7709.2004.00428.x.

Smart Approaches to Marijuana (SAM). "How Legalizing Marijuana Affects Your Health and Safety (extended)." YouTube video, October 19, 2022. https://www.youtube.com/watch?app=desktop&v=lko7ufmgYag&ab_channel=SmartApproachestoMarijuana%28SAM%29.

Smith, Bill. "Evanston's Population Has Dropped: How to Respond?" *Evanston Now*, January 3, 2020. https://evanstonnow.com/evanstons-population-has-dropped-how-to-respond/.

Smith, Jean Edward. *FDR*. New York: Random House, 2007.

Smith, Jeff P. (@jeffpsmith). "CSNA Mayoral Forum Qs. #9, #10: Gentrification; People's Republic of Evanston." Blog post, Central Street Neighbors Association, March 23, 2009. Archived at https://archive.vn/20120707064753/http://centralstreetneighbors.com/?q=node/530.

Smith, Mikki L. "A Generation at Risk: The Ties Between Zero Tolerance Policies and the School-to-Prison Pipeline." *McNair Scholars Research Journal* 8 (2015): 125–41. https://commons.emich.edu/cgi/viewcontent.cgi?article=1094&context=mcnair.

Smith, Stephen F. "Clarence X? The Black Nationalist Behind Justice Thomas's Constitutionalism." *New York University Journal of Law & Liberty* 4 (2009): 583–625.

Sorkin, Amy Davidson. "The G.O.P.'s Matt Gaetz Problem." *New Yorker*, April 19, 2021. https://www.newyorker.com/magazine/2021/04/19/the-gops-matt-gaetz-problem.

Spector, Joseph, and Jon Campbell. "Why Legalizing Marijuana in New York Failed, but Decriminalizing It Passed." *Democrat & Chronicle* (Albany, NY), June 21,

2019. https://www.democratandchronicle.com/story/news/politics/albany/2019/06/21/why-legalizing-pot-new-york-failed-but-decriminalizing-passed/1521505001/.

State Farm. "Halloween Is 'Deadliest Day' of the Year for Child Pedestrian Fatalities." News release, October 23, 2012. https://www.prnewswire.com/news-releases/halloween-is-deadliest-day-of-the-year-for-child-pedestrian-fatalities-175397121.html.

Statista. "Craft Beer Share of Retail Beer Market in the United States from 2012 to 2021." 2022. https://www.statista.com/statistics/1093653/craft-beer-dollar-share-of-us-beer-market/.

Stein, Sanford. "What Happened in Illinois Part I." *Cannabis Law*, March 15, 2022. https://cannabislaw.com/what-happened-in-illinois-part-i/.

Stillman, Frances A., Lee R. Bone, Adam J. Milam, Jiemin Ma, and Kathleen Hoke. "Out of View but in Plain Sight: The Illegal Sale of Single Cigarettes." *Journal of Urban Health* 91, no. 2 (2014): 355–65. https://doi.org/10.1007%2Fs11524-013-9854-3.

Stine, Andy. *Building Excellent Schools Today (BEST) Annual Report.* Denver: Colorado Department of Education, February 2022. https://www.cde.state.co.us/capitalconstruction/bestfy21legislativereport.

Strategy Network, LLC. *Prospectus 2015: Ohio Marijuana Legalization and Regulation*. Columbus, OH: Strategy Network, 2014. Archived at https://www.documentcloud.org/documents/2096463-ro-prospectus.html.

Stryker, Alyssa. *Rethinking the "Drug Dealer."* New York: Drug Policy Alliance, 2019. https://drugpolicy.org/sites/default/files/dpa-rethinking-the-drug-dealer_0.pdf.

Sudhoff, Helen K. *Blowing Smoke at the Second Amendment*. Los Angeles: Reason Foundation, 2021. https://reason.org/wp-content/uploads/blowing-smoke-at-the-second-amendment.pdf.

Sundaresh, Ram, Youngmin Yi, Brita Roy, Carley Riley, Christopher Wildeman, and Emily A. Wang. "Exposure to the US Criminal Legal System and Well-Being: A 2018 Cross-Sectional Study." *American Journal of Public Health* 110, no. S1 (2020): S116–22. https://doi.org/10.2105/AJPH.2019.305414.

Sykes, Stefan. "Cannabis Drinks Pop Up As Companies Bet on the Growing Market for Legal Marijuana." *CNBC*, updated August 31, 2022. https://www.cnbc.com/2022/08/30/cannabis-drinks-companies-hope-to-capitalize-on-growing-market.html.

Taughtme, Hazey, and K. Michael Williams. "Driven by Necessity." *Black Cannabis*, April 2021. https://blackcannabismagazine.com/april2021/.

Taylor, Matthew, and Gary R. Potter. "From 'Social Supply' to 'Real Dealing': Drift, Friendship, and Trust in Drug-Dealing Careers." *Journal of Drug Issues* 43, no. 4 (2013): 392–406. https://doi.org/10.1177/0022042612474974.

Taylor, Paul S. "Crime and the Foreign Born: The Problem of the Mexican." In Edith Abbott, *Report on Crime and Criminal Justice in Relation to the Foreign Born for National Commission on Law Observance and Enforcement*, 200–25. Washington, DC: Government Printing Office, 1931. https://www.ojp.gov/pdffiles1/Digitization/44548NCJRS.pdf.

Teh, Cheryl. "Trump Has Been Asking His Advisers Questions Like 'What Do You Think of Firing Squads' When Planning His Campaign Messaging: *Rolling Stone*." *Business Insider*, February 14, 2023. https://www.businessinsider.com/donald-trump-firing-squad-guillotine-ask-advisers-report-2023-2.

Thornton, Mark. "Alcohol Prohibition Was a Failure." Cato Institute Policy Analysis No. 157, July 17, 1991. https://www.cato.org/policy-analysis/alcohol-prohibition-was-failure#notes.

Title, Shaleen. "Bigger Is Not Better: Preventing Monopolies in the National Cannabis Market." Ohio State Legal Studies Research Paper no. 678. Drug Enforcement and Policy Center (2022), 10–11. https://dx.doi.org/10.2139/ssrn.4018493.

Tobias, Andrew J. "After Paying $500k in Settlement, Medical Marijuana Company Can Open Three Ohio Dispensaries." Cleveland.com, March 6, 2020. https://www.cleveland.com/open/2020/03/after-paying-500k-in-settlement-medical-marijuana-company-can-open-three-ohio-dispensaries.html.

Tracy, Sam. "Stop Using a Superhero Mascot to Campaign for Marijuana Legalization in Ohio." Petition, Change.org, 2015. https://www.change.org/p/yeson3ohio-stop-using-a-superhero-mascot-to-campaign-for-legalization-nomarijuanamascots.

Transform Drug Policy Foundation. "Legalising Cannabis for Good | Chris Alexander." YouTube video, December 7, 2022. https://youtu.be/mrqI3SiPgAE.

Treisman, Rachel. "In Likely First, Chicago Suburb of Evanston Approves Reparations for Black Residents." *NPR*, March 23, 2021. https://www.npr.org/2021/03/23/980277688/in-likely-first-chicago-suburb-of-evanston-approves-reparations-for-black-reside.

Tribune News Service. "Matt Gaetz Helped Set Off Florida's Marijuana 'Green Rush': Some of His Friends, Allies Scored Big." *Tampa Bay* (FL) *Times*, May 9, 2021. https://www.tampabay.com/news/florida-politics/2021/05/09/matt-gaetz-helped-set-off-floridas-marijuana-green-rush-some-of-his-friends-allies-scored-big/.

Unitarian Church of Evanston. "Unitarian Church of Evanston Land Acknowledgement." https://ucevanston.org/land-acknowledgment/.

University of Mississippi School of Pharmacy. "Marijuana Research: History." https://pharmacy.olemiss.edu/marijuana/history/.

US Census Bureau. "Explore Census Data." https://data.census.gov/.

US Department of Justice. "Justice Department Issues Memo on Marijuana Enforcement." News release, January 4, 2018. https://www.justice.gov/opa/pr/justice-department-issues-memo-marijuana-enforcement.

US Drug Enforcement Administration. "Narcotics." Drug Fact Sheet. April 2020. https://www.dea.gov/sites/default/files/2020-06/Narcotics-2020.pdf.

———. "Schedules of Controlled Substances: Removal of (18F)FP-CIT from Control." *Federal Register* 86, no. 211 (November 4, 2021): 60785–90. https://www.govinfo.gov/content/pkg/FR-2021-11-04/pdf/2021-23852.pdf.

US Food and Drug Administration. "FDA Regulation of Cannabis and Cannabis-Derived Products, Including Cannabidiol (CBD)." Content current as of January 22, 2021. https://www.fda.gov/news-events/public-health-focus/fda-regulation-cannabis-and-cannabis-derived-products-including-cannabidiol-cbd.

———. "FDA Warns Consumers About the Accidental Ingestion by Children of Food Products Containing THC." News release, June 16, 2022. https://www.fda.gov/food/alerts-advisories-safety-information/fda-warns-consumers-about-accidental-ingestion-children-food-products-containing-thc.

———. "Think E-Cigs Can't Harm Teens' Health?" Content current as of June 29, 2022. https://www.fda.gov/tobacco-products/public-health-education/think-e-cigs-cant-harm-teens-health.

US Government Accountability Office. *Youth Illicit Drug Use Prevention: DARE Long-Term Evaluations and Federal Efforts to Identify Effective Programs*. GAO-03–172R, January 15, 2003. https://www.gao.gov/assets/gao-03-172r.pdf.

US House of Representatives. H.Amdt.332 to H.R.2578. 114th Cong. (2015–2016). https://www.congress.gov/amendment/114th-congress/house-amendment/332.

US Office of the Comptroller of the Currency. "The Freedman's Savings Bank: Good Intentions Were Not Enough; A Noble Experiment Goes Awry." https://www.occ.treas.gov/about/who-we-are/history/1863-1865/1863-1865-freedmans-savings-bank.html.

US Secret Service. "Our Drug Policy." https://www.secretservice.gov/careers/drug-policy.

US Senate. *Final Report of the Special Committee to Investigate Organized Crime in Interstate Commerce*. Washington, DC: Government Printing Office, 1951. Archived at http://stoppredatorygambling.org/wp-content/uploads/2012/12/Kefauver-Committee-Final-report.pdf.

US Senate Historical Office. "The Senate Overrides the President's Veto of the Volstead Act." https://www.senate.gov/artandhistory/history/minute/Volstead_Act.htm.

US Senate Joint Economic Committee Democrats. *The Economic Toll of the Opioid Crisis Reached Nearly $1.5 Trillion in 2020*. Issue brief, 2021. https://www.jec.senate.gov/public/_cache/files/67bced7f-4232-40ea-9263-f033d280c567/jec-cost-of-opioids-issue-brief.pdf.

Vaccaro, Adam. "Medical Marijuana Lobbyist to Oppose Pot Legalization Push." Boston.com, January 21, 2016. https://www.boston.com/news/untagged/2016/01/21/medical-marijuana-lobbyist-to-oppose-pot-legalization-push.

VanderHart, Dirk. "Addiction Experts Tell Oregon Lawmakers the State Has Been Too Lax on Drug Use." OPB.org, September 21, 2022. https://www.opb.org/article/2022/09/21/oregon-decriminalize-drugs-measure-110-addiction-treatment/.

Vaz, Matthew. *Running the Numbers: Race, Police, and the History of Urban Gambling*. Chicago: University of Chicago Press, 2020.

Vinicky, Amanda. "The Illinois Marijuana Industry Was Supposed to Bring Equity: Advocates Say Those Promises Are Falling Short." *WTTW*, September 28, 2022. https://news.wttw.com/2022/09/28/illinois-marijuana-industry-was-supposed-bring-equity-advocates-say-those-promises-are.

———. "More Than 2 Years After Illinois Legalized Recreational Marijuana, Some Say Law Falls Short of Promise." *WTTW*, April 21, 2022. https://news.wttw.com/2022/04/21/more-2-years-after-illinois-legalized-recreational-marijuana-some-say-law-falls-short.

Virdi, Jay. "Understanding the Federal SAFE and CLAIM Acts." *mg Magazine*, June 23, 2021. https://mgmagazine.com/business/understanding-the-federal-safe-and-claim-acts/.

Wall, Craig, and Sarah Schulte. "Illinois Marijuana Law Signed by Governor JB Pritzker Tuesday, Takes Effect January 1, 2020." *ABC 7 Chicago*, June 25, 2019. https://abc7chicago.com/illinois-marijuana-law-in-jb-pritzker-recreation-weed-2020/5362982/.

Wallace, Lewis. "Issue 3 Divided Taft Family." *WOSU*, November 5, 2015. https://news.wosu.org/news/2015-11-05/issue-3-divided-taft-family.

Walsh, Maeve, and Natalie Fahmy. "How Marijuana Could Become Legal in Ohio in 2023." *NBC4i*, updated January 24, 2023. https://www.nbc4i.com/news/local-news/how-marijuana-could-become-legal-in-ohio-in-2023/.

Walters, Ronald G. *American Reformers, 1815–1860*. Rev ed. New York: Hill and Wang, 1997.

Wang, George Sam, Katelyn Hall, Daniel Vigil, Shireen Banerji, Andrew Monte, and Mike VanDyke. "Marijuana and Acute Health Care Contacts in Colorado." *Preventive Medicine* 104 (2017): 24–30. https://doi.org/10.1016/j.ypmed.2017.03.022.

Wang, Qi, Nolan Edward Phillips, Mario L. Small, and Robert J. Sampson. "Urban Mobility and Neighborhood Isolation in America's 50 Largest Cities." *PNAS* 115, no. 30 (2018): 7735–40. https://www.pnas.org/doi/10.1073/pnas.1802537115.

Wang, Vivian. "Cynthia Nixon Puts Legalizing Marijuana Front and Center of Campaign." *New York Times*, April 11, 2018. https://www.nytimes.com/2018/04/11/nyregion/cynthia-nixon-marijuana-legalization.html.

———. "Democratic Insurgents Topple 6 New York Senate Incumbents." *New York Times*, September 13, 2018. https://www.nytimes.com/2018/09/13/nyregion/state-senate-election-results-idc-klein.html.

Wang, Vivian, and Jesse McKinley. "Marijuana Legalization Isn't Dead Yet in New York." *New York Times*, June 17, 2019. https://www.nytimes.com/2019/06/17/nyregion/ny-marijuana-legalization.html.

Ward, Andrew. "Most Affected: Craig Cesal Remained Positive and Defiant Despite Life Behind Bars." *High Times*, March 11, 2021. https://hightimes.com/activism/most-affected-craig-cesal-remained-positive-defiant-despite-life-behind-bars/.

Warner, Joel. "Dismantling Denver's 'Pot Capital Misnomer." *Westword*, January 6, 2010. https://www.westword.com/news/dismantling-denvers-pot-capital-misnomer-5825956.

———. "Meet the Unlikely Champions of Legalized Weed in Mass." *Boston Globe Magazine*, October 18, 2016. https://www.bostonglobe.com/magazine/2016/10/18/why-marijuana-opposition-effective-liberal-mass/QAN3Chb4AxpXCQKFKJ1M5M/story.html.

Warren, Mark. *Fire in the Heart: How White Activists Embrace Racial Justice*. New York: Oxford University Press, 2010.

Washnock, Kaylynn. "Prohibition in Georgia." In *New Georgia Encyclopedia.* Last edited July 20, 2020. https://www.georgiaencyclopedia.org/articles/history-archaeology/prohibition-in-georgia/.

Watson, Stephanie. "Medical Marijuana FAQ." WebMd.com, December 18, 2021. https://www.webmd.com/a-to-z-guides/medical-marijuana-faq.

Webb et al. v. United States, 249 U.S. (1919). https://tile.loc.gov/storage-services/service/ll/usrep/usrep249/usrep249096/usrep249096.pdf.

Weekend Edition Sunday. "New York Is Debating Bringing Back Cash Bail." *NPR*, April 3, 2002. https://www.npr.org/2022/04/03/1090498735/new-york-is-debating-bringing-back-cash-bail.

Weisner, Lauren. "The Illinois Restore, Reinvest, and Renew (R3) Grant Program: Examining Grant Applicant Feedback." Illinois Criminal Justice Information Authority, October 22, 2021. https://icjia.illinois.gov/researchhub/articles/the-illinois-restore-reinvest-and-renew-r3-grant-program-examining-grant-applicant-feedback/.

Wessler, Mike. "Updated Charts Provide Insights on Racial Disparities, Correctional Control, Jail Suicides, and More." Prison Policy Initiative (blog post), May 19, 2022, https://www.prisonpolicy.org/blog/2022/05/19/updated_charts/.

West, Steven L., and Keri K. O'Neal. "Project D.A.R.E. Outcome Effectiveness Revisited." *American Journal of Public Health* 94, no. 6 (2004): 1027–29. https://doi.org/10.2105%2Fajph.94.6.1027.

Whitehill, Jennifer M., Mark Melnick, April Pattavina, et al. *Identifying Disproportionately Impacted Areas by Drug Prohibition in Massachusetts*. Worcester: Massachusetts Cannabis Control Commission, March 2021. https://donahue.umass.edu/documents/MA_Cannabis_Control_Commission_Study_Report1_3-11-21_FINAL.pdf.

White House Office of National Drug Control Policy. "National Drug Control Budget: FY 2023 Funding Highlights." March 2022. https://www.whitehouse.gov/wp-content/uploads/2022/03/FY-2023-Budget-Highlights.pdf.

Whitfield, Chandra Thomas. "Capitalizing on Cannabis: Meet Colorado's Black 'Potrepreneurs.'" *NBC News*, April 20, 2015. https://www.nbcnews.com/news/nbcblk/capitalizing-cannabis-meet-colorados-black-potrepreneurs-n344556.

Wiersema, Alisa, Kendall Karson, and Josh Margolin. "'Draft Cuomo 2020' Groundswell Emerges Amid the New York Governor's Coronavirus Response." *ABC News*, March 31, 2020. https://abcnews.go.com/Politics/draft-cuomo-2020-groundswell-emerges-amid-york-governors/story?id=69879290.

Williams, Mason B. "How the Rockefeller Laws Hit the Streets: Drug Policing and the Politics of State Competence in New York City, 1973–1989." *Modern American History* 4, no. 1 (2021): 67–90. https://doi.org/10.1017/mah.2020.23.

Windle, Sarah B., Crystal Sequeira, Kristian B. Fillon, et al. "Impaired Driving and Legalization of Recreational Cannabis." *Canadian Medical Association Journal* 193, no. 14 (2021): E481–85. https://doi.org/10.1503/cmaj.191032.

Winter, Jessica. "Pot, Porn, and Strawberries." *Village Voice*, May 6, 2003. https://www.villagevoice.com/2003/05/06/pot-porn-and-strawberries/.

Wolf & Company, P.C. "Massachusetts Passes Income Tax Relief for Cannabis Business." Blog post. https://www.wolfandco.com/resources/alerts/massachusetts-income-tax-relief-cannabis-businesses/.

Wolf, Jeffrey. "New Medical Marijuana Rules Pass, Ritter Says He'll Sign It." *9News*, May 11, 2010. https://www.9news.com/article/news/local/politics/new-medical-marijuana-rules-pass-ritter-says-hell-sign-it/73-338221418.

Wolff, Eli A., and Mary Hums. "'Nothing About Us Without Us'—Mantra for a Movement." *HuffPost*, updated September 6, 2017. https://www.huffpost.com/entry/nothing-about-us-without-us-mantra-for-a-movement_b_59aea450e4b0c50640cd61cf.

Wolters Kluwer. "Do States Allow Income Tax Deductions for Marijuana Business Expenses?" Blog post, September 15, 2021. https://www.wolterskluwer.com/en/expert-insights/do-states-allow-income-tax-deductions-for-marijuana-business-expenses.

Wood, Sam. "Harvest, the Big Marijuana Company on the Ropes in Pennsylvania, Accused of Misleading Ohio Regulators." *Philadelphia Inquirer*, July 31, 2019. https://www.inquirer.com/business/weed/harvest-health-cannabis-marijuana-pennsylvania-ohio-20190731.html.

Wriggins, Jennifer. "Rape, Racism, and the Law." *Harvard Women's Law Journal* 6 (1983): 103–41.

WXYZ-TV Detroit. "Police Warn of Marijuana Edibles That Look Like Candy Ahead of Halloween." YouTube video, October 21, 2021. https://www.youtube.com/watch?v=7G07RJAZLFo&ab_channel=WXYZ-TVDetroit%7CChannel7.

Yacovone, Donald. "The Transformation of the Black Temperance Movement, 1827–1854: An Interpretation." *Journal of the Early Republic* 8, no. 3 (1988): 281–97. https://doi.org/10.2307/3123691.

Yakowicz, Will. "The Sexiest Story of Taxes and Marijuana: The History of Tax Code 280e." *Inc.*, June 29, 2016. https://www.inc.com/will-yakowicz/how-cpas-tax-lawyers-fighting-irs-for-marijuana.html.

———. "Weed vs. Greed: How America Botched Legalizing Pot." *Forbes*, August 2, 2022. https://www.forbes.com/sites/willyakowicz/2022/08/02/how-america-botched-legalizing-cannabis-berner-cookies-kim-rivers-trulieve-steve-deangelo/?sh=70693b874489.

Yates, Shanique. "Meet the Only Black Woman Licensed to Grow, Dispense and Sell Cannabis in the State of Ohio." *AfroTech*, October 12, 2021. https://afrotech.com/first-black-cannabis-dispensary-owner-ohio.

YesOn3Ohio.com "Last Chance to Make History." Accessed November 3, 2015. Archived at https://web.archive.org/web/20151103173155/http://yeson3ohio.com.

YesOnQuestion2.com. "Lt. Tom Nolan." YouTube video, October 21, 2008, https://www.youtube.com/watch?v=-00FVeU4_T8&ab_channel=YesOnQuestion2.

Young, Colin A. "Cannabis Commission to Revisit Regulations Around Equity, Host Agreements in Massachusetts." *New England Public Media*, September 20, 2022. https://www.nepm.org/regional-news/2022-09-20/cannabis-commission-to-revisit-regulations-around-equity-host-agreements-in-massachusetts.

———. "Latest Appointee Ensures Question 4 Opponents Will Have Majority on Cannabis Commission." *WBUR*, September 1, 2017. https://www.wbur.org/news

/2017/09/01/latest-appointee-ensures-question-4-opponents-will-have-majority-on-cannabis-commission.

———. "Lawrence Seeks Equity from State Cannabis Regulators." *Boston Business Journal*, October 15, 2021, https://www.bizjournals.com/boston/news/2021/10/15/lawrence-seeks-equity-status-from-state-cannabis-r.html.

———. "Task Force Would Target Illegal Marijuana Sellers." SouthCoastToday.com, December 18, 2019. https://www.southcoasttoday.com/story/news/2019/12/18/task-force-would-target-illegal/2059356007/.

Young, Jabari. "Former NBA Forward Al Harrington Wants to Make 100 Black Individuals Millionaires Through the Cannabis Business." *CNBC*, updated June 15, 2020. https://www.cnbc.com/2020/06/13/al-harrington-wants-to-make-100-black-people-millionaires-with-cannabis.html.

Zarkin, Gary A., Alexander J. Cowell, Katherine A. Hicks, et al. "Benefits and Costs of Substance Abuse Treatment Programs for State Prison Inmates: Results from a Lifetime Simulation Model." *Health Economics* 21, no. 6 (2011): 633–52. https://doi.org/10.1002/hec.1735.

Zeff, Blake. "Another Cuomo Noninterference Story Falls Apart." *Politico*, September 2, 2014. https://www.politico.com/states/new-york/albany/story/2016/05/another-cuomo-noninterference-story-falls-apart-049022.

Zhang, Mona. "The *High Times* Interview: Wanda James." *High Times*, June 24, 2016. https://hightimes.com/business/the-high-times-interview-wanda-james/.

Zippia.com. "Restaurant Owner Demographics and Statistics in the US." Last updated September 9, 2022. https://www.zippia.com/restaurant-owner-jobs/demographics/.

Index

About the Author

Dr. **Jeffrey Moyer** is originally from the Lehigh Valley region of Pennsylvania and currently lives and works in eastern Massachusetts as a dedicated researcher, practitioner, and educator specializing in drug policy. He earned his Ph.D. in public policy from the University of Massachusetts, where he conducted research on state policy innovation, racial equity, and cannabis legalization policy. Dr. Moyer has led courses on public policy, public administration, and various aspects of American politics at Northeastern University and Suffolk University, among other institutions. He has contributed to the field through publications—including *Stoneover: The Observed Lessons and Unanswered Questions of Cannabis Legalization* (co-edited with Nikolay Anguelov, 2022)—and public presentations, covering topics such as social equity in cannabis legalization, educational activism, and election law. Driven by a genuine passion for advancing evidence-driven public policy while promoting equity, Dr. Moyer strives to make a meaningful impact across academia and state and local government, as well as through service to the broader community.

www.ingramcontent.com/pod-product-compliance
Ingram Content Group UK Ltd.
Pitfield, Milton Keynes, MK11 3LW, UK
UKHW041449071026
15587UKWH00010B/703